WHAT MOTIVATES WORKERS to work harder? What can management do to create a contented and productive workforce? Any discussion of these questions would be incomplete without reference to the Hawthorne experiments, among the most famous pieces of research ever conducted in the social and behavioral sciences. Drawing on the original records of the experiments and the personal papers of the researchers, Richard Gillespie has reconstructed the intellectual and political dynamics of the experiments as they evolved from tentative experimentation to seemingly authoritative publications. *Manufacturing Knowledge* raises fundamental questions about the nature of scientific knowledge and about the assumptions and evidence that underlie debates on worker productivity.

Manufacturing knowledge

STUDIES IN ECONOMIC HISTORY AND POLICY
THE UNITED STATES IN THE TWENTIETH CENTURY

Edited by
Louis Galambos and Robert Gallman

Other books in the series:

Peter D. McClelland and Alan L. Magdovitz: *Crisis in the making: The political economy of New York State since 1945*

Hugh Rockoff: *Drastic measures: A history of wage and price controls in the United States*

William N. Parker: *Europe, America, and the wider world: Essays on the economic history of Western capitalism*

Richard H. K. Vietor: *Energy policy in America since 1945: A study of business–government relations*

Christopher L. Tomlins: *The state and the unions: Labor relations, law, and the organized labor movement in America, 1880–1960*

Leonard S. Reich: *The making of American industrial research: Science and business at GE and Bell, 1876–1926*

Margaret B. W. Graham: *RCA and the VideoDisc: The business of research*

Michael A. Bernstein: *The Great Depression: Delayed recovery and economic change in America, 1929–1939*

Michael J. Hogan: *The Marshall Plan: America, Britain, and the reconstruction of Western Europe, 1947–1952*

David A. Hounshell and John Kenly Smith, Jr.: *Science and corporate strategy: Du Pont R&D, 1902–1980*

Simon Kuznets: *Economic development, the family, and income distribution: Selected essays*

Moses Abramovitz: *Thinking about growth: And other essays on economic growth and welfare*

W. Bernard Carlson: *Innovation as a social process: Elihu Thomson and the rise of General Electric, 1870–1900*

Manufacturing knowledge

A history of the Hawthorne experiments

RICHARD GILLESPIE

CAMBRIDGE
UNIVERSITY PRESS

Published by the Press Syndicate of the University of Cambridge
The Pitt Building, Trumpington Street, Cambridge CB2 1RP
40 West 20th Street, New York, NY 10011-4211, USA
10 Stamford Road, Oakleigh, Melbourne 3166, Australia

First published 1991
First paperback edition 1993

Library of Congress Cataloging-in-Publication Data
Gillespie, Richard, 1952–
Manufacturing knowledge : a history of the Hawthorne experiments /
Richard Gillespie.
p.   cm. – (Studies in economic history and policy)
Includes bibliographical references and index.
ISBN 0-521-40358-8
1. Industrial management – Research – United States – Case studies.
I. Title. II. Series.
HD30.42.U5G55   1991
658–dc20   90-25639
                                                                CIP

British Library Cataloguing in Publication Data
Gillespie, Richard
Manufacturing knowledge : a history of the Hawthorne
experiments – (Studies in economic history and policy :
the United States in the twentieth century).
1. Organizational psychology, history
I. Title   II. Series
158.70973

ISBN 0-521-40358-8 hardback
ISBN 0-521-45643-6 paperback

Transferred to digital printing 2003

Contents

Editors' preface

As the large corporation developed in the United States and abroad, the institution's professional managers gradually worked out new means of improving their control of the firm's internal operations and external sociopolitical and economic environments. Out of these efforts came formal departments for public relations and public affairs, as well as personnel (more recently, human resources). Quasi-professions arose to satisfy the need for practitioners. In the case of the personnel function, the practitioners in turn created elaborate networks of relationships with the evolving social science disciplines. One of the most interesting and important of these networks produced the Hawthorne experiments and the human relations school of industrial sociology.

The experiments were conducted at the Hawthorne Works of the Bell System's Western Electric Company between 1924 and 1933. Elton Mayo, his colleagues at the Harvard Business School, and company researchers and supervisors cooperated to generate the data. The dominant interpretation that emerged stressed the role of informal human relationships – rather than material or formal organizational factors – in yielding a contented, productive workforce. The experiments became famous, and the interpretation became a foundation of modern industrial sociology and personnel management.

Richard Gillespie has dissected that interpretation, shown how it emerged, and analyzed with great insight the social context in which it was enthroned as scientific knowledge. His book forces us to reconsider what we know about these important experiments, the disciplines that used the Hawthorne findings, and for that matter the development of the social sciences in the United States during these decades. Appearing at a time when the sources of productivity are of central significance to U.S. business and government, *Manufacturing Knowledge* should give pause to those who are prepared to jump quickly on the latest bandwagon and transform industrial relations in this country. We are pleased and proud to include this volume in the series Studies in Economic History and Policy: The United States in the Twentieth Century.

<table>
<tr><td>LOUIS GALAMBOS
Professor of History
Johns Hopkins University</td><td>ROBERT GALLMAN
Kenan Professor of Economics
and History
University of North Carolina
at Chapel Hill</td></tr>
</table>

Glossary of manuscript collections

AT&T	American Telephone and Telegraph Company Archives, Bell Telephone Laboratories, Warren, New Jersey
CEM	Charles E. Merriam Papers, Joseph Regenstein Library, University of Chicago
DCJ	Dugald Caleb Jackson Papers, Institute Archives and Special Collections, Hayden Library, Massachusetts Institute of Technology, Cambridge
EM	Elton Mayo Papers, Baker Library, Harvard University, Graduate School of Business Administration, Boston
FJR	Fritz Jules Roethlisberger Papers, Baker Library, Harvard University, Graduate School of Business Administration, Boston
HSC	Hawthorne Studies Collection, Baker Library, Harvard University, Graduate School of Business Administration, Boston
HSCM	Hawthorne Studies Collection – Microfiche Set, Baker Library, Harvard University, Graduate School of Business Administration, Boston
LSRM	Laura Spelman Rockefeller Memorial Records, Rockefeller Archive Center, Pocantico Hills, North Tarrytown, New York
NAS–NRC	National Academy of Sciences, National Research Council Central File, Archives, Washington, D.C.
OMR	Office of the Messrs. Rockefeller Records, Rockefeller Archive Center, Pocantico Hills, North Tarrytown, New York
RF	Rockefeller Foundation Records, Rockefeller Archive Center, Pocantico Hills, North Tarrytown, New York
TAE	Thomas Alva Edison Papers, Edison National Historic Site, West Orange, New Jersey

WE   Western Electric Company Records, Bell Telephone Laboratories, Warren, New Jersey

WJD   William J. Dickson Papers, Bell Telephone Laboratories, Warren, New Jersey

Introduction

ALTHOUGH IT IS NOW more than half a century since they were conducted, the Hawthorne experiments are still among the most frequently
cited and most controversial experiments in the social sciences. Generations
of students in the social sciences have committed to memory the findings
of the experiments. They are acclaimed as a landmark study in both sociology and psychology and have acquired the status of a creation myth in
such subdisciplines as industrial sociology, the social psychology of work,
industrial psychiatry, and the anthropology of work. Surveys of the key
developments in organization and management theory consistently note the
seminal contribution of the experiments to their field. Yet paradoxically,
social scientists still disagree about what the experiments actually revealed.

The accounts of the Hawthorne experiments in disciplinary histories and
textbooks are beguilingly straightforward and unproblematic. From 1924
to 1933, we are informed, managers at the Hawthorne Works of the Western
Electric Company, in collaboration with Elton Mayo and his colleagues at
the Harvard Business School, conducted a series of experiments on worker
productivity, job satisfaction, and workplace organization. They began by
attempting to measure the effects of different levels of lighting on the productivity of several groups of workers, but found it impossible to isolate
the effects. Indeed, popular accounts delight in telling the reader that the
workers' production actually remained the same or increased as lighting
levels were reduced, contrary to common sense and the expectations of the
researchers. This seemingly inexplicable result drove the researchers to conduct further experiments, all of which attempted in some way to identify
the other variables that might be influencing the level of production.[1]

[1] The "standard account" of the experiments that I present in this and the following paragraphs
can be found, with variations and occasionally wild inaccuracies, in any number of historical
surveys and textbooks of industrial sociology, industrial psychology, management theory,
and organization theory. See, e.g., Thomas J. Peters and Robert H. Waterman, Jr., *In Search
of Excellence: Lessons from America's Best-Run Companies,* New York: Warner, 1984, 5–
6, 92–4; Jonathan L. Freedmen, David O. Sears, and J. Merrill Carlsmith, *Social Psychology,*
3d ed., Englewood Cliffs, N.J.: Prentice-Hall, 1978, 413–15; C. S. George, Jr, *The History*

The relay assembly test room experiment, the most famous of the experiments, was conducted to isolate through experimental control the other factors affecting production and worker satisfaction. Six women were placed in a test room, where their production, working conditions, health, and social interactions were carefully recorded. Production increased as the researchers introduced improvements in working conditions, such as rest periods and a shorter working day; at the same time, the workers expressed satisfaction with the improvements and attributed the rise in their production to these experimental changes. But when in the crucial twelfth test period the researchers removed the special conditions, production continued to increase. One of the researchers later described this moment as "the great *éclaircissement*, the new illumination, that came from the research." It seemed that the workers' attitude toward their work was more important than the changes in working conditions; separated from their fellow workers and given special consideration by researchers and supervisors, the workers responded so enthusiastically that the total experimental environment overwhelmed the individual changes in conditions. (The phrase "Hawthorne effect" has subsequently been used in textbooks to refer to unexpected influences of nonexperimental variables in any experiment in the social or behavioral sciences.)[2]

Thereafter the researchers developed further experiments, all designed to explore this new insight. Textbook descriptions and popular accounts tend to emphasize different aspects of these later experiments, depending in large measure on the disciplinary concerns of the authors, but two aspects are commonly discussed. First, a massive program of interviews with the factory workers revealed that complaints about working conditions and supervision could not be taken at face value but had to be understood in the context of the workers' personalities; workers brought to the factory a host of attitudes and sentiments that shaped their reactions to the work environment. Second, a study based on the observation of a group of male workers in an experimental setting much closer to the normal work environment revealed the existence of an informal social group among the workers. The most dramatic effect of the group was that it enabled the workers to restrict

of Management Thought, Englewood Cliffs, N.J.: Prentice-Hall, 1968, 128–30; Charles Perrow, *Complex Organizations: A Critical Essay*, 2d ed., New York: Random House, 1979, 92–8; William S. Sahakian, *History and Systems of Social Psychology*, 2d ed., Washington, D.C.: Hemisphere, 1982, 183–93; Steven R. Cohen, "From Industrial Democracy to Professional Adjustment: The Development of Industrial Sociology in the United States, 1900–1955," *Theory & Society*, 1983, 12: 47–67. For two typical textbook accounts from the 1950s, see Delbert C. Miller and William H. Form, *Industrial Sociology: An Introduction to the Sociology of Work Relations*, New York: Harper, 1951, 34–64, and Morris S. Viteles, *Motivation and Morale in Industry*, New York: Norton, 1953, 181–206.

[2] The quotation is from F. J. Roethlisberger, *Management and Morale*, Cambridge, Mass.: Harvard University Press, 1941, 15.

their output and, to a degree, protect themselves from the directives of engineers and supervisors. In sum, the Hawthorne experiments seemed to show that managers had to look beyond the technical organization of the factory; the behavior of workers and supervisors and their productivity were influenced as much by personal attitudes and informal social organization as they were by the formal lines of organization and authority.

The most striking characteristic of all these accounts of the Hawthorne experiments is their emphasis on the drama of scientific discovery, of comfortable assumptions being overturned by the force of unexpected and irrefutable experimental evidence. Discoveries in one experiment suggested new methodological approaches in the following experiment, until it too yielded results that propelled the researchers to the next stage. This portrayal of the dynamics of scientific discovery at Hawthorne is not confined to textbooks and popular accounts. The official publications of the Hawthorne experiments, of which the most frequently cited are Fritz Roethlisberger and William Dickson's *Management and the Worker* (1939) and Elton Mayo's *Human Problems of an Industrial Civilization* (1933), describe in great detail the tortuous path taken by the researchers on the way to scientific enlightenment. The message of these disarming descriptions of error and false assumption is that the final conclusions were forced on the researchers by the weight of the experimental evidence. The objectivity of the findings seems to be guaranteed by the researchers' confessions.

The rhetorical persuasiveness of the official accounts has not prevented the appearance of a vast literature criticizing and reinterpreting the Hawthorne experiments. After the Second World War, an initial round of critics, writing during a peak of union activity and amid widespread public interest in industrial relations, attacked the researchers for identifying too closely with the interests of managers. Some sought to discredit the ideological assumptions of the researchers, primarily by exposing the conservative political beliefs of Elton Mayo, while others identified what they regarded as methodological weaknesses in the research. Since the 1960s there have been repeated attempts to reinterpret the experimental data, particularly those from the relay assembly test room. Critics have questioned the researchers' conclusion that production increased because the special considerations given to the workers changed their mental attitudes and forged them into a small group; instead, they have variously proposed that economic incentives or supervisory discipline were the major factors or that the increase simply reflects a normal learning curve. Complex statistical techniques have been sent in to do battle with the more qualitative interpretations of the original researchers. The Hawthorne experiments have been constantly reshaped in the light of contemporary disciplinary debates or to provide supporting evidence for the latest technique for improving worker motivation and productivity. The interpretations of the experiments are now so varied that many would agree with the discouraging observation of one writer on management theory that "we shall never know exactly what happened at Hawthorne."[3]

In this book I try to provide the historical assessment of the Hawthorne experiments that has been missing from fifty years of commentary and criticism. There are three major streams to this assessment. First, I undertake a detailed analysis of the actual process of the "production" of the experiments, showing the subtle interplay among theoretical assumptions, experimental data, and the social and ideological concerns of the participants. The dynamics of the experiments can be reassembled from a rich source of archival material, including the entire collection of original experimental records (consisting of raw data, progress reports, and the researchers' correspondence) and the personal papers of three of the principal researchers (Elton Mayo, Fritz Roethlisberger, and William Dickson). Second, I seek to locate the experiments in a specific historical context. The experiments were variously a practical contribution to the management of industrial workers, an exploration of the social scientific study of work, and an expression of paternalistic corporate ideology. It is not possible to understand the development of the experiments, the researchers' interpretations, or the application of the experimental results without exploring in detail the institutional and intellectual contexts of the research. Third, I attempt to assess the impact of the Hawthorne experiments on managerial practices, industrial relations, and the social sciences, concentrating on the 1940s and 1950s, when the influence of the experiments was at its height.

I have chosen the title "Manufacturing Knowledge" to emphasize that scientific knowledge is produced in specific social, institutional, and ideological contexts and that these contexts leave their imprint on the knowledge claims made by scientists. In the case of the Hawthorne experiments, the different social interests of the many participants – academics, company researchers, workers, supervisors, and executives – shaped their interpretations of the results and their opinions as to the practical consequences of the research; controversies over the meaning of the Hawthorne experiments did not originate after publication, but were an intrinsic part of the production of the experiments themselves. One of the key concerns of this book is to demonstrate the extraordinary diversity of interpretations generated by the Hawthorne researchers in the course of their research and to show why one interpretation eventually dominated.

Meaning is not discovered; it is imposed. To understand the significance of the Hawthorne experiments it is necessary to explore how a body of

[3] Michael Rose, *Industrial Behaviour: Theoretical Developments Since Taylor*, Harmondsworth: Penguin, 1978, 118. For references to criticisms of the relay assembly test room, see the final section of Chapter 3, this volume; the reception of the experiments by social scientists is analyzed in Chapter 9.

complex and uncertain data, tenuous hypotheses, and conflicting interpretations was transformed into a relatively dependable body of social scientific
knowledge that, while criticized, is accepted as an important contribution
to several disciplines and has influenced managerial practice. The experiments were conducted in an environment shaped by a complex network of
social interest and institutions, including Western Electric and its parent
company, American Telephone and Telegraph, the Rockefeller Foundation,
the Harvard Business School, and the National Research Council. This
network, with Elton Mayo at its center, stabilized the initially problematic
interpretations of the Hawthorne experiments and facilitated the elaboration
of a single, authoritative account, then ensured that the official version was
widely disseminated and applied. Social scientists' "discoveries" about
worker productivity and contentment were the product of specific institutional structures, which shaped both the production and consumption of
the scientific knowledge.

The experiments occurred in a period that saw major changes in the social
sciences, in the organization of industry, and in labor relations; indeed, they
exemplify and offer a window on these transformations in academic and
industrial work. In 1920, shortly before the experiments commenced, social
and behavioral scientists were just starting to move out of the university
and laboratory and into society; claims for the social utility of the social
sciences had been common since the last decades of the nineteenth century,
but only after the First World War did experts try in any coherent fashion
to develop techniques of social control based on academic research, mod-
eling themselves explicitly on the successes of scientific medicine over the
previous three decades. By 1950, this professional program of social scientists was firmly in place, even if some of the more extreme technocratic
visions had not been realized; the social and behavioral sciences were being
applied to the planning of all aspects of society, from the economy and
industry to the school and the home, and to the adjustment of individuals
and groups to the social order. The Hawthorne experiments were widely
seen by social scientists in the 1950s (even those who had some reservations
about the particular arguments and theories of the Hawthorne researchers)
as a social scientific model for combining intellectual progress with practical
intervention in society.

Fundamental changes in the management of workers and industrial relations meant that industrial managers were more receptive to social scientists' ideas. During the 1910s and 1920s the major industrial corporations
had started to recognize that the existing system of powerful and capricious
supervisors and harsh conditions did not necessarily achieve high levels of
productivity or create a loyal workforce. Various benefits were introduced
in an attempt to attract and retain workers, and many of the personnel
functions of supervisors were transferred to a new group of employment
or personnel managers, who became responsible for everything from the

selection of workers to pensions and labor relations. Eager for practical techniques to guide their daily work, as well as for a professional ideology that would strengthen their position in the managerial hierarchy, personnel managers turned to social scientists for assistance in increasing productivity and achieving a more contented workforce. These issues became even more important with the dramatic rise of industrial unions in the 1930s and 1940s; managers were now confronted by workers who had transferred their loyalties to the labor movement and were prepared to challenge managerial authority on the shop floor. Personnel executives were convinced that this battle could be won only if supervisors had the appropriate personnel techniques to assert their authority and regain the allegiance of their workers, and they increasingly turned to social scientists for assistance. The Hawthorne experiments were the most important collaboration between personnel managers and social scientists in this period, and they were the key social scientific contribution to the elaboration of both management ideology and practical personnel management techniques after the Second World War.

This book thus combines a detailed analysis of the production of the Hawthorne experiments with a broader study of the intellectual and political context in which they were produced and an assessment of how they were "consumed." The analytical approach adopted here is informed by theoretical and empirical work in the sociology of scientific knowledge and the history of science, which argues that science is fundamentally a social activity in which knowledge claims can never be said to be determined solely by empirical data. Social interests, institutions, and ideologies shape the topics scientists choose to work on, the technologies they use to investigate the natural and social world, and the theories they use to guide their research; social interactions determine which scientists have authority in a scientific discipline to advance or reject knowledge claims and which knowledge claims will be regarded as "true" or "useful." [4] My concern, therefore, is to show why social scientists and managers – and even the workers themselves – arrived at particular interpretations of the Hawthorne experiments and why one interpretation came to be accepted as "correct."

[4] Bruno Latour integrates the theoretical literature and informative case studies in his entertaining *Science in Action*, Milton Keynes: Open University Press, 1987. For useful surveys of the literature and themes of the historical sociology of scientific knowledge, see Henrika Kuklick, "The Sociology of Knowledge: Retrospect and Prospect," *Annual Review of Sociology*, 1983, 9: 287–310; Steven Shapin, "History of Science and Its Sociological Reconstructions," *History of Science*, 1982, 20: 157–211; Michael Mulkay, *Science and the Sociology of Knowledge*, London: Allen & Unwin, 1979; and Steve Woolgar, *Science: The Very Idea*, Chichester: Horwood; London: Tavistock, 1988.

1

The management of work

IN MARCH 1927 an industrial delegation appointed by the prime minister of Australia arrived in the United States in order to examine methods of manufacturing, factory working conditions, and the system of industrial relations. They came, as did delegations and observers from Europe, to see at first hand the productive base of America's economic prosperity and international power, to learn the secret of a nation where it was claimed every worker would soon be able to own an automobile, a radio, and a telephone. As visitors to Japan were to do fifty years later, they came away impressed, indeed overwhelmed, by many aspects of U.S. industry, but were unsure whether these methods could be imported to Australia without the introduction of what they considered undesirable aspects of U.S. culture. The delegates were particularly impressed by their visit to a Chicago factory, which the journalist accompanying them dubbed a "workers' paradise":

> There, surely, was the highest development of American industry on the lines of factory organization, mass production, piece-work, and care for the welfare of employees. I could not help being deeply impressed by the beauty, the orderliness, and the smoothness of modern industry on a scale unimagined in Australia, and by the comfort and well-being of the workers in a place where the management was genuinely concerned for their welfare.[1]

The factory was the telephone manufacturing plant of Western Electric Company, the manufacturing subsidiary of American Telephone and Telegraph Company (AT&T) and site of the Hawthorne experiments.

The very factors that attracted the attention of the Australian visitors were necessary conditions for the development of such a large-scale research effort in worker productivity and supervisory techniques. In its report the delegation stressed several developments that it considered critical to the

---

[1] Hugh Grant Adam, *An Australian Looks at America*, London: Allen & Unwin, 1928, 62–4, quote on 63; and his report in *The Sun*, Sydney, 19 March 1927. The findings of the Australian delegation are gathered in Australian Industrial Delegation to the United States, *Report of Industrial Delegation*, Canberra: Government Printer, 1927.

success of U.S. industry: the growth of large corporations and the concomitant development of specialized management; mass production, resulting from the reorganization of the workplace and the application of scientific management; the existence of a quiescent and malleable workforce, attributable in part to the U.S. system of industrial relations and personnel practices; and the organized application of scientific and technical research to industrial production, including the growth of industrial research laboratories. In order to comprehend why managers at the Hawthorne Works of Western Electric embarked on the experiments, we must understand the broad changes that were taking place in industrial organization and discover why Western Electric and its parent company AT&T were at the forefront of these transformations. The Australian delegation correctly recognized the significance of the Hawthorne Works as a model of American industrial production. The central characteristics of American production identified by the delegation go a long way toward explaining why the Hawthorne Works was the site of the first major undertaking of social scientific research on the organization of work, managerial practices, and worker satisfaction.

The rise of corporations and modern management

The development of the telephone industry coincided with an extraordinary expansion of U.S. industry between the Civil War and the First World War. Equipment manufacturers built machines capable of producing goods cheaply and efficiently, in areas as diverse as agriculture, textiles, steel, and power. New industries based on scientific and technical innovation appeared with bewildering regularity – photography, the telegraph, electrical lighting and power, urban transit, the automobile, and of course the telephone. This expansion involved complex changes in the organization and management of industry. Companies integrated in order to achieve an efficient system of production and distribution, to bring about a continuous and rapid throughput of goods and services, and to ensure long-term stability. Common strategies involved both horizontal integration – the reduction of competition through mergers with similar companies – and, most importantly, vertical integration – the combination of manufacturing, purchasing, distribution, and marketing functions in a single firm. The administrative coordination required by such integration required the emergence of professional managers, both middle managers who concentrated on the day-to-day running of the firm and top managers who made long-term decisions regarding the allocation of capital and personnel. By the First World War large oligopolistic enterprises, controlled by a new elite of professional managers, dominated many sectors of U.S. industry.[2]

---

[2] For an overview of industrial and company growth in the late nineteenth and early twentieth centuries, see Alfred D. Chandler, "The United States: Seedbed of Managerial Capitalism,"

The telephone industry exemplifies this industrial growth and change in business structure.[3] On 14 February 1876 Alexander Graham Bell filed a patent application for an "improvement in telegraphy" that permitted the transmitting of vocal or other sounds telegraphically; later that same day Elisha Gray filed a caveat for a patent on his "harmonic telegraph," a device similar in function to Bell's. Bell and his associates formed the Bell Telephone Company in July 1877 and commenced to license local entrepreneurs in major cities, who in turn leased Bell telephones to customers, primarily businesses and wealthy individuals. The Bell company soon faced stiff competition from the Western Union telegraph company, which owned Gray's patent caveat and did not welcome encroachment on its communications business. After a brief battle, the companies decided in 1879 to carve up the market: Western Union agreed to withdraw from the telephone industry and assigned its telephone patents to Bell in exchange for Bell's agreement not to enter the telegraph market. Freed from the threat of direct competition, at least until the expiration of the basic telephone patents in 1894, the Bell company sought to take complete control of the telephone industry.[4]

The drive to integrate the manufacturing and operating licensees into the Bell company was directed by its first general manager, Theodore N. Vail. Aware that patent rights would not provide complete protection for the company, Vail and an emerging group of professional managers sought to control the industry organizationally. In 1880 a new controlling company was formed to take on the role of coordinating and directing the local telephone companies, or "operating companies" in headquarters parlance. The American Bell company invested in these operating companies and provided them with financial and technical assistance. In 1881 American Bell began the purchase of its licensed telephone manufacturers, including

in Alfred D. Chandler and Herman Daems, eds., *Managerial Hierarchies: Comparative Perspectives on the Rise of the Modern Industrial Enterprise*, Cambridge, Mass.: Harvard University Press, 1980, 9–40. Chandler's analysis of organizational and managerial changes is treated in his *The Visible Hand: The Managerial Revolution in American Business*, Cambridge, Mass.: Harvard University Press, 1977, passim; on horizontal integration see 315–20; on vertical integration, 363–5; on the role of managers, esp. chaps. 12 and 13.

[3] For the history of the telephone industry and the Bell System, see John Brooks, *Telephone: The First Hundred Years*, New York: Harper & Row, 1976; Gerald W. Brock, *The Telecommunication Industry: The Dynamics of Market Structure*, Cambridge, Mass.: Harvard University Press, 1981; N. R. Danielian, *A.T.&T.: The Story of Industrial Conquest*, New York: Vanguard Press, 1939; R. J. Tosiello, "The Birth and Early Years of the Bell Telephone System, 1876–1880," Ph.D. dissertation, Boston University, 1971; and Robert Garnet, *The Telephone Enterprise: The Evolution of the Bell System's Horizontal Structure, 1876–1909*, Baltimore: Johns Hopkins University Press, 1985. For the early development of the Bell company and its purchase of Western Electric, see George David Smith, *The Anatomy of a Business Decision: Bell, Western Electric, and the Origins of the American Telephone Industry*, Baltimore: Johns Hopkins University Press, 1985.

[4] Brock, *Telecommunications Industry*, 89–99; Smith, *Anatomy of a Business Decision*, chaps. 2 and 3.

the Chicago-based Western Electric Company, and in the following year it gave Western Electric exclusive rights to manufacture telephone equipment under Bell patents. Vail also sought to extend the company's patent protection and its technical advantages over future competitors by institutionalizing the process of invention and development. In 1881 an Electrical Department was established to oversee patents and technical developments, and by the time the original patents expired in 1894 the company held some nine hundred additional patents. Vail realized too the importance of developing long-distance telephony, which would tie together the local exchanges and make entry by competitors after 1894 even more difficult. Accordingly, in 1885 American Telephone and Telegraph Company was formed as a subsidiary, with the responsibility of developing and operating long-distance telephone communications. By 1885, then, American Bell had integrated the manufacturing, operating, long-distance, and financial and technical arms of the telephone industry. In that year the nascent Bell System operated 155,751 telephones and collected revenues of just over $10 million; by 1905 the number of telephones in service had risen to 2,284,587 and by 1925 to more than 12 million.[5]

A major reorganization occurred in 1908 under the direction of Vail, who had spent the previous decade engaged in entrepreneurial activities outside the Bell System. Vail owed his return in 1907 as president of AT&T, now the parent company, to the intervention of J. P. Morgan. Since 1902 Morgan and other New York financiers had assumed increasing control over the operation of AT&T, which was facing competition from the independent phone companies that had emerged since the expiration of the original patents in 1894. Vail set about allocating the functions of the various elements of the Bell System more precisely: AT&T was to be responsible for determining the overall business strategy of the system and for operating the long-distance service; the operating companies were to provide local service; and Western Electric was to take on research, development, quality control, and exchange installation in addition to its manufacturing responsibilities.[6]

A three-pronged strategy to reestablish Bell System control of the market was undertaken. First, AT&T bought up many independent companies and merged them with its operating companies, until the threat of antitrust action led to the so-called Kingsbury Commitment of 1913; henceforth, AT&T undertook not to purchase competitors and agreed to allow the independents to interconnect with the Bell System. Second, AT&T and the operating companies embraced growing state and federal regulation, which they were

5   Brock, *Telecommunications Industry*, 99–109; Chandler, *Visible Hand*, 200–2; Smith, *Anatomy of a Business Decision*, 96–126; Charles G. DuBois, "A Half Century of Western Electric Achievement," *WE News*, 1919, 8(9): 1–6; Danielian, *A.T.&T.*, 15.
6   Danielian, *A.T.&T.*, 50–69; Brock, *Telecommunications Industry*, 148–51.

confident would sanction the monopoly of the Bell System as long as profits were kept at reasonable levels. Third, Bell began a concerted program in basic scientific research to ensure that the system was not threatened by outside scientific and technical developments. Thus, by the First World War the Bell System had gained effective control of the telephone industry, had completed the process of vertical integration begun in the 1880s, and, by accepting government regulation, had acquired a degree of public acceptance of its monopoly.[7]

Scientific management and factory organization

While the corporate managers at AT&T concerned themselves with these financial, political, and technical accommodations, managers at Western Electric focused on the reorganization of production and the introduction of scientific management. Through their efforts Western Electric became one of the leaders of U.S. industry in the scientific planning and rigorous control of manufacturing methods.

The essential principles of the new "scientific" management were codified and disseminated by Frederick W. Taylor in his seminal "Shop Management" (1903) and later in his famous (and notorious) *The Principles of Scientific Management* (1911). Taylor argued forcefully that the organization of production had to be wrested from workers and placed under the control of management. In existing systems of production, he argued, workers kept craft secrets to themselves, worked at a collectively agreed-upon rate that meant most did not work to the maximum of their ability, and were more interested in maintaining regular work than in achieving maximum output. Scientific management could achieve higher levels of production by undertaking a scientific analysis of each job, breaking it down into its component parts, and assigning these new simple tasks to carefully selected workers, who were expected to work at maximum output throughout the day. Taylor claimed that managers could dramatically increase production by implementing a system of job analyses, including time and motion studies, and by carefully applying incentive payments. In his most frequently quoted example, Taylor claimed that he had increased the output of a pig-iron handler from 12½ to 47½ tons per day by the simple expedient of directing the worker precisely when and how to work and rewarding him for this obedience.[8]

Taylor and the efficiency engineers who followed him insisted that scientific management was in the interests of both capitalists and workers. For workers it brought higher wages and cultivated sobriety and thrift, while

---

[7] Brock, *Telecommunications Industry*, 151–74.
[8] Frederick Winslow Taylor, *The Principles of Scientific Management*, New York: Harper, 1911.

for managers it increased productive efficiency, improved quality, and undermined the craft knowledge that helped sustain union power. Of course, Taylor reassured workers, they would now no longer need unions, because scientific management would deliver the high wages and job security they had long sought to achieve through senseless militancy. Efficiency engineers assured workers that production quotas and pay rates were based on firm scientific principles and would not be changed unless production processes were altered. Organized workers were not so sure; they soon discovered that piece rates had a nasty way of falling whenever they increased their productivity, leaving them earning the same as before. Moreover, the reorganization of production meant that skilled workers in particular lost control over the content, pace, and social organization of their work. In many places workers resisted the introduction of scientific management, especially the reviled time and motion studies and stopwatch, but with only limited success.[9]

The changes in factory organization codified by Taylor were already under way at Western Electric before "scientific management" became a well-known term. The extraordinary growth of the manufacturing arm of the Bell System provided a major impetus to find new methods of planning and controlling production. In 1879, at the time of the settlement between American Bell and Western Union, Western Electric employed about 200 workers each in its Chicago and New York factories. By 1900 the Clinton Street factory in Chicago employed 5,200 and a further 3,500 were at work in the New York plant, giving the company two of the thirty largest manufacturing plants in the United States. When in 1927 the Australian delegation visited the Hawthorne Works outside Chicago, nearly 22,000 workers were employed there with a further 9,000 at the company's Kearny plant in New Jersey. The increasing complexity of the technology, combined with the need to standardize the system, also encouraged the refinement of production methods, for such products as loading coils and large exchange switchboards required fine tolerances and precise calibration. It seems probable, too, that the renewed competition in the telephone industry from 1894 to 1913 placed pressure on Western Electric to keep production costs as low

---

[9] On the application of scientific management to U.S. industry, see Harry Braverman, *Labor and Monopoly Capital: The Degradation of Work in the Twentieth Century*, New York: Monthly Review Press, 1974, chaps. 4 and 5; David Montgomery, *The Fall of the House of Labor*, Cambridge University Press, 1987, chap. 5; Daniel Nelson, *Frederick W. Taylor and the Rise of Scientific Management*, Madison: University of Wisconsin Press, 1980; A. G. H. Aitken, *Taylorism at the Watertown Arsenal: Scientific Management in Action, 1908–1915*, Cambridge, Mass.: Harvard University Press, 1960; and Daniel Nelson, *Managers and Workers: Origins of the New Factory System in the United States, 1880–1920*, Madison: University of Wisconsin Press, 1975, chaps. 3 and 4. For a major survey of the development of U.S. manufacturing methods, see David A. Hounshell, *From the American System to Mass Production, 1800–1932: The Development of Manufacturing Technology in the United States*, Baltimore: Johns Hopkins University Press, 1984.

as possible in order to give the Bell companies every possible advantage. Finally, the factory managers were committed to undermining the considerable control held by craftsmen and their unions over the production process and conditions of work.[10]

Production at the Chicago and New York plants until the end of the nineteenth century was highly decentralized, in keeping with contemporary manufacturing practices. The foreman in each shop or department was an independent contractor who entered into agreements with the company to supply a certain amount of apparatus at a given price and by a given time. Company managers simply provided the factory, supplies, tools, and power; it was left to the foreman to hire, supervise, and pay the workers and determine the best method of production. Although this could permit a capricious and tyrannical foreman to drive and exploit the workers, in practice a mutuality of interest existed between them, especially when the foreman was the leader of a group of skilled workers rather than an independent entrepreneur. Skilled workers could have considerable control over the system of production through the establishment of union shop rules.[11]

The replacement of the contract system with a centralized production system under the control of specialized management was a gradual process. Beginning in 1888 a "chaser" was employed to keep track of the orders placed with foremen and check daily on their progress. From 1896 management began to follow the orders down the line to the subforemen and gang bosses and intervene in any problems holding up production. Finally, around 1897, the contract system was abolished; responsibility for planning and supervising production now lay with company managers.

The first steps were taken in the area of standardization. From 1899 every piece was manufactured according to specifications and tolerances taken from technical drawings, rather than by the old technique of comparing the manufactured part with a sample. At the same time inspectors began to inspect tools, gauges, and parts as well as finished products – an innovation that was resisted fiercely by both foremen and workers. Although information is scarce, it is apparent that managers also introduced piecework payment schemes and began to direct the way in which work was to be

[10] H. F. Albright, "Fifty Years' Progress in Manufacturing," *WE News*, 1919, 8(9): 22–9; U.S. Industrial Commission, *Report*, Washington, D.C.: U.S. Government Printing Office, 1901, testimony of Enos M. Barton, president of Western Electric, 8: 296, 298; Nelson, *Managers and Workers*, 7–8.

[11] Albright, "Fifty Years," 25–6; U.S. Industrial Commission, *Report*, testimony of Enos M. Barton, 8: 295–301. For discussions of the contract system and control of production by skilled workers, see Katherine Stone, "The Origins of Job Structures in the Steel Industry," *Review of Radical Political Economics*, Summer 1974, 6: 113–73; David Montgomery, *Workers' Control in America: Studies in the History of Work, Technology, and Labor Struggles*, Cambridge University Press, 1979, esp. chap. 1; and Nelson, *Managers and Workers*, chap. 3.

performed. A strike by 214 machinists in 1900, ostensibly over the company's refusal to permit a union shop, was in essence a challenge to management's right to direct production methods, since union rules prohibited piecework. That other skilled workers in the plant saw this as a crucial fight is reflected in the fact that seventy-eight brass molders and metal polishers went out in support of the machinists' demands. The strike, however, was a failure, and the reorganization of the factory proceeded apace.[12]

The major changes in production came with the building of the Hawthorne Works on the outskirts of Chicago in 1905, which gradually absorbed Western Electric's other two factories. By 1914 the entire manufacturing plant of the company was centralized in a single factory employing twelve thousand workers (Figure 1). Under the leadership of engineer Henry F. Albright, general superintendent at Hawthorne from 1908 to 1923, the company undertook a complete reorganization of production. New functional departments gathered similar equipment in one location and served the entire plant. No longer did each product department have its own collection of machines with skilled workers moving from one machine to the other, varying their work. Now each worker was confined to working in a department of drill presses, or lathes, or punch presses, assigned to a task that had been designed, timed, and priced according to precise measurements by a force of engineers and managers. Semiskilled and unskilled operators ran machines into which the skill had been designed or sat at benches assembling a single product. The modern factory had arrived.[13]

Behind the physical organization of the factory lay a complex technical organization of engineers and managers. For example, once the decision had been made to introduce machine switching, or automatic telephone exchanges, shortly after the First World War, the Manufacturing Department worked closely with the Engineering Department (later Bell Laboratories) to determine the appropriate equipment and manufacturing methods. Machine switching equipment consisted of some two hundred pieces of apparatus, made from approximately three thousand parts and requiring some thirty-six thousand manufacturing and inspection operations. Manufacturing methods had to be determined for each of these parts and operations, and time standards and piece rates established for the workers. By 1922 such tasks had grown so immense that a separate Time Standards Department was established, which by 1929 was employing sixty personnel to establish rates with the use of stopwatches and a micromotion camera. Only thirty years previously workers set their own pace and determined

[12] Albright, "Fifty Years," 26–8; U.S. Industrial Commission, *Report*, testimony of E. M. Barton, 8: 295–301; Barton to J. F. Hudson, 21 April 1900, AT&T/1316.

[13] Albright, "Fifty Years," 28–9; "Pioneer Factory Builder Rose from Office Boy to Executive," n.d., WE/Albright; Western Electric, *Organization of the Western Electric Co., Inc.,* [1922], 19.

Figure 1. Hawthorne Works, Western Electric Company, 1929. The main assembly plant is at the bottom center of the picture with its landmark tower at the corner of Cicero Avenue and Cermak Road. Railroad tracks intersect the site of more than two hundred acres, which extends from the cable plant on the far left to a lumber yard on the center right. Rows of workers' houses extend along two sides of the factory. Courtesy of AT&T Archives.

how they would produce an article, while management had to request a foreman to expedite a job.[14]

Functional organization was also applied to the process of hiring and firing, the keeping of employment records, and the training of apprentices. Under the contract system the foreman had complete responsibility for hiring and firing workers of his choice and for determining their wage rates. In 1896 an Employment Department was established as part of the process of abolishing the contract system; henceforth, workers were to be hired through this central department, and foremen would be required to justify their decisions to fire workers. From 1913 a superintendent of employment and welfare at Hawthorne controlled a sophisticated system of personnel records. Prospective workers were required to fill out a detailed application

[14] W. F. Hosford, "Preparation for Manufacture of Machine Switching Equipment," Western Electric, *Engineering-Manufacturing Conference, Chicago, 27–31 October 1919,* 1–3 WE; E. C. Tessman, "Report on the Organization and Operation of the Wage Incentives, Time Standards and Labor Grades Departments," 5 Oct. 1936, HSC/6/Research & Special Studies.

form and to be interviewed by a personnel officer; only in the case of some skilled workers did the foreman have an opportunity to interview them before they were hired. If an applicant was successful, and passed a physical examination, numerous forms were completed: an identification card, a clock number, notices to the employee's department and the payroll office, and a personnel record. The new employee's rate of pay was set by the department head, but within the range of rates set for that class of work, and could be changed only with the approval of higher management. The foreman or department chief, as much as the worker, was now bound into a hierarchical and bureaucratic system in which his power was severely curtailed.[15]

The new employment managers, now in charge of detailed employment records, soon began to analyze their data, compiling statistics on such subjects as labor turnover and stability, the reasons given by workers for resigning, and employees' length of service. For the first time Western Electric managers had detailed statistics showing the characteristics of their workforce and changing trends. The workforce profiles of branches and departments could be compared, and the performance of managers in handling their employees judged thereby. Pay scales could be compared with those of similar factories in the Chicago area to ensure that they were high enough to attract a desirable workforce – but not so high as to be excessive. And with reports such as these in their hands, top managers began to turn their attention to the management of personnel. The behavior and attitudes of workers and supervisors were becoming a management concern.

Industrial relations and personnel policies

Bell managers were not alone in their attempts to improve the motivation and loyalty of their workers. From about 1910 until the middle of the 1920s large U.S. corporations expended considerable energy on reforming industrial relations systems and in developing a sophisticated package of personnel practices. Various developments fueled this concern. The labor movement had matured into a powerful industrial and political force under the leadership of Samuel Gompers of the American Federation of Labor (AFL). Corporate leaders tried every possible means to contain union power, from negotiation and agreements to the use of spies and private militia; but whatever the tactics, they realized they faced a guerrilla war in which they had to win the hearts and minds of the rank and file. A powerful network of social reformers emerged at the same time in Progressive Era America

---

[15] J. W. Bancker, "Records and Reports of Work," *Annals of the American Academy of Political and Social Science,* 1916, 65: 252–72; C. W. Berquist, "Industrial Relations," Western Electric, *Engineering-Manufacturing Conference, Chicago, 27–31 October 1919,* WE; "History of Personnel Practices," 1949, WE/Personnel. For a general discussion of employment departments, see Nelson, *Managers and Workers,* 79–86.

and took as one of their central goals the improvement of the living and working conditions of the industrial worker. A spate of labor legislation was passed in the first two decades of the century, notably workers' compensation, factory inspection, and the regulation of women's and children's labor. Muckraking journalists brought to light endless examples of the carelessness and callousness of corporations and trusts. Companies suddenly had to win the hearts and minds of the public as well.

Apart from these external pressures, companies discovered that there were sound financial and organizational reasons to improve working conditions and the social relations of production. The large corporations had by the First World War completed the major phase of vertical and horizontal integration. Now in control of the national markets, they could begin to plan for long-term stability and growth and were earning profits that they could afford to share with their workforce. Personnel managers had sufficient evidence and arguments to persuade their superiors that improved personnel practices would increase productivity. The best example was the extraordinary waste to a company caused by labor turnover, which exceeded 300% per annum in many factories. The small investment required to make a job sufficiently remunerative and satisfying would be more than repaid by a stable, dedicated, and efficient workforce. By the end of the First World War business leaders had begun to perceive the advantages of expressing concern for the economic and political rights of the common worker, and they sought ways that would accommodate those rights within their corporate strategies.

Like many of the other major corporations that could afford a full-scale campaign, the Bell System combined a series of measures designed to win worker loyalty, known collectively as welfare capitalism, with strategies to limit or even eliminate union organization, primarily through company-controlled unions or employee representation plans. Individual firms often picked up only aspects of these plans, and in many cases they did not become permanent features. The Bell System, however, was a huge corporation with a high public profile and an excellent profit rate, and it applied the new personnel philosophies to an extent unsurpassed by any other company. The growth of personnel schemes in the Bell System was not the result of a clearly defined managerial philosophy – that came later – but was a response to labor unrest inside the companies and external political and social pressures.[16]

---

[16] Analyses of the corporate strategy of welfare capitalism and descriptions of the programs introduced are provided in Stuart D. Brandes, *American Welfare Capitalism, 1880–1940*, Chicago: University of Chicago Press, 1976; Sumner H. Slichter, "The Current Labor Policies of American Industries," *Quarterly Journal of Economics*, 1929, 43: 393–435; Nelson, *Managers and Workers*, chap. 6; David Brody, *Workers in Industrial America: Essays on the Twentieth Century Struggle*, New York: Oxford University Press, 1980, chap. 2; Montgomery, *Workers' Control*, chap. 2; Stephen Meyer, *The Five Dollar Day: Labor*

Western Electric's first step in the implementation of welfare plans for its employees occurred in 1906 with the introduction of a pension system. Workers over sixty-five who had worked for at least twenty years were eligible for a modest pension of 1 percent of their salary times the number of years they had worked. It was hoped that the scheme would help the company attract and retain workers and discourage them from striking. The capacity of the plan to avert strikes lay not so much in the inculcation of responsible attitudes among the workforce as in the fact that the awarding of a pension to any individual was discretionary, the decision remaining in the hands of a management committee.[17]

Welfare policies were also shaped by the political climate in which the company operated. A significant factor in the introduction in 1913 of a package of welfare benefits throughout the Bell System was the need to demonstrate to insistent state regulators, federal antitrust interests, and the public that Bell was a socially responsible trust and public utility. In addition to a pension scheme the plan included sickness and disability benefits; these were intended in part to satisfy recent workmens' compensation legislation passed in many states. As with the earlier Western Electric plan, it was hoped that welfare policies would discourage unionization. The International Brotherhood of Electrical Workers (IBEW) in 1910 had commenced a campaign to organize telephone operators; accordingly, the original memorandum to Vail recommending the introduction of a benefit plan listed "freedom from Labor Unions" as a major reason.[18]

AT&T also pioneered in the implementation of a stock purchase plan for its employees, which by the mid-1920s was the largest of its kind in the country. Introduced in 1915, the plan permitted employees in the Bell System to purchase AT&T stock on installments, with provisions for withdrawing the money at any stage. The stock was sold to employees at below market price; for example, one AT&T share in 1926 cost an employee $130, whereas the market price varied from $140 to $150. The purposes of the

Management and Social Control in the Ford Motor Company, 1908–1921, Albany: State University of New York Press, 1981; and U.S. Bureau of Labor Statistics, *Welfare Work for Employees in Industrial Establishments in the United States* (bulletin no. 250), Washington, D.C.: U.S. Government Printing Office, 1919.

[17] C. G. DuBois to the Board of Directors, Western Electric, 1 Feb. 1906, AT&T/1380. A similar provision was included in most company pension schemes of the period; for the use of this provision against strikers at International Harvester, see Robert Ozanne, *A Century of Labor–Management Relations at McCormick and International Harvester*, Madison: University of Wisconsin Press, 1967, 82–5.

[18] On the introduction of the plan, see J. D. Ellsworth to T. N. Vail, 6 Apr. 1910, AT&T/47; Vail to U. N. Bethell, 8 Oct. 1910, AT&T/47; H. J. Brandt, "The History of the Employees' Benefit Plan," *Bell System Benefit Secretaries' Conference, New York, March 23–8, 1925*, AT&T/75; R. E. McEwen, "The Why of Our Benefit Plan," 1927, WE/Personnel. See Brock, *Telecommunications Industry*, 151–61, for an account of increased government regulation and public concern regarding the telephone trust.

plan were threefold. First, it was expected that employee stockholders would be more likely to stay with a company in which they had an investment. Second, the company hoped that its employees would work harder because, as company literature constantly stressed, workers who bought stock became "partners as well as employees." Third, and most important, the plan was part of a concerted campaign by AT&T to increase the number of stockholders so that it could argue that the Bell System was, as Chairman Walter Gifford never tired of stressing, not a private monopoly but a "public utility, publicly owned." While technically employees had no obligation to purchase stock, considerable pressure was applied: Supervisors at Hawthorne lectured workers on the need for thrift and pestered them to subscribe to shares, while comparative statistics of companies and plants turned the affair into a competition. Such campaigns increased participation at Hawthorne from 19 percent of employees in 1925 to 75 percent in 1929, when 18,374 workers at the factory subscribed to 104,907 shares.[19]

Welfare capitalism was extended in several other directions at the Hawthorne Works. A medical department and hospital were opened in 1908; from 1909 a band gave lunch-hour concerts once a week; in 1921 an athletic field consisting of six baseball diamonds, thirteen tennis courts, and a running track was constructed; and in 1927 the Albright Gymnasium was built in memory of the first factory superintendent (Figure 2). The Hawthorne Club, however, was the pinnacle of social activities at the works. Formed in 1911, the club organized social activities, vacations, sports competitions (including a baseball league, gun, golf, and swimming clubs, and a women's basketball team called the "Ruthless Babes"), evening classes, a club store, a savings and loan association, and even beauty contests. The major event each year was the club elections, conducted in the style of a political campaign, with lunchtime political rallies and speeches over the factory public address system. Candidates were carefully chosen by a nominating committee and were invariably managers or office workers rather than factory workers. Despite this, voter turnout was always high, reaching 94 percent in 1931. The club was enormously popular, especially among the large number of young and single men and women and those who lived in the working-class suburbs adjacent to the works. Evening courses attracted about 2,500 participants each year during the 1920s, although, as with stock purchases, there is evidence that supervisors were given quotas and directed to encourage their workers to attend – women were particularly pressured into attending a course on health and hygiene. All these activities were coordinated through the *Hawthorne Microphone*, a bimonthly mag-

[19] National Industrial Conference Board, *Employee Stock Purchase Plans in the United States*, New York, 1928, esp. 81, 101, and app. 1; Walter S. Gifford, *Addresses, Papers, and Interviews*, New York, 1928–49, 1: 61–72, 84, 115; Danielian, *A.T.&T.*, 173–99; *Hawthorne Microphone*, 25 May 1925, 5 Nov. 1928, 26 Aug. 1929.

Figure 2. Hawthorne Club track and field meet, 1927. Welfare capitalism at its peak. The center included the imposing Albright Gymnasium, baseball field, and basketball and tennis courts. The Telephone Apparatus building can be seen in the background. Courtesy of AT&T Archives.

azine combining factory and company news with social activities and paternalistic messages from works managers.[20]

Welfare capitalism was designed to dissuade workers from joining unions; the employee representation plan introduced in the Bell System in 1919 was intended to stifle the existing unions. To understand the development of this scheme we must consider the history of the companies' attitudes toward unions. Some of Western Electric's skilled workers had become union members in the 1880s and 1890s, and machinists and molders made more than one attempt to establish a union shop in the early 1900s. The company resisted formal union representation on the shop floor, although it did sign

[20] Western Electric, *History of Personnel Practices*, WE/Personnel; Western Electric, *Opportunities with the Western Electric Company, Hawthorne Station, Chicago*, n.p., 1914; Western Electric, *A Good Place to Work*, n.d., WE/Hawthorne; *Hawthorne Microphone*, 1922–33. The evidence for supervisor pressure on workers to subscribe to stock and to attend evening classes comes from Relay Assembly Test Room, Daily History Record, 7 Oct. 1927, HSCM/11–15.

one-year contracts with a few groups of workers in 1902. The Bell operating companies adopted a similar strategy of resistance to organizing attempts by the IBEW, including the use of spies at union meetings and the firing of union members. Bell particularly feared the organization of its army of telephone operators, especially after the IBEW commenced a serious organizing effort in 1910 and succeeded in establishing a local among the Boston operators in 1912; it was during this period of union activity that the pension and stock purchase plans were developed.[21] A common theme in Bell arguments against recognizing unions was that it did not want outside parties (union organizers) to come between the company and its employees, thereby destroying the intimate relationship that had been established between manager and worker. But there was a flaw in this argument, as a Massachusetts state arbitration board observed during its adjudication of a strike among Western Electric workers in 1917: "The rights of the employer as to employees brought in close touch and contact with the management, may be as claimed by the company, but not so with a corporation whose employees are numbered by thousands and with whom there is not the personal touch that may be found in smaller units of industry." The employee representation plan introduced in 1919 was intended to circumvent that objection by conceding a form of worker representation without recognizing unions.[22]

Pressure from outside political forces was again necessary before Bell took this new step in industrial relations. From 1 August 1918 to 31 July 1919 the telephone and telegraph industries were placed under government control as a means of ensuring wartime security. The Wire Control Board and postmaster general took control of the telephone companies, but the present managers and executives continued the day-to-day operation of services. The AFL saw a golden opportunity for extending the policies of the government War Labor Board to the telephone industry, including its direction

[21] Brief overviews of early unionization are given in Jack Barbash, *Unions and Telephones: The Story of the Communications Workers of America*, New York: Harper & Bros., 1952, 1–10; John N. Schacht, *The Making of Telephone Unionism, 1920–1947*, New Brunswick, N.J.: Rutgers University Press, 1985, 6–18; AT&T, "A Chronological Summary of Management–Labor Relations in the Bell System, 1880–1950," AT&T. Detailed evidence of industrial relations in the Bell System is thin, but see U.S. Industrial Commission, *Report*, testimony of Enos M. Barton, 8: 295–301; H. B. Thayer to Hudson, 16 Apr. 1900, Barton to Hudson, 21 Apr. 1900, AT&T/1316; Barton to Fish, 6 Dec. 1902, AT&T/1316; F. J. McNulty to Officers and Members of IBEW Locals, 9 May 1907, AT&T/1365; Samuel Gompers to Vail, 25 June 1907, Gompers to Vail, 2 Nov. 1907, AT&T/1365; B. E. Sunny to Vail, 2 Mar. 1911, AT&T/2018.

[22] For example, U.S. Industrial Commission, *Report*, testimony of Enos M. Barton, 8: 295–301; Thayer to Senator W. Murray Crane, 22 May 1918, WE/Thayer. Quote from Commonwealth of Massachusetts State Board of Conciliation and Arbitration, "In the Matter of a Strike by Employees of the Repair Plant of the Western Electric Company, Inc., at Boston," 30 Oct. 1917, AT&T/47.

that unions be permitted to organize in those industries with war contracts. Postmaster General A. S. Burleson at first resisted demands by the telephone unions and the War Labor Board to permit union officials to bargain with the companies or the Wire Control Board, until the threat of a national strike forced him to issue a directive in June 1919 that the Bell companies must bargain collectively with their workers.[23]

By the following year most of the employees of the Bell System were covered, the specifics of the plan varying from company to company. Elected or appointed employee representatives would meet with managers once a month in "joint conference committees" to discuss issues raised by either group. At first workers used the meetings to address long-held grievances, but management increasingly used the occasion as a means of disseminating and explaining company policy. The employee representation plan was, as an AT&T personnel manager put it, "both an extension of management practices and a supplementation of regular organization arrangements."[24] The AFL was quick to attack the premises on which employee representation plans, or company unions, were based:

> In establishing wages, hours, and working conditions, in their plant, employers habitually use their great economic power to enforce their will. Therefore, to secure just treatment, the only recourse of the workers is to develop a power equally strong and to confront the employers with it. . . . In this vital respect, the company union is a complete failure. With hardly a pretense of organization, unaffiliated with other groups of workers in the same industry, destitute of funds, and unfitted to use the strike weapon, it is totally unable to force its will.[25]

[23] See documents in file on Government Control, AT&T/14; John B. Colpoys (Department of Labor) and Julia O'Connor (president, Telephone Operators' Union, New England) to A. S. Burleson, 6 Jan. 1919, AT&T/14; Burleson to W. B. Wilson (secretary of labor), 15 Mar. 1919, AT&T/2; J. Epps Brown to Thayer, 10 June 1919, W. H. Lamar to U. N. Bethell, 14 June 1919, AT&T/2; Barbash, *Unions and Telephones*, 1–10. For discussion of the National War Labor Board policies, which guaranteed collective bargaining but did not concede union recognition and consequently recommended a form of shop committee or works council, see Carroll E. French, *The Shop Committee in the United States*, Baltimore: Johns Hopkins University Press, 1923, 21–6; and Nelson, *Managers and Workers*, 160–1.

[24] On the introduction of the plan see Vail to Presidents of Associated Companies, 3 June 1919, Vail to F. H. Bethell, 3 June 1919, Thayer to President of Associated Companies, 6 June 1919, AT&T/2. The employee representation plan in the Bell System is described in E. K. Hall, "The Personnel Job – What It Is and What It Is Not," *Bell System Personnel Conference, Washington, DC, October, 1925*, WE, 1–6; B. Gherardi, "Some Suggestions and a Summary of the Discussion of Employee Representation and Personnel Work in the Bell System," *Bell System Personnel Conference, Rye Beach, N.H., October 1923*, WE; E. K. Hall, "What Is Employee Representation?" *Personnel*, Feb. 1928, 4: 71–84. The quote is from W. A. Griffin, "Possibilities of Joint Conference Committees as a Means of Getting Information to Employees," *Bell System Publicity Conference, Southern Pines, N.C., 1928*, WE, 49.

[25] AFL convention resolution, 1919, quoted in U.S. Bureau of Labor Statistics, *Characteristics*

However, combined with welfare policies and rigorous antiunion practices, employee representation succeeded in halting and then reversing the process of unionization started during the First World War. As in many other major corporations, union membership in the Bell System declined rapidly under the pressure of a nation-wide open-shop drive, a "Red scare," and a postwar economic depression. By 1922 AT&T president H. B. Thayer could look forward to the time when, "before very long, the employees of the Bell System throughout the country will have no affiliation with any outside labor organizations and will co-operate thoroughly with the management for the good of the business."[26]

Several other major corporations established employee representation plans during 1919 in the face of massive industrial unrest and public and government pressure. All of the plans, including that at Bell, drew directly or indirectly on the so-called Rockefeller Plan, established at the Colorado Fuel and Iron Company (CF&I) in 1915. A strike in the Colorado coal fields in 1914 had exploded into violence when company police and state militia attacked the miners' tent camp at the Rockefeller-owned CF&I mine. Eleven children and two women died in the "Ludlow massacre." In the face of public outrage and the probings of the U.S. Commission on Industrial Relations, the recently formed Rockefeller Foundation appointed Canadian politician William L. Mackenzie King to devise an industrial relations plan for CF&I and to undertake a detailed study of the whole field of industrial relations. Labor leaders, progressives, and liberal members of the U.S. commission were appalled. Only four years previously Rockefeller had failed to have his foundation publicly incorporated by the U.S. Congress, because a majority of politicians adopted the view that such foundations were built on the ill-gotten gains of the "robber barons" and that philanthropic programs would be used to undermine the democratic process. But King and John D. Rockefeller, Jr., persisted, and in the following year an Industrial Representation Plan was introduced amid much fanfare, including a visit to Colorado by Rockefeller. Although King saw employee representation as a supplement to rather than a replacement of trade unions, in practice the plan excluded unionists and collective bargaining.[27]

of Company Unions, 1935 (bulletin no. 634), Washington, D.C.: U.S. Government Printing Office, 1938, 17–18.

[26] Barbash, *Unions and Telephones*, 10–19; quote from Thayer to Herbert J. Wells, 2 June 1922, AT&T/1.

[27] For the Ludlow massacre and federal government inquiry see U.S. Senate, Commission on Industrial Relations, *Final Report and Testimony*, Washington, D.C.: U.S. Government Printing Office, 1916, vols. 7–9; Graham Adams, *The Age of Industrial Violence, 1910–1915: The Activities and Findings of the United States Commission on Industrial Relations*, New York: Columbia University Press, 1966; Howard M. Gitelman, *Legacy of the Ludlow Massacre: A Chapter in American Industrial Relations*, Philadelphia: University of Pennsylvania Press, 1988. The plan and Rockefeller's views are gathered in John D. Rockefeller, Jr., *The Colorado Industrial Plan*, n.p., 1916. Mackenzie King's role is described in F. A.

The experience transformed John D. Rockefeller, Jr., who had previously been overshadowed by his father. The events surrounding the Ludlow massacre proved to be a rite of passage, and he continued to involve himself in industrial issues for years afterward. For the most part this involvement occurred out of the public eye, with the exception of his chairmanship of the public group in President Wilson's Second Industrial Conference of 1919–20. On this occasion Rockefeller and King conferred closely with Vice-Chairman Herbert Hoover. The report of the conference, written largely by Hoover, endorsed employee representation plans as a means of "collective bargaining."[28] Privately, Rockefeller encouraged the introduction of plans and offered King's services to those companies in which he was a major shareholder. Through 1918 and 1919 King assisted in the introduction of plans at Bethlehem Steel, General Electric, International Harvester, Standard Oil of Indiana, Standard Oil of New Jersey, and Youngstown Sheet and Tube. With these eminent examples and that of the Bell System before them, many other large companies followed suit; by 1924 some 1,240,000 U.S. workers were covered by employee representation plans.[29]

For reasons not explicit in existing documentation, the Bell representation plan was not applied at Western Electric. Two reasons can be adduced, however. First, the manufacturing subsidiary was not subject to government control since it did not engage in telephone communications and Postmaster General Burleson's order therefore did not apply to the company. Second, Western Electric was not subject to state or federal regulation as a communications company, with the notable exception that regulatory authorities might examine its pricing structure for telephone equipment. Its labor relations were therefore never a matter of government scrutiny as they were at AT&T and Bell operating companies. Nevertheless, the plan influenced Western Electric personnel managers in many indirect ways, for it established underlying assumptions about the roles of managers and workers that permeated all parts of the Bell System, and it encouraged the development of elaborate personnel policies.

The most important result of the representation plan was that it estab-

McGregor, *The Fall and Rise of Mackenzie King, 1911–1919,* New York: Macmillan, 1962, 92–109; see also Mackenzie King to J. D. Rockefeller, Jr., 6 Aug. 1914, RF/3/900/20/149, and Mackenzie King, "The Relation of the Industrial Representation Plan to Trade-Unions," 31 May 1916, RF/3/900/20/151. On public views of the new philanthropies, see Barry D. Karl and Stanley D. Katz, "The American Private Philanthropic Foundation and the Public Sphere, 1890–1930," *Minerva,* 1981, 19: 236–70.

[28] Peter Collier and David Horowitz, *The Rockefellers: An American Dynasty,* New York: Holt, Rinehart & Winston, 1976, 108–34; U.S. Department of Labor, "Report of Industrial Conference Called by the President," *Annual Report,* 1920, 234–69.

[29] Rockefeller, Jr., to Walter Teagle (president, Standard Oil of New Jersey) 9 May 1919, OMR/2F/133; Rockefeller, Jr., to Col. Robert W. Stewart (Standard Oil, Indiana) 30 Apr. 1919, OMR/Business Interests/87.1-S5; Clarence Hicks (Standard Oil of New Jersey) to Rockefeller, Jr., 7 Mar. 1933, OMR/2F/133/87.1S9; McGregor, *Mackenzie King,* 249–72; U.S. Bureau of Labor Statistics, *Characteristics of Company Unions,* 19–25.

lished a new group of managers within the corporate structure of the Bell System. Henceforth, personnel managers would be responsible for codifying and disseminating industrial relations policy. Following the introduction of the plan in June 1919, AT&T established a Personnel Committee, chaired by Vice-President Walter S. Gifford, and directed that each operating company appoint a manager to be responsible for personnel relations. In November 1919 these managers met in the first of the Bell System personnel conferences, which were held every few months until the plan was regularized and then became an annual event. By 1922 these conferences had developed into a week-long affair at a resort, where managers exchanged ideas and received the latest directives from AT&T headquarters.[30]

Western Electric quickly followed suit, even though it did not introduce a representation plan. In 1920 personnel managers were established in each of the major branches at the Hawthorne Works, and in 1922 a General Personnel Committee was formed at the New York head office. As at AT&T, personnel matters were now considered so important that they were placed under the control of a vice-president reporting directly to the president. Lacking a company union through which it could publicize its policies, the Western Electric General Personnel Committee composed a personnel policy consisting of ten "commandments." President Charles Dubois himself wrote the tenth commandment:

> To carry on the daily work in a spirit of friendliness. As the Company grows it must be more human – not less so. Discipline, standards and precedents become more necessary with size, but the spirit in which they are administered must be friendly as well as just. Courtesy is as important within the organization as in dealing with outsiders. Inefficiency and indifference cannot be tolerated, but the effort of supervisors must be increasingly directed at building up in every department a loyal and enthusiastic interest in the Company's work.[31]

This emphasis on the need to take into account the "human element" echoed again and again through Bell System discussions of personnel management. E. K. Hall, vice-president in charge of personnel of AT&T, developed this theme extensively in talks and articles during the 1920s. Technical developments in industry, he argued, had been introduced without regard for their effect on workers. Complex managerial structures isolated workers from those making decisions. The result was that workers, encouraged by

[30] Thayer to W.S. Gifford, 3 July 1919, Thayer to Gifford, 18 Mar. 1921, AT&T/56; E. K. Hall, "Opening of Conference," *Bell System Personnel Conference, Washington, DC, October, 1925*, AT&T/2017; J. Walter Dietz, *Walter Dietz Speaking*, Summit, N.J.: Walter Dietz, n.d., 58–9. From 1922 the proceedings of the conferences were published and disseminated through the system; incomplete sets are held at WE and AT&T.

[31] Quoted in J. W. Dietz, "Some Aspects of Personnel Research in a Manufacturing Organization," *Annals of the American Academy of Political and Social Science*, 1925, 119: 3. See Dietz, *Walter Dietz Speaking*, 59–60, for an account of the writing of the ten commandments. On the introduction of Western Electric personnel policies, see Western Electric, "History of Personnel Practices," WE.

the doctrines of "demagogues" and "yellow newspapers," began to perceive themselves as members of a separate class. Personnel management was intended to integrate the three "human forces" in industry – executives, intermediate managers, and workers – so as "to make sure that the entire human element and manpower in the industry is mobilized." It would transform the worker into a partner in a collective industrial enterprise. And since the average worker's contribution to the development of civilization could occur only through work, personnel management would ensure that "his whole attitude toward his job and often toward life itself becomes more wholesome and he becomes a more contented citizen." Personnel management was in no way seen as a replacement for scientific management. Rather, personnel management, with its various means of making workers feel part of a larger enterprise, was necessary precisely because scientific management and modern production techniques had, with few exceptions, reduced workers' control over their work and sentenced them to performing a series of repetitive, meaningless tasks.[32]

Personnel management thus became a cornerstone of corporate political philosophy. Walter S. Gifford, president of AT&T from 1925 to 1948 (and later U.S. ambassador to Great Britain, 1950–3) devoted much time to enunciating this philosophy during the 1920s. "Democracy in business," he asserted, has "three important manifestations – in the ownership of business enterprises, in the relations between management and labor, and in the reaction of business practices to public sentiment."[33] Seemingly disparate corporate policies dovetailed as AT&T sought to create the image of "Ma Bell" as a corporation that was owned by the public and operated in its interest through the cooperation of managers and workers. A campaign to increase the number of stockholders was undertaken; by 1928 the company could point to 437,000 stockholders, a threefold increase since 1920, and claim that not one of them held as much as 1 percent of the stock (it refrained from noting that such a holding would entail an investment of the order of $17 million). While large numbers of small stockholders gave the appearance of public ownership, top management increased its control of the company. Stockholders lacked the power to challenge sitting directors and executive officers, who held sufficient proxies to ensure control of the annual general meeting. In their classic study of large corporations, citing AT&T as a prime example, Adolph Berle and Gardiner Means concluded that "the separation of ownership and control has become virtually complete." The large number

---

[32] E. K. Hall, "Management's Responsibility for and Opportunities in the Personnel Job," American Management Association, Convention Address Series, no. 1, 1922, quotes from 5, 6, 13, respectively. See also E. K. Hall, "New Objectives in Personnel Relations," *Bell System General Plant Operation Conference*, Pinehurst, N.J., October 1928.

[33] Walter S. Gifford, "Democracy in Business," *Saturday Evening Post*, 29 Mar. 1930, in Gifford, *Addresses*, 2:57. For a more candid discussion by Gifford of the function of Bell policies, see Gifford, "A Statement of the Fundamental Policies of the Bell System," *Bell System Publicity Conference*, Southern Pines, N.C., 1928.

of employee stockholders, as we have seen, also provided evidence of the supposedly democratic nature of the business.[34] Personnel policies and the employee representation plan demonstrated that managers were as responsive to workers as they were to stockholders and the public. "We don't shout at people nowadays and hammer the desk," Gifford observed. "We really hardly give orders. We suggest certain courses of action."[35] In the hands of Bell publicists, the company shed the tarnished image of a monopoly and took on the rosy glow of something that at times seemed to approach a workers' soviet, captured in Vail's motto of "One System, One Management, Universal Service."

It is tempting to see such employee representation and employee stock purchase plans as nothing more than a simple ploy by large companies to avoid unionization and collective bargaining, and as we have seen, this was certainly an important motivation. Yet as the example of Walter Gifford and other Bell executives suggests, corporate leaders saw these plans as a permanent solution to the antagonism between labor and capital and as a crucial element in the building of a democratic society free of social and industrial unrest. Thus, Herbert Hoover shared the views of Rockefeller and Bell executives that U.S. industry had to "re-establish through organized representation that personal cooperation between employer and employee ... that was a binding force when our industries were smaller." Ellis Hawley has shown that Hoover and postwar Republican progressives such as Rockefeller and Gifford shared a vision of an "associative state" in which public-spirited business leaders would join with private associations and the state to build a mass society. Professional managers, unlike the earlier "robber barons," were not a threat to democratic values – indeed, through such means as economic growth and employee representation, business was to be the central mechanism for building the new society.[36]

Science at work

Science was to play a central role in the building of this modern industrial society. The final attribute noted by the Australian industrial delegation in

[34] Adolf A. Berle, Jr., and Gardiner C. Means, *The Modern Corporation and Private Property*, New York: Commerce Clearing House, 1932, 47–9, 84–90, quote on 89; Danielian, *A.T.&T.*, 173–99.

[35] Gifford, "Democracy in Business," 56–7.

[36] Ellis W. Hawley, *The Great War and the Search for a Modern Order*, New York: St. Martin's Press, 1979, 52–5, 66–71, 83–5, 90–4; idem, "Herbert Hoover, the Commerce Secretariat, and the Vision of an 'Associative State,' 1921–1928," *Journal of American History*, June 1974, 61: 116–40; Robert H. Zieger, "Herbert Hoover, the Wage-Earner, and the 'New Economic System,' 1919–29," in Ellis Hawley, ed., *Herbert Hoover as Secretary of Commerce*, Iowa City: University of Iowa Press, 1981, 80–114, quote on 83. For a description of the debate among intellectuals over industrial democracy as a critical social reform, see James B. Gilbert, *Designing the Industrial State: The Intellectual Pursuit of Collectivism in America, 1880–1940*, Chicago: Quadrangle, 1972, 80–122.

1927 was the level of scientific and technical research conducted in U.S. industry and the systematic application of that research to new industrial products and processes. Frederick Taylor and his followers stressed that industrial management must also be conducted on scientific principles. Although Taylor concentrated on the technical organization of work and the physical abilities of the worker, he underlined the need for scientific investigation into the "motives which influence men."[37] Taylor's system stressed primarily the economic incentive of higher pay for workers, but by the 1920s specialists in such fields as psychology, physiology, and psychiatry began to conduct research on industrial relations and personnel management. The growing faith of U.S. business leaders in the utility, indeed absolute necessity, of industrial research provided the basis for a ready acceptance of social and behavioral scientists who promised that their expertise was relevant to the problems of industry.

Industrial research had commenced in the late nineteenth century with the emergence of science-based industry, the electrical and chemical industries being the most conspicuous cases. As company engineers faced more and more complex research tasks, they turned to universities as a source of highly trained scientists and began to conduct laboratory research. Executives found that only by conducting continuous research and patenting the results could they maintain technical and market superiority over competitors. By 1920 some 296 industrial research laboratories in the United States employed 9,300 research personnel, with major corporations, including General Electric, Eastman Kodak, and Du Pont, leading the field. A decade later the field had expanded to 1,625 laboratories employing more than 34,000 researchers.[38]

The industrial research program of the Bell System was the largest of them all. The company had recognized early on the need to conduct research in order to improve the quality and distance of telephone transmission; in 1883 it established an experimental shop, and in 1907 centralized all engineering and research for the Bell System in the Western Electric Engineering Department. Fundamental scientific research was seen as the key to staying at the forefront of communications technology and locking out competitors. By 1915 the Engineering Department employed more than forty researchers, seven of whom had Ph.D.'s, and when the department was reorganized in 1925 as Bell Telephone Laboratories, it had a budget of more than $12 million and 3,500 employees. The Bell System was now engaged in the manufacture of science as well as telephones.[39]

---

[37] Taylor, *Principles of Scientific Management*, 119–120.
[38] The history of industrial research is analyzed in David F. Noble, *America by Design: Science, Technology, and the Rise of Corporate Capitalism*, New York: Knopf, 1977, esp. chaps. 1 and 7. See Malcolm Harrison Ross, ed., *Profitable Practice in Industrial Research*, New York: Harper, 1932, for the views of leaders in industrial research in the 1920s.
[39] Danielian, *A.T.&T.*, chaps. 5 and 6; Leonard S. Reich, *The Making of American Industrial*

Bell's chief researchers and executives become public advocates of the importance of scientific research for industrial and national growth, and they set out to forge links between universities, government, and industry. The First World War provided the opportunity for the rapid development of these institutional ties. The Council of National Defense was established by the government in 1916 as a means of coordinating industrial resources for the war; future AT&T president Walter Gifford acted as its administrative director. For the coordination of scientific resources the National Academy of Sciences, with government approval, established the National Research Council (NRC), which proved so successful that it was reestablished in 1918 as a peacetime organization. With funding from the Engineering Foundation, Carnegie Corporation, and Rockefeller Foundation, the NRC took on the role of coordinating scientific research in both universities and industry, acting as a clearinghouse for scientific information, and providing research fellowships for young scientists. Several Bell personnel held influential positions; for example, Bell Labs president Frank B. Jewett became chairman of the Division of Engineering and Industrial Research in 1923 and worked tirelessly to bring university scientists and engineers into closer contact with industry.[40]

This new awareness of the importance of scientific research for industrial progress created a favorable environment for the application of the social, behavioral, and medical sciences to industrial problems. Two other factors were also critical. First, members of these new or revolutionized scientific disciplines saw the application of their expertise to social problems as an intrinsic part of the professionalization of their field; hitherto intractable and divisive social issues could be resolved, they felt, by empirical observation and scientific judgment. Moreover, the application of science would result in a society at once more harmonious and rational – "efficiency" in all areas of social endeavor remained a slogan well into the 1920s.[41]

Second, personnel managers were gaining a measure of professional con-

Research: Science and Business at GE and Bell, 1876–1926, Cambridge University Press, 1985, esp. chaps. 7 and 8.

[40] Noble, *America by Design,* chap. 7; Dugald C. Jackson, "A History of the National Research Council: III. Division of Engineering and Industrial Research," *Science,* 1933, 77: 500–3. The optimistic spirit of scientific leaders coming out of the war is captured in Robert M. Yerkes, ed., *The New World of Science: Its Development During the War,* New York: Century, 1920.

[41] For the professionalization of the social sciences see Henrika Kuklick, "Boundary Maintenance in American Sociology: Limitations to Academic 'Professionalization,' " *Journal of the History of the Behavioral Sciences,* 1980, 16: 201–19; Dorothy Ross, "The Development of the Social Sciences," in Alexandra Oleson and John Voss, eds., *The Organization of Knowledge in Modern America, 1860–1920,* Baltimore: Johns Hopkins University Press, 1979, 107–38; for psychology see Donald S. Napoli, *Architects of Adjustment: The History of the Psychological Profession in the United States,* Port Washington, N.Y.: Kennikat, 1981.

sciousness and searching for knowledge and techniques that would mark them as experts in their field, distinct from other levels and types of management. Specialization, apparent in the development of employment departments and welfare programs in the 1910s, was greatly accelerated by the First World War, when labor shortages and National War Labor Board policies encouraged the selection of managers in charge of personnel relations. A conference of employment managers in 1918 attracted six hundred participants and resulted in the formation of the National Association of Employment Managers, which in 1923 was renamed the American Management Association. Meanwhile, the National Industrial Conference Board was formed in 1916 to serve in part as a clearinghouse for developments in personnel management (two AT&T presidents, Frederick P. Fish and Theodore N. Vail, were keen supporters of its establishment). Scientists proposing solutions to industrial problems thus had a ready audience.[42]

Harvard psychology professor Hugo Münsterberg was one of the first social scientists to suggest the value of his field for the industrialist. Scientific management, he wrote, had successfully increased rationality in the workplace by restructuring the work process and by increasing managerial control over the worker; psychology could now penetrate the psychological realm of the factory, placing workers in jobs that corresponded to their mental types and aiding in the adjustment of the worker to the job. "Experimental psychology," Münsterberg wrote in 1913 in *Psychology and Industrial Efficiency*, "offers no more inspiring idea than this adjustment of work and psyche by which mental dissatisfaction in the work, mental depression and discouragement, may be replaced in our social community by overflowing joy and perfect inner harmony."[43] Theories about the psychological and social behavior of workers were not strictly confined to social scientists, of course. Frederick Taylor had assumed that workers, while incapable of organizing their work, were rational economic creatures who would seize the opportunity to work harder if they could share in the rewards. But Münsterberg and a growing band of psychologists offered something more than this; they brought from the laboratory a battery of mental tests that, they claimed, would permit the selection of the most capable worker for

[42] W. J. Donald, "The Work and Program of the American Management Association," *Annals of the American Academy of Political and Social Science*, 1925, 119: 140–2; *Proceedings of the Employment Managers' Conference, Rochester, N.Y., May 9–11, 1918* (U.S. Bureau of Labor Statistics, bulletin no. 247, Jan. 1919), 181–5. See also Montgomery, *The Fall of the House of Labor*, 236–44; H. M. Gitelman, "Management's Crisis of Confidence and the Origins of the National Industrial Conference Board, 1914–1916," *Business History Review*, 1984, 58: 153–77; Henry Eilbert, "The Development of Personnel Management in the United States," *Business History Review*, 1959, 33: 345–64.

[43] Hugo Münsterberg, *Psychology and Industrial Efficiency*, Boston, 1913, 309; Matthew Hale, Jr., *Human Science and Social Order: Hugo Münsterberg and the Origins of Applied Psychology*, Philadelphia: Temple University Press, 1980, esp. chap. 8.

each job and thereby would increase worker contentment and reduce industrial unrest.[44]

Psychology thrived in the hothouse environment of the First World War. Where before psychology had been an academic discipline with mere pretensions to social utility, by the end of the war psychological tests were a household word and psychologists found their skills in great demand. Psychologists found two niches in the war effort. Robert M. Yerkes, a student of Münsterberg, headed the development of an intelligence test to be administered to all recruits for the purposes of selection and classification. From his position as chairman of the Psychological Committee of the NRC and head of the Psychological Section in the Army Surgeon General's office, Yerkes oversaw the universal testing of recruits from the beginning of 1918. In the meantime, Walter V. Bingham and Walter Dill Scott, psychologists who had already experimented with the use of psychological tests in industry, persuaded the army to establish a Committee on Classification of Personnel. During the course of the war some 3 million men were rated by means of personality tests and Yerkes's alpha and beta tests. Army officers' opinions of the tests and rating schemes were mixed, but by Armistice Day psychologists were looking to new applications of their skills, confident that they would find receptive audiences.[45]

Full of confidence and hope, applied psychologists directed their zeal toward building institutional bases that would provide the framework for their campaign. Scott and several other members of the Committee on Classification of Personnel established the Scott Company in Philadelphia in 1919, which offered consulting services to business and industry. Two years later several of the leading psychologists in the country, including James McKean Cattell, J. B. Watson, Lewis M. Terman, Scott, Bingham, and Yerkes, formed the Psychological Corporation to persuade industry of the utility of psychology and to undertake consultancy work.[46] But the major institutional breakthrough came with the establishment of the Personnel Research Federation under the auspices of the NRC. In June 1919 the Engineering Foundation had suggested to the NRC the need for "concurrent, coordinated research in . . . industrial medicine, in psychology, in management, and in engineering . . . a broad plan of investigation covering the whole

---

[44] For a comprehensive overview of industrial psychology in America, see Loren Baritz, *The Servants of Power: A History of the Use of Social Science in American Industry*, Middletown, Conn: Wesleyan University Press, 1960.

[45] Daniel J. Kevles, "Testing the Army's Intelligence: Psychologists and the Military in World War I," *Journal of American History*, 1968, 55: 565–81; Franz Samelson, "World War I Intelligence Testing and the Development of Psychology," *Journal of the History of the Behavioral Sciences*, 1977, 13: 274–82; Baritz, *Servants of Power*, chap. 3; Michael M. Sokal, ed., *Psychological Testing and American Society, 1890–1930*, New Brunswick, N.J.: Rutgers University Press, 1987.

[46] Baritz, *Servants of Power*, 51–3; Michael M. Sokal, "The Origins of the Psychological Corporation," *Journal of the History of the Behavioral Sciences*, 1981, 17: 54–67.

question of personnel in industry – intellectual, moral, physical, psychological."[47] Accordingly, a Committee on Industrial Personnel Research, directed by Yerkes, was charged with discussing the proposal with interested parties. At the same time Bingham and Beardsley Ruml, a member of the Committee on Classification of Personnel and now with the Scott Company, coordinated the work of a Committee on Personnel Research in Business and Industry of the NRC's Division of Anthropology and Psychology. Two conferences were held at the NRC in November 1920 and March 1921, at which representatives from professional and industry associations ranged over the field of industrial relations. In March 1921 the Personnel Research Federation (PRF) began operation with Beardsley Ruml as its director and Robert Yerkes as chairman. A year later the PRF founded the *Journal of Personnel Research* to aid in the dissemination of new research and practices in personnel management.

In his address at the first annual meeting of the PRF, Yerkes delineated the field of personnel relations and specified the important contribution he believed it could make to social progress:

> We stand on the threshold of a new era in which attention and interest are beginning to shift from the material to the personal; from the things that are worked with, to the worker; from the machinery of industry, to the man who made, owns, or operates it. There is every reason to believe that human engineering will shortly take its place among the important forms of practical endeavor.[48]

Both capital and labor, he argued, had been forced into acting from narrow self-interest, for the wage system was inherently divisive, emphasizing only material rewards. Personnel research, by taking into account the material, mental, and spiritual traits of every individual, could lead to a new system of "cooperation" in which each worker would fit into a vocation that utilized his or her particular attributes. It was essential, however, that it be conducted in a disinterested manner, for the plan of the PRF could succeed only if all members of society, whatever their abilities, accepted its objective judgment. Social scientists and business leaders never doubted that scientific knowledge was objective and that scientific experts could therefore stand above the special interests of social classes and determine what was best for the whole society. Personnel researchers generally felt quite comfortable with the professional ideology of the new corporate managers, for both groups assumed that their expertise would bring about the organic cohesion of a divided society.[49]

[47] Alfred Flinn to John Merriam, 16 June 1919, NAS-NRC Central File/Exec. Bd./Comm. on Industrial Personnel Research/1919.

[48] Robert M. Yerkes, "What Is Personnel Research?" *Journal of Personnel Research*, 1922, 1: 56–63, quote on 56–7.

[49] Sanford Jacoby suggests that it is possible to draw a distinction between a conservative personnel management promoted by major corporations and the American Management

The achievements of personnel research in the 1920s never quite lived up to the programmatic statements of its proponents. By the end of the decade they remained optimistic, but with a sounder appreciation of the complexities of social scientific research. Psychological tests were applied with much excitement in many companies, large and small, but the results were equivocal. Tests were often crude. Drivers, for example, might be tested for basic motor skills and knowledge of traffic laws – the resultant score was called an index of "accident proneness." It was difficult to see how intelligence scores could aid in anything but the simplest sorting of job applicants: Most companies preferred to start unskilled employees at the bottom level and then train and promote them if they showed potential. And if reaction time tests measured learned skills rather than inherited abilities, it was not clear that they would assist in choosing the most suitable workers for assembly line jobs. Companies experimented with psychological tests, but if they used them at all it was as adjuncts to application forms and interviews rather than as the great sorting mechanism envisaged by industrial psychologists.[50]

Of the remaining social sciences that might have been expected to address issues in labor relations and personnel management – sociology, economics, and political science – only economics developed a sizable field of research, and here too the study of industrial relations was a special case. The study of "labor problems" was confined to a handful of labor economists, the majority of them students of John R. Commons of the University of Wisconsin. Committed to the positive role played by trade unions and government legislation in protecting workers from the ravages of the "free market," labor economists hardly endeared themselves to business leaders. Although, as Commons noted, he "was trying to save capitalism by making it good," managers found the field too tainted with principles of social reform. For example, although labor economist Summer H. Slichter noted the necessity of introducing personnel management, promotion schemes, and grievance

Association, and a liberal, professionally based personnel management advanced by the Personnel Research Federation; see Jacoby, *Employing Bureaucracy: Managers, Unions, and the Transformation of Work in American Industry, 1900–1945*, New York: Columbia University Press, 1985. However, the evidence is inconclusive and there are too many counterinstances. For example, John D. Rockefeller, Jr., encouraged antiunion personnel policies in major corporations in which he had a shareholding and provided funds to both the American Management Association and the Personnel Research Federation.

50 See Herman Feldman, *Survey of Research in the Field of Industrial Relations, by the Advisory Committee on Industrial Relations of the Social Science Research Council*, New York: Social Science Research Council 1928, 71–5, and Baritz, *Servants of Power*, 58–76, for an assessment of psychological tests in industry. Sokal, "Origins of the Psychological Corporation", 60–2, discusses the more general features of applied psychology in the 1920s. The best overview of industrial psychology in the 1920s is provided in a textbook, Morris S. Viteles, *Industrial Psychology*, New York: Norton, 1932; see also H. S. Person, "Industrial Psychology: A Layman Considers Its Status and Problems," *Bulletin of the Taylor Society*, 1924, 9: 163–71; W. V. Bingham, "Industrial Psychology: Its Progress in the United States," *Bulletin of the Taylor Society*, 1928, 13: 187–98.

procedures if such problems as labor turnover were to be reduced, he clearly regretted the way industrial relations policies had increased workers' dependence on paternalistic employers and stifled union membership. Nor was it apparent that economists had anything practical to offer to managers other than historical assessments of the impact of policies already introduced.[51]

The application of the medical sciences to the organization of work proved equally difficult. Before the war, social reformers had coined the term "industrial fatigue" in order to argue that working hours, especially for women and children, should be based on sound physiological principles. The industrial requirements of the First World War had wedded the concept of fatigue to the drive for efficiency and increased production: Only by understanding the physiological behavior of the worker's body in the industrial environment could maximum production be obtained with minimal effects on the worker. The Council of National Defense appointed a Sub-Committee on Industrial Fatigue, which oversaw research conducted by the Public Health Service and issued guidelines on how to reduce industrial fatigue. Support for the research waned after the war, and for much of the 1920s U.S. physiologists and physicians drew on the research of the British government's Industrial Fatigue Research Board. As more research was conducted, however, the concept of fatigue became more vague. Although some correlations could be made between the tiredness of the worker and a decline in production, the physiological mechanisms were complex, and the hope of developing a test for fatigue declined, as did the expectation that it would be possible to grade workers on their ability to withstand fatigue. A 1928 survey on personnel research concluded that "the study of fatigue seems to be more or less at a standstill; we do not know what fatigue is and we do not know how to measure it."[52]

There had also been the hope that psychiatry, prominent through its wartime success in the treatment of shell shock, would be adaptable to industrial problems. In 1919 the Engineering Foundation funded an inquiry into the mental hygiene of industry by psychiatrist E. E. Southard, director of the Boston Psychopathic Hospital. Southard was one of the founders of

---

[51] Paul J. McNulty, "Labor Problems and Labor Economics: The Roots of an Academic Discipline," *Labor History*, 1968, 9: 239–61, John R. Commons quoted on 251; Sumner Slichter, *The Turnover of Factory Labor*, New York: Appleton, 1919; idem, "Current Labor Policies"; Feldman, *Survey of Research*, 112–14, 142–3; William M. Leiserson, "Contributions of Personnel Management to Improved Labor Relations," in *Wertheim Lectures in Industrial Relations, 1928*, Cambridge, Mass.: Harvard University Press, 1929, 125–64.

[52] Feldman, *Survey of Research*, 85. The major U.S. works on industrial fatigue are Josephine Goldmark, *Fatigue and Efficiency: A Study in Industry*, New York: Survey Associates, 1912; and Frederick S. Lee, *The Human Machine and Industrial Efficiency*, New York, 1919. See Richard Gillespie, "Industrial Fatigue and the Discipline of Physiology," in Gerald L. Geison, ed., *Physiology in the American Context, 1850–1940*, Bethesda, Md.: American Physiological Society, 1987, 237–62.

the mental hygiene movement, which stressed that the mental problems of the normal community required as much attention as the more dramatic illnesses of institutionalized mental patients. Psychiatrists, psychologists, and psychiatric social workers were joining forces in the outpatient clinics of psychopathic hospitals; Southard urged that their skills be directed at the individual problem worker and, more generally, at industrial unrest: "The problem of the mental hygiene of industry is not only a problem of the individual laborer or worker who goes into unemployment. It is also a problem with important bearings on the nature, causes, and proper handling of anarchism and Bolshevism. Proof can probably be adduced that psychopaths play an enormous role in anarchism and Bolshevism." He foresaw the day when factory social workers would meet with those from the community and psychopathic hospitals to discuss the problems of an individual worker. Little came from the suggestion, however, with the exception of some articles by Southard and his colleague Mary C. Jarrett, a founder of psychiatric social work. Southard died suddenly in 1920, leaving no one to take on the leadership, and psychiatric social workers concentrated their energies in the area of community social work.[53]

Personnel research during the 1920s was thus of a decidedly mixed character. An extraordinary amount of research was published in the 1920s, much of it in new journals created for the purpose, including *Bulletin of the Taylor Society* (1915), *Journal of Applied Psychology* (1917), *Personnel* (1919), *Journal of Industrial Hygiene* (1919), and *Journal of Personnel Research* (1921). A whole genre of semipopular books on worker psychology – with titles like *Instincts in Industry*, *Mind and Work*, and *What's on the Worker's Mind* – promised to unlock the mysteries of worker behavior for puzzled managers.[54] But while academic researchers and personnel managers retained confidence that their grand plans for a rationally selected and socially engineered workforce would one day be realized, they

[53] E. E. Southard, "Mental Hygiene of Industry," in Southard to Flinn, 5 May 1919, 1, NAS-NRC Central File/Exec. Bd./Comm. on Industrial Personnel Research/1919; E. E. Southard, "The Movement for a Mental Hygiene of Industry," *Mental Hygiene*, 1920, 4: 43–64; E. E. Southard, "Trade Unionism and Temperament: Notes upon the Psychiatric Point of View in Industry," *Mental Hygiene*, 1920, 4: 281–300; Frederick P. Gay, *The Open Mind: Elmer Ernest Southard, 1876–1920*, Chicago: Normandie House, 1938. On the mental hygiene movement, see Gerald N. Grob, *Mental Illness and American Society, 1875–1940*, Princeton, N.J.: Princeton University Press, 1983, 144–66; and David Rothman, *Conscience and Convenience: The Asylum and Its Alternatives in Progressive America*, Boston: Little, Brown, 1980, 293–323. A mental hygiene program was established for workers at R. H. Macy & Company during the 1920s, but the program would appear to have taken on the functions of a personnel department and developed no new techniques or theories of note; it is described in V. V. Anderson, *Psychiatry in Industry*, New York: Harper, 1929.

[54] Ordway Tead, *Instincts in Industry: A Study of Working-Class Psychology*, Boston: Houghton Mifflin, 1918; Charles S. Myers, *Mind and Work*, New York: Putnam's, 1921; Whiting Williams, *What's on the Worker's Mind, By One Who Put on Overalls to Find Out*, New York: Scribner's, 1920.

were aware that current research was fragmentary and often unsatisfactory. By the late 1920s many social scientists and personnel managers felt that future research should be more rigorously conducted, better coordinated, and more effectively disseminated.[55]

The Hawthorne experiments were the most successful realization of the hopes and plans of those personnel managers and social scientists trying to develop a science of work. Five weeks after the Australian industrial delegation visited the Hawthorne Works of Western Electric in March 1927, managers and scientists there completed a three-year series of tests on the effects of lighting on worker productivity and commenced a study of six women relay assemblers that over the next few years would expand into a variety of other experiments and programs. Funded variously by the NRC, Western Electric and AT&T, and Rockefeller philanthropies, the experiments were carried out on an unparalleled scale. The participation of Elton Mayo and his colleagues at the Harvard Business School ensured that the research was influenced by a wide range of social sciences, at different times drawing on the disciplines of psychology, psychiatry, sociology, physiology, and anthropology. Following the research with close interest were company managers, personnel executives from major corporations, Rockefeller Foundation officials, and academic leaders in the social science community. When the Hawthorne experiments ceased in 1933, their results were already known to an influential network of personnel managers and social scientists in North America and Europe. Culminating in 1939 with *Management and the Worker,* articles and books on the Hawthorne research disseminated a new philosophy and practice of industrial management that, it was claimed, was firmly grounded in objective scientific research. Here, it seemed, was the first step in the human engineering of industrial work.

---

[55] See, e.g., the conclusions of a 1928 Social Science Research Council survey, Feldman, *Survey of Research;* and R. W. Stone, "Personnel Management: An Appraisal," American Management Association, Personnel Series, no. 14, 1932, including the discussion.

2

The T Room

THE RELAY ASSEMBLY TEST has always been the most famous and most controversial part of the Hawthorne experiments. It was the longest running of the tests and programs conducted by the researchers, it was the test from which many of the key ideas emerged, and the official accounts of the experiments devoted more space to the relay test than to any other aspect. Subsequently, social scientists have engaged in a heated debate over what really happened in the relay assembly test room and over what is the correct interpretation of the experimental data. For example, the official accounts stressed that the relay assembly test demonstrated that production increased when workers were treated humanely by their supervisors, while critics have argued that the marked increase in output was due to economic factors such as the system of payment and the effects of the depression or to the more rigorous supervision of the workers. Behind these interpretations lie fundamental differences over how managers should organize production and supervise their workers.

In this and the following chapter I will try to show that the participants in the Hawthorne experiments also disagreed over the correct interpretation of the relay test results. Company researchers, academic consultants, supervisors, and the workers who were the subjects of the experiments all had different explanations for the increase in production in the test room. The results of the experiments were complex, the data uncertain, seemingly objective production figures infuriatingly open to interpretation, and working hypotheses uncomfortably vague. As is always the case in science, meaning had to be imposed rather than discovered. There are good reasons why commentators have not perceived the diversity of opinion among the experimenters themselves. Most commentaries rely on the official published accounts of the relay assembly test, which adopt a relatively consistent and uniform interpretation. Recent authors who have had access to the original records of the relay test have used them selectively to support their arguments for a particular interpretation of the test.

My major concern in analyzing the relay assembly test is not to provide one more supposedly definitive account of "what really happened during the relay assembly test." Instead, I focus on understanding the diversity of interpretation and on trying to explain why participants emphasized different aspects of the results and at times came to quite different conclusions. Of course, in writing a narrative of the experiments I cannot avoid constructing an interpretation, and I leave it to the reader to judge the plausibility of my account. But like the Hawthorne researchers, who were interested in examining the social relations of production rather than a particular manufactured product, I have focused less on the finished product of scientific knowledge so that I can examine the nature of the scientific production process itself.

In this and the following chapter I present a detailed narrative of the relay assembly test, based on the original experimental records and the correspondence of several of the participants. This chapter deals with the experiments before the involvement of the two academics, Elton Mayo and Clair Turner, in April 1928, while Chapter 3 analyzes the interpretations of the relay assembly data by the academic consultants, company researchers, and recent commentators and critics. However, before examining the relay assembly test, it is necessary to look at the series of experiments on industrial lighting that preceded the relay test. The lighting tests have been the subject of considerable confusion, both in the official accounts and in subsequent discussions. When the official accounts of the Hawthorne experiments were written in the 1930s, the authors did not have access to any of the participants in the lighting tests or to the reports that had been drafted but left unpublished. However, enough of the reports and correspondence surrounding the lighting tests have survived in personal papers and institutional archives to reconstruct their history.

The industrial illumination tests

The set of three experiments on the effect of industrial lighting on productive efficiency commenced at the Hawthorne Works in November 1924. These were not isolated experiments conducted at the instigation of factory management, but part of a broader series of experiments and research being conducted under the auspices of the National Research Council (NRC). The impetus for the lighting tests came primarily from the electrical industry, which was conducting a major campaign to encourage industry to install artificial lighting rather than rely solely on the vagaries of natural illumination. Electrical manufacturers and utilities claimed that lighting would reduce accidents, save workers' sight, and raise production by as much as 25 percent. Most significantly, good lighting was claimed to be profitable; an engineer with the major electrical manufacturer General Electric calculated on the basis of tests in nine companies that "raising the average initial illumination from about 2.3 to 11.2 foot-candles resulted in an increase in production of more than 15 per cent, at an additional cost of only 1.9 per cent of the payroll."[1]

More persuasive proof was needed than compilations from the experience of a few companies, however. Accordingly, E. P. Hyde, chairman of the Illuminating Engineering Society's Committee on Research and director of research at General Electric's National Lamp Works, suggested in early 1923 that the NRC undertake a program of experimentation. A series of meetings with members of the NRC's Division of Engineering and Industrial Research resulted in the establishment of a Committee on the Relation of Quality and Quantity of Illumination to Efficiency in the Industries, subsequently shortened to the Committee on Industrial Lighting. Chairing the committee was Dugald C. Jackson, professor of electrical engineering at Massachusetts Institute of Technology (MIT) and one of the leaders of the electrical engineering profession. In addition, the father of the electrical industry, Thomas A. Edison, was persuaded to assume the symbolic position of honorary chairman.[2]

By channeling the research through a public organization such as the NRC and attaching Edison's prestige to the research, the electrical industry was seeking to ensure that the research would be viewed as disinterested and objective. But behind the apparent impartiality of the NRC lay a network of interconnecting corporate and professional interests. This was particularly the case in the Division of Engineering and Industrial Research, since the engineering profession was so closely allied with industry: Chairman of the division was Frank B. Jewett, vice-president of research at Western Electric, and Western Electric chief engineer Edward B. Craft was vice-chairman.[3] This convergence of interests was evident too in the Committee on Industrial Lighting, where industrial engineers and executives sat in roughly equal numbers with academic engineers and psychologists.[4]   A

[1] Ward Harrison, "The Necessity for Standards in the Relation Between Illumination and Output," *Bulletin of the Taylor Society,* 1920, 5: 113–19; Earl A. Anderson, "Better Lighting Increases Production 35 Per Cent," *Electrical World,* 30 June 1923, quote on 1530. For increases in recommended lighting levels in codes established by the Illuminating Engineering Society and the lighting companies, see L. P. Alford, "Technical Change in Manufacturing Industries," in *Recent Economic Changes in the United States,* New York: McGraw-Hill, 1929, 143–5; it is notable that codes written by the lighting companies always suggested higher levels of illumination than those set by the professional society.

[2] E. P. Hyde to Vernon Kellogg, 26 Jan. 1923, NRC/Divn. Engineering/Comm. Industrial Lighting/Proposed; "Summary of National Research Council Committee on Industrial Lighting, October 1924," TAE/NRC/1924; Maurice Holland to Albert L. Barrows, 9 Apr. 1924, NAS–NRC/Engineering & Industrial Research/Committee on Industrial Lighting (henceforth NAS–NRC/E&IR/CIL)/1924–5.

[3] E. F. Nichols, "Report of the Committee on Research," *Transactions of the Illuminating Engineering Society,* 1924, 19: 125–30; NRC, *Annual Report,* 1922–3, 20, 1924–5, 79. See David F. Noble, *America by Design,* New York: Knopf, 1977, on the shared interests and vision of the engineering profession and corporate capitalism.

[4] NRC Committee on Industrial Lighting, "General Directive Board," TAE/NRC/1924.

conference of the preliminary committee and additional industrial representatives was held in New York on 15 April 1924, at which funding and locations for the research were resolved. Gerard Swope of General Electric and John W. Lieb of New York Edison undertook to raise the $50,000 required for two years' research from electrical manufacturers and utilities. Jewett reported that he had talked with Clarence G. Stoll, superintendent of the Hawthorne Works of Western Electric, who had expressed his willingness to cooperate in research and indicated that the company would bear the costs of installing lighting and maintaining production records. The committee enthusiastically accepted Western Electric's offer and promptly recruited Stoll as a member.[5]

The Committee on Industrial Lighting conducted a broad program of research over the following three years, of which the tests at the Hawthorne Works were only a part, albeit an important part. Harvard psychologist Leonard Troland carried out an exhaustive analysis of the literature on the relationships between illumination and visual acuity; psychologists C. E. Ferree and G. Rand of Bryn Mawr College undertook a wide range of laboratory experiments on light and vision, hoping thereby to establish basic parameters for industrial lighting codes; and psychologists and engineers at Boston University, MIT, and General Electric experimented under laboratory conditions with the effect of different types of lighting on workers. Industrial trials of the effects of lighting on production were intended to test the findings from this more basic research; these trials were conducted at several factories, including the Hawthorne Works. The literature survey and laboratory experiments resulted in several published papers, but the final report of the industrial trials was never completed. Involved in numerous NRC, MIT, and consulting projects, Jackson managed to compile a draft of the final report, but it was always a last priority and was finally abandoned around 1930. The electrical industry representatives never seem to have pressed for its completion, probably because they were unhappy with the results of the committee's research, especially the experiments at Hawthorne, which questioned the simplistic correlation between lighting and production promoted by the electrical industry.[6]

[5] "Conference re Project of National Research Council on Industrial Lighting, New York, April 15, 1924," Minutes, DCJ/5/326; Holland to Committee on Projects, NRC, 15 Apr. 1924, NAS–NRC/E&IR/CIL/1924–5.

[6] The draft report by Jackson is in DCJ/5/329; the NRC annual reports from 1927–8 to 1930–1 noted the impending publication of the report. The poor work of one of the two research assistants also impeded publication; see Jackson to J. W. Barker, 16 Aug. 1928, DCJ/326. The published work arising from the committee includes C. E. Ferree and G. Rand, "The Effect of Mixing Artificial Light with Daylight on Important Functions of the Eye," *Transactions of the Illuminating Engineering Society*, 1926, 21: 588–612; C. E. Ferree and G. Rand, "Intensity of Light and Speed of Vision Studied with Special Reference to Industrial Situations," *Transactions of the Illuminating Engineering Society*, 1927, 22: 79–110, 1928, 23: 507–46, 642–5; C. E. Snow, "Research on Industrial Illumination," *Tech Engineering*

Table 1. *Hawthorne illumination tests, 1924–7*

Department	Test conditions
First series: 24 Nov. 1924 to 11 Apr. 1925	
Relay assembly	Experimental lighting
Inspection	Experimental lighting
Coil winding	Experimental lighting
Coil winding	Normal lighting
Second series: 15 Feb. to 24 Apr. 1926	
Induction coil winding	Experimental lighting
	Experimental supervision
Induction coil winding	Normal lighting
	Normal supervision
Receiver coil winding	Experimental lighting
	Normal supervision
Relay assembly	Normal lighting
	Experimental supervision
Third series: 13 Sept. 1926 to 30 Apr. 1927	
Induction coil winding	Experimental lighting
	Experimental supervision[a]
Induction coil winding	Steady lighting
	Experimental supervision[a]

[a]The researchers also varied the payment scheme in one period and supervision in two periods.

Lighting tests commenced at the Hawthorne Works in November 1924 and continued intermittently over the next two and a half years (Table 1). Plans for the first stage of the tests were finalized at a meeting of several members of the committee at the factory in August 1924. It was agreed that tests would be undertaken in three departments, each with different payment schemes: relay assembly, which worked on a group piece rate; coil winding, with an individual piece rate; and inspection, where work was paid on a day rate. Production records and lighting levels were to be measured several times a day, and after a base period had been established, lighting was to be increased in stages and its effects on production noted.[7] The day-to-day

News, Nov. 1927, 257, 272, 274, 282; J. W. Barker, "Technique of Economic Studies of Lighting in Industry," *Transactions of the Illuminating Engineering Society*, 1928, 23: 174–88; Dugald C. Jackson, "Lighting in Industry," *Journal of the Franklin Institute*, 1928, 205: 285–303; and Leonard T. Troland, "An Analysis of the Literature Concerning the Dependency of Visual Functions upon Illumination Intensity," *Transactions of the Illuminating Engineering Society*, 1931, 26: 107–96.
[7] Dugald C. Jackson, "Memorandum Respecting Conference at the Hawthorne Works," 26 Aug. 1924, TAE/NRC/1924.

supervision of the experiments was conducted by C. E. Snow, a recent MIT graduate in electrical engineering, who was assisted by Homer Hibarger, a Hawthorne piece-rate analyzer. At Hawthorne they were supported by the active interest of works manager Clarence Stoll and technical superintendent George Pennock, both members of the general directive board of the Committee on Industrial Lighting. Meanwhile, at MIT Jackson was assisted by Joseph W. Barker, an electrical engineer who acted as chief research assistant on the entire industrial lighting program, and Vannevar Bush, a professor of electrical engineering who would go on to become one of the most powerful scientists in the United States and director of scientific research during the Second World War. The Hawthorne lighting tests were thus controlled by an elite group of academic and industrial engineers.[8]

The committee was aware from the beginning that human factors could influence production and thereby interfere with the experimental results. In order to obtain the workers' cooperation in the tests, it was considered necessary to inform them of the nature of the experiment. The committee realized that the workers might be influenced by the knowledge that they were experimental subjects, and the researchers did all they could to minimize this effect. Changes from one level of lighting to another were made on weekends so as to reduce the psychological effects on the workers (although it is apparent that the workers were aware of the changes, for they were later asked to express their preferences). It was also agreed that at least some of the workers would be questioned about their personal reactions to the changing conditions, because Stoll and Pennock, the Hawthorne engineers, were especially interested in gauging the effects of improved lighting on the employees' attitudes and behavior as well as on production.[9]

The first winter's tests, from November 1924 to April 1925, revealed the difficulty of isolating the contribution to productivity of specific factors such as lighting. In none of the three test groups did there appear to be any relation between the level of lighting and output, which varied between 93 and 112 percent of the base production level; while production in all three test groups showed an improvement, it could not be correlated with those periods in which lighting was higher. Further, in a control group of coil winders working under normal lighting conditions, production increased almost as much as it did among the group of coil winders working under improved lighting. Other factors were obviously affecting the results. The researchers suspected that a major factor was the increased supervision during the tests: The ratio of supervisors to workers had necessarily increased so that detailed measurements of illumination, production, and atmospheric conditions could be

---

[8] Snow, "Research on Industrial Illumination"; M. Howarth, "Development of the Illumination Study," HSCM/2,A1–7; on Hibarger, see *Hawthorne Microphone*, 19 July 1926, 2.
[9] Jackson, "Memorandum," 26 Aug. 1924; NRC, "Industrial Illumination Tests, Progress Report No. 4, 1 March 1925," TAE/NRC/1924; NRC, Division of Engineering and Industrial Research, Minutes, 21 Nov. 1924, NAS–NRC/E&IR/CIL/1924–5.

taken, and the workers were interviewed at each stage by the foreman or gang chief. While the control group of coil winders had not been subjected to increased supervision, it was suspected that their increased output was due to competition with the test group of coil winders.[10]

When the lighting tests were resumed in February 1926, "it was decided that every effort would have to be made to either eliminate the effect of increased supervision and the effect of other psychological factors incident to test conditions, . . . or to evaluate these effects before any conclusive statement as to the effect of illumination on production could be made."[11] The major experiment involved the induction coil winders, who were split into a test group and a control group and placed in separate buildings in order to deter competition. The experimenters tried to ensure that each group would "be subjected to exactly the same supervision and psychology": The same supervisors directed both groups and tried to equalize all conditions. Two further tests were designed to assess the effects of supervision. First, a group of receiver coil winders was to be subjected to the same lighting conditions as the test group of induction coil winders, but supervision was to be no different from normal; that is, the increased supervision of the tests was to be avoided. Second, a group of relay assemblers was to be subjected to test supervision while lighting was left as normal; this would provide a control on the previous year's experiment with relay assemblers.[12]

Results from the second series of tests confirmed the suspicion that "the effects of increased supervision and the psychological factors incident to test conditions are of much larger degree of magnitude than the increases which might possibly be ascribed to illumination, even though the illuminations during this test were extremely high." Output among the test and control groups of induction coil winders remained almost parallel, despite much higher illumination in the test group. In the receiver coil winding department, where increased lighting was introduced under normal shop supervisory conditions, production remained almost steady. In the relay assembly department, output during the 1926 test was higher than in the 1924–5 test, although illumination was lower. In contrast to the inflated claims of the lighting industry, the researchers concluded that "no increase in production could be definitely credited to the illumination increases." Medium levels of lighting, of the order of 10 to 15 foot-candles, seemed sufficient for regular tasks; any higher levels could not be expected to return their investment.[13]

But how *low* could illumination go before production would begin to fall

[10] Appendix H, "Factory Illumination–Production Tests at Hawthorne Works of the Western Electric Co." (henceforth Appendix H), 1–7, DCJ/5/330.
[11] Ibid., 8.
[12] Ibid., 8–9; quote from Dugald C. Jackson, "Memorandum to Committee on Industrial Lighting," 17 Feb. 1926, TAE/NRC/1924.
[13] Appendix H, 8–12, quotes on 10, 12; Dugald C. Jackson, "Progress Report of the Committee on Industrial Lighting," 1 Apr. 1926, TAE/NRC/1924.

off? The third series of experiments, conducted from September 1926 to April 1927, were directed toward this question. Even more elaborate care was taken in the execution of this test, the experimenters refining their methods to control as many variables as possible. Two groups of induction coil winders were matched so that their average production and length of service were equal. In previous tests, artificial lighting had always been provided in addition to natural illumination, which varied throughout the day and seasons. In order to regulate the level of illumination precisely, a special test room was constructed that excluded all natural light. In one section of the divided test room, the control group worked under a steady illumination of 11 foot-candles throughout the test, while in the other section the test group was subjected to progressively lower levels of lighting. Jackson and the other experimenters expected that the level of production in the test group would "be maintained until the illumination intensity arrives at a point where it becomes impossible for the group to produce at the previous rate." There were two reasons for this: First, the workers would tend to maintain the rhythm of work established during adequate illumination, even when lighting was poor; and second, they would try to maintain production in order to sustain their wage earnings, "and with each succeeding decrease in illumination the tendency will be to work harder and harder."[14]

The committee's predictions proved correct. As was to be expected from the previous tests, production in both the control and test groups increased during the experiment (Table 2). Most significantly, the test group maintained its production in the face of decreasing illumination, complaining only when the lighting had been reduced to 1.4 foot-candles. (However, it is important to note that coil winders had been working in levels as low as 3 foot-candles in the regular department back in 1924, before the first series of tests.)[15] Two further variables were introduced into the test, although for such a short time (three weeks) that conclusions were necessarily tentative. Assuming that the coil winders were working harder as lighting decreased in order to maintain their wages, the experimenters shifted them onto an individual day rate from their individual piece rate. Production declined, although not significantly. However, it is not clear how this was explained to the workers, or whether the workers seriously believed that if they slowed production they would not be penalized financially. Supervision was also altered slightly by shifting the gang boss's headquarters from the room housing the test group to that containing the control group; clerical duties required that he spend 30 to 40 percent more time in the test room where his desk was located. Again, no significant difference in production could be detected. However, it was claimed that the significance of increased

[14] Dugald C. Jackson, "Progress Report of the Illumination Test," [September 1926], in Barker to Edison, 11 Sept. 1926, TAE/NRC/1924, quotes on 3; Appendix H, 12–14.
[15] Appendix H, 3.

Table 2. *Output data for coil winding illumination test, 1926–7*

Test period	Commenced	Test group			Control group		
		Lamps (watts)	Illumination (foot-candles)	Production index[a]	Lamps (watts)	Illumination (foot-candles)	Production index[a]
1	13 Sept. 26	100	11.0	111.8	100	11.0	106.8
2	4 Oct. 26	100	9.0	113.5	100	11.0	110.2
3	25 Oct. 26	75	7.0	112.7	100	11.0	107.6
4	15 Nov. 26	75	6.0	115.2	100	11.0	110.2
5	6 Dec. 26	60	5.0	115.2	100	11.0	111.0
6	27 Dec. 26	50	4.0	116.1	100	11.0	111.0
7a	17 Jan. 27	40	2.7	118.6	100	11.0	111.9
7b	8 Feb. 27	40	2.7	117.0	100	11.0	111.0
8	28 Feb. 27	25	1.4	113.5	100	11.0	109.3
9	1 Mar. 27	100	11.0	116.1	100	11.0	114.4
10	21 Mar. 27	100	11.0	119.5	100	11.0	115.2
11	11 Apr. 27	50	4.0	119.5	100	11.0	117.0

Note: The following additional changes were made: 7b, Employees paid on an individual day rate; all other periods on an individual piece rate. 9, Test and control groups swap rooms, which means gang boss is now in same room as control group, i.e., additional supervision for control group. 10, Gang boss moves with control group back to their original room, i.e., continued increased supervision for control group. 11, Gang boss returns to test group room. [a]The production index was calculated as a percentage of the 1924 base established in the first series of experiments for coil winders.

supervision during the tests was clearly demonstrated by the production curves of the induction coil winders *after* each of the annual experiments, for then their production curves would revert to the standard production rate for piece workers throughout the Hawthorne Works.[16]

While the Committee on Industrial Lighting was committed to concentrating on the role of illumination on production, the Hawthorne managers were free to pursue independent lines of inquiry. Works manager Clarence Stoll and technical superintendent George Pennock kept in close contact with Charles Snow and Homer Hibarger, the technical assistants in the tests, and were quickly alerted to the role that supervision appeared to be playing in the experimental results. For example, Snow reported to Stoll that there was a major leap in production among the inspection group in the first series of tests not because of improved illumination, but because a new foreman "told them what would happen if they raised their percentage and if this did not attract

[16] Ibid., 14–18. F. J. Roethlisberger and William J. Dickson, in *Management and the Worker*, Cambridge, Mass., Harvard Univ. Press, 1939, 16–17, citing Snow, "Research on Industrial Illumination," incorrectly state that the workers complained when the level was reduced to 3 foot-candles.

them told them what would happen if they didn't."[17] The managers' involvement in the research, both as members of the committee and as factory executives, began to make itself felt in the second and third series of lighting tests; the second series of tests in particular was aimed more at measuring the effect of supervision than at measuring that of lighting, while the third series also explored the role of supervision and wage payment schemes.

Before the illumination tests had even been completed, the Hawthorne managers began independent experiments on a modest scale. Hibarger obtained Pennock's approval to test his belief that cooperative workers would be willing and able to work in almost total darkness. Accordingly, on 4–7 February 1927 Hibarger placed two relay assemblers in a cloakroom and reduced the light in stages from 1.0 to 0.060 foot-candle – roughly the level of moonlight. Only at this last stage did output decline markedly.[18] Yet it was not at all clear what the results of this test indicated: Was it measuring cooperation, the irrelevance of high levels of lighting, or simply the manual skills of two relay assemblers? (That the workers could continue at such low levels of light, when the coil winders complained at 1.4 foot-candles, can probably be attributed, at least in part, to the different natures of the jobs. Skilled relay assemblers were able to put together the thirty or so pieces by memory and feel, while coil winders had to be able to see the progress of their winding task.) Yet while the result might be problematic, the short test was symbolic of the Hawthorne managers' awakened interest in the application of the experimental method.

For the Committee on Industrial Lighting, Hibarger's brief experiment underscored the difficulty of basing lighting codes on such production tests, or of even showing a close relationship between lighting and production. Jackson remained committed to producing a final report of the NRC research, but difficulties overwhelmed his efforts: Jackson and Barker, the principal research assistant, were too busy to take on the task, while Snow's digests of the committee's wide-ranging research were dismissed by Jackson as a inadequate basis for the report.[19] Meanwhile, the members of the committee from the electrical industry appear to have remained silent, doing nothing to encourage publication of a report that would have undermined their extravagant claims. On the basis of a presentation given by Jackson and Barker to the NRC in 1928, we can assume that the final report would have recommended a basic lighting level of 7 to 10 foot-candles for normal industrial production, which was roughly the range recommended by the electrical industry and Illuminating Engineering Society. But the committee had clearly failed to sat-

[17] Quote from Charles D. Wrege, "Solving Mayo's Mystery: The First Complete Account of the Origins of the Hawthorne Studies: The Forgotten Contributions of Charles E. Snow and Homer Hibarger," Paper delivered to Academy of Management Conference, History Division, Kansas City, Mo., Aug. 1976, 13.

[18] Ibid., 24–5.

[19] Jackson to Barker, 16, Aug. 1928, DCJ/326.

isfy the electrical industry's expectations that the research would provide the scientific justification for these or even higher levels of illumination.[20]

How, then, did the illumination tests influence the Hawthorne experiments? Textbook writers typically assert that the failure to isolate the effects of lighting on production pointed to a far more significant discovery – that human factors have an important influence on worker productivity. The lighting tests are seen as a triumph of the human factors studied by psychologists and sociologists over the mechanistic assumptions of engineers and managers. This view of the lighting tests is based on the official accounts of the Hawthorne experiments, which gave only a brief history based on the few details available to the authors. For example, Fritz Roethlisberger, coauthor of *Management and the Worker*, wrote in 1941 that after the lighting tests "a few of the tough-minded experimenters already were beginning to suspect their basic ideas and assumptions with regard to human motivation." This narrative of scientific defeat transformed into victory by a leap of insight has played a major role in investing the Hawthorne experiments with their mythic power.[21]

These textbook accounts of the illumination tests exaggerate the initial ignorance of the experimenters and misrepresent the process of discovery. Far from the active members of the Committee on Industrial Lighting being surprised by the fact that the coil winders maintained production in the face of inadequate lighting, they had actually predicted it – indeed, it was a necessary part of the experimental protocol, which was designed to set a lower limit on lighting levels. Similarly, the experimenters never supposed that the relationship between lighting and production was a simple one. From the inception of the tests they were aware of the importance of other factors; they did not ignore them, but sought to *control* them so as to bring out the individual effect of illumination. As it turned out, this was a fruitless task, but since the explicit mandate of the committee was to determine the effect of lighting, the researchers had little choice but to continue to make attempts at isolating the chosen variable. The Hawthorne managers did not face such constraints, and throughout the course of the lighting tests they were interested in other variables.

Managers had, of course, long been manipulating such factors as supervision, wage schemes, and worker solidarity on a daily basis. For example,

---

[20] J. W. Barker and D. C. Jackson, "The Industrial Illumination Research," Exhibit A of minutes of NRC Division of Engineering and Industrial Research, 14 Nov. 1928, NAS–NRC/E&IR/CIL/1926–31; Alford, "Technical Changes in Manufacturing Industries," 144–5. Leonard Troland of the Committee on Industrial Lighting later summarized the psychological studies on lighting and visual acuity and similarly concluded that 10 foot-candles was sufficient for normal industrial work; see Troland, "An Analysis of the Literature," 195.

[21] F. J. Roethlisberger, *Management and Morale*, Cambridge, Mass.: Harvard University Press, 1941, 11.

Frederick Taylor's scientific management relied on the judicious combination of close supervision, economic incentive, and some basic assumptions about worker motivation in order to break down worker solidarity and replace it with unquestioning obedience to the supervisor and machine. But a significant change was taking place. Previously, Hawthorne managers such as Stoll and Pennock had regarded the skills of personnel management and supervision as a craft acquired on the job, under the guidance of immediate superiors. The illumination tests suggested that these skills could be transformed into variables and subjected to scientific analysis and experimentation.

Stoll and Pennock would have been well aware of the high prestige attached to research and experimentation in the Bell System. Only two years previously, responsibility for industrial research in the Bell System had been shifted from Western Electric to a separate organization, Bell Telephone Laboratories, which quickly attained an international reputation for its basic and applied research. The creation of Bell Labs posed a problem for Western Electric, which was left with the more mundane task of manufacturing equipment according to needs and specifications determined by AT&T and Bell Labs. In fact, Western Electric soon acquired the reputation of being the poor sister of AT&T, Bell Labs, and the operating companies; managers from other parts of the system viewed its engineers as dull and unadventurous, protected from the pressures of the marketplace and the frontiers of research. The only ways in which Western Electric could hope to impress its importance on AT&T executives were by improving manufacturing methods and increasing productivity. Stoll and Pennock were both academically trained engineers in midcareer and in 1927 were in crucial positions within the company to implement changes in these areas. Stoll had just moved to New York to become vice-president in charge of manufacturing, and Pennock was technical superintendent at Hawthorne, with oversight of manufacturing methods. The lighting tests demonstrated to these Western Electric engineers that the experimental method so successfully applied to technology in the Bell System could also be directed at the social organization of production.

The relay assembly test room

On 25 April 1927, a week before the completion of the third series of lighting tests, Western Electric embarked on a new series of experiments. Planned as an extension of the experimental method into the study of factors other than lighting and supervision, the relay assembly test room studies continued for more than five years and spawned several other studies, collectively known as the Hawthorne experiments. This grand evolution was not planned. The relay assembly test was expected to run for a few months; only gradually did experimentation become formalized and institutionalized.

The decision to establish the relay assembly test room lay with George Pennock, who as superintendent of the Technical Branch at the works was responsible for production methods, which included the development of machines and methods for new products, the setting of piece rates, and plant layout. Pennock gathered a small group of researchers from his organization, including himself, Homer Hibarger, the piece-rate analyst who supervised the lighting tests, E. H. Kraft, chief of the Piece Rates Division, and his assistant R. H. Fauquier. They had at their disposal the resources of the Technical Division, the approval of senior managers in the company, and a well-lit test room that would soon become available at the conclusion of the lighting tests. Pennock and his assistants agreed that the object of the relay test would be "to determine what effects rest periods and various hours of work will have in increasing the efficiency of an operator," and they prepared a list of questions they hoped the test would help to answer:

1. Why does output drop in the afternoon?
2. Do operators actually get tired out?
3. Desirability of establishing rest periods.
4. Changes in equipment.
5. What is the attitude of the operators?
6. Effects of a shorter working day on output.[22]

The majority of these questions came directly out of the wartime studies on industrial fatigue, which had shown that shorter hours and rest periods could sometimes result in increased production and efficiency. The Hawthorne engineers were aware of this research, and the start of the relay test can be seen in large measure as an attempt to explore how these findings could be applied to production at Hawthorne. Only the fifth question about workers' attitudes was a departure from the industrial fatigue research. Wartime researchers had argued that shorter hours would result in less fatigue, both physical and mental, but they had not explored how workers' attitudes might be affected. The interest in attitudes arose out of the postwar expansion of personnel management, which emphasized the importance of establishing industrial relations policies and welfare programs that would constrain unions and mold a workforce that identified with company goals. Personnel managers sought not just obedience, but cooperation. This is not to say that the Hawthorne researchers were interested at this stage in the general issue of the relationship between worker attitudes and production – a question that would be explored in detail in the later stages of the experiment. Nor were they interested in making breakthroughs in the analysis of fatigue or furthering scientific knowledge. Their concern was with the organization of production in their own factory and with determining the most appropriate technical and social arrangements for specific production processes.

Relay assembly was chosen for study because it involved the kind of highly

---

[22] Relay Assembly Test Room (henceforth RATR) Progress Report no. 1, 3 Dec. 1927, Sec. I, HSCM/3,B1–F11.

Figure 3. Relay Assembly Department, c. 1925. The rows of benches and regimented atmosphere were characteristic of many of the assembly operations at Hawthorne. Courtesy of AT&T Archives.

repetitive work with which fatigue was commonly associated. Equally important, relay assembly was one of the major production departments at Hawthorne, absorbing a large number of "unskilled" workers (Figure 3). Relays are electromagnetic switches that are activated by a weak signal and then send out a new, stronger signal. They played a central role in the Bell System, especially after the decision in 1918 to introduce automatic exchange switching and with the continued growth of long-distance calling. For example, a typical operator-assisted call required the use of about 20 relays in the 1920s, whereas a direct call used as many as 150 relays. Types of relays varied considerably, depending on their use in the system; by the late 1920s Hawthorne was manufacturing 75 different types and 6,500 separate kinds of relays, with production reaching more than 7 million each year. With the exception of the coils, which required manual wiring, most of the parts of the relay could be produced by specialized machines that punched and machined the pieces in massive quantities. But then the 35 or more parts had to be hand assembled, adjusted, and inspected – all labor-intensive operations in which the speed of the individual assembler determined productivity.[23]

The researchers' interest in a close analysis of individual productivity was reflected in the design of the test room. Upon completion of the illumination tests, one of the test rooms was adapted for use in the relay assembly test, primarily by the introduction of elaborate equipment designed to record automatically the individual production of the workers, as well as temperature and humidity. Five relay assemblers sat side-by-side at a bench; to their right a sixth worker, the layout operator, prepared trays of relay parts for the five to assemble. The finished relay was dropped down a chute in the bench, where it triggered a recording mechanism to punch a hole in a paper tape moving at a constant speed. The strips of paper thus recorded not only the individual production for each worker, but also the interval of time that elapsed between the fall of each relay down the chute, that is, the individual production time for each relay (Figures 4–6).[24]

The task of assembling relays required manual dexterity, along with a willingness to repeat the same task every minute or so for almost nine hours per day, five and a half days per week. The assembly of a relay required the simultaneous use of both hands to place pins, bushings, springs, terminals, and insulators between plates, insert a coil and armature, then screw the assembly together. A motion analysis of the operations required to put together the thirty-two parts of R-1498 relay identified thirty-two separate operations for each hand. Although the layout of parts was identical, each worker, or "operator," had a slightly different way of assembling, perhaps using a different hand for a certain operation or piling up parts closer to the fixture on which the relay was held while being assembled. (The term "operator" was normally used at Hawthorne to describe unskilled manual workers; it is not clear whether the term was used because these workers were regarded merely as agents that carried out series of operations or whether it was chosen to suggest that unskilled occupations at Hawthorne were different from those traditionally performed by manual workers.)[25]

Across the test room opposite the work bench sat Homer Hibarger, whose role was a combination of supervisor and experimenter. Since the test room was far removed from the regular Relay Assembly Department (so as to reduce possible competition between the two groups), Hibarger was responsible, informally at least, for supervising the five workers and layout operator

[23] M. D. Fagen, ed., *A History of Engineering and Science in the Bell System: The Early Years, 1875–1925,* [Murray Hill, N.J.]: Bell Telephone Laboratories, 1975, 519–23; S. P. Shackleton and H. W. Purcell, "Relays in the Bell System," *Bell System Technical Journal,* 1924, 3: 1–42; "Relays Pass the Word Along the World's Telephone Lines," *Hawthorne Microphone,* 3 Nov. 1930, 2.

[24] RATR Progress Report no. 1, sec. II.

[25] "Stock List and Bench Layout Used in Assembling R–1498 Relay," HSC/2.

Figure 4. Relay assemblers, relay assembly test room, 1927. In the foreground are the chutes through which the completed relays pass into the boxes below. The measuring equipment is on the bench in the rear. The workers are, from the left, Anna Haug, Wanda Blazejak, Theresa Layman, Irene Rybacki, and Adeline Bogatowicz. Courtesy of AT&T Archives.

and for organizing a regular flow of materials through the room. As experimenter, he ensured that the recording equipment was functioning, that experimental conditions were maintained, and that his chiefs in the Piece Rates Division and Pennock were kept informed of all developments. He was responsible too for analyzing the output tapes, recording the relay types assembled, adjusting individual and group output figures to account for the fact that the workers were assembling various types of relays, and calculating pay and incentives. A junior clerk was soon added to the test room to aid Hibarger in the more mundane aspects of the work.[26] Two documents were prepared daily. The Log Sheet recorded work times, personal time out for each worker, time taken for repairing relays that failed inspection, time spent waiting for parts, and any other fluctuations in production. Every fifteen minutes the output tape was counted and the totals entered. The History Sheet, or Daily History Record, was intended to be a diary of the test. It included "what changes

[26] RATR Report no. 1, secs. II and III.

Figure 5. Relay assembly test room. The workers' view of the test room, showing the layout of the relay parts. The boxes at the front of each position contain coils. The supervisor/researcher's desk is visible in the background. The layout operator, Beatrice Stedry, is at the far right of the picture. Courtesy of AT&T Archives.

are made; what transpires during the day; operators' remarks; our own observations and anything that will assist as an explanation when rationalizing the performance curve."[27] Intended to provide Pennock and the other experimenters with a window on the test room, it subsequently would prove invaluable to Mayo and his colleagues – and to the historian trying to understand the social dynamics of the tests.

The six test room workers were loosely representative of the relay assemblers at Hawthorne. They were all young women – at the start of the test, four of the workers were eighteen or nineteen, the fifth worker was twenty-eight, and the layout operator was twenty-four (or so the experimenters believed; in fact, one of the women was only fifteen years old but had lied in order to obtain a job at Hawthorne). All came from the large ethnic communities of Chicago. The four younger workers came from the local Polish community, although all had been born in the United States; the fifth worker had been born in Norway and had emigrated only three years before;

27 Ibid., sec. 3.

Figure 6. Recording equipment, relay assembly test room. On the right is the tape that recorded each worker's output; on the left is the equipment for recording temperature and humidity. Courtesy of AT&T Archives.

and the layout operator came from a Bohemian family (Table 3). With one exception, all were single and lived with their parents, contributing to the family income. Like many of the other unskilled workers at Hawthorne, the relay assembly test room workers were young women for whom work was a means of providing additional income for the family, along with some measure of financial independence from their families until they married.[28]

Personal details on the workers are available because the experimenters extended their investigation into the young women's personal lives. Persuaded that "home and social environs" and "more personal elements" could affect the workers' performance, Hibarger and Pennock questioned the six young women about their home lives, families, and social activities and inspected their employment records. The women's physical condition was checked during monthly visits to the factory hospital. These visits provided an opportunity for the experimenters to probe further into the work-

[28] "List of Employees Who Worked in Relay Assembly Test Room Study," FJR/3; see also notes in WJD/1/21.

Table 3. *Relay assembly test room workers*

Worker I.D. no.	Name	Age on entering test room	Ethnicity	Date began at Western Electric
1A	Adeline Bogatowicz	18	Polish	Sept. 1925
2A	Irene Rybacki	19	Polish	July 1923
3	Theresa Layman	15[a]	Polish	June 1925
4	Wanda Blazejak	19	Polish	Oct. 1923
5	Anna Haug	28	Norwegian	Mar. 1926
Layout	Beatrice Stedry	24	Bohemian	Dec. 1920
From 25 Jan. 1928				
1	Mary Volango	18	Polish	July 1926
2	Jennie Sirchio	20	Italian	Feb. 1924

[a] Western Electric believed Theresa Layman to be 18.

ers' private lives; the doctors exploited the doctor–patient relationship to ask the workers questions, prepared by Hibarger, that the women might otherwise have been unwilling to answer, including the timing of their menstrual periods.[29] A heavy paternalism suffused the relationship of the researchers to the workers and colored their perceptions. The experimenters and authors of the official accounts typically referred to the women as "girls" – a practice still adopted by many recent commentators.

The illumination tests provided the model for the experimental protocol of the relay assembly test. A base production rate was established by checking the workers' production in the regular department; indeed, the five seem to have been chosen because they were experienced workers with almost identical levels of output. After this first test period, the workers were moved into the remodeled test room for a period of acclimatization. In the third period they were shifted onto a special group rate of payment, where instead of sharing the bonus of the regular department, they became in effect a separate gang, keeping for themselves any bonuses accruing from increased production. The effects of this move should not be underestimated. In the regular department the workers were sharing a bonus among some one hundred workers in a large department of about three hundred workers; in the test room the workers were a group of six sitting at a single bench, for whom an increase in production would have measurable effects on their wages in the following pay period. The experimenters reasoned that unless such a payment scheme was introduced, "the operators would not respond with the fullest cooperation that would be essential to a test of this nature."

[29] Ibid.; RATR Daily History Record, 9 Aug. 1927, HSCM/11–15.

A controversy has raged ever since over whether the change in pay system served only to ensure the workers' cooperation or whether it became the most significant experimental variable introduced, with the workers increasing their production because of the direct financial incentive.[10]

Finally, in August 1927, three months after the workers had started in the test room, rest periods were introduced: at first, two five-minute rests at 10 a.m. and 2 p.m., then two ten-minute rests, then six five-minute rests spaced through the day. In November the experimenters introduced a fifteen-minute morning rest and a ten-minute afternoon rest, with the company providing free tea and food during the morning rest period. These innovations held until the twelfth test period in September 1928, while the experimenters tried out the effects of a shorter working day and week (Table 4). Production was carefully monitored, and the individual and group average hourly output for each period calculated and compared with that of the preceding periods. Monthly hospital visits provided data on the health of the workers, and Hibarger religiously entered the daily events of the test room in the Log Sheet and Daily History Record. The results were notable. Average hourly output for the group increased steadily in every period up to and including the introduction of the morning lunch in period 7 – from 49.7 to 55.8 relays per hour. Before considering the reasons proffered by the experimenters and workers for this increase, however, it is necessary to examine the relay assembly test from the workers' standpoint.

The workers' view of the test room

The six young women sitting at the bench in the test room took an active role in the experiment. They pressured the experimenters into altering working conditions in the room, they developed their own interpretations of the experimental results, and they tried to control their level of production, sometimes restricting and sometimes increasing output.

The workers were deliberately drawn into the process of running and interpreting the experiment. It was not possible, as it had been in the lighting tests, to prevent the workers from being aware of changes in experimental conditions; their knowledge of the introduction of rest periods was necessary if they were thereby to be encouraged to produce steadily, aware that they could rest so many times a day. Before each experimental stage was introduced, the workers met with Hibarger and the other experimenters in Pennock's office, where a discussion would be held regarding the progress of the tests to date, the factors affecting production, and whether the workers thought they could increase production despite the reduction of working

---

[10] RATR Progress Report no. 1, sec. IV. The size of the bonus group in the regular relay assembly department is given in Roethlisberger and Dickson, *Management and the Worker*, 34.

Table 4. Average hourly output, relay assembly test room

Period	Starting date	Duration (weeks)	Special test feature	Hours per week	Worker's average hourly output of relays						
					1	2	3	4	5	Group	Period
1	25 Apr. 27	2	Regular department	48:00	50.5	49.7	49.7	49.7	48.3	49.6	1
2	10 May 27	5	Test room	48:00	47.8	48.0	49.5	51.1	48.9	49.1	2
3	13 June 27	8	Special group pay	48:00	48.4	50.4	53.6	52.1	50.5	51.0	3
4	8 Aug. 27	5	Rests: 2 × 5 min	47:05	51.5	50.7	53.6	53.6	50.8	52.0	4
5	12 Sept. 27	4	Rests: 2 × 10 min	46:10	54.1	55.4	56.9	56.1	52.9	55.1	5
6	10 Oct. 27	4	Rests: 6 × 5 min	45:15	54.0	53.6	55.7	55.7	53.5	54.5	6
7	7 Nov. 27	11	Rests: 15 min a.m., 10 min p.m.; morning tea	45:40	54.0	53.9	58.9	58.2	54.2	55.8	7
8	23 Jan. 28	7	As for 7, with 4:30 stop; two new workers	43:10	62.8	64.5	62.2	63.1	56.8	61.9	8
9	12 Mar. 28	4	As for 7, with 4:00 stop	40:40	65.5	68.0	63.0	63.5	59.5	63.9	9
10	9 Apr. 28	12	As for 7	45:40	63.9	64.9	62.1	62.8	55.2	61.8	10
11	2 July 28	9	As for 7, Sat. morning off	41:40	65.6	66.4	63.9	62.9	55.0	62.8	11
12	3 Sept. 28	12	Repeat period 3	48:00	62.5	63.9	59.7	61.3	56.1	60.7	12
13	26 Nov. 28	31	As for 7[a]	45:40	67.4	71.9	64.3	69.1	59.7	66.5	13
14	1 July 29	9	Sat. morning off[a]	41:40	64.5	70.6	62.0	69.4	Sub.[b]	66.6	14
15	2 Sept. 29	31	—[a]	45:40	68.8	73.9	64.0	71.3	Sub.[b]	69.5	15
16	7 Apr. 30	4	Workers change positions[a]	45:40	72.7	76.8	67.5	73.0	Sub.[b]	72.5	16
17	5 May 30	25	4:15 stop; Sat. morning off[a]	37:55	69.6	75.9	65.6	73.7	61.5	69.3	17
18	27 Oct. 30	15	4:15 stop; Fri. p.m. and Sat. morning off[a]	34:35	69.1	76.4	64.9	72.8	64.9	69.6	18
19	9 Feb. 31	15	Workers return to original positions[a]	34:35	72.9	74.8	64.1	69.6	65.3	69.3	19
20	25 May 31	25	4:15 stop; Sat. morning off[a]	37:55	72.5	76.3	63.4	66.5	64.0	68.5	20
21	16 Nov. 31	3	4:15 stop; Mon. and Sat. off[a]	30:20	70.2	72.5	67.0	68.9	67.7	69.3	21
22	7 Dec. 31	9	4:15 stop; Sat. off[a]	37:55	75.0	76.4	68.6	73.1	65.8	71.8	22
23	8 Feb. 32	3	4:15 stop; Mon. and Sat. off[a]	30:20	77.1	78.0	66.9	73.1	67.1	72.4	23
24	1 Mar. 32 17 June 32	17	3- and 4-day week, with no work for 5 weeks[a]	—	71.4	73.0	67.9	69.1	Sub.[b]	69.6	24

[a] Morning tea, 15-minute morning rest, and 10-minute afternoon rest continue through the remainder of the test periods.
[b] Anna Haug replaced by Antoinette Parillo from 5 Sept. 29 to 14 May 30 and from 8 Mar. 32; group output calculated on four workers only.

hours through rests and a shorter day. Further, the workers were even informed of what changes were expected in the periods; on the day that two ten-minute periods were introduced, for example, they were "given the suggestion that the increased rest periods... would possibly have an increasing result insofar as uniform activity is concerned."[31]

The workers' knowledge of daily production figures was also formalized, with Hibarger telling them each morning the results of the previous day's work. Production figures were given to the workers as a percentage of the "bogey" – the rate at which piece-rate engineers believed workers could theoretically work. When production increased to its highest level on the first day of ten-minute rests, the workers responded enthusiastically to Hibarger's announcement:

> *Bogatowicz:*   80.6 per cent! No? Hurrah for our side, and on Monday too, isn't that nice?
> *Rybacki:*   Gee we made 80% yesterday, today we ought to make 90%.[32]

And as they became more confident, the women would stroll across to the junior clerk's desk during the rest period in order to inspect the output figures.[33]

It did not take long for the workers to realize that their special position endowed them with hitherto undreamed of power. That they had become a privileged elite among relay assemblers, even among the entire Hawthorne workforce, they did not doubt. Did they not participate in meetings in the office of one of the plant managers, during which their opinions were earnestly solicited? Did not the doctors and nurses fuss over them at the monthly hospital visit? Was not the company providing them with a free meal each morning and allowing them rests that no other worker in the factory had? Still, there was clearly room for improvement, and the workers, especially Adeline Bogatowicz and Irene Rybacki, asked for further changes, at first hesitantly and then more insistently. Most of the changes were small, although not insignificant. Bogatowicz requested that a screen be placed in front of their workbench to provide privacy from the male experimenters' gaze. When Hibarger was slow to act on this request, she commented ironically, "I'll bet we could get out more work if we had screens in front so we wouldn't have to keep pulling our dresses down." The screens were duly installed. In November the workers complained collectively that the lighting was too bright; testing revealed that it was indeed 50 percent higher than desired and it was accordingly lowered.[34]

A more protracted struggle ensued over the hospital visits. From the

[31] Daily History Record, 12 Sept. 1927.
[32] RATR Progress Report no. 1, sec. VI.
[33] Daily History Record, 13 Oct. 1927.
[34] Ibid., 28 May 1927, 25 June 1927, 10 Nov. 1927.

beginning the women resented the physical examination and the personal questions of the doctors and nurses, and Bogatowicz was, Hibarger recorded, "somewhat antagonistic." The doctor visited the test room so as to make more informal contact with the workers, but their dislike of the hospital visits remained. The experimenters attempted to lessen this by turning the visits into parties – cake, ice cream, and tea were served, and a radio provided entertainment. These constituted such a dramatic change in the workers' normal work experience that they accepted future hospital visits in exchange for the parties, which became duly ritualized, the workers taking turns to bake a cake or cookies. Repeated attempts by the experimenters to stop the parties failed (the engineering sensibilities of Kraft and Fauquier were especially offended by this carnival atmosphere and upsetting of work discipline). The parties remained, symbols of the women's ability to influence the test room environment in exchange for their participation in the experiment.[35]

Adeline Bogatowicz and Irene Rybacki proved especially willing to exploit the possibilities to the fullest. Underpayment of their wages, due to miscalculations by the foreman of the regular department, brought threats of a strike. These were in jest, but the women realized that they could rely on Hibarger and Pennock to intervene on their behalf over any difficulties with other supervisors. The next time an error occurred in their pay packets they had the satisfaction of receiving a personal apology from the relay assembly foreman – something that would never occur in the regular department.[36] On other occasions they could play the foreman against the experimenters, getting permission from the foreman for a Saturday morning off after the experimenters had refused it because it would make their calculations more difficult.[37]

Privileged status and a modicum of control over their workdays brought about a strong identification with the test room among the workers. At their own initiative they requested prints of a photograph taken of the test room and its occupants. The hospital parties, supplemented by a Christmas party and birthday celebrations, provided social occasions unheard of in the factory, at least during working hours. In time the friendly and cooperative Homer Hibarger became "Hi," and the junior clerk was treated as a younger brother and teased. With the introduction of refreshments during the morning rest period, the women's status soared higher still. When workers in other departments learned that tea was being served in the test room, they quickly dubbed it the "T Room."[38]

As each of the experimental stages was completed, experimenters and

[35] RATR Progress Report no. 1, sec. V; Daily History Record, 24 May 1927, 6 July 1927, 14 Sept. 1927, 13 Jan. 1928, 23 Feb. 1928.
[36] Daily History Record, 17 Sept. 1927, 17 Oct. 1927.
[37] Ibid., 23 Dec. 1927.
[38] Ibid., 26 Sept. 1927, 4 Oct. 1927, 22 Dec. 1927, 6 Feb. 1928.

workers would analyze the data together, both in meetings in Pennock's office and in conversation with Hibarger in the test room. The women were never considered equals in these discussions – they were treated instead as experimental subjects who might be able to contribute something to the debate – but this did not prevent them from trying to present their own collective interpretation of the results. They gave two reasons for their increased output. First, the rest periods and morning refreshments prevented them from becoming tired and were a vast improvement over normal work arrangements. Second, as a result of the reduction in the variety of relays (to simplify standardization of the output data) they could become proficient on a few relays; in the regular department they might be required to work on as many as twenty-five different types of relays in a day. When it was suggested that the daily report of output might also be an incentive, Bogatowicz rejected this, and Rybacki pointed out that the foreman in the regular department would "bawl you out" if you did not make your rate. Thus, the workers emphasized the factors they liked about the test room – rests, morning lunch, fewer relay types – and discounted traditional techniques of maintaining production, including pressure from supervisors. If new factors were to be discovered in the test room, the women wanted to ensure that they were to their liking.[39] The workers also commented on the differences in supervision between the test room and the regular department, although they never explicitly linked this factor to production during the first eight test periods. Anna Haug commented: "Out there there are too many bosses and in here it's different.... I used to hate to come to work in the morning out there.... When I didn't make my rate I was afraid to come down the next day." And Rybacki explained: "We don't have to worry about getting bawled out about our rates. I wish this test would last two more years."[40] There is no doubt that the test room was a more friendly and egalitarian environment than the Relay Assembly Department, especially under Hibarger's benevolent guidance.

But supervision in the test room, even if conducted in a less confrontational fashion, was probably more intense and more focused than it was in the department. To be sure, Hibarger was officially the test room observer, and as such he had no supervisory control over the women, nor did he seek it. Disciplinary power remained with the Relay Assembly Department foreman, Mr. Platenka, who could pay only occasional visits to the test room. But the very organization of the test room entailed increased supervision. Each time a worker completed a relay and dropped it down the chute, she was reminded that the time she took to assemble that relay had been mea-

[39] On rests, see ibid., 17 Aug. 1927; RATR Progress Report no. sec. 9, 6. On relay types, see Daily History Record, 5 July 1927, 7 Oct. 1927, 9 Mar. 1928; and RATR Progress Report no. 1, sec. IX, 6. On reports of output, see Daily History Record 17 Aug. 1927; RATR Progess Report no. 1, sec. IX, 6.
[40] Daily History Record, 9 Dec. 1927, 21 Oct. 1927.

sured automatically on the tape. The sound of falling relays told her how rapidly her fellow workers were proceeding. Each morning Hibarger would announce the previous day's output and translate that into wages. And if output was particularly low, Platenka would visit the room to inform the workers of their poor performance. On at least one occasion the experimental variables were used as a stick; Pennock directed Hibarger to hint to the workers that the morning lunches would be discontinued if production and cooperation did not improve.[41]

The major confrontation was over the extent to which the workers could talk in the test room. Talking was permitted as long as it did not disturb production, but this was an impossible line to hold. Conversations about movies, clothes, or boyfriends naturally gained momentum, until work slowed and the women laughed and talked freely. Hibarger was powerless to stop this, confining his role to making notations in the daily record and marking "19" on the tape to indicate talking. This in turn prompted a threat from Bogatowicz and Rybacki to go on strike if he continued to put "so many 19s on the tape." The experimenters resolved to stop what they regarded as disruptive talking and warned the women that it must cease. This appeared to have the desired effect – except with Adeline Bogatowicz and Irene Rybacki. Both continued to talk on occasion, and this led to a series of confrontations that resulted in their removal from the test room.[42]

The talking was symptomatic of a more independent spirit in these two workers than was evident in the others. Both had explored to a fuller extent the possibilities of altering the test room conditions and influencing the experimenters' conclusions. They formed a close friendship and became increasingly confident about asserting their independence, summed up in Rybacki's chant, "We do what we want, we work how we feel and we say what we know."[43] Meanwhile Bogatowicz had become engaged and then married in November, and this provided a further topic of conversation. The catalyst for the women's removal seems to have been their discovery in December that Hibarger was writing down parts of their conversation in the Daily History Record. Bogatowicz and Rybacki in particular resented this practice, for it brought home to them just how "nosy" the experimenters had been, both in the test room and in the hospital.[44] Soon after this affair, the chief of the Piece Rates Division called Rybacki to his office and spelled out her shortcomings: She was moody, she talked too much, and her output was lower than that of the other workers. Two weeks later she was dressed down by Pennock. She refused to give way. A race between two other workers prompted her to ask rhetorically, "Do you think I've got holes in

[41] Ibid., 21 June 1927, 2 Aug. 1927, 4 Aug. 1927, 9 Aug. 1927, 16 Aug. 1927, 8 Dec. 1927.
[42] Ibid., 27 July 1927, 1 Aug. 1927.
[43] Ibid., 28 July 1927.
[44] Ibid., 11 July 1927, 6 Dec. 1927, 15 Dec. 1927.

my head to work like Theresa and Wanda do?" And when Hibarger showed her production figures that revealed her poor performance, she exclaimed: "For the love of Mike! They tell you to work how you feel, and when you do it, it isn't good enough. . . . I work like I feel and I don't feel like working any different."[45]

The complaint struck home at a basic contradiction in the tests. Pennock and the other experimenters were trying to be dedicated researchers by changing only one variable at a time and holding other factors steady. This meant telling the workers to work as they felt and not to make any increased effort, for that would disguise the effect of the changes in rest periods. Yet at the same time they were senior factory supervisors, unaccustomed to having teenage women challenge their authority. To complain to Bogatowicz and Rybacki that their production was unsatisfactory made nonsense of the experimental method, but the experimenters were committed to making the experiment work, which meant in this case demonstrating the efficacy of rests. The charges against the two women shifted, therefore, from their low production to the assertion that they were "uncooperative." But some guilt remained, especially on the part of Hibarger, who started entering old occurrences into the Daily History Record so as to build the case against them, such as an occasion on which one of the other workers had complained about Rybacki's behavior.[46]

The showdown came when Hibarger obtained some direct evidence that Bogatowicz was restricting output. Her friend had been heard to brag about the number of relays she could make in a day, to which Bogatowicz had replied: "Don't do it, don't be a fool." Pennock decided that both women should be removed, and on 25 January 1928, two days into period 8, they were replaced by Mary Volango, an eighteen-year-old Polish woman, and Jennie Sirchio, a twenty-year-old Italian.[47] Hibarger's entry in the log for that day reviewed the reasons for the removal of the two workers, emphasizing that a major factor was the animosity that had built up between these two women and the other workers. It is not clear how much credence should be given to this explanation. The Log Sheet does record two occasions in January on which Wanda Blazejak and the layout operator Beatrice Stedry requested that Rybacki be removed from the test; but one of these was Hibarger's recollection of an earlier incident, and Stedry's complaint came only two days before the women's removal, and then from the worker who as layout operator was encouraged by the experimenters to adopt an informal supervisory role. In the course of an interview held four years later, Theresa Layman, who sat closest to Bogatowicz and Rybacki, recalled that the two women did exclude the other workers from their conversation but

[45] Ibid., 16 Dec. 1927, 28 Dec. 1927, 4 Jan. 1928, 12 Jan. 1928.
[46] Ibid., 11 Jan. 1928, 23 Jan. 1928.
[47] Ibid., 23 Jan. 1928, 25 Jan. 1928.

stressed that while she disliked Bogatowicz, she thought Rybacki was "swell." Her explanation for the workers' removal was that "they were cutting down on their work and they said they couldn't do any more and then they were always talking about... I can't remember." Even four and a half years into the relay test, the workers' responses to the experimenters were carefully edited. Despite claims by a recent commentator that the women were removed "at their coworkers' initiative," tensions among the workers were of only secondary importance to the experimenters and received attention only once the more serious problem of the women's restriction of production had become evident.[48]

The replacement of the two women had a dramatic effect on production in the test room. Output in periods 2 through 7, covering thirty-seven weeks, had risen 12.3 percent over the starting level for the group; now, in the seven weeks of period 8, it jumped a further 12 percent. There appear to be two reasons for this extraordinary change. First, the two new workers were much faster than the women they replaced (in period 7, Volango produced 17.5 percent more relays than did Bogatowicz, and Sirchio produced 21.3 percent more than Rybacki); indeed, Jennie Sirchio held the record as fastest relay assembler in the regular department. Of the increase in the group's productivity from the periods 1 to 8, fully 31 percent can be attributed to these faster assemblers. Second, the removal of the two women constituted an explicit threat to the remaining workers of their own removal from the privileged conditions of the test room if they did not perform adequately. This is not as easily measured, for the other test room conditions could have had their cumulative effect on these three women. It is noteworthy, however, that in this period Blazejak and Haug registered their highest increases in output yet for a single period. Hibarger noted too, somewhat elliptically, that the attitudes of Layman and Blazejak "seem to tend slightly toward resentment."[49]

Their resentment seems to have been directed not only at the experimenters, but also at Sirchio, who quickly took on the role of leader, even driver, of the team. A fast worker, she had a reputation for breaking the rates in the regular department; the test room provided a providential opportunity to exercise this ability further. Immediate personal circumstances also increased her desire to work hard and increase her wages. A sister had died in January, shortly before she entered the test room, her mother died in

[48] Ibid., 25 Jan. 1928; RATR, "Record of Interviews," Theresa Layman, 20 Jan. 1932, HSCM/ 32–42, 62. The two major official accounts of the Hawthorne experiments gave considerable space to the removal; see T. N. Whitehead, *The Industrial Worker*, Cambridge, Mass.: Harvard University Press, 1938, 1; 117–18; and Roethlisberger and Dickson, *Management and the Worker*, 53–5. The "recent commentator" is Jeffrey A. Sonnenfeld, "Shedding Light on the Hawthorne Studies," *Journal of Occupational Behaviour*, 1985, 6: 111–30, quote on 121.

[49] Daily History Record, 20 Mar. 1928, 4 Apr. 1928.

early March, and then her father and a brother learned they were to be laid off work at the end of April. Jennie Sirchio was rapidly transformed into the housekeeper of the family and was about to become its major bread-winner. She therefore did everything she could to increase group production in the test room. When daily output fell, she would chastise the worker most responsible for the decline. If the junior clerk was slow to call the workers back to work after rest periods, she would hurry him up. If Layman and Blazejak slowed down to talk, she would admonish, "Come on you, do some work and shut up" – only to be told, "Oh shut up ambitious!" But it had the desired effect. Shortly after these exchanges Layman declared she was going to try to beat Sirchio's output, and in early April the workers decided (temporarily as it turned out) to dispense with the party at the hospital since it affected their earnings – an index as to how production for a time became more important than the social relations of the test room. On Good Friday the women achieved a new output record, and in period 9 they posted individual and collective records.[50]

It would be a mistake, however, to conclude that the atmosphere of the test room had changed considerably or that the women had caved in to the pressure to work faster, thereby dispensing with their hard-won freedoms. With the exception of Anna Haug, the workers engaged in much laughing and talking, duly noted by Hibarger in the record. Indeed, Sirchio quickly became the leader in more than production, and as we shall see in the next chapter, she was soon challenging the experimenters in a manner reminiscent of the departed workers.[51]

The researchers' view of the test room

As the confrontation with Bogatowicz and Rybacki brewed, the experiment-ers were also busy trying to make sense of the test room results. A lengthy report, dated 3 December 1927, described meticulously the setting up of the tests, the test periods, and the results and offered some tentative con-clusions. The experimenters were well aware that in moving the workers to the test room they had altered a large number of variables simultaneously, including the changes in supervision, the decrease in relay types, the small size of the working group, uniform lighting, and the psychological effects of selecting and isolating the workers in the test room.[52] Indeed, the report stressed the importance of psychological factors in a discussion of the reason for the improvement in the workers' health reported by the company doctor:

> This improvement in the general health and gain in weight is felt to be
> due to the psychological effects which produce a more contented state

---

[50] Ibid., 24 Mar. 1928, 29 Mar. 1928, 31 Mar. 1928, 3 Apr. 1928, 4 Apr. 1928, 7 Apr. 1928.
[51] Ibid., 21 Mar. 1928, 27 Mar. 1928.
[52] RATR Progress Report no. 1, sec. II.

of mind and which in turn is fostered by the novelty aspect, the realization of their having been chosen; the experiencing of something new;
the anticipation of impending and continued changes, etc. all of which
tend as a whole to assist in accomplishing the thing we are endeavoring
to accomplish, and that is, to determine the essential features required
to overcome monotony and the establishing of the relationship existing
between monotony and efficient performance.[53]

From the beginning of the relay assembly test (before Mayo and other
academics were brought in to aid in interpreting the results) the company
experimenters were well aware that the changed psychological conditions
in the test room were having a positive effect on the workers' outlook and
production.

Yet while they recognized that test room conditions altered workers'
attitudes significantly, Pennock and the other experimenters were concerned
primarily to determine whether rest periods were successful in reducing
monotony and mental and physical fatigue in repetitive assembly work,
thereby increasing production. Although sensitive to the full array of social
and psychological factors at work in the test room, their eyes were always
firmly focused on the bottom line − average hourly output. They were
industrial engineers and managers interested in developing more productive
management techniques, not social scientists studying the social psychology
of the factory. In this respect, their choice of the term "test," rather than
"experiment," to describe the research is suggestive: The test room was
intended to be a place for testing innovations in the organization of production to see if they could be applied throughout the factory. Thus, after
the apparent success of the rest periods in the test room, they were introduced in the regular Relay Assembly Department in February 1928, where
they were received enthusiastically.[54] To the managers this seemed a more
orderly way of proceeding than experimenting directly in the regular department, only to be faced with the difficulty, if rest periods did not work
out to management's liking, of trying to take them away from the workers
without incurring protests.

The "Observations and Conclusions" of the first progress report balanced
an interest in practical results with an awareness of the significance of the
social and psychological findings. Much of the analysis of the test room
data focused on the standard concerns of industrial fatigue research. The
wartime fatigue researchers had noted that the rate of production started
slowly in the morning, then increased toward midmorning, only to slow
down again before lunch; a similar bell-shaped curve was evident in the
afternoon. These "fatigue curves" had been taken by industrial physiologists
as evidence of industrial fatigue toward the end of each work session. They
argued that by experimenting with work hours and rest periods and by

[53] Ibid., sec. 5.
[54] Daily History Record, 27 Feb. 1928, 9 Mar. 1928.

analyzing the resulting output curves, it would be possible to find the most efficient organization of production and at the same time avoid industrial fatigue.[55]

Half of the fourteen conclusions in the relay test report concerned production curves and the effects of rest periods. The slump in production in the late morning was found to be due not to fatigue, but to the workers taking time to go to the bathroom. Similarly, the early afternoon slump apparently resulted from the workers feeling tired after having had a heavy lunch – hence the introduction of the midmorning meal to lessen the time between breakfast and lunch and reduce the size of lunch. The ten-minute rests and morning lunch and afternoon rest periods resulted in the highest production, but the five-minute rests brought the most consistent production rate; in every case total daily production increased with rests, despite the reduction in the amount of time actually at work. From the managers' viewpoint, rest periods were clearly beneficial to both workers and managers. Whether one wanted to ascribe the increase in production to a reduction of fatigue or not, the results fit squarely into the findings of industrial fatigue research.[56] Six of the remaining conclusions dealt specifically with social and psychological influences in the test room. Major incentives consisted of the "novelty" and "psychology of the test," along with the "absence of the closer supervision customary in the regular department." By comparison, increased earnings were considered a minor factor – although the logic behind this conclusion was not spelled out. In addition, outside influences such as home and social environment played a role, especially in determining "a buoyant or morbid spirit which is reflected in production." Interactions among workers partly accounted for their similarity of performance in many periods, but the experimenters attributed this to "instinctive imitation" and not to conscious control of production.[57]

In several respects the report downplays factors that appear to have been important. First, the absence of a bullying foreman yelling at the workers did not necessarily mean that there was less supervision. Although the report was written before the removal of the two rebellious workers, there had been consistent supervision by the experimenters, primarily through reprimands and the recording of output. Indeed, a second report issued a month after the removal of the two workers continued to assert that supervision was less strict in the test room.[58] Second, the experimenters assumed that a majority of the increase in production attributable to the special group payment would have occurred during the eight weeks of period 2, when it was introduced. Yet the small-group rate applied in all experimental periods,

---

[55] See, e.g., Frederick S. Lee, *The Human Machine and Industrial Efficiency*, New York, 1919.
[56] RATR Progress Report no. 1, sec. VIII.
[57] Ibid.
[58] RATR Progress Report no. 2, 25 Feb. 1928, HSCM/4, A1–E4.

and there was no reason to suppose that it would not provide a continuing incentive, especially when daily output could be so easily translated into daily earnings. Certainly Jennie Sirchio was expressly motivated by the need to increase her wages. Third, the conclusions omitted a major reason given by the women: that the reduction in the variety of relay types made work easier and faster. Finally, the researchers set aside any idea that the workers might be consciously controlling their production, whether by increasing or restricting it. The researchers believed that period 2 had exhausted the effect of economic incentive, a prime motive for conscious control of production. They had redefined the restriction of output by Bogatowicz and Rybacki as an unwillingness to cooperate with the test protocol. The male managers found it hard to credit working-class "girls" with the capability for such planning. But probably most significantly, as managers they could not accept that they might not be in complete control of production, and that included workers' behavior.

Is there a consistent perspective that explains these omissions and particular interpretations? It is not immediately apparent why managers should downplay the effect of wages or production difficulties – until one realizes that these were factors out of their control. Relays would continue to be required in bewildering styles, often only a small number ordered at a time, and wages were determined by a separate department in collaboration with the works manager and head office in New York. Pennock and the piece-rate engineers accordingly directed their attention to factors that could be adjusted without further expenditure. Rest periods, as they carefully argued, could be introduced at little or no expense, and actually increased production. And in their comparison between the test room and regular department, they pointed tentatively to the effects of "reduced" supervision, although at this stage there was no indication that this was a variable that could be introduced outside the test room. The experimenters were attempting to intensify work within the existing technical and social parameters of production, not alter those boundaries. This is clearly revealed in their attitude toward talking and laughing by the workers. Rather than consider this a natural and necessary aspect of work, a constituent of an enjoyable work environment, the report cited this continued hilarity as evidence that the workers were not yet working at full capacity and that further tests might reveal how to exploit this unutilized productive capacity. The researchers therefore concentrated on those factors that they had deliberately manipulated in the test room, with a view to intensifying managerial control.

The two groups in the relay assembly test, workers and production managers, therefore had conflicting views of the meaning of the test and of the appropriate interpretation. Severely limited in their power, the workers regarded the test as an opportunity to gain hitherto unrealizable status and to manipulate the experimental conditions to their advantage. They naturally chose to emphasize the conditions in the test room they most enjoyed

– rest periods, the morning lunch, fewer relay types, increased earnings, and the "freedom" to work as they wished. Similarly, the managers chose to highlight the factors they were free to manipulate – rest periods and supervision.

Contrary to the standard accounts of the Hawthorne experiments, the Hawthorne managers and industrial lighting experimenters did not ignore the significance of psychological factors when accounting for the variation of production in the lighting tests and early stages of the relay assembly test. We have seen that the Hawthorne and MIT engineers recognized the importance of psychological factors from the very first series of tests and sought to design experimental protocols that controlled for these factors. They did not emphasize them, because their express concern was to determine the effects of different levels of lighting on production, although they did expand the tests by introducing different degrees of supervision as a variable. The Hawthorne managers conducting the relay test were not working under the constraints of an NRC committee, and they did wish to explore the significance of the workers' personal life and attitudes on production, clearly indicated by the collection of personal data, interviews, and the noting of workers' conversations. But the Hawthorne engineers were operating under a different set of constraints – their paramount concern was to increase production by adjusting those aspects of the technical and social relations of production that were under their control.

This does not mean that the Hawthorne engineers were confident about their observations and conclusions. The results remained inconclusive and puzzling, a problem borne out when Pennock tried to explain the progress of the test to the works manager Charles L. Rice and Vice-President Clarence Stoll in early 1928. After this round of meetings Pennock seemed less sure of the interpretations voiced in the progress report, telling the women: "The rate of working has gone up approximately 25%. That's a lot, we do not know whether it's due to the small gang; the lunches; the rest periods; small number of different types or what?" At this stage Pennock started casting around for guidance, at first from the published literature on fatigue and related subjects held by his fellow engineers and in the works library. It was probably Stoll who suggested that the researchers approach some experts for assistance. Stoll had been a member of the Committee on Industrial Lighting, with its mixture of industrial engineers and academics, and was now at New York headquarters, where contacts with leading educational institutions were taken for granted. Only two weeks after conferring with Stoll, Pennock reported to the relay test workers that "we're going to have a man come out from one of the colleges and see what he can tell us about what we've found out."[59]

[59] Quotes from Daily History Record, 9 Mar. 1928; see also 28 Jan., 20 Feb. 1928.

3

Interpreting the relay test

TWO ACADEMIC CONSULTANTS joined the group of company researchers during 1928 – Clair Turner from MIT and Elton Mayo from the Harvard Business School. Both Mayo and Turner brought new approaches to the test room study. The test room women were now subjected to a barrage of tests and questionnaires, as the two scientists sought, independently, to highlight the physiological relationships between production and the workers' lifestyles. In so doing they shifted some of the emphasis in the test room away from the manipulation of variables through the introduction of new test periods, focusing instead on the workers themselves, individually and collectively. The company researchers had hoped that their academic consultants would be able to clarify some of the confusing results of the relay assembly test. However, Mayo and Turner brought their own preconceptions and intellectual commitments to the test room, and two additional perspectives were added to those of the workers and company researchers. The achievement of a consensus among the various parties as to what the experiments meant seemed as far away as ever.

The relay assembly test room always remained the heart of the Hawthorne experiments, to the researchers and subsequent commentators. Although by the end of 1928 the researchers had shifted their attention to other studies, they would periodically try to apply the approaches developed in the other studies to the relay test room, hoping to revitalize the relay test. Commentators on the experiments over the past two decades have become preoccupied with the relay assembly test almost to the exclusion of the other research conducted at Hawthorne. The official accounts of the test have been subjected to a series of critical analyses, and sophisticated statistical techniques have been applied to the test room production data. All of these reanalyses, by both the Hawthorne researchers and subsequent commentators, have generated further controversy and uncertainty over how to interpret the events that took place in the relay assembly test room between 1927 and 1932. In this chapter I shall set out the variety of interpretations of the relay assembly test and explore why different participants and commentators have generated such diverse accounts.

Scientists to the test

Once Clarence Stoll and George Pennock had agreed that it was time to bring some outside expertise to bear on the relay test results, they wasted no time in locating suitable collaborators. Stoll and T. K. Stevenson, the Western Electric personnel director, approached Harvard Business School professor Elton Mayo. Stevenson and other company executives had been impressed by a speech Mayo had given five months previously to a luncheon group of personnel directors from large corporations entitled "What Psychology Can Do for Industry in the Next Ten Years." During the lunch Stevenson talked with Mayo and told him of the experiments with rest periods at the Hawthorne Works. Now, in March 1928, Stevenson sent Mayo a copy of the relay test progress report and suggested that Mayo visit Chicago. Meanwhile Pennock arranged for a visit by Clair Turner, professor of biology and public health at MIT. Pennock had close ties with MIT, reinforced by the participation of Jackson and his colleagues in the lighting tests; it is possible that Turner was recommended by Jackson. The choice of an expert in public health reflects Pennock and Hibarger's interest in expanding the relay test to examine the personal and social background of the workers, factors that had been mentioned in the lighting tests as possibly affecting production but had so far remained unexamined. Both Mayo and Turner agreed to visit the test room at the company's expense and subsequently became consultants to the experiments.[1]

It seems likely that Pennock and the Hawthorne researchers deliberately kept their academic consultants apart. In the fifteen documented visits made by Turner or Mayo to Hawthorne in 1928 and 1929, they were never there at the same time; minimal planning could have ensured that their visits coincided had any of the parties desired it. Available evidence indicates that Mayo and Turner never conferred over the test room results or their contributions to the tests, which is surprising when one considers that the two academics worked in institutions only two miles apart. Pennock may possibly have considered it prudent to discourage collaboration between the two men, fearful that they might join forces and dominate the tests. With the two experts working separately, it was left to the Hawthorne managers to integrate their research.[2]

---

[1] T. K. Stevenson to Elton Mayo, 15 Mar. 1928, HSCM/161, A1–2; Mayo to Stevenson, 19 Mar. 1928, EM/1.087. Turner claims in his autobiography that Pennock approached him one "mild late September morning" to ask for his assistance, but it seems more likely to have occurred in February 1928, for Pennock first mentions him in early March. Turner's account is so inaccurate on almost every other fact that there is no reason to take this discrepancy seriously. Further, Progress Report no. 3 of 30 June 1928 notes that Turner has joined the experiment; he is not mentioned in Report no. 2 of 25 Feb. 1928. See Clair Elsmere Turner, *I Remember*, New York: Vantage Press, 1974, 83–4; Daily History Record, 9 Mar. 1928; RATR Progress Report no. 3, 30 June 1928, HSCM/5–6, D1.

[2] Visits by Mayo and Turner were recorded in the Daily History Record. Although we cannot be certain that this was done consistently, the record lists all visits for which there is inde-

Mayo's initial participation in the relay assembly test was remarkably brief, although he would later play a significant role in interpreting the results. After reading the second progress report sent to him by Stevenson in New York, Mayo arranged to visit Hawthorne in April 1928, accompanied by his assistant Emily Osborne and a student at the business school, Osgood "Steve" Lovekin. They went to Hawthorne to look over the experiment, but Mayo also had a plan to conduct an intensive series of blood pressure measurements on the workers. To understand why Mayo wished to take blood pressure measurements on the relay assemblers we must briefly examine his research and theories before his visit to Hawthorne.

While conducting research in factories in Philadelphia from 1923 to 1925, Mayo had developed an elaborate theory of the relationship between working conditions and workers' mental states and their impact on productivity and industrial relations. His thesis was that poor working conditions, long hours, and awkward postures led to industrial fatigue and, most importantly, to mild psychiatric disturbances, which in turn could collectively lead to industrial unrest. I shall examine the source of Mayo's ideas in more detail in the next chapter, but here it is sufficient to note that Mayo sought to combine the physiological study of fatigue with a psychiatric study of workers' mental states. Mayo believed that his research in a Philadelphia textile mill had given clear evidence of the interaction of physiological and psychological states. When he had introduced rest periods, there had been a significant reduction in fatigue and increase in productivity, and this had been associated with a decline in the incidence of "melancholy preoccupations."

Mayo also began to experiment with blood pressure measurements as an index of fatigue, hoping that they could be used to identify those workers with poor physiological integration and, by extension, those most susceptible to falling into reveries and obsessions that could lead to industrial strife. Since moving to Harvard in 1926 Mayo's interest in blood pressure had been cemented by his friendship with physiologist L. J. Henderson, who was conducting extensive research on the physiology of fatigue and the biochemistry of the blood. For the past two years Mayo had been collecting blood pressure data on workers in several factories in the Boston area, and for a time Emily Osborne had been installed to act as an industrial nurse and observer of workers' mental states. Initially the Hawthorne Works seemed to offer just one more opportunity to expand his series of data, a particularly interesting series given that the workers were working with rest periods, Mayo's favorite remedy for fatigue and industrial unrest.[3]

---

pendent confirmation from correspondence. In addition, there is no extant correspondence between the two men, nor does one mention the other in correspondence to others. In his autobiography Turner claims that he met Mayo at the plant "occasionally"; this seems doubtful. See Turner, *I Remember*, 85.

[3] Elton Mayo, "Mental Hygiene in Industry," *Transactions of the College of Physicians of Philadelphia*, 1924, 3d ser., 46: 736–48; idem, "Revery and Industrial Fatigue," *Journal of*

Mayo and his assistants obtained five separate measurements of blood pressure and pulse rate on each of two days for the five relay assemblers and for three women in an adjacent department. From these they calculated the Addis index – pulse pressure by pulse rate, where pulse pressure is the difference between diastolic (or maximal) and systolic (or minimal) blood pressure. This index, Mayo maintained, was the best available measure of what he called the "organic integration" of the worker, by which he meant the ability of the worker to sustain production at a steady and optimal rate. Workers with a low Addis index and one that remained steady throughout the working day were more likely to maintain a consistently high level of production. Mayo was drawing directly on the work of Henderson and his researchers at the Harvard Fatigue Laboratory, who had experimented with marathon runners on a treadmill in the laboratory. In addition to measuring blood pressure and pulse rate, they were able to undertake a more complex analysis of expired air and blood samples – tests that could not easily be applied in factory conditions. Mayo nevertheless saw a direct parallel between the laboratory tests and industrial work: Industry needed marathon runners, not sprinters, and Mayo hoped that the Addis index would provide an "objective standard" of a worker's productive capacity. By talking of organic integration Mayo also hoped to set to one side the question of what caused fatigue. Both physiological and psychological factors were present in fatigue; the important issue at present was to find a measure that could be compared with production figures. This was something of a shift from Mayo's previous conception of fatigue, in which he had thought of fatigue as a physiological precursor to psychiatric disturbance.[4]

The results of the measurements were ambiguous. As he had hoped, Mayo found that a low and steady index, indicating an efficient vascular system, correlated moderately with the most productive workers in the test room. More persuasively, the index was much higher for three women working without rests in the Coil Winding Department. Here was evidence that rest periods helped to maintain organic equilibrium and consequently boosted production. However, the Addis index did not correlate at all well with individual or collective fluctuations in output during the working day, so it was a crude tool at best and in need of refinement. Mayo therefore

---

Personnel Research, 1924–5, 3: 273–81. Mayo gave a personal account of his Philadelphia research in a letter to his superior at the University of Pennsylvania; see Mayo to J. H. Willits, 28 Dec. 1923, LSRM/75/790. On the Boston research, see Emily Osborne, "What Is the Future of the Industrial Research Department?" [early 1930], EM/3.073; the blood pressure data are gathered in EM/3.084.

[4] Mayo to Stevenson, 7 May 1928, HSCM/159, D8–13; L. J. Henderson, *Blood: A Study in General Physiology,* New Haven, Conn.: Yale University Press, 1928, esp. 354–62. On the history of the Harvard Fatigue Laboratory, see S. M. Horvath and E. D. Horvath, *The Harvard Fatigue Laboratory: Its History and Contribution,* Englewood Cliffs, N.J.: Prentice-Hall, 1973.

proposed that he return to take further measurements when rests were suspended in a later experimental period.[5]

The recent removal of the two workers from the test room provided Mayo with an unexpected opportunity for demonstrating his view that physiological and psychiatric states were intimately connected. To turn the incident to his advantage required a good deal of reinterpretation. Mayo described the incident to Stevenson, the personnel director in New York, as one in which "a former worker in the test room...was permitted to withdraw because she complained of fatigue, became paranoid and 'turned Bolshevik.'" On examining Rybacki's medical record, Mayo discovered that her blood analysis showed a low hemoglobin level and red blood cell count, indicating anemia. He believed that this was a clear demonstration of the intimate connections between "pessimistic or paranoid preoccupations, fatigue and organic disability."[6] Of course, this "accounted" only for the case of Irene Rybacki, while ignoring that of Adeline Bogatowicz, whose blood counts were normal. Mayo's account of Rybacki's removal from the test room demonstrates a persistent tendency in Mayo's work to transform any challenge by workers of managerial control into evidence of psychiatric disturbance. Thus, Rybacki's assertions that she would work as she liked became evidence to Mayo of fatigue and Bolshevism, and her objections to having her conversations secretly recorded were indications of paranoia. By comparison, the company researchers' interpretation of Mayo's discovery of anemia was more sociological. They concluded that while Rybacki's physical condition had contributed to the slump in her output, it was the remarks of the other workers about her low production (not recorded in the Daily History Record) that had goaded her into saying that she would not hurt herself working.[7]

Contact between Mayo and Hawthorne then fell into abeyance. Mayo spent the summer in Britain, where he compared notes with researchers at the Industrial Fatigue Research Board. On returning he found a letter from Pennock enclosing the third progress report and informing him that rest periods would be suspended in the test room as of September. Fresh from his travels and able to make comparisons with British research, Mayo began to realize the potential of the Hawthorne studies, telling Pennock that "your experiment is by way of becoming something that will be almost classic in the literature of industrial investigation." He proposed taking a more active part in the tests, suggesting that Emily Osborne visit the plant for several weeks to make "observations" of the mental state of the workers and social situation in the test room. Pennock appears to have declined, or tactfully

[5] Mayo to Stevenson, 7 May 1928; RATR Progress Report no. 3, 30 June 1928, sec. V, 6–7; Mayo to G. Pennock, 9 May 1928, EM/1.087.

[6] Mayo to Stevenson, 7 May 1928; Mayo to B. Ruml, 30 Apr. 1928, LSRM/53/572.

[7] RATR Progress Report no. 3, 30 June 1928, sec. V.D.

ignored, this request; when Mayo visited in October it was to take further blood pressure readings. His involvement in the test was restricted by Pennock to the blood pressure study, and when Mayo's participation did broaden in 1929, he became involved in the new activities of the researchers in employee interviewing and supervisory training, with only a marginal role as commentator on the test room findings.[8]

Clair Turner, by contrast, became intimately connected with the relay test. He had preceded Mayo's first visit by a week and quickly agreed to act as a consultant on the test room experiments. Turner was a curious choice for the role, for he had no particular talents in the field of industrial health or physiology. He held a certificate of public health from MIT, had worked as a sanitary engineer for the Public Health Service during the war, and had subsequently devoted his energies to the field of health education. He appears to have been chosen because he was the only likely candidate at MIT. Drawing on his expertise in health education, with its emphasis on individual responsibility for cleanliness and healthy behavior, Turner probed the data for any possible relationships between output and the personal habits of the workers. On Turner's instructions Hibarger completed a questionnaire on the women's diets, health, menstrual cycles, recreation, and hours of sleep, but Turner could find no obvious link to the improvements in production. Figures on temperature, humidity, and output were subjected to statistical analysis, but again no new insights emerged.[9] The factors that doctors typically found to be associated with disease and physical well-being did not seem to apply in any straightforward way to industrial output. Turner's attempts to measure fatigue were equally frustrating. Guided by the literature on fatigue, he administered blood pressure measurements and a vascular skin reaction test (which measured the time that a white line scratched across the wrist took to disappear). But while there were noticeable differences between morning and evening readings, these did not correspond to variations in daily output. Taking into account these findings and the fact that there was no evidence of declining output during the course of the week, which might indicate cumulative fatigue, Turner decided that the increased production in the test room could not be attributed to a reduction in neuromuscular fatigue.[10]

Turner was unable to develop a satisfactory alternative explanation for the increasing production. He proposed vaguely that "it is the nervous system which controls the rate of production in this type of process"; but

[8] Pennock to Mayo, 16 Aug. 1928, EM/1.087; Mayo to Pennock, 7 Sept. 1928, HSCM/159, C14–D1.

[9] RATR Progress Report no. 3, 30 June 1928, sec. V.D; Daily History Record, 16 Apr. 1928, 23 Apr. 1928, 10 May 1928, 23 Nov. 1928; RATR Progress Report no. 4, 11 May 1929, 70, 79–80, HSCM/7–8, F13.

[10] RATR Progress Report no. 4, 82–92; C. E. Turner to Pennock, 5 Feb. 1929, HSCM/161, C5–6.

by this he seemed to mean a long list of factors that had already been considered by the company researchers, including test room conditions, supervision, fatigue of the nervous system, changes in mental attitude, and so on. Gathering all these factors under a single term did not really aid interpretation or guide future research. Turner's contributions to the relay test were thus of marginal value. After the initial flurry of tests on fatigue and personal habits, his role shifted to that of collaborator with Hibarger on the choice of experimental periods and the writing of progress reports. A domineering man, whose letters to the Hawthorne researchers issued directives rather than made suggestions, Turner was excluded from the other research projects as they developed.[11]

If Pennock and Hibarger had been expecting rapid clarification of their problems upon consultation with Mayo and Turner, they must have been disappointed. Both scientists brought new perspectives to the relay assembly test room, but their measurements proved as ambiguous as did those made by the Hawthorne experimenters. This was not due to a failure on the part of the two experts; the data were intrinsically recalcitrant, and one needed faith and a willingness to choose one's facts judiciously in order to select any particular interpretation. Objective measurements such as blood pressure and vascular skin reaction required interpretation if they were to be slotted into the other data, as Mayo's physiological explanation of Rybacki's "Bolshevism" demonstrates.

The experiments, however, were now more scientific in the formal sense. In addition to output measures and controlled experimental periods, physiological and psychological tests now appeared in the progress reports. Not all of these were conducted by the academic consultants. The Psychological Investigation Department, which administered a wide range of psychological tests to applicants for technical jobs at Hawthorne, gave pegboard and finger-dexterity tests to the workers and discovered that the rank for dexterity among the five women accorded exactly with their rank in production.[12] Hibarger and the other researchers began to read books on industrial fatigue and attend lectures on the subject. A watershed was reached with the fourth progress report of May 1929, which included a two-page bibliography on scientific studies of fatigue. Under the guidance of their academic consultants, the company researchers were starting to look past the direct benefits for production and ask how their findings could be integrated into the literature on personnel research.[13]

Most important, under Mayo's tutelage the Hawthorne managers became

[11] Turner to Pennock, 5 Feb. 1929 (quote); Turner to Putnam, 6 Nov. 1930, HSCM/161, B8–9; Turner to Putnam, 4 Dec. 1930, HSCM/161, B6–7.

[12] Elinor G. Hayes, "Selecting Women for Shop Work," *Personnel Journal*, 1932–3, 11: 69–85, esp. 74–6; RATR Progress Report no. 4, 11 May 1929, 47.

[13] Daily History Record, 6 Sept. 1928, 16 Oct. 1928; RATR Progress Report no. 4, 11 May 1929, 134–5.

less concerned that the tests were not providing easy answers or clear conclusions. Mayo emphasized that confusion and apparent failure were an intrinsic part of the scientific method: "That this should be so is a sign of health and not of failure; one has to welcome such moments, to 'hang on' closely to the work and to wait for a new illumination to reveal itself." This was somewhat self-serving, for it allowed Mayo to suggest that evidence for his theories of the relations between organic integration, mental attitude, and production would subsequently appear, even if it was not presently available. But it also allowed Pennock and the company researchers to relax their expectations, to look for gradual developments rather than instant solutions, and to see the experiments as exploratory investigations as much as tests of specific measures that could be introduced throughout the factory. Mayo directed the researchers to the work of L. J. Henderson, whose recent book on the physiology of blood had demonstrated the impossibility of isolating single variables in a complex physicochemical system; instead, Henderson used graphical representations that revealed the interrelations between several variables at a time. Mayo clearly hoped that such an approach might work in ordering the interrelated variables in the relay test.[14]

The researchers learned their epistemological lessons well. Informing Jackson of the developments at Hawthorne since the lighting tests, Pennock explained the impossibility of isolating a single variable, whether it be lighting or something else, and concluded, "We have become so skeptical of being able to prove anything in connection with the behavior of human beings under various conditions during the six years we have been making tests that it is hard to get us to commit ourselves to anything."[15] Pennock was exaggerating for effect, but the frustration and skepticism were real enough; for while Turner and Mayo's scientific tests were producing highly uncertain data, the results of the test periods were equally problematic.

The relay test continues...

Hibarger, increasingly in collaboration with Turner, continued to establish new test periods and analyze the results. In the periods starting with the removal of the two workers he experimented with stopping the working day at 4:30 p.m., half an hour early, and then at 4:00 p.m., and finally gave the women Saturday morning off. Output continued its upward trend, with the highest average hourly output being reached in the period with the 4:00 p.m. stopping time. When in period 12 all rests and the morning lunch were removed, conditions thus being returned to those in period 3, pro-

---

[14] Mayo to Pennock, 29 April 1929 (quote), HSCM/159, C6–10; Mayo to Putnam, 1 Apr. 1929, EM/1.088; Henderson, *Blood*, esp. 11–12.
[15] Pennock to Jackson, 22 Oct. 1930, DCJ/5/326; Pennock to Jackson, 4 Aug. 1930, DCJ/5/326.

duction did fall but remained 19 percent higher than in period 3. Excluding
the two new workers, the production of the three remaining workers had
still increased 13 percent during the year and a half. With period 13 the
workers were once again given two rest periods, although they were now
required to furnish their own food for the morning snack, and the company
supplied beverages.[16] From period 17, beginning in May 1930, the experimental periods were at the mercy of company employment policy as it
struggled to cope with the depression. The working week declined steadily,
so that by period 21 in late 1931 the women were working only a four-
day week.

The next two progress reports, prepared in June 1928 and May 1929,
built on the conclusions already reached in the first two reports. The analysis
of production figures became more rigorous, since Turner had a statistician
at MIT check the reliability of the data by calculating standard deviation
and probable error. New measures of output were constructed, presenting
individual production as a percentage of each worker's highest fifteen-
minute output. The women managed to work for the four weeks of period
9 at an average of 80 to 84 percent of their highest fifteen-minute rate –
an indication of the intensification of work in the relay test room. Yet it
was not clear what all this extra analysis was meant to reveal, or what
practical value it held. The reports reiterated the earlier findings that production increased for several reasons, including the small-group payment
rate, rest periods, and the novelty of the test room. And they ruled out any
substantial role for the factors that Turner had investigated so thoroughly
– neuromuscular fatigue, personal habits, health, and the physical conditions
of work.[17]

Much has subsequently been made of the fact that production in period
12 remained 19 percent higher than that in the identical period 3, with
commentators suggesting that this constituted the major intellectual discovery of the Hawthorne experiments. This view can be traced back to the
official accounts of the experiments. For example, Fritz Roethlisberger
concluded:

> After Period XII in the Relay Assembly Test Room, the investigators
> decided to change their ideas radically. What all their experiments had
> dramatically and conclusively demonstrated was the importance of em-
> ployee attitudes and sentiments. It was clear that the responses of work-
> ers to what was happening about them were dependent upon the
> significance these events had for them.... This was the great *éclaircisse-
> ment*, the new illumination, that came from the research.

[16] RATR Progress Report no. 4, 11 May 1929, 34, 126–31.
[17] RATR Progress Report no. 3, 30 June 1928, secs. VI and VIII; RATR Progress Report no.
4, 11 May 1929, 125–31. The dates of the reports are not totally reliable; they appear to
have indicated when they were drafted rather than when they were released.

But contrary to such claims, the research records provide no evidence that period 12 triggered a flash of insight and a revolution in the understanding of the social relations of work. The fourth progress report, prepared during period 13, did note that average hourly output had been maintained in spite of the return to regular hours of work and the removal of rest periods. But far from emphasizing this as a major discovery, this observation was listed twelfth in a series of twenty-four new observations and conclusions since the previous report. It was also mentioned in a five-page section of the report, which argued that the reduction of physiological fatigue could not be the major factor in the increase in production, but simply one piece of evidence among discussions of variations in output during the day and week, hours of work, and the failure of fatigue tests, all of which pointed in the same direction. Period 12 came as no surprise to the researchers. They had already introduced a check period in the series – period 10 was the same as period 7 – and noted that production was significantly higher in the latter period. But most important, it had never been supposed by the company researchers that physiological fatigue was the only significant factor influencing output. Period 12 was not a discovery, but a neat piece of evidence that confirmed established views.[18]

The most significant change of emphasis in the new progress reports (written on either side of period 12) was their more extensive consideration of the improved mental attitude of the workers. This was attributed to "greater freedom, less strict supervision and the opportunity to vary from a fixed pace without reprimand from a gang boss." Summarizing a questionnaire answered by the women, the reports noted that "the operators have no clear idea as to why they are able to produce more in the Test Room; but ... there is the feeling that better output is in some way related to the distinctly pleasanter, freer, and happier working conditions."[19] The implications for the supervision of workers in all parts of the factory seemed clear. The gang boss or other immediate supervisor tended to assume that workers were "thick-skinned and that his thrusts must go deep"; but workers, especially those of "limited mental scope," were now discovered to be emotionally sensitive and should be treated accordingly. Perhaps, the reports hesitantly suggested, it would be possible to supervise and organize workers along the lines used for directing managers, for whom work was a "pleasant, cooperative, friendly and interesting activity."[20]

How accurate was this depiction of a friendly and minimally supervised test room? A researcher placed in the test room in 1932 to observe the

[18] Fritz Roethlisberger, *Management and Morale*, Cambridge, Mass.: Harvard University Press, 1941, 15; RATR Progress Report no. 4, 11 May 1929, 83–7, 125–9.

[19] RATR Progress Report no. 3, 30 June 1928, sec. VIII, 3; RATR Progress Report no. 4, 11 May 1929, 131.

[20] RATR Progress Report no. 3, 30 June 1928, sec. VIII, 3–5; RATR Progress Report no. 4, 11 May 1929, 131–3.

interactions between the supervisors and workers stressed the special relationship that had grown up between Hibarger and the women:

> [Hibarger] probably had more to do with breaking down the barriers in the employee–supervisor relationship than any other factor. It was he who injected a spirit of play in the group by his comical antics, encouraging them to call everyone by first name, to take strangers into their facetious conversations, to "ride" supervisors and fellow operators alike.[21]

The researchers had realized this possibility, and in early 1930 Hibarger was replaced by Donald Chipman. However, Chipman had been in the test room since October 1928 as Hibarger's assistant and consequently had absorbed the relaxed supervisory style, and he was taking over a well-established social group. There is no evidence that the social dynamics of the test room changed under Chipman, and production continued its slow climb.

By a different measure, supervision actually intensified in the test room. When the relay test room was established, Hibarger had been the only person present besides the five workers and layout operator. By 1930 the test room personnel had increased to five to include Chipman as supervisor, a junior clerk, a calculator, a typist, and an inspector of finished relays. These additional members were not supervisory personnel, but they could have some control over the women, especially when Hibarger or Chipman was absent, by reporting events or entering them in the record. There is evidence, too, that the layout operator, technically only a somewhat better paid worker, was also used as a supervisory conduit between the researchers and the workers. When Pennock wanted the women to know that their excessive talking had been noticed, it was the layout operator who was directed to tell them. Another supervisory technique entailed reading the Daily History Record to the workers to emphasize to them the amount of time they spent talking and not working. While the workers no longer had to contend with a driving gang boss, they were pressured in more subtle ways – by reprimands from managers, entries in the test records, and the threat of removal from the test room.[22] Even granting that a change in supervision did contribute to the increased production, it is not clear whether this was because the supervision was more relaxed and friendly, as the researchers supposed, or because it was more intense, with continual oversight of the workers' behavior.[23]

[21] D. D. Davisson, "An Observer's Impressions of the Relay Assembly Test Room," 7 July 1932, HSCM/58, A1–9.

[22] RATR, Questionnaire, Sept. 1931, HSCM/27, C9–12; see also Daily History Record, 8 Nov. 1928, 9 Oct. 1929.

[23] Daily History Record, 17 May 1928, 31 Oct. 1928. On test room personnel, see T. N. Whitehead, *The Industrial Worker*, Cambridge, Mass.: Harvard University Press, 1938, vol. 2, fig. A–1.

Certainly the workers did not accept the incessant observation of their work by the researchers, and this was revealed by constant small battles between the workers and their researcher-supervisors. Every day the women tried to extend their domain of control in the test room or protect their rights from encroachment by the supervisors. Jennie Sirchio was the leader of these tests of power. Although she was the fastest worker and often drove the other women to work faster, she was also their de facto shop steward, always prepared to challenge the supervisors and organize the test to the women's benefit. The researchers noted that she encouraged the women to talk quietly if they did not want the researchers to hear what they were saying; quiet conversation between the workers would not carry over to Hibarger or Chipman on the other side of the room because of the noise from the adjacent department, the noise of the automatic screwdrivers, and the screening effect of the cardboard boxes of parts immediately in front of each worker. The workers therefore had considerable control over what the researchers could hear and therefore what was recorded in the Daily History Record. Similarly, when the women's positions at the bench were changed in one experimental period, Sirchio led the opposition. A meeting in the washroom (presumably reported by the layout operator) was held, at which Sirchio told the other women, "If you girls keep hollering about the change they'll change us back."[24]

On that occasion they failed, but there were many victories. Poor relay parts during the summer of 1929 slowed the women's work and increased the amount of time required for repairs. This in turn triggered complaints by the workers that the inspector in the regular department was unfairly failing the relays, due to jealousy over not having been chosen to replace Anna Haug, who had just resigned. Sirchio led the demand for an inspector in the test room, who would be working under the eyes of the workers and answerable to their complaints. The following month an inspector was established in the test room.[25] A major battle occurred during period 12, when the rest periods and morning lunch were abandoned. The women disliked this period intensely and did everything possible to sabotage the test. They took time out when the rests would normally have occurred and complained that the absence of rests made the job "monotonous" – a term, Hibarger noted, that they had picked up from reading the progress reports. When they started to bring their own morning refreshments, Pennock stepped in and threatened to extend the period if the women refused to cooperate. They curbed their protests, and the period finished on schedule.[26] And they continued to talk and laugh, moderating only when pressure was

[24] Daily History Record, 15 Oct. 1929; quote from 7 Apr. 1930. Control of conversation was still firmly institutionalized in 1932; see RATR, Record of Observations, 27 Jan. 1932, HSCM/59–62.
[25] Daily History Record, 9 Sept. 1929, 25 Sept. 1929, 21 Oct. 1929.
[26] Ibid., 4 Sept. 1929, 5 Sept. 1929, 7 Sept. 1929, 7 Nov. 1929.

applied. Despite these victories, the women knew that their power was severely limited, their privileged position fragile. As far into the test as September 1930, two and a half years after the removal of Bogatowicz and Rybacki, Sirchio remarked, "I've been complaining so much lately that they will kick me out of here."[27]

The workers controlled their production as well as their work environment. Although anxious to produce at a level that would ensure the continuation of the test and maintain their earnings, they never sought to produce as much as possible. By late 1928 they had organized a system whereby each of the workers would take turns keeping group production at the desired rate for the day (with the exception of Haug, a slower worker who was given smaller runs of many relay types). If production fell behind during the week, they sped up to maintain weekly output. If a worker was feeling ill and working slowly, the other women would compensate. And because the absence of a worker could affect group earnings, a worker wishing to take a day off for some special reason had to get permission from her fellow workers as well as from her supervisor.[28] The women thus balanced increased earnings against a pleasant pace of work. This did not mean that earnings were unimportant, however. In 1929 the workers were disappointed when they received only a one cent per hour raise – the same as the regular relay assemblers – when they had asked for five cents per hour. On this occasion even the normally quiet Haug threatened to quit, for her wages supported her husband's farming venture. Indeed, she did resign in August, returning only in May 1930 as the depression started to bite.[29]

There is little evidence that the depression had a direct effect on the rate of production in the test room, as some later commentators claimed.[30] The women did not increase production out of fear that they would otherwise be fired. They were well aware that their supervisors would do everything to protect the experiment and therefore their jobs. Employment policy at Hawthorne was bureaucratic and systematic; as the effects of the depression began to be felt in mid-1930, hours were reduced across the board for all workers, including those in the test room. Then workers were laid off by seniority, the remaining workers shuffled into jobs they had not done before. For a considerable time the researchers managed to forestall the application of seniority rules to the test room workers. Although the women feared the depression, there is no evidence that their fate would be affected by their level of production. Nor is there any evidence that they tried to earn more

---

[27] "Operators' Comments," 11 Sept. 1930, HSCM/26–31.

[28] Daily History Record, 19 Oct. 1928, 17 Nov. 1928, 22 Feb. 1929, 27 Sept. 1929.

[29] Ibid., 27 May 1929.

[30] See, e.g., Richard Herbert Franke and James D. Kaul, "The Hawthorne Experiments: First Statistical Interpretation," *American Sociological Review* (henceforth *ASR*), 1978, 43: 623–43.

to compensate for the lost income of unemployed family members. They were more concerned to use their special status to preserve their jobs for as long as possible.[11]

The reports of the test room never conceded that the workers' demands might constitute a concerted attempt to shape the relay test room to their own liking. The company researchers were engineers and managers accustomed to seeing workers as "operators" who performed a series of tasks on command. Even though the researchers came to appreciate the women as individuals, they could not accept that the workers might be active agents in the workplace. Thus, to the extent that the researchers accepted that the test room environment was different, indeed superior, to the regular Hawthorne working environment, they attributed this to supervision, that is, to the actions of those in charge of production.

Nevertheless, the researchers recognized that the relay assembly test did not provide definitive answers, and they initiated several new research projects on other groups of Hawthorne workers. By 1929 studies were being undertaken on groups of typists, mica splitters, armature straighteners, and a second group of relay assemblers. Two in particular were intended to throw new light on the results of the relay test. The second relay assembly test was designed to isolate and measure the effect of paying the relay assembly test room workers as a small gang. In the third period of the first test a special group rate had been introduced, but it was maintained for only eight weeks before further variables, such as rests, were added. Pennock suspected that the effect of being paid as a small group continued to be significant during subsequent periods but that the effect was concealed by the new variables. In October 1928 he ordered that a group of five relay assemblers be selected and paid as a small gang but that they remain in the relay department under regular supervision and under normal working conditions.

The second project involved the establishment of a new test room. The initiative appears to have come from Hibarger, who suggested to Pennock as early as June 1928 that establishing a test room of mica splitters would enable them to test the effect of rests, working hours, and test room conditions on workers who were paid on an individual piece rate. Mica splitting was one of the highest paid and most sought after jobs for women at Hawthorne. The job required more skill than did relay assembly; sheets of mica had to be split to a thickness of 0.0012 to 0.0016 of an inch, then trimmed for use as insulating material. The mica splitting test room was established with five women workers on 22 October 1928 and was to continue until March 1931. The two new tests were clearly conceived as parallel pieces of research. In the second relay assembly test, the payment

[11]   Daily History Record, 3 May 1930; RATR, Record of Observations, 14 June 1932, 16 June 1932.

system was altered while all other conditions were held steady. In the mica splitting test the payment system was kept the same while test room conditions and variables were imposed. By comparing the results of these two tests with those from the relay assembly test, it should be possible to obtain a crude measure of the separate effects of wage incentives and test room conditions.[32]

The results of the two new studies did little to clarify the relay test. The output of the second relay group increased 13.8 percent in their first week as a special group and remained 10 to 15 percent above the base for all nine weeks of the test; it then fell below the base when the workers returned to being paid as members of the department. Hibarger concluded that "the basis of pay has been an important item in increasing output in the [relay assembly] test room."[33] Indeed, the effect may have been even greater in the initial test room, where the workers came to realize that no matter how high their output and pay, the company would not reduce the piece rates, something it would do as a matter of course in regular departments.[34]

The mica splitters' output fell at first, as it had in the relay test, then gradually began to pull above the base period after two ten-minute rests had been introduced. By the fall of 1929 average hourly output had risen to 15.6 percent above the base, a rise in keeping with both groups of relay assemblers if one attributed half of the approximately 30 percent rise in the relay assembly test room to the changed payment scheme. But then output began to decline so that by March 1930 it had fallen to a level only 4.4 percent above the base. The only change in experimental periods since the introduction of rests had been the cessation of overtime in June 1929; before that, the women had worked most Saturday afternoons and some Sundays in addition to their regular week of five and a half days. However, production had continued to increase during this period for several months before beginning its decline. The researchers were puzzled, although this was expressed only by their silence; Hibarger appears not to have produced a report on the mica splitting test, and it received only cursory coverage in other reports.[35]

This is perhaps not surprising, for the two new studies provided evidence

[32] "An Investigation of Rest Pauses, Working Conditions, and Industrial Efficiency; Supplementary Progress Report as of 11 May 1929," HSCM/7–8, F13.

[33] Daily History Record, 10 Oct. 1928, 19 Nov. 1928; "An Investigation of Rest Pauses, Working Conditions, and Industrial Efficiency; Supplementary Progress Report as of 11 May 1929," 93–4, quote on 94.

[34] This observation was never made by the company researchers, but was noted by Mayo's assistant, the economist R. S. Meriam; see Meriam to Mayo, 12 Nov. 1930, EM/1.089.

[35] "An Investigation of Rest Pauses, Working Conditions, and Industrial Efficiency; Supplementary Progress Report as of 11 May 1929," 104–7. Because of the lack of reports on the mica test by the researchers, I have had to rely in part on the published account in F. J. Roethlisberger and William J. Dickson, *Management and the Worker*, Cambridge, Mass.: Harvard University Press, 1939, 134–60.

that seemed to contradict the relay assembly test findings. The second relay group showed the significance of payment schemes, a factor that had been recognized but played down in the initial relay test. Yet the results of the mica splitting test seemed to undermine the argument that the test room conditions, in particular the change in supervision, were a major factor in increasing output in the relay test.

Although the relay assembly test ran until February 1933, the fourth progress report of May 1929 was the last detailed analysis of the test room data by the company researchers. Several factors contributed to the researchers' waning interest in the test room. First, it was difficult to identify with any precision the causes of the fairly steady increase in production. As we have seen, the experimental data were amenable to a variety of interpretations, and each group involved in the experiments emphasized different factors. In particular, the academic consultants brought into the test to resolve these interpretative difficulties introduced further interpretations, based on their own research interests and knowledge of the literature. Second, the focus of personnel research at Hawthorne shifted from the relay test to a range of other experiments and programs conducted by a new Industrial Research Division. Pennock and the expanded group of company researchers, along with Mayo and his Harvard colleagues, were now more interested in the developments in interviewing, supervisory training, and new test groups. The relay test was left under the control of Hibarger and Turner, although the interest of the latter had waned by the end of 1929. Third, the result of these changes was that the relay test became completely routinized, its test periods determined more by the company's responses to the depression than by any explicit research strategy. Apart from switching the workers' positions and replacing Hibarger with his assistant, no significant variables were introduced after period 12. An observer brought into the test room in an attempt to revitalize the research noted that "the entire study was too mechanized, too much governed by routine, and too concealed; this in the face of the knowledge that the Test Room was originated solely to experiment with the effect of certain variables upon production curves. The objectives changed but its techniques ever remained at a standstill."[36]

Only sporadic attempts were made to reanalyze the test room data or generate different types of experimental data from the relay test. In each case the impetus came from outside the test room, from company researchers applying techniques developed in other parts of the Hawthorne research program with the aid of the Harvard scientists. In 1931 and 1932 the researchers attempted to revitalize the relay test by introducing programs of intensive interviewing and anthropological observation of the workers.

[36] D. D. Davisson, "An Observer's Impressions of the Relay Assembly Test Room," 7 July 1932, HSCM/58, A1–9.

The idea for interviewing the relay workers derived from the huge program of interviewing all Hawthorne workers between 1928 and 1930. From this program the researchers believed that they had generated a better picture of workers' complaints and aspirations, and under Mayo's guidance they began to see interviewing as a means of penetrating the irrational or emotional aspects of workers' attitudes and behavior. The anthropological approach had previously been established in a new test room of bank wiring workers under the guidance of Mayo's colleague W. Lloyd Warner. The idea was that rather than test variables being introduced and the changes in production measured, the ethnographer was inserted into an existing workplace culture and expected to observe all aspects of its social relations. The sources and development of these techniques will be dealt with in subsequent chapters; here we shall focus on their application in the relay test room.

The company researchers expected that repeated interviews would facilitate a detailed psychological and sociological study of the behavior, motives, and relationships of each member of the test room. The initial plan entailed interviews with everyone in the test room, workers and the experimenter-supervisors, but this was abandoned as being too "academic." The researchers were still wedded to the idea that the interview material should be related to production, the only objective measure of change available in the test room, and consequently decided to interview only the five workers and the layout operator. In May 1931 Imogen Rousseau began interviewing the workers on a regular basis. Rousseau was an experienced member of the interviewing team, and the researchers hoped that a woman could more easily win the confidence of the female relay assemblers.[37]

However, the test room workers disliked Rousseau's interviews intensely and resisted her probing in any way they could. By 1931 the women had been interviewed several times and felt that they had already told the researchers everything about their personal lives that they were willing to reveal. When Rousseau told worker Mary Volango that she would be interviewing the women frequently, Volango suggested that this was a needless imposition:

> I don't think the girls will be glad to hear that.... They won't have anything to say. They've got it all up there [in the managers' offices]. You know they take down everything about us. They've got a lot of stuff up there all written down and you get tired of telling it.[38]

The women resisted in two ways. First, they collectively protested when the frequency of the interviews was increased to once per week and succeeded

---

[37] I. Rousseau to Wright, 15 Oct. 1931, "Report on Special Relay Assembly Test Group Study," HSCM/63, A1–9; RATR, "Record of Interviews, May 1931–May 1932, Apr.–May 1933," HSCM/32–42, 62.

[38] "Record of Interviews," Mary Volango, 27 May 1931.

in having them returned to once every two weeks. Second, they learned to prepare for the interview, each worker borrowing Wanda Blazejak's watch, presumably with the object of keeping track of the time and ending the interview as soon as possible. With experience they also became adept at filling the time with chat on meaningless topics such as films and clothes, thereby avoiding more personal subjects. Only Theresa Layman became more confidential, giving Rousseau glimpses of the workers' concerns, including their suspicion that Rousseau was trying to get the women to tell things about one another. But even Layman was cynical about the interviewing; heading off to see Rousseau on one occasion, she told the other women: "I guess I'll have to wear my coat down there. My dress is too short. That shows depression."[39]

The difficulties in breaking through the workers' defenses were compounded by the lack of any clear sense of what the interviews were intended to accomplish. In her report Rousseau reiterated constantly that the study was about the "relation between personal and social factors and employee effectiveness," a safe enough definition but too vague to give any direction to her research. Confronted with the resistance of the workers and the particularistic character of the personal information she did obtain, Rousseau never produced an analysis of the more than twenty interviews she conducted with each of the women. Nor did she provide any new insights into the relations between the workers and the supervisors in the test, another of the avowed aims of the interviews.[40]

The observation program was equally unsuccessful, for the observer found it impossible to gain the confidence of either the workers or the other experimenters in the test room. D. D. Davisson, previously an interviewer, joined the test room staff in December 1931 and began a detailed "Record of Observation" in late January 1932. The plan was that he use Warner's anthropological techniques to study the interactions among all members of the relay test room, including the experimenters, now consisting of Hibarger, Chipman, a clerk, and a calculator. Hibarger and Chipman disliked this intrusion from the start, for Davisson's presence was a clear statement of their inadequacies and a sign that the relay test was moving out of their control and into the hands of the interviewing department. A week after Davisson joined the test, Chipman's Daily History Record was halted in favor of the new Record of Observation, a change that Chipman protested vigorously, doubtful that Davisson's technique was any different. Chipman was shifted to recording and calculating production, a job of lower status and one that he found boring. Hibarger also felt cast aside, and in April he

[39] "Record of Observations," 5 Feb. 1932 (quote); RATR, "Weekly Activity Summary, 8 August–26 December 1931," HSCM/22, esp. 5 Sept., 18 Sept., 14 Nov. 1931; "Record of Interviews," Theresa Layman, 4 Nov. 1931.
[40] Rousseau to Wright, "Report on Special Relay Assembly Test Group Study," 15 Oct. 1931, quote on 7.

returned to the Technical Branch, after having been in charge of the test room for exactly five years. Aware of their antagonism, Davisson returned the compliment. In his Record of Observation he criticized Hibarger's clowning relationship with the workers, suggesting that it was responsible for what he regarded as infantile behavior among the workers, notably their resistance to the removal of any test room privileges. Thus, having come to study the social solidarities and antagonisms in the test room, Davisson channeled much of his energy into coping with the experimenters' antagonism toward him.[41]

The test room workers were friendly toward Davisson, but he could never gain their confidence. They began to pay attention to him only once they realized in late March that he was recording their conversation; then Volango and Sirchio began to flirt with him at his desk, trying to find out exactly what he was recording. They were unsuccessful, but Davisson had equal difficulty in learning what they were saying to one another, for they had long ago learned how to converse at a level that could not be heard by the experimenters. He did note that the workers in the test room were divided into two groups, Volango, Sirchio, Layman, and Blazejak in one and Anna Haug and the inspector in another, with the layout operator mediating between the groups; but this was hardly an original observation, nor could he relate it to production or any other variable.[42]

The entry of Davisson and Rousseau did provide an opportunity for a new assessment of the reasons for the increased production in the test room. In September 1931 Hibarger and Turner prepared, although they never formally issued, a belated fifth and final report of the relay assembly test, in which they continued to downplay changes in working conditions as the major reason for increased production. Drawing on Mayo's theories, which he had elaborated in the interviewing program, they insisted that the major cause was the changed "mental attitude" of the workers. Rousseau and Davisson were not so sure. After interviewing the women several times and reading the previous reports, Rousseau concluded that "explanations of test group behavior may not lie in as obscure causes as is generally supposed." She particularly stressed the importance of increased earnings as a motive, noting that the women had been most concerned that her repeated interviewing would affect their wages. Davisson was equally critical of what he saw as undue emphasis on the supposed lack of supervision in the test room. He claimed that insufficient attention had been paid to such factors as the excellent supply of parts to the test room, the limited number of relay types, and in particular the pay incentive, observing that the women had a keen interest in their daily percentages and a much clearer understanding of the

[41] "Weekly Activity Summary," 5 Dec. 1931, HSCM/22; RATR, "Record of Observations," esp. 22 Jan. 1932, 4 Mar. 1932, 27 Apr. 1932; Davisson, "An Observer's Impressions."
[42] "Record of Observations," 21 Jan. 1932, 1 Apr. 1932.

piecework system than other workers. Even Chipman, who had been in the test room since August 1928, doubted Hibarger's interpretations, as the following discussion over the 1931 report, recorded by Davisson, reveals:

> *Chipman:* I thought it was good. Of course I could give a different set of explanations for some of those things myself, but I agree with you.
>
> *Hibarger:* Well, we know now that we could take either side of any question and prove or disprove it [in] whatever [way] we want.
>
> *Chipman:* Yes, they say that figures don't lie, but we have shown that we can take a set of figures and prove anything we want to.

Thus, as the depression brought the experiments to a close, the company researchers closest to the relay assembly test differed over how to interpret the results and had become doubtful that any conclusive interpretation was possible.[43]

Two new projects were undertaken or proposed before the relay test closed, and both are worth brief mention because they demonstrate that Mayo's interests remained primarily with the psychopathological and physiological model he had first developed in Philadelphia. One of Mayo's Harvard collaborators, Thomas North Whitehead, was conducting a detailed statistical analysis of the relay assembly data (see Chapter 7). In the early stages of his research, Whitehead believed that he had found statistical evidence for the influence of physiological factors on production. Mayo was ecstatic, Roethlisberger noted, because "it looked as if the organization of the girls in the test room was more conditioned by biological factors rather than anything so naive as economic incentive. As this fits in with what Mayo has been saying for the last five years we were very pleased." Just what Whitehead believed he had discovered is unclear, because his early correspondence and papers have not survived, and his subsequent publications explicitly reject the relevance of physiological factors.[44]

At about the same time, in early 1932, Mayo proposed a new project to examine the relationship between physiological and psychiatric changes in the relay test women. Pennock gave his permission for Emily Osborne to conduct a study of the "interrelationship between the organic cycle, emotional attitudes to work and to people, and the relation of both these to domestic and industrial events." Mayo hoped that the physiological changes produced by the menstrual cycle might be found to affect the women's mental attitudes, and hence their adaptation to work and family. The idea was not entirely original. Turner had looked for an obvious link between the menstrual cycle and fluctuations in production among the relay test women, with no success, and the Industrial Fatigue Research Board in

[43] RATR, "Outline for Progress Report," [Sept. 1931], 20–3, HSCM/9, B11–13; Rousseau to Wright, "Report on Special Relay Assembly Test Group Study," quote on 3; Davisson, "An Observer's Impressions"; "Record of Observations," 26 Feb. 1932 (quote).
[44] Roethlisberger to Osborne, 5 Apr. 1932, FJR/1.

Britain had recently come to the same negative conclusion. However, it seems probable that Mayo was searching for more subtle changes in behavior and adaptation than noticeable changes in output. Even at the end of the Hawthorne experiments, Mayo remained strongly committed to his psychopathological model, and he believed that he would eventually be able to show the interrelationship between the physiological and mental states of workers. In the event, Pennock had to cancel the project, explaining to Mayo that given the dramatic layoffs under way at Hawthorne, no new research could be undertaken; managers and supervisors would regard it as a frivolous expense, unaware that the research was being funded by Mayo. This aborted research would prove to be Mayo's last attempt to find experimental evidence of these links, and he would not conduct further industrial research until the Second World War.[45]

The relay assembly test continued after all the other components of the Hawthorne experiments had been halted by the depression. But in mid-1932, the relay test workers began to be laid off and replaced by women with greater seniority. They left without bitterness, believing that the company and their bosses had kept them on as long as possible; they knew of companies that had shown much more disregard for their workers. Feeling the loss of the companionship of the test room, Blazejak suggested sardonically that the women start their own test room. The test room limped on for several more months, a symbol of hope to the researchers rather than a place of research, but on 8 February 1933 it closed permanently. With the exception of Haug, the relay assemblers remained good friends and had occasional social gatherings. But they did not maintain contact with any of the researchers with whom they had shared the test room for so long. When Emily Osborne, now living in Chicago, tried to contact the women for Mayo in 1933, she found that none of the researchers knew their whereabouts. Eventually she tracked down Jennie Sirchio, who organized a luncheon for the relay assemblers, Osborne, and Rousseau, the interviewer from the test room. The distance between the relay assemblers and the researchers was humorously captured by Sirchio, who closed her letter to Osborne by signing it "Your Blood Pressure Subject."[46]

The interpretations continue...

Why did production increase so significantly in the relay assembly test room: by some 34 percent over the first two years and by 46 percent over the entire five years? How was it that over a five-year period the same group

---

[45] Mayo to Frank L. Smith (Medical Department, Hawthorne Works), 23 Dec. 1931, EM/1.090; Pennock to Mayo, 11 Mar. 1932, EM/1.091. On menstruation and production, see Industrial Fatigue Research Board, *Eighth Annual Report to 31st December 1927*, London, 1928, 8–10.

[46] Osborne to Mayo, 14 Dec. 1932 and 29 Jan. 1933, Jennie Sirchio to Osborne, 26 Jan. 1933, EM/1.067.

of workers (with two notable exceptions), assembling the same relay types under the same production system, could increase their productivity so dramatically? Ever since the results of the relay assembly test were published, social scientists have argued over which factors were most important. As we have seen, the various participants in the experiments also found it difficult to settle on a single interpretation. In some ways the most fascinating aspect of the relay assembly test is not the dynamics of the experiment or its results, but the interpretative edifices that have been built on the test data. This is not the place to undertake a detailed exegesis of the many interpretations; an exhaustive study of the analyses by social scientists would require a separate monograph. The ways in which the Hawthorne researchers integrated the relay test results into the rest of the Hawthorne studies and their broader theoretical commitments will be dealt with in Chapter 7. Here I shall briefly review the interpretations of the relay test data by the Hawthorne researchers and subsequent commentators, first to stress the interpretative flexibility of the data and second to ask how particular interpretations came to be accepted as the most authoritative.

As we have seen, the company researchers by no means agreed on the significant causes of increased productivity, and they emphasized different variables on different occasions, depending on the circumstances and on the current influence of their academic consultants. Initially they emphasized those factors that could be easily introduced into other parts of the plant, especially the small-group payment rate and rest periods, and discounted the role of fatigue and the physical conditions of work. As the researchers shifted their attention to the programs of interviewing workers and supervisory training and came under the influence of Mayo's ideas, they tended to stress the improved mental attitude of the relay workers, which they thought was due to the more friendly and relaxed supervision in the test room. The relay test thus bolstered their claims that supervisory styles at Hawthorne had to be revolutionized to take into account the human relations of work. In essence, different aspects of the relay test were emphasized in order to justify to senior company executives the latest project of the company researchers. Indeed, what really mattered in the relay test room was that production had increased so significantly; the company researchers believed that it showed that "a great deal more can be done to increase human productivity ... without any change whatsoever in the set-up of the work itself."[47] The increase in production justified the research in the only way that really mattered to company executives and gave the researchers freedom to explore the entire area of the social relations of production.

When Mayo and his colleagues at Harvard came to write their monographs on the experiments, they too emphasized different elements of the relay test. Still committed to his physiological and psychiatric model, Mayo

[47] RATR Progress Report no. 5, Sept. 1931, 22, HSCM/9, B11–C1.

attributed the increased production to the physical and mental steady state or integration achieved by the workers with the demands of their work. Irene Rybacki, with her Bolshevism and anemia, exemplified the unbalanced worker; her replacement, Jennie Sirchio, the productive leader, exemplified the integrated worker. The official account of the experiments, *Management and the Worker*, written by Mayo's protégé Fritz Roethlisberger and Hawthorne personnel manager William Dickson, adopted a more sociological approach, attributing the increased production to the development of a "spontaneous type of informal organization" in the relay test room, brought about because the experimenters adopted a supervisory style that paid attention to the human needs of the workers.[48] Still, although they emphasized different aspects of the relay test, the company researchers and academic consultants agreed that the major changes had occurred in what came to be called the "human relations" of the test room rather than in those factors stressed in existing managerial practice, such as payment schemes, supervision, and the physical conditions of work.

There have been several attempts in the past twenty-five years to reinterpret the relay test data, with the intention of either undermining or defending the conclusions of the Hawthorne researchers. An exhaustive analysis of these reexaminations would be a tedious affair – although it would provide some insight into the methodological and ideological assumptions of the authors and their disciplines. But it is proper to consider briefly some of the major recent critiques of the original interpretations and assess the value of their arguments in the light of this detailed history.

In 1967 Alex Carey launched a scathing attack on the Hawthorne experiments, arguing that they were scientifically worthless and that the researchers had subjected the data to a "massive and relentless reinterpretation." Undertaking a "radical criticism" of the original published accounts, Carey argued that the researchers had suppressed the importance of the economic incentive and given a misleading impression of the nature of supervision in the test room. Carey's essay was intended as a Marxist critique of contemporary management ideology and a reassertion of the importance of the traditional mechanisms of capitalist exploitation, but similar reinterpretations have also come from conservative management circles. In 1978 Richard Franke and James Kaul subjected the original relay test data, still available in the archives, to sophisticated multiple regression analysis. They concluded that 97 percent of the variance could be accounted for by the combined effects of managerial discipline, the economic incentive provided by the depression, and rest periods; subsequently they adjusted the variance explained down to 87 percent, still an impressive figure. They

---

[48] See Elton Mayo, *The Human Problems of an Industrial Civilization*, New York: Macmillan, 1933, esp. 53–73; Roethlisberger and Dickson, *Management and the Worker*, esp. 179–86, 551–68.

suggested this new analysis showed that the traditional managerial techniques of close supervision and economic incentive were more important than worker participation and industrial democracy. But as others have been quick to point out, Franke and Kaul achieved their sophisticated statistical analysis only by creating dummy variables for discipline (which they assume commenced when the two workers were replaced) and economic incentive (which they assume became important after the Wall Street crash in October 1929). This seems a rather crude way to analyze complex social dynamics.[49]

While economic incentive and managerial discipline were far more important in the test room than was conceded by the Hawthorne researchers, their effects were more long term and subtle than the aforementioned critiques suggest. As we have seen, managerial discipline was present throughout the five years of the relay test. The intensive observation by the experimenters, the detailed recording of production, the threats of withdrawing privileges, the removal of two workers, and the admonishment for excessive talking all contributed to tight supervision, backed up by inducements and benefits for the workers if they cooperated and by the continuance of the relay test.

Other commentators have sought to interpret the data in the light of subsequent social scientific theories. For example, in the 1970s H. M. Parsons argued that the incentive of financial reward offered by the small-group payment scheme, combined with the daily feedback of production figures, created an environment in which the relay assemblers learned to work faster through a process of operant conditioning. This model has found support in Brian Pitcher's 1981 statistical analysis, which aimed to show that the production figures fit a learning curve and accounted for more than 80 percent of the variance for the three workers who were in the relay test for the entire five years. Although it is certainly possible that the workers may have learned to produce relays faster while in the test room, several points tend to discount the view that this was the central factor. First, the relay assemblers were already skilled workers when they entered the test room; Sirchio was the fastest assembler in the department's history. Second, it is apparent that the assemblers in the regular department were aware of their

[49] Alex Carey, "The Hawthorne Studies: A Radical Criticism," *ASR*, 1967, 32: 403–16; Richard Herbert Franke and James G. Kaul, "The Hawthorne Experiments: First Statistical Interpretation," *ASR*, 1978, 43: 623–43; Walter I. Wardwell, "Critique of a Recent Professional 'Put-Down' of the Hawthorne Research," *ASR*, 1979, 44: 858–61; Richard Herbert Franke, "The Hawthorne Experiments – Re-View," *ASR*, 1979, 44: 861–7; Robert Schlaifer, "The Relay Assembly Test Room: An Alternative Statistical Interpretation," *ASR*, 1980, 45: 995–1005; Richard Herbert Franke, "Worker Productivity at Hawthorne," *ASR*, 1980, 45: 1006–27. For more recent radical critiques that have prompted an additional flurry of defenses of the experiments, see Dana Bramel and Ronald Friend, "Hawthorne, the Myth of the Docile Worker, and Class Bias in Psychology," *American Psychologist*, 1981, 36: 867–78; replies in *American Psychologist*, 1982, 37: 855–62, 1397–1401.

rate of production; the number of boxes of coils used by each worker made it easy to keep track of daily progress, and supervisors were quick to crack down on workers who were not producing enough. Third, the workers did not assemble relays at a steady pace throughout the day, but produced rapidly for short runs of ten or so relays, then slowed for a while before picking up another run. There is no suggestion in the relay test data that the experienced workers actually increased the speed with which they assembled a single relay, but rather that the intensification of work increased – that is, that the women worked at full pace for larger amounts of the day. It seems inappropriate to ascribe such increases to learning.[50]

Finally, Jeffrey Sonnenfeld and others have attempted to refute those critics whom they see as being ideologically inspired and statistically obsessed. They defend the original insights of the researchers through a mixture of methodological defense and citing of the more measured and judicious claims in *Management and the Worker*. They also adopt a new tactic by interviewing the surviving participants, three of the workers and the relay test supervisor Donald Chipman, who not surprisingly confirm that the "cooperative group culture" created in the test room was the major factor. The interviews with the workers are rather naively presented as a source of the true perceptions of the workers back in the relay test room, free of any interpretative gloss. But the workers were always aware of the researchers' interpretations, even if they did not read the published accounts, and they have participated in anniversaries of the experiments in which they have conversed with surviving researchers and imbibed the official accounts. The "real" Hawthorne experiments cannot be discovered in individuals' accounts of events that occurred fifty years previously.[51]

What, then, readers may be asking, really happened in the relay assembly test room? Although the desire for an answer is understandable, the question is misplaced. The meaning of the relay test does not lie waiting to be discovered in the production data, or the transcripts of conversations in the test room, or the unpublished reports, or the official accounts, or the latest statistical analyses. Meaning has to be imposed on a complex set of statistics and reports of complex social relations – which were themselves refracted through the experimenters' own assumptions. In this and the preceding chapter I have tried to show that the most important thing to understand about the relay test was not what really happened, but how different par-

[50] H. M. Parsons, "What Happened at Hawthorne?" *Science*, 1974, 183: 922–32; H. M. Parsons, "What Caused the Hawthorne Effect?" *Administration and Society*, 1978, 10: 259–83; Brian L. Pitcher, "The Hawthorne Experiments: Statistical Evidence for a Learning Hypothesis," *Social Forces*, 1981: 133–49.

[51] Jeffrey A. Sonnenfeld, "Shedding Light on the Hawthorne Studies," *Journal of Occupational Behaviour*, 1985, 6: 111–30; Ronald G. Greenwood, Alfred A. Bolton, and Regina A. Greenwood, "Hawthorne a Half Century Later: Relay Assembly Participants Remember," *Journal of Management*, 1983, 9: 217–31.

ticipants and observers developed accounts of what they believed happened and how the various interpretations were shaped by the practical and political concerns and intellectual commitments of their authors.

My account has stressed several key factors in the relay test that seem to have contributed to the increase in production – although like Roethlisberger and Dickson in *Management and the Worker* I must emphasize that one has to see these factors as operating within their entire social (and, I would add, political) context. Supervision became more intense in the test room, although presented in a more friendly and personable style. Managerial authority was underscored by the removal of two workers for threatening to maintain their production at existing levels; henceforth, the women always worked under the threat that they would be removed or the test halted if the researchers were dissatisfied with the productivity levels. In addition, part of the increase in production was an artifact caused by the introduction of faster workers into the test room. The small-group payment system whereby the five workers were paid according to their collective output was undoubtedly a significant factor in forging social cohesion and encouraging the collective determination of output. Moreover, the test room workers could increase their production significantly, knowing that the piece rates would not be cut, which they certainly would have been had the workers increased production by the same amount in the regular department. In this respect, the depression could have had an effect, not because the workers faced the threat of being laid off if they did not produce faster, but because they were able to ameliorate the effect of steadily declining hours on weekly income by working harder.

In short, there is considerable evidence that the assemblers were not passive workers subject to the invisible effects of the experimental conditions, but women actively controlling their production individually and as a group, exploiting the parameters set by the experimenters. This was never fully perceived by the Hawthorne researchers, even though they would subsequently observe that the men in the bank wiring test room did restrict their production by setting collective output norms. There are several reasons for this. The relay assemblers were young women, "girls" to the researchers, who it was felt were driven by their emotions and personal problems rather than active agents in constructing the test room environment. Managers and observers of worker behavior were also accustomed to seeing worker organizations in purely negative terms, especially in the restriction of production; they would have found it strange to attribute the large increases in output in the relay test to the collective action of the workers. Further, the design of the test room, with its emphasis on the manipulation of experimental variables, meant that the researchers were inclined to attribute any changes in production to changes they had brought about and to see the workers as objects on whom the variables operated, not as active agents.

The political character of the relay test does not stop with the interpretations of the data, however. The very act of experimentation at the Hawthorne Works was itself political. By isolating a group of relay assemblers in the test room, the Hawthorne researchers were making problematic the existing technical and social relations of production. Experimentation implicitly questioned the existing order in two ways. First, it suggested that alternative social relations of production were possible; the experimental periods were possible industrial worlds, with changes in productivity the sole arbiter of their efficacy and desirability. Second, the authority to construct and interpret the experiments lay with personnel managers, not with the workers' immediate supervisors – and certainly not with the workers. The removal of the two women from the test reveals the political character of experimentation itself. The workers responded to demands that they work faster by arguing that they were only following experimental directives to work at the rate that seemed comfortable to them. But for the researchers it was simply inconceivable that the dependent variable in the test, hourly production of relays, was not intimately (and positively) correlated with the workers' happiness and with good worker–supervisor relations. They perceived any attempts to restrict production as an indication that the women were failing to be good experimental subjects. Experimentation was embedded in the existing politics of production and therefore naturalized those social relations.

During the 1930s and 1940s, when the Hawthorne experiments were at their most influential, particular interpretations were certified as correct and were disseminated in the official accounts and popular summaries. Those interpretations gained credibility because they were located within a network of authority that stretched across the Hawthorne Works, the Bell System, managers in major industrial corporations, the Harvard Business School, and social scientists studying the organization of work. In the following chapter I shall begin to explore how that network of authority was constituted and how it could stabilize the interpretations of the relay test.

4

Elton Mayo and the research network

THE TRANSFORMATION of the Hawthorne experiments from an obscure and confusing piece of industrial research into a stunning social scientific "discovery" was due in large part to the network that developed around Elton Mayo. Most commentators have seen Mayo as the conceptual designer and popularizer of the experiments, but he was both less and more than this. Mayo was only one of several interpreters of the experiments, and the experimental design was shaped by various practical and intellectual concerns. But he was also far more than a popularizer whose writings conveyed the excitement of the experiments to a diverse readership. Mayo became the central figure in a complex network of Western Electric managers, Bell System executives, social scientists, industrial relations experts, business educators, and foundation officials. It was within this network that the interpretations of the experiments would be stabilized and then disseminated.

Elton Mayo's career followed an extraordinary trajectory before his participation in the Hawthorne experiments. When the Personnel Research Federation (PRF) was established with much fanfare and optimism in 1921, Elton Mayo was a professor of philosophy in a small Australian university and had never undertaken industrial research. In 1924, when the industrial lighting tests commenced at Hawthorne, Mayo held a temporary research position at the University of Pennsylvania and was struggling to find a suitable workplace for undertaking industrial research. By 1928, when Mayo first visited the Hawthorne Works, he was a professor of industrial research at Harvard Business School, he was funded by a major grant from the Laura Spelman Rockefeller Memorial, and he had established close ties with executives and personnel managers in some of America's largest corporations. In this chapter I shall examine Mayo's early career in Australia and Philadelphia, and then his emerging role as the key figure in the network that guided the Hawthorne experiments. By analyzing the difficulties Mayo faced during his industrial research in Philadelphia, it is possible to highlight how the Hawthorne research network overcame some of the problems that typically confronted personnel researchers.

The Australian career of Elton Mayo

When Mayo arrived in the United States in the summer of 1922 his credentials as a student of the labor problems in modern industry were slight. George Elton Mayo was born in 1880 into an upper-middle-class family in Adelaide, South Australia; his grandfather had been the leading surgeon in the colony, and his father was a successful businessman. Elton disappointed his parents, who had expected that he would pursue a medical career. He failed the second year of his medical studies at the University of Adelaide and lost interest in the medical courses his parents cajoled him into taking in Edinburgh and London. After several months of working as a clerk in West Africa, he fell ill and returned to London, depressed and painfully aware of his failure. His only success was his teaching, without pay, at the Working Men's College in London; he apparently got on very well with his students and later looked back on these months as the beginning of his long study of worker attitudes and behavior.

Mayo was summoned back to Australia by his family in 1904, and after completing a degree in philosophy and psychology at the University of Adelaide, he was appointed lecturer in mental and moral philosophy at the newly established University of Queensland. In 1919 he became foundation professor of philosophy. Mayo found the atmosphere in subtropical Brisbane physically and intellectually stifling; throughout his eleven years there he constantly sought a means of escape, either back to England or to a better position in Melbourne or Sydney. At the end of 1921, failing to find alternative employment, he took one year's leave from the university (although he had little intention of returning to Brisbane). He spent several months in Melbourne and then set sail for the United States, arriving in San Francisco in August 1922, now forty-two years old.[1]

This marginal man nevertheless had a seductive message for American political and industrial leaders. Mayo had developed a coherent social and political philosophy while in exile in Queensland. As one of seven teachers for the entire arts faculty, he had found himself teaching metaphysics, ethics, psychology, education, and economics; it seemed natural to attempt to synthesize his reading in these diverse fields. And caught in the turmoil of the First World War, especially in the conflict over industrial relations policy,

---

[1] For further biographical details, see Richard C. S. Trahair, *The Humanist Temper: The Life and Work of Elton Mayo*, New Brunswick, N.J.: Transaction Books, 1984; and J. H. Smith, "The Significance of Elton Mayo," in Elton Mayo, *The Social Problems of an Industrial Civilization*, London: Routledge & Kegan Paul, 1975, pp. ix–xlii. This section is also based on Mayo's correspondence with his wife Dorothea, held in the Mayo Papers, South Australian Archives; a microfilm of these letters is held in the Mayo Papers, Baker Library (cited as EM/film). Mayo's younger daughter has written an autobiography that provides revealing glimpses of his family life; see Gael Elton Mayo, *The Mad Mosaic*, London: Quartet Books, 1983.

he tried to apply his theories to current political problems. In 1918 he informed the anthropologist Bronislaw Malinowski that he was at work on a short book. Mayo and Malinowski had first met at the 1914 British Association meeting in Brisbane and developed their acquaintance whenever Malinowski passed through Brisbane on his way from his base in Melbourne to his ethnographic research in the Trobriand Islands. Malinowski's high regard for Mayo's abilities and his exhortations to his friend to join him in Melbourne and spend a year writing had a powerful influence on Mayo's decision to escape from Queensland.

In 1919 Mayo published *Democracy and Freedom,* a seventy-page outline of his philosophical and political views. Surveying political and social developments in Australia and abroad, Mayo saw an imminent danger of social disintegration. The terms "democracy" and "freedom," he asserted, were erroneously assumed to be synonymous. Democracy was not an ideal; it was a form of government that might or might not guarantee freedom and ensure social growth. He could only conclude on the basis of recent history that democracy in its present form was a failure, for the democratic party system polarized society into two irreconcilable camps and politicians trivialized serious issues by playing on the emotional fears of the public. For Mayo the true source of social growth and development lay not in the political controversies of democratic government, but in the social collaboration that took place in social institutions like the professions and business. Each member of society had a different and partial conception of society, based primarily on his or her occupational identity; only by rising above theories such as socialism and conservatism could society become more rational:

> The way in which each of us sees the world is determined in the main by the occupational group which claims us as a member. Educated or uneducated, logical or unreasoning, we are all creatures of an occupation; it is the work we do for the community that determines the angle from which we see society and the world.... Taking this fact into account, psychology – the science of human nature and human consciousness – is able to make at least one general assertion as to the form a given society must take if it is to persist as a society. It must be possible for the individual to feel, as he works, that his work is socially necessary; he must be able to see beyond his group to the society. Failure in this respect will make disintegration inevitable.

The workplace for Mayo was the key to social cohesion as a whole, and he therefore turned his attention to the vexing problem of industrial relations.[2]

Mayo insisted that existing methods of industrial relations served only to produce the same divisions in industry as occurred in politics; class

---

[2] Elton Mayo, *Democracy and Freedom: An Essay in Social Logic,* Melbourne: Macmillan, 1919, quote on 37.

hostility between workers and employers was exacerbated, not resolved. He was particularly critical of the Australian arbitration system, in which the government could force a settlement of industrial disputes, for it attempted to impose solutions where only spontaneous accord could be effective. Similarly, he held that collective bargaining between employers and unions, by transforming their different views into rival social logics, served to reinforce class warfare. But he reserved his greatest contempt for U.S. and British industrial democracy schemes: "The elective method would most probably enthrone 'collective mediocrity' within the industry" and "would be an unqualified social disaster." If unskilled workers were allowed to dominate industry, new developments such as Taylor's scientific management would be resisted, and society would suffer. Yet Mayo blamed employers as well as workers for the present system, for they too had ignored the need to consult with labor and ensure social collaboration: "So long as commerce specialises in business methods which take no account of human nature and social motives, so long may we expect strikes and sabotage to be the ordinary accompaniment of industry."[3]

The role of the intellectual in modern society was to forge the social and industrial collaboration that the political system was clearly incapable of achieving. Mayo argued repeatedly that democracy had failed "to appreciate the social importance of knowledge and skill" and that professional and technical skills must be accorded their proper status in society. We would not decide the correct method of treatment for typhoid by a referendum, he observed; nor should we allow misguided democratic principles to dilute and subvert the technical skills required in industry. "Civilization," he wrote to his wife, "was progressive rationalization or nothing"; it therefore followed that society could grow only if it accepted the guidance of experts – engineers, social scientists, managers, and doctors. These arguments echoed the views of progressives in the United States and Fabians in Britain that the emerging professional middle class must assume a central role in modern industrial society.[4]

Less typical was Mayo's view that psychology and psychiatry could be profitably applied to the analysis of industrial conflict. Mayo had expanded his knowledge in these fields considerably over the previous few years, through extensive reading in psychiatry and psychoanalysis, including Jung, Freud, Charcot, and Janet. In addition, he had collaborated with a Brisbane physician, T. H. R. Matthewson, in the use of psychoanalytic techniques on Matthewson's patients, including shell-shocked soldiers. In a series of articles on industrial conflict published shortly before he left Australia, he

[3] Ibid., esp. 45–60, quotes on 53 and 56; see also Elton Mayo, "The Australian Political Consciousness," in Meredith Atkinson, ed., *Australia: Economic and Political Studies*, Melbourne: Macmillan, 1920, 127–44.

[4] Mayo, *Democracy and Freedom*, 55–9, quote on 59; Mayo to Dorothea Mayo, Mar. 1919, EM/film.

suggested that psychological research would reveal the irrationality and mental disorder that produced industrial unrest: "To any working psychologist, it is at once evident that the general theories of Socialism, Guild Socialism, Anarchism and the like are very largely the phantasy constructions of the neurotic." Although the nature of the therapeutic intervention might remain unclear, Mayo was convinced that industrial and political turmoil could be resolved only by the application of psychological and psychiatric knowledge. He was not alone in making such suggestions. Although Mayo was unaware of his writings, Boston psychiatrist E. E. Southard was making similar programmatic statements for the development of industrial psychiatry. In due course Southard's proselytizing would open the way for Mayo to find a professional niche in the United States.[5]

Mayo in Philadelphia

On 1 August 1922 Mayo sailed into San Francisco, £50 and several letters of reference in his pocket, including one from the Australian prime minister, and a desperate hope that he would be able to make contacts and find some useful work before his money ran out. As the £50 disappeared rapidly in hotel bills, Mayo tried to establish himself in all kinds of work: university research, magazine articles, the lecture circuit, and personnel work for Standard Oil in California. But on every occasion promising leads tapered off into frustrating dead ends. Only one lead seemed to offer any hope. At the end of his first month in San Francisco Mayo met Vernon Kellogg, secretary of the National Research Council (NRC), who was most receptive to Mayo's ideas about strike control and suggested that Mayo visit him in Washington to talk further about his ideas and plans. From this point on Mayo perceived that his views on the application of psychiatry and psychology to industrial conflict were sufficiently novel to attract the interest of academic and government leaders. Several weeks later Kellogg finally wrote to Mayo inviting him to talk with social scientists and industrialists on the East Coast, and buoyed by the receipt of £200 cabled by his family to sustain his adventure, Mayo set out for Washington. Mayo had by now been long enough in the United States to understand the nature of the stakes, explaining to his wife:

> This is the best thing that ever happened to us. It means that both the financial and the psychological leaders will be wanting to discuss research with me.... Kellogg says that "a representative of one of the

---

[5] For a more detailed analysis of Mayo's social and political views, see Helen Bourke, "Industrial Unrest as Social Pathology: The Australian Writings of Elton Mayo," *Historical Studies*, 1982, 20: 217–33, quote from Mayo on 229. Elmer Ernest Southard's writings on industrial psychiatry include "The Movement for a Mental Hygiene of Industry," *Mental Hygiene*, 1920, 4: 43–64; and "Trade Unionism and Temperament: Notes upon the Psychiatric Point of View in Industry," *Mental Hygiene*, 1920, 4: 281–300.

major foundations" is anxious to meet me and talk things over in New York. This means a financial magnate or Rockefeller Trust.[6]

The timing was fortunate. The PRF had been established only eighteen months previously and was still looking for suitable researchers. Upon arriving in Washington Mayo was carefully looked over by NRC and PRF leaders, including James McKeen Cattell (pioneer psychologist and founder of the Psychological Corporation), Raymond Dodge (president of the Division of Anthropology and Psychology of the NRC), and Robert Yerkes (first president of the PRF). Kellogg and his colleagues saw in Mayo a person who could open up new areas of industrial research, especially in industrial psychiatry, where no one had emerged to replace E. E. Southard since his death in 1920. They were particularly attracted by Mayo's interdisciplinary approach, especially his ability to range freely across what in the United States were the strictly demarcated disciplines of psychology, psychiatry, and sociology. Realizing this, Mayo liked to paint himself as an interdisciplinary renegade, although his approach primarily reflected his training in the British tradition of social and behavioral sciences, which lacked clear disciplinary divisions. Whatever the reason, Mayo's intellectual breadth impressed the Washington scientific administrators, who believed that personnel problems could be fruitfully addressed only if the perspectives of various disciplines were coordinated. Moreover, Mayo shared their view that the social sciences could bring objective knowledge to the field of industrial relations and the organization of work and that experts in personnel research could stand above the partisan attitudes of workers and employers. At the personal level, Mayo was a fluent and spontaneous speaker, and by his own (somewhat exaggerated) account related well with workers. If a kind of religious zeal inspired the leaders of the PRF, then Mayo seemed to them a very promising preacher.

With the imprimatur of the PRF and NRC, Mayo traveled to New York to meet Beardsley Ruml, director of the Laura Spelman Rockefeller Memorial. Again, his timing was perfect. Ruml had become director only five months previously and had just begun to develop a strategy that was to transform the funding of social science research in America. Only twenty-eight years old, Ruml had trained in psychology with Walter Bingham and James R. Angell and then worked as an industrial psychologist in Bingham's division at Carnegie Institute of Technology and for the Committee on Classification of Personnel during the war. When he arrived at the Memorial its policy was to fund social welfare organizations; it had been created by John D. Rockefeller in 1918 as a memorial to his late wife. Ruml found

---

[6] Mayo wrote detailed letters to his wife in Melbourne, which amount to a diary of his life in America before she joined him in Philadelphia in June 1923. Used in this and the following paragraphs are letters written between August 1922 and January 1923, EM/film. See also Mayo to Vernon Kellogg, 30 Aug. 1922, NAS–NRC/Institutions/Mayo/1922–3.

this policy of social amelioration to be fundamentally misguided and re-
directed funding to the support of the social sciences, which he believed
would provide scientific solutions to social problems. Ruml's plan was that
the Memorial, with its annual income of more than $4 million, would
encourage in the social sphere the development of the same kind of basic
knowledge that lay at the foundation of modern medical and engineering
practice. By citing the development of scientific medicine in the late nineteenth and early twentieth centuries, Ruml knew that he was drawing on
an example in which the Rockefeller philanthropies had played a major
role; John D. Rockefeller's gifts established the Rockefeller Institute for
Medical Research in 1901; the Rockefeller Sanitary Commission, dedicated
to the eradication of hookworm disease in the American South, in 1909;
and the International Health Commission in 1913. The model of basic
scientific research applied to widespread social problems of disease inspired
Ruml's plans for the social sciences.[7]

Mayo's interests seemed to Ruml to be in exactly the kind of research
that the Memorial should be supporting, and he dedicated himself to finding
Mayo a suitable institutional location from which he could undertake research. But attempts to place Mayo at Cornell or in New York failed, and
at one point in November Mayo seriously contemplated throwing in the
towel and returning to Australia. Finally Ruml sent him to visit Joseph
Willits, head of the University of Pennsylvania's Department of Industrial
Research. Willits had started the department at the Wharton School of
Business in March 1921, with funds provided by local Philadelphia firms
and the Carnegie Corporation (where Ruml had then been assistant to the
president). The aim of the department was to coordinate research on personnel problems in the Philadelphia area, improve knowledge of the labor
market in Philadelphia by gathering uniform statistics from a range of companies and follow the changes over time, and provide data that would guide
the activities of employers and unions alike. At present, however, the department consisted solely of economists, and Willits saw in Mayo an opportunity to branch out into areas of research other than labor mobility
and turnover. Willits agreed to take Mayo if Ruml could find the funds.[8]

Finally, on 18 January 1923, almost six months after Mayo's arrival in
America, Ruml obtained a grant of $3,000 for Mayo to work in Philadelphia

[7] For a detailed discussion of Ruml's vision and achievements, see Martin Bulmer and Joan
Bulmer, "Philanthropy and Social Science in the 1920s: Beardsley Ruml and the Laura
Spelman Rockefeller Memorial, 1922–29," *Minerva*, 1981, 19: 347–407, esp. 362–3; on
the Rockefeller funding of science, see Robert E. Kohler, "Science, Foundations, and the
American Universities in the 1920s," *Osiris*, 1987, 2d ser. 3: 135–64.
[8] On the Wharton Industrial Research Department, see Joseph H. Willits, "An Industrial
Personnel Research Program," *Journal of Personnel Research*, 1924–5, 3: 125–8; Steven A.
Sass, *The Pragmatic Imagination: A History of the Wharton School, 1881–1981*, Philadelphia: University of Pennsylvania Press, 1982, 208–13.

for a trial period of six months. This hardly seemed a major victory, but the size of the grant underestimates Ruml's commitment to Mayo. Ruml had been unable to persuade the Memorial trustees to provide funds; they were still not convinced by Ruml's plans to change the course of the philanthropy to the funding of social science, and more important, they saw Mayo's work as dangerously political. The memories of the Rockefeller Foundation's embroilment in the Ludlow massacre were still fresh, and the Rockefeller philanthropies continued to shy away from funding projects that might be interpreted as overtly political. The private wealth of John D. Rockefeller, Jr., was a different matter, however. He had developed an active interest in industrial relations since the Ludlow massacre; in addition to encouraging the introduction of his employee representation plan in corporations in which he was a major shareholder, he had the previous year given Princeton University $12,000 per year for five years to establish an industrial relations library. In December 1922 he had contributed $5,000 toward the deficit of the American Management Association and subscribed an annual sum of $1,000. In due course the PRF would also benefit from his largesse, with a grant of $5,000 per year for five years, commencing in 1924. It was in the context of this private support for industrial relations that Rockefeller approached Ruml after the Memorial meeting and offered to fund Mayo personally.[9]

The structure of the financial support had a significant influence on Mayo's research style. With the university, the Memorial, and Rockefeller arguing over who should provide support, it always seemed possible that he would fall between the cracks, and this produced an element of uncertainty that haunted Mayo for several years. Although Ruml could informally reassure Mayo that funding would continue as long as Mayo made progress, the formal messages were always more pessimistic, suggesting that the grant was only to tide Mayo over until he found alternative sources of support. This uncertainty played on Mayo's insecurities, and for the next few years he always harbored a fear that his U.S. supporters would suddenly decide that they had been taken in by a charlatan from a colonial backwater. Mayo was also plagued by a sense of inadequacy, stemming from his youthful failures and the success of other members of his family; it took time for him to come to terms with his success. The pressure on Mayo to achieve rapid and demonstrable results in order to please his patrons would play a significant role in the development of his ideas.

Mayo's research program in Philadelphia industries underwent a process

[9] Mayo to Dorothea Mayo, 12–20 Jan. 1923, EM/film; Beardsley Ruml, "University of Pennsylvania, Department of Industrial Research," 17 Jan. 1923, LSRM/75/790. On John D. Rockefeller, Jr.'s, private funding of industrial relations, see Rockefeller, Jr., to C. J. Hicks, 26 June 1922, OMR/Educational Institutions/Princeton; W. S. Richardson to National Personnel Association, 26 Dec. 1922, OMR/2F/12/93; Richardson to Alfred Flinn, 15 July 1924, OMR/Civic Interests/81.4/Personnel Research Federation.

of elaboration and adaptation in a suspicious and at times hostile environment. In all of his Philadelphia work there was a constant tension between
his desire to do fundamental research that would form the basis of his
overarching social theories and the need for practical results that would
bring acclaim from the employers who gave him access to their factories.
As his research unfolded, Mayo discovered that the major challenge would
be to balance the practical and theoretical demands of his research agenda.

Settling into Philadelphia at the start of 1923, Mayo contemplated how
he could perfect his ideas on industrial psychiatry or, as he now preferred
to call it, psychopathology. Mayo's choice of the term "psychopathology"
indicated his readiness to adapt to circumstances in the United States. The
term had come to represent the treatment of milder forms of mental illness
and behavioral problems, the neuroses found throughout the population
rather than the psychoses of institutionalized mental patients. The new
European psychiatry of Freud and Jung and the growing mental hygiene
movement in America combined to emphasize the fact that mental illness
could be found everywhere in society. Freudian ideas had spread slowly but
surely after Freud's visit to America in 1909 and by the 1920s found influential adherents in psychiatry and psychology. Meanwhile, mental hygiene
activists – psychiatrists, psychologists, and psychiatric social workers – had
begun to define whole new social domains in which mental treatment was
required; they were most successful at establishing programs in child guidance, general hospitals, and community social work. By referring to the
psychopathology of industry, Mayo located his own work in these broader
developments.[10]

In two articles for the PRF's *Journal of Personnel Research* he outlined
his theory of psychopathology and indicated how it illuminated industrial
conflict. The European psychiatrists, he argued, had demonstrated that organic causes of mental illness were not as important as previously believed.
Irrationality and delusion were more often due to personal maladaptation
to the environment, they were problems of education and development, and
sanity was "an achieved, rather than a merely natural condition of mind."
Citing clinical cases from his Australian experience, he argued that the
symptoms of irrationality in a patient did not indicate the real, underlying
irrationality, which was due to unacknowledged reveries, that is, the work-
ings of the unconscious: "The human expression of a maladjustment or
disorientation is no guide to the actual disorientation except by the road of
psychological investigation and interpretation."[11] Every individual suffered

[10] David Rothman, *Conscience and Convenience: The Asylum and Its Alternatives in Pro-
gressive America*, Boston: Little, Brown, 1980; Roy Lubove, *The Professional Altruist: The
Emergence of Social Work as a Career, 1880–1930*, Cambridge, Mass.: Harvard University
Press, 1965.

[11] Elton Mayo, "The Irrational Factor in Society," *Journal of Personnel Research*, 1922–3,

from irrationalities and reveries, which, while they did not affect the well-integrated individual, might interact with the reveries of others to cause a "breakdown" in industry or society.

Strikes and the political disturbances of mass democracy therefore were not rational attempts to gain an increase in wages or the acceptance of a political program. They were expressions of underlying reveries, and it was these reveries that had to be addressed, not the political demands or "symptoms." The case of an Australian worker demonstrated Mayo's method at the clinical level:

> A medical colleague was once consulted by a young artisan who desired relief from certain hysterical symptoms. We speedily discovered that he was what he proudly called a "rebel." In other words, he objected to all authority, and to such an extent that if a "boss" or foreman gave him a direct order, it was his habit to walk off the job. This "response to situation," we found, was determined by the facts of his early childhood. His father, a drunkard, had brutally mishandled his mother and himself. His reaction to authority, individual or social, was his reaction to his father; he had never discriminated between paternal and other commands. His recovery from hysteria was accompanied by a complete change of attitude to authority. He took a job and kept it, and recognised the necessity of legitimate authority as part of social and industrial organization.

The psychiatrist's role in industry, as conceived by Mayo, was to undermine the extreme political positions of workers and employers (who were also prone to irrational responses) by reinterpreting their political stances as merely irrational manifestations of underlying personal maladjustment. Ideally, his approach provided both ideological and practical benefits to industry: Psychopathology would enable employers to argue that worker radicalism was irrational, and the psychopathologist could offer to cure any psychiatric disturbances that existed among the workforce, thereby reducing industrial conflict.[12]

In practice Mayo found it difficult to balance his theoretical commitment to criticize both workers and employers with the fact that he was dependent on employers for access to their factories. He began his research in the carpet mill of C. H. Masland & Sons in the textile district in north Philadelphia, but the unionized workers declined to discuss their personal problems and reveries with Mayo, and he was highly critical of the owners for discouraging all social organization in the factory. His research came to an abrupt end when one of the owners learned that Mayo had offered a book

1: 419–26, quote on 424; idem, "Irrationality and Revery," *Journal of Personnel Research*, 1922–3, 1: 477–83, quote on 482.

[12] Ibid., 483; see also Elton Mayo, "The Application of Psychopathology to Industry," typescript, 1 Mar. 1923, LSRM/75/790.

on the physiology of sex to a female worker, apparently to correct her faulty knowledge of the subject.[13]

In subsequent research at Collins & Aikman Company, a manufacturer of plush and pile fabrics, Mayo found that the president of the company wanted him to develop psychological tests to reduce labor turnover. Psychological tests were very appealing to employers in the early 1920s: Their apparent success in selecting recruits in the First World War had been highly publicized, and they seemed a practical and readily administered solution to an immediate problem. But Mayo felt that such tests were too simplistic to be of much value and that they ignored the psychiatric dimension, or what he called the "total situation." Of course, neither did such tests utilize Mayo's special skills. Unwilling to pass up the opportunity for research, Mayo attempted to balance his interests with that of the employer. He indicated that he would develop tests, but insisted that turnover was due to factors other than a poorly selected workforce; poor work conditions, dislike of nightwork, and psychiatric disturbances were more to blame. The president rebutted Mayo's suggested remedy of a nine-hour night shift in place of the existing shift of eleven and a half hours. After further friction Mayo abandoned his research, and the president employed an industrial psychologist to develop tests.[14]

Mayo had greater success in a third textile factory, the woollen mill of Continental Mills, Inc. Here he managed to strike a balance between theoretical and practical concerns by tying the two together in a study of labor turnover. The model of physiological fatigue and psychiatric disturbances that he elaborated during his Continental Mills research ensured his continued funding and shaped his initial research at Hawthorne. Apart from the Hawthorne experiments and some research during the Second World War, the work at Continental Mills was the only other industrial investigation conducted by Mayo that he reported on in any detail in print, and it constituted a chapter in his seminal *Human Problems of an Industrial Civilization* (1933). Mayo was invited to the mill by its general manager, who was concerned with the high turnover in the spinning department, which was running at an annual rate of 250 percent compared with 5 to 6 percent in other parts of the mill. Mayo studied the factory operation without incurring any direct opposition from the workers, whose unions had been broken by management campaigns during the 1921 depression. Conditions in the mill were bad: The temperature and humidity were high and

[13] Mayo to Dorothea Mayo, 18 Feb.–11 Mar., 22–6 Mar., 1923, EM/film; Mayo to Willits, 14 May 1923, LSRM/75/790.
[14] See correspondence between Mayo and Melville Curtis in EM/4.008; for Mayo's views on the causes of turnover, psychological tests, and his experience at Collins & Aikman, see his "The Irrational Factor in Human Behavior: The 'Night-Mind' in Industry," *Annals of the American Academy of Political and Social Science*, 1923, 110: 117–30, esp. 120–1, 125.

the air choked with wool. In addition, the manager of the spinning department informed Mayo that the machines were run faster than in comparable plants. Poor conditions did not seem to explain the high turnover among spinners, however, since these conditions also obtained in the carding department, where the turnover was low.[15]

Observing the spinning operation more closely, Mayo hypothesized that the awkward posture that spinners had to adopt to join the yarn was causing fatigue, due to the "relative inco-ordination of blood pressure in upper and lower zones" of the body. He was not content to rely solely on a physiological explanation for the high turnover, however, and asserted that the workers' pessimistic reveries exacerbated the problem, citing as evidence the frequency of statements such as "piecers get disgusted – they are always getting disgusted." The combination of these two approaches – physiological and psychiatric – constituted a neat balancing act between the conflicting interests of the employers and workers. The physiological account tended to place responsibility on the employer for the turnover, while the psychiatric part attributed the problem to the workers' mental state. Mayo's hypothetical explanation reflected his tenuous position in the mill, wanting to antagonize neither the workers nor the managers, and reflected his commitment to the view that both labor and capital were to blame for industrial conflict. In October 1923, at Mayo's suggestion the company introduced rest periods into the troublesome spinning department. The rest periods seemed eminently successful: "The effect was immediate – symptoms of melancholy preoccupation disappeared, the labor turnover ceased, production was maintained, the morale generally improved."[16]

Mayo used the Continental Mills research to construct a model of labor turnover that linked physiological studies of fatigue with his commitment to psychiatry. The following representation of their relationship is what Mayo had in mind:

work conditions → fatigue → reveries → turnover

This model was attractive for several reasons. First, it inserted into the relationship between work conditions and turnover two of Mayo's fields of scientific expertise, medicine and psychiatry. Second, by introducing fatigue

---

[15] The account of the Continental Mills research is based on Mayo's reports to Willits, 14 May 1923 and 28 Dec. 1923, LSRM/75/790; a draft report to Willits of Apr. 1925, EM/1.099; letters of Mayo to Dorothea Mayo, March–May 1923, EM/film; Continental Mills personnel files, EM/4.015–019, 4.021–033. Mayo reported the Continental Mills research primarily in "Irrational Factor in Human Behavior"; "Mental Hygiene in Industry," *Transactions of the College of Physicians of Philadelphia*, 1924, 3d ser., 46: 736–48; "Revery and Industrial Fatigue," *Journal of Personnel Research*, 1924–5, 3: 273–81; "The Basis of Industrial Psychology," *Bulletin of the Taylor Society*, 1925, 9: 249–59; "The Surrey Textile Company: Manufacturer – Textiles," *Harvard Business Reports*, 1927, 4: 100–15.

[16] Mayo, "Revery and Industrial Fatigue," quote on 275.

into the "equation," Mayo could draw on a substantial body of literature on industrial fatigue written by physiologists and psychologists in the United States, Britain, and Germany. In particular he could utilize the reports of the British Industrial Fatigue Research Board, a government research committee established in 1919 to discover means of reducing fatigue and increasing production. The efficacy of rest periods in checking the onset of fatigue had already been noted by the board and its wartime predecessor, the Health of Munitions Workers Committee. Mayo's concentration on the problems of turnover may also have been influenced by the board, which used turnover as a test of the "health" of a factory.[17] Third, the model paralleled Mayo's explanation of the behavior of shell-shocked patients, whose condition often improved once they were removed from the front and could rest. If one assumed that battle conditions had similar effects on soldiers as working conditions had on workers, the "transient hysteria" of shell shock could be likened to the irrational behavior of workers. Finally, the model reinforced Mayo's belief that reveries had a substantial influence on worker behavior.

Mayo was well aware that he must prove to the factory managers that rest periods would not only reduce turnover but also maintain levels of production. The measure of production used in the factory was based on estimates of the time that spinning a particular weight of yarn should take. If the department attained more than 75 percent of the ideal productive efficiency in a month, then a bonus was paid, based on the additional percentage of efficiency. In fact, according to Mayo a bonus had never been paid. But once the rest periods were introduced, albeit as rewards for production, productive efficiency leaped to about 80 percent. He felt he could use the measure of production to confirm his assessments of the workers' levels of reveries. He therefore placed great emphasis on the following, otherwise fairly innocuous, occurrence. On visiting the mill in late February 1924 he detected what he felt was an increased incidence of pessimistic reveries and symptoms of fatigue. Inquiry revealed that the department had dropped the rest periods a week earlier because of the demand for yarn, and when figures of efficiency were examined they showed a precipitous decline. Here was apparently independent confirmation of Mayo's observations of fatigue and revery. Mayo also reported that labor turnover had virtually been eliminated through the introduction of rest periods, although he never provided statistical evidence.

Many problems remained with Mayo's explanatory model, although he tended to gloss over them in his reports to Ruml and Willits and in his

---

[17] On industrial fatigue, see Richard Gillespie, "Industrial Fatigue and the Discipline of Physiology," in Gerald L. Geison, ed., *Physiology in the American Context, 1850–1940*, Bethesda, Md.: American Physiological Society, 1987, 237–62; for an example of the British research see H. M. Vernon, *Fatigue and Efficiency in the Iron and Steel Industry* (Industrial Fatigue Research Board, report no. 5), London: HMSO, 1920.

published accounts. The evidence for a close relationship between rest periods and increased production was inconsistent – fatigue researchers were constantly frustrated by confusing results, just as they were in the relay assembly test room. Production at Continental Mills did not return to its previous high levels when rest periods were reintroduced after Mayo's discovery of renewed fatigue and reveries. In the following year Mayo's assistant noted that production remained above 80 percent even though the foreman of the spinning department had once more abandoned rest periods.[18]

The most serious problem for Mayo was to show some link between fatigue and reveries. Without this his model could simply be collapsed into the more conventional account of fatigue as a physiological overload that could be relieved by rests. Mayo therefore attempted to gain more detailed information on the psychiatric states of the workers at Continental Mills. But as an outsider he was unable to "press too hard for intimate details of their lives and thoughts. . . . I have had in certain instances to relax an inquiry because indications of possible doubt as to my purpose began to show."[19] With additional financial assistance from Rockefeller, Mayo employed a nurse in the factory to act as a "listening post," gathering whatever information she could about the workers' personal lives and thoughts. Mayo made arrangements so that any interesting cases identified by the nurse would be sent to a local hospital for a physical examination and then referred to Mayo for psychiatric treatment. The scheme was to serve as a trial of the whole concept of extending mental hygiene clinics into industry. At the same time the nurse, Emily Osborne, began taking blood pressure measurements sixteen times a day from several workers as a rough measure of their fatigue. Mayo hoped that he might be able to link blood pressure measurements to groups of psychiatric states and thereby demonstrate unequivocally that fatigue and reveries were related. As in the later blood pressure measurements during the relay assembly test, the results were infuriatingly ambiguous, but Mayo remained committed to pursuing this line of research.[20]

Although Mayo's model of worker behavior had its problems, he had succeeded in developing a model that reflected his own intellectual interests and at the same time fit comfortably with the practical concerns of employers and the corporate ideology of his backers. In reports to Willits and Ruml and in several articles he argued that his Continental Mills investigations showed that few, if any, workers were free from reveries:

> Everyone, worker or executive, probably carries with him a private grief
> or discontent. Wherever the conditions of work are unsuitable, physi-

[18] Emily Osborne, "Fact of Interest," 16 Feb. 1925, EM/4.034.
[19] Mayo to Willits, 28 Dec. 1923, 27–8.
[20] Mayo, "Fatigue in Industry," typescript, 1925–6, EM/2.052.

cally or mentally, the immediate effect seems to be an increase of pessimistic or bitter reflection.

He noted that many of the textile workers had an abiding fear of losing their good health and ability to carry out their job. Mayo conceded that workers might indeed lose their good health prematurely, but argued that such a revery was irrational and that unionists exploited this fear to organize labor. He seemed unwilling to accept that workers who lost their agility and speed in the textile industry would no longer have jobs and would have no guarantee of finding other work. He even argued that the drop in a worker's performance was due not to a decline in agility and speed, but to the fear of that decline; physiological facts were transformed into psychological states, and concern about them by the worker thus rendered irrational. Mayo rejected the notion that the worker was able to identify poor working conditions: "The opinion of the worker as to the suitability or otherwise of his working conditions is apparently of no value in this respect." For example, not all monotonous jobs were necessarily bad, only those that produced abnormal preoccupations. Only the psychopathologist or, at the very least, the executive trained in psychopathological techniques could identify and rectify such problems.[21]

The power of Mayo's approach came from his conviction that he was providing an objective scientific analysis of the problems of modern capitalism. He firmly believed that he was being equally critical of both workers and employers and that both could benefit from his intervention. Indeed, he went out of his way to point out that he was not introducing a management efficiency scheme such as Taylorism or psychological testing. Presenting a chart showing the increased production at Continental Mills following the introduction of rests, he stressed, "I use this chart not because we are necessarily interested in increasing production, but rather because it offers an interesting, and so far accurate, measure of the general effect of the humaner organization of work upon the men."[22] Whether he was being disingenuous is unimportant; what mattered was that there was an audience of social scientists, foundation officials, corporate executives, and managers ready to listen to and support Mayo's approach. They accepted that his modest criticism of employers was the prelude to a program offering them more efficient techniques of control.

Yet just as he was achieving some success, the difficulties and limitations of industrial research became increasingly apparent. Continental Mills provided the greatest opportunity for research, yet severe practical constraints hampered the conduct of rigorous experiments. Rest periods were set aside when periods of high demand required intensive production, thereby making

---

[21] Mayo, "Revery and Industrial Fatigue," quotes on 279; Mayo to Willits, 28 Dec. 1923, 16–17.
[22] Mayo, "Revery and Industrial Fatigue," 275–6.

the interpretation of results highly problematic. Foremen, skeptical of out-side interference in their domain by personnel managers and university researchers, refrained from cooperating in the research and undermined its value when they altered experimental conditions without the researchers' knowledge. Nor were any but a handful of workers willing to share their personal problems with Osborne and Mayo, even when the subterfuge of using a nurse was introduced. Workers given appointments to see Mayo at his center city office, a hospital specialist, or a social worker would rarely attend after the first visit, thus making intensive study of individual workers impossible. Subsequent research at the textile mill of Aberfoyle Manufac-turing Company in Chester, south of Philadelphia, also proved unrewarding.

Mayo's difficulties were symptomatic of those confronted by personnel researchers in the 1920s. Scientists were intervening in complex technical and political relationships in the workplace, and it was by no means certain that all parties – employers, managers, foremen, and workers – would welcome their presence. Mayo and his fellow researchers had to move warily through a jungle of conflicting interests. There was constant tension over whether researchers should be developing fundamental or applied science. Personnel researchers often found themselves in a dilemma when they had to prove to industrialists that their research was practical and likely to produce valuable personnel techniques, while at the same time they had to gain the scientific approval of their university colleagues. Thus, despite Walter V. Bingham's success in developing army tests during the First World War, in 1924 the Carnegie Institute of Technology abruptly dismantled his Division of Applied Psychology, the most prestigious research group in industrial psychology in the country.[23]

Finances posed a further restraint. Universities were unable or unwilling to provide research funds in such applied fields, while the meager offerings of employers practically ensured that research and any resulting techniques would be very crude. The PRF had been established in part to overcome the fragmentation and underfunding of research, but its experience in the 1920s only confirmed these problems. Bingham, now director of the fed-eration in New York, was continually frustrated in his attempts to obtain long-term funding that would support sustained fundamental research. Most companies expected direct payoffs for their contributions, and Bingham was driven into performing a large number of small special studies of doubtful long-term benefit to the field of personnel management. A similar fate had befallen the PRF's British equivalent, the National Institute of Industrial Psychology, which was forced by its reliance on company support to conduct

[23] Loren Baritz, *The Servants of Power: A History of the Use of Social Science in American Industry*, Middletown, Conn.: Wesleyan University Press, 1960, 39–40; Walter V. Bingham, "Walter Van Dyke Bingham," in E. G. Boring et al., eds., *A History of Psychology in Autobiography*, New York: Russell & Russell, 1952, 4: 1–26.

repetitive and simplistic research. Mayo's career might have followed a path similar to that of Bingham, who had to wait until the Second World War before attaining a prominent position as the army's chief psychologist. But by 1926 Mayo had moved to Harvard University as a professor of industrial research, and within two years he was intimately involved in the development of the research at Hawthorne. The major difference between Bingham and Mayo was that the latter had powerful friends.[24]

A network for industrial research

The network in which Mayo and the Hawthorne experiments became embedded drew its power from the fact that it successfully straddled the intellectual and corporate worlds. Three men played key roles in the development of the network. Beardsley Ruml ensured that Mayo found a secure academic position at the Harvard Business School from which he could pursue his industrial research, using generous funds provided by the Rockefeller philanthropies. Ruml also encouraged Mayo's interdisciplinary approach and drew Mayo into the elite circle of U.S. social scientists seeking to weaken the boundaries between their disciplines. For the first time Mayo acquired some real confidence in his intellectual abilities. Mayo found a more secure academic position in the Harvard Business School with the assistance of Ruml and Wallace Donham, the school's dean, who believed that Mayo's type of social scientific research would help transform business management into a science-based profession. At the same time Mayo's approach to personnel research was encouraged and facilitated by Arthur Young, the key figure in an industrial consulting firm created by John D. Rockefeller, Jr. Young drew Mayo into the inner circle of industrial relations executives of major corporations, fostered Mayo's long-term involvement in the Hawthorne research, and ensured that Western Electric and AT&T executives realized the importance of the research.

Mayo was always acutely aware that he needed to please his sponsors. Throughout his period of industrial research in Philadelphia he wrote detailed reports for Ruml and Willits, in which he candidly set out his research plans, achievements, hopes, and frustrations. With no colleagues to share his broad intellectual interests, and with his wife still in Australia during the first year of his adventure in the United States, Mayo relied on Ruml for intellectual and emotional support. Ruml and Willits judged that Mayo's progress was sufficient to warrant continued support, and Mayo's original

[24] The Personnel Research Federation's difficulties are discussed in W. V. Bingham to J. D. Rockefeller, Jr., 13 Oct. 1926, LSRM/112/1138; J. D. Rockefeller, Jr., Committee on Benevolence Minutes, 13 Dec. 1928, OMR/Civic Interests/81.4-PRF. On the National Institute of Industrial Psychology, see Henry J. Welch and Charles S. Myers, *Ten Years of Industrial Psychology: An Account of the First Decade of the National Institute of Industrial Psychology*, London: Pitman, 1932.

six-month grant was continued by a series of annual grants from Rockefeller, Jr.'s, Committee on Benevolence – in 1925–6 at the rate of $13,300, to cover the salaries of Mayo and his industrial nurse and expenses.

But by 1925 Mayo was beginning to become frustrated by his industrial research in Philadelphia, and he turned increasingly to consider more general social problems and to embrace a wider range of intellectual disciplines. Even while in the thick of industrial research on turnover in 1923 and 1924, Mayo had not neglected the wider ramifications of his experiments. He had long believed that the problems of industry were symptomatic of more general social ills, notably the development of class consciousness and the failure of democracy. He spelled out these problems for a general audience in articles in *Harper's Magazine,* stressing the current ignorance of human nature and the disinclination of social and industrial leaders to draw on the insights of the human sciences: "If some inorganic material cannot readily be adapted to industrial processes we employ a chemist or a physicist to discover why. But should a group of workers show signs of resisting adaptation to some industrial system, we usually lose our tempers and endeavor to force them to accept it." Until the role of irrationality in society was dealt with scientifically, he suggested, it left us "in doubt whether Frazer's volume on *Taboo and the Perils of the Soul* is not a better guide to the problems of industry than learned treatises on economics."[25]

The reference to anthropology was a new thread in Mayo's social critique. Although he had been friendly with Malinowski since 1914, he did not begin to consider the relevance of anthropology to his own research until after he arrived in Philadelphia. The work of Lucien Levy-Bruhl, who argued that all primitive thinking was prelogical and obsessional, seemed particularly useful. Mayo thought it likely that fatigue in the industrial worker brought about a reversion to primitive thinking; the worker whose reveries led to obsessive and radical views had in a sense regressed to the evolutionary stage of the savage. Another way to view the problem was to see the worker as a child whose mental state echoed (even recapitulated) that of the primitive; soon Mayo was absorbing Jean Piaget's research on the mental development of the child, seeking in it evidence that would support his own theories. In 1926 Mayo, in the draft of a report to Willits, actually contemplated referring to his studies as "anthropological."[26]

This broad approach was complemented by research in psychiatry and physiology that sought to elucidate some of the mechanisms of mental disturbance that Mayo considered so prevalent. He was most excited by the results of his collaboration with a Philadelphia psychiatrist:

---

[25] Mayo, "Civilization: The Perilous Adventure," *Harper's Magazine,* 1924, 149: 590–7, quotes on 591, 592.
[26] Mayo to Willits, draft report, Apr. 1925, draft report, 30 June 1926; see also Mayo, "Civilization," 593–5; Mayo, "The Basis of Industrial Psychology," 253.

Two days ago we were looking at a man's stomach (X-rays & fluorescent screen) in a laboratory. He was in a somnambulic condition, standing, his eyes shut. I suggested to him a great anxiety he had when awake about his wife's health. The effect was immediate – he gave no external sign of hearing or of awaking but his stomach immediately fell into violent spasm (under the observation of a medico and a psychologist of Vassar) which ceased only when I began to reassure. Where does this kind of fact come in in politico-psychological research?[27]

This research reflected part of a widespread interest in the connection between physiological and psychological states, spurred on by the publication in 1915 of experimental research on the physiological basis of the emotions by Harvard physiologist Walter B. Cannon.

Always prepared to draw from diverse disciplines and to integrate his eclectic interests, Mayo constructed a model that tied together laboratory experiments in physiology and findings in psychiatry with his political and social observations. Mayo never published this model for the integration of the human sciences – he was well aware that it was highly speculative. But he did set it out for Charles E. Merriam, the eminent political scientist at the University of Chicago, who was committed to the introduction of knowledge from psychology and the social sciences into political science and was a key figure in redirecting the field into a study of political behavior. Introduced by Ruml, the two men began a lengthy and detailed correspondence on the psychological causes of political attitudes; in due course Merriam would send his best student, Harold D. Lasswell, to study psychopathology with Mayo.[28]

Mayo suggested that one could characterize two basic types of abnormal personality. On the one hand, there were people who were inclined toward hysteria; physiologically, they were dominated by the sympathetic nervous system, had high blood pressure, and had dilated intestines; sociologically, they were usually uneducated. On the other hand, obsessive or neurotic people were dominated by the parasympathetic nervous system, had low blood pressure and contracted intestines, and were generally educated. The hysteric was a more primitive type, Mayo felt, whereas the obsessive or neurotic was associated more with urban civilization. He suggested that industrial unrest was led by obsessive parasympathetics and followed by hysteric sympathetics and that the same model could be applied to political revolutions. He had learned, he told Merriam, that a representative of the Soviet government was to visit in autumn, and he proposed trying to get permission to conduct an experiment in Russia:

[27] Mayo to C. E. Merriam, 16 Mar. 1925, CEM/35/17.
[28] On Merriam, see Barry D. Karl, *Charles E. Merriam and the Study of Politics*, Chicago: University of Chicago Press, 1974. Merriam's views on the relevance of the social and natural sciences to the study of politics are stated concisely in C. E. Merriam, "The Significance of Psychology for the Study of Politics," *American Political Science Review*, 1924, 18: 469–88.

This, if it could be worked, would be such an opportunity as there has never been – because the Soviet could give us factories and village communes to be made the subject of our investigations and experiments – reinforced by the high authority of the Soviet. This would enable us to demonstrate the effect of doing away with fatigue, of altering the salt-balance; of changing the metabolism from alkaline to acid or of dealing with hysteria in a psychopathological fashion. The mere discovery of the facts would be so important to politics and social research as to be worth while, even if remedies acted slowly. Suppose, for example, we discovered (as I think we should) that the majority of the peasants and workers were of the hysteric-sympathetic type, and the majority of the leaders of the obsessional-parasympathetic [type]. This alone, I think, would be of the highest value – though I should expect also to be able to demonstrate our capacity to handle situations after investigation, backed by the arbitrary authority of the Soviet.[29]

Merriam was deeply impressed by Mayo's proposal and asked him to outline the probable cost and the type of researchers needed. The following year Merriam visited the Soviet Union and talked with a psychiatrist who was studying "disorganizers," but the project never eventuated.

Nevertheless, Mayo's breadth of approach tantalized Ruml and Merriam. Ruml in particular sought to use his position as director of the Laura Spelman Rockefeller Memorial to bring together the diverse social sciences to study the common problem of human behavior. By 1925 the Memorial was funding a number of interdisciplinary programs, notably the Local Community Research Committee at the University of Chicago (of which Merriam was a member), the Yale Institute of Human Relations, a wide range of research at the London School of Economics (where Malinowski was Ruml's key confidant), and the Social Science Research Council. Ruml reinforced these institutional developments by organizing an interdisciplinary conference to discuss trends in the sciences of human behavior. Mayo was one of thirty or so representatives from psychology, psychiatry, physiology, neurology, economics, sociology, and political science who spent two weeks at Dartmouth College in the summer of 1925; here Mayo was encouraged to propose his model of hysteric and obsessive types. Later that year Merriam, in his presidential address to the American Political Science Association, cited Mayo's industrial research as evidence of the value of studying the physiological and psychiatric bases of political behavior. Not that Mayo impressed everyone. Merriam delightedly informed Mayo that Chicago psychologist L. L. Thurstone "regards you as unorthodox, and what is more irritating, unclassifiable."[30]

Mayo's research, then, both industrial and psychiatric, gained the atten-

[29] Mayo to Merriam, 21 July 1925, CEM/35/17.
[30] Bulmer and Bulmer, "Philanthropy and Social Science," esp. 185–97; "Conference of Psychologists, 1925," LSRM/53/566–8; C. E. Merriam, "Progress in Political Research," *American Political Science Review*, 1926, 20: 1–13, esp. 10–11; quote from Merriam to Mayo, 24 July 1925, CEM/35/17.

tion of a wide range of social scientists because it represented a significant attempt to integrate approaches in a period when scientists of many disciplines were expressing the desire to develop a unified science of behavior. Merriam, Ruml, and Mayo all believed that modern society could be administered or "controlled" only by the rigorous application of scientific techniques and principles; social and political conflicts, and even personal maladjustments, were to be resolved scientifically and thus objectively. There was plenty of room for differences within such a broad commitment. Whereas Mayo was highly skeptical of the political process and in the 1930s remained critical of Franklin Delano Roosevelt's populist and interventionist administration, Merriam was a former politician who sought to embed scientific administration within the political process and embraced the New Deal.

Yet just as he was beginning to receive this recognition, Mayo found his position in Philadelphia less and less satisfactory. Opportunities for conducting extensive research in industry had not been forthcoming; the psychiatric community in Philadelphia was not very interested in Mayo's ideas; and lectures at the university, which Mayo felt obliged to give, crowded in on his time. Accordingly, Ruml undertook to assist Mayo in finding an alternative location. Several institutions were considered during 1925, but by the end of the year it had become apparent that the Harvard Business School offered the most potential for both industrial and psychopathological research. Mayo's funding was shifted from Rockefeller, Jr., to the Memorial, which agreed to support Mayo for five years at $12,000 per annum, commencing in July 1926. The political climate had changed, and the Rockefeller philanthropies were now less concerned about the political implications of projects they funded. In return President A. Lawrence Lowell of Harvard agreed to appoint Mayo an associate professor in industrial research with the understanding that the university's future commitment would be settled at the end of the five years.

The Harvard Business School seemed the ideal location for Mayo. Founded in 1908 with a grant from the Rockefeller General Education Board (GEB), the school was the first business school devoted exclusively to graduate training. At a time when big business was being attacked by muckraking journalists and politicians, the school constituted an attempt by Lowell and the GEB to raise business leadership above these taints by introducing professional training for future executives. During the 1920s the business school took on its familiar institutional and physical form under the direction of Wallace B. Donham, its dean from 1919 to 1942. In 1924 Donham secured $5 million from George F. Baker, president of the First National Bank and a director of AT&T since 1902; the gift was based on close professional and personal ties, since both had worked in the New York group of banks led by J. P. Morgan. It was therefore appropriate that when the new business school campus was completed in 1927, the two men most responsible for the reorganization of the Bell companies in 1902–7 should be honored in the naming of its two major buildings, Baker Library and Morgan Hall. Delivering the dedication address of the new buildings in 1927, General Electric president Owen D. Young declared that "today and here business formally assumes the obligations of a profession." Business, he went on, was now the major social force, eclipsing church and state, and it was therefore imperative that it develop the knowledge and social responsibility commensurate with this position.[31]

Under Donham the Harvard Business School gained preeminence in the field of business education, especially in graduate education and in the training of corporate leaders. Donham emphasized the need for research, primarily to provide case material for teaching, but also to develop a more basic understanding of business practice. The school had a responsibility to develop an "adequate intellectual background which will enable business leaders to assume their social responsibility wisely among the most critical problems of civilization."[32] Only then could business assume its proper position as a profession alongside medicine and engineering. Mayo's work, in Donham's view, constituted precisely the kind of basic research that could prove of value to industry and business. He was convinced that the business school offered the perfect location for this research, for it could provide Mayo with industrial contacts and also disseminate his research findings throughout the business world.[33]

Boston also seemed an attractive location for Mayo's research because of the interest shown in his work by scientists outside the business school. C. Macfie Campbell, who had replaced pioneer industrial psychiatrist E. E. Southard as director of the Boston Psychopathic Hospital, was deeply interested in the development of psychiatry as an "immunological" technique that would reduce individual and social conflict, including that in industry; he gladly offered Mayo access to the clinics of the Boston Psychopathic Hospital and looked forward to collaboration on industrial psychiatry. Of still greater importance was the support of physiologist and biochemist L. J. Henderson, who headed his own research laboratory at Harvard and was willing to provide the laboratory facilities and staff Mayo needed for his physiological research. Mayo and Henderson quickly discovered that they

---

[31] Owen D. Young, "Dedication Address," *Harvard Business Review*, 1926–7, 5: 385–94, quote on 394; see also Wallace B. Donham, "The Social Significance of Business," *Harvard Business Review*, 1926–7, 5: 406–19. On the history of the Harvard Business School and business education in America, see Melvin Thomas Copeland, *And Mark an Era: The Story of the Harvard Business School*, Boston: Little, Brown, 1958, 8–16; and James H. S. Bossard and J. Frederick Dewhurst, *University Education for Business*, Philadelphia: University of Pennsylvania Press, 1931.

[32] Donham to Rockefeller, Jr., 24 Feb. 1927, LSRM/53/572; Wallace B. Donham, "Essential Groundwork for a Broad Executive Theory," *Harvard Business Review*, 1922, 1: 1–10.

[33] Donham's plans for Mayo are outlined in Young to Fosdick, 17 Feb. 1926, LSRM/53/572.

shared a love of fine wine, conservative political values, and a commitment to applying insights drawn from medicine and physiology to social instability and maladjustment.[34]

Discussions among Mayo, Henderson, Ruml, and Donham resulted in an expanded program whereby the Laura Spelman Rockefeller Memorial agreed to increase Mayo's grant to encompass Henderson and physiologists Arlie V. Bock and David B. Dill. The combined grant from the Memorial was now substantial: Mayo and Henderson were receiving an annual appropriation of $42,000 per annum for five years, plus an additional $35,000 to equip the laboratory. To his amazement Donham found himself agreeing to the establishment of a physiological and biochemical laboratory in a business school. The Harvard Fatigue Laboratory's members differed somewhat in their conception of the function of the laboratory. Mayo and Henderson hoped to conduct research integrating as far as possible approaches in physiology, biochemistry, psychiatry, psychology, and anthropology; they called their program "human biology," using the term favored by Rockefeller Foundation official Edwin Embree to describe his interdisciplinary program of funding. By contrast, Bock and Dill remained interested primarily in research on physiological fatigue. Industrial fatigue provided a framework within which quite diverse research interests could be pursued.[35]

With a secure institutional base and the opportunity for collaboration with colleagues in several disciplines, Mayo cast around for a factory in which he could conduct research. He hoped to find a business in which Emily Osborne, the industrial nurse he had brought with him from Philadelphia, could establish an industrial mental hygiene clinic, conducting observations and taking blood pressures. But it proved difficult to find an appropriate setting. Mayo and Osborne were unable to persuade managers that they had anything useful to offer them in the way of controlling workers or improving production, while several of the companies lacked the employment department and data necessary for extensive research. Two years and six companies later, Mayo had little to show besides an inconclusive collection of blood pressure data. Reflecting on the first two years of his work at Harvard, Mayo told Ruml that he had achieved a great deal in terms of establishing contacts and writing and elaborating his theories, but

---

[34] C. Macfie Campbell, "Conference of Psychologists, 1925," esp. 162–3, LSRM/53/566–8; C. Macfie Campbell to Mayo, 15 May 1926, EM/3.079. On Henderson's career, see Walter B. Cannon, "Lawrence Joseph Henderson, 1878–1942," *National Academy of Sciences Biographical Memoirs*, 1945, 23: 31–58; and Stephen J. Cross and William R. Albury, "Walter B. Cannon, L. J. Henderson, and the Organic Analogy," *Osiris*, 1987, 2d ser., 3: 165–92.

[35] A history of the Harvard Fatigue Laboratory by Dill's daughter and son-in-law provides a useful overview, although it is based primarily on recollections; see S. M. Horvath and E. D. Horvath, *The Harvard Fatigue Laboratory: Its History and Contribution*, Englewood Cliffs, N.J.: Prentice-Hall, 1973.

the one difficulty remaining was to secure a "convenient niche in the industrial structure from which we can push investigation and experiment." Two weeks after writing that sentence Mayo visited the Hawthorne Works for the first time.[36]

Mayo's incorporation into the Hawthorne experiments resulted from the intervention of John D. Rockefeller, Jr.'s, corporate associates. When Mayo moved to Harvard, it had been agreed that he would maintain close contact with members of the Rockefeller interests involved in industrial relations issues. In 1926 Rockefeller, Jr., had financed the establishment of Industrial Relations Counselors, Inc., to provide research and guidance to large companies in the development of personnel policies. The need for such an organization had been demonstrated by the large amount of corporate advising conducted by Rockefeller's law firm since he had encouraged the development of employee representation plans. Secretary of the company was Arthur H. Young, a former manager at Colorado Fuel and Iron and former director of industrial relations at International Harvester, where he had implemented the Rockefeller-sponsored representation plan. Young and the staff of Industrial Relations Counselors maintained a close watch on Mayo's work, a situation encouraged by Dean Donham, who felt that their oversight ensured that the research would be guided by the practical requirements of Mayo's corporate underwriters.[37]

Young was also a member of a complementary organization of personnel executives from major corporations, most of which had implemented employee representation plans after the war. Formed in 1919, the Special Conference Committee included representatives from Bethlehem Steel, Du Pont, General Electric, General Motors, Goodyear, International Harvester, Standard Oil of New Jersey, U.S. Rubber, Westinghouse, and, from 1925, AT&T. Presumably concerned about antitrust investigations, the organization was secret: There was no letterhead, telephone, or bank account, and minutes of meetings were marked "confidential." Edward S. Cowdrick, like Young a former executive at Colorado Fuel and Iron, acted as secretary, organizing the monthly meetings in New York at which executives would discuss developments in industrial relations. In November 1927, at Young's request, Mayo addressed the group at the Harvard Club in New York; among those present were E. K. Hall, vice-president in charge of industrial relations of AT&T, W. A. Griffin, assistant vice-president of AT&T, and T. K. Stevenson, personnel director of Western Electric. During the lunch Mayo talked with Stevenson from Western Electric and learned that the company was conducting experiments on the effect of rest periods at its

[36] Emily Osborne, "What Is the Future of the Industrial Research Department?" [early 1930], EM/3.073; the blood pressure data are gathered in charts in EM/3.084. Quote from Mayo to Ruml, 11 Apr. 1928, LSRM/53/572.

[37] Fosdick to Rockefeller, Jr., 7 May 1926, OMR/2/2F/16/127; Donham to Ruml, 14 Dec. 1926, LSRM/53/572.

Hawthorne Works. Mayo's message and style of address were a great success. Young informed Mayo that "they are all of them in sympathy with your methods and I think would not have as much confidence in anyone else. You will be able to get the unstinted cooperation of every member of the group."[38]

Five months later Mayo was invited by Stevenson to come to Hawthorne and observe the relay test room experiments. As we have seen, Mayo's participation in the relay test was restricted to taking blood pressure measurements and speculating about the physiological causes of the behavior of the two workers removed from the test room. Mayo's suggestion that Emily Osborne be permitted to make more detailed observations of the mental state of the workers was politely ignored by the Hawthorne researchers, who were still trying to define an appropriate role for their outside consultants.

Mayo returned from his trip to England in the summer of 1928 imbued with confidence that, in collaboration with the Hawthorne researchers, he could make original contributions to the "intelligent control of men and situations." In his discussions with members of the British Industrial Fatigue Research Board, Mayo learned that their research was suffering from the same problems that Mayo had encountered in Philadelphia – lack of funds, industry's obsession with short-term results, and the difficulties of trying to observe workers and alter variables without interfering with production. The research at Hawthorne offered a unique opportunity to become involved in experiments that were instigated by company managers who were prepared to devote considerable resources to research.[39]

It soon became apparent to both the Hawthorne researchers and the Western Electric executives in New York that Mayo was the ideal person to be entrusted with presenting the findings of the relay assembly test to a wider audience. At first they were concerned that Mayo's interests were too academic. A report that Mayo had written for Donham and Ruml on his English trip and intellectual orientations had been circulated among Western Electric managers, presumably by Arthur Young; personnel director F. W. Willard confessed to Pennock at Hawthorne that much of the report was "clean over my head." However, Pennock reassured Willard that Mayo's visit to the plant in October 1928 had been very productive; most important,

[38] Young to Mayo, 22 Nov. 1927, EM/1.102. The activities and documents of the Special Conference Committee were obtained by the U.S. Senate in the late 1930s; see U.S. Senate, Committee on Education and Labor, *Violations of Free Speech and the Rights of Labor. Hearings. Part 45, "The Special Conference Committee,"* Washington, D.C.: U.S. Government Printing Office, 1939, esp. 16785–9.
[39] Mayo to W. B. Donham, [17 Sept. 1928], LSRM/53/57, quote on 16. For repeated discussions by the British researchers of the constraints on their research, see the annual reports of the Industrial Fatigue Research Board, esp. its *Second Annual Report*, London, 1921, 5–8, and *Third Annual Report*, London, 1922, 28–35.

Mayo had proved himself adept at talking "in words of one syllable which we could readily understand."[40]

A further opportunity to test Mayo soon arose. In part because Mayo was enthusiastically spreading news of the experiments, the personnel managers in the New York headquarters of Western Electric began to receive requests from other companies and researchers for further information about the experiments. After considerable discussion between the personnel managers and company executives, it was agreed that a report would be presented to a luncheon meeting of personnel directors of corporations allied with the Special Conference Committee. The secrecy stemmed from an attitude, deeply ingrained in Bell System managers, that the public image of the companies had to be carefully protected. While the New York personnel managers felt that the Hawthorne research might prove to be, as Willard acknowledged, "the biggest contribution to the problem of management that has ever been made in the System," they were cautious about releasing reports that might attract unnecessary and unwelcome attention to the system, especially in the sensitive area of industrial relations. The New York managers were clearly impressed by Mayo's presentation of the Hawthorne research to the Special Conference Committee lunch, Willard writing to Pennock:

> He unquestionably has a true scientific spirit. That is evidenced by the fact that he took particular pains to give you complete credit. I personally feel that you could not have done better than to cultivate him for technical advice. He is wholly disinterested so far as personal gain is concerned. The next time I see you I want to talk over a number of things about the future development of your contact with him.

Clair Turner's name never came up in these discussions; his role was confined solely to assisting Hibarger in the relay assembly test. Although the evidence is inconclusive, it seems probable that Pennock and Willard found Turner unsatisfactory because they felt he was domineering and would take over the experiments if given too great a role.[41]

By early 1929 Western Electric was so pleased with Mayo's contributions to the research that Pennock offered him a job as director of one of the new research projects at Hawthorne, the program to interview all workers at the plant. But Mayo was unwilling to take on that responsibility on either a part-time or full-time basis; he proposed to Pennock that he continue to visit Hawthorne occasionally "to extend and intensify your inquiries" and hinted that the company might place him on a retainer. Accordingly, for the next four years Mayo received an annual retainer of $2,500 from West-

[40] Willard to Pennock, 16 Oct. 1928, HSCM/159, G6–7; Mayo to Donham, [17 Sept. 1928], LSRM/53/572; Pennock to Willard, 25 Oct. 1928, HSCM/159, G1–2.
[41] Willard to Pennock, 1 Oct. 1928, HSCM/159, F13–14; Willard to Pennock, 2 Nov. 1928, HSCM/159, G4.

ern Electric, in addition to the reimbursement of his expenses. Mayo also received the imprimatur and financial backing of Arthur Young, who offered him a retainer of $1,000 per annum to act as a consultant for Industrial Relations Counselors. Mayo accepted the retainer, and his assistant, Emily Osborne, also received $1,000 per annum as payment for the preparation of monthly reports describing Mayo's and his colleagues' research. Mayo reciprocated by arranging for Young to be appointed as an occasional lecturer in industrial relations at Harvard. These payments reflected the commitment by all parties that Mayo should take on the strategic role of communicating the results of the ongoing research at Hawthorne through the network.[42]

This informal network was strengthened by the establishment of a formal research organization at Hawthorne that gave the experiments a secure institutional base inside the factory. In November 1928, Western Electric president Edgar S. Bloom and other top executives visited Hawthorne and were impressed with the personnel research program, which now included the relay assembly test and new programs in interviewing and supervisory training. Willard in New York assured Pennock:

> [The] work that you are doing... is fundamental to our whole problem of employee–management relations, and out of it I believe can come a new technique of management.... I believe that this can be accomplished only by careful, painstaking, controlled experiments such as the ones you have conducted. From these experiments I believe that most of the essential data can be obtained to direct all of our employee relations policies.[43]

Approval was given for the establishment of an Industrial Research Division within the Industrial Relations Branch at Hawthorne. Chief of the division was Mark L. Putnam, who had worked in personnel positions at Hawthorne for four years since graduating from college. The division comprised four departments: the Employee Relations Research Department, where the employee interviewing program was directed by H. A. Wright, also a young college graduate; the Supervisory Training Department, headed by Putnam; and a Research Studies Department, in which Hibarger directed the test rooms. In August 1929 an Industrial Development Department, led by F. E. Byron, was created to undertake analysis of the interview material. The 1929 budget for the division totaled $112,000, and by the end of the year fifty-eight people were employed in its activities. Although this was only a fraction of the $7 million spent annually by the Bell System on personnel activities, it indicated a huge commitment by the company to personnel research.[44]

[42] Mayo to Pennock, 25 Mar. 1929, EM/1.088 (quote); Pennock to Mayo, 3 Apr. 1929, EM/1.088; Young to Mayo, 24 Jan. 1929, EM/1.103.
[43] Willard to Pennock, 2 Nov. 1928, HSCM/159, G4; Willard to Pennock, 28 Feb. 1929, HSCM/160, C11–13.
[44] "Organization of Industrial Research Division, 6088," HSCM/131, D4; "Plan for the In-

Expansion of the research at Hawthorne was paralleled by a substantial increase in funding of the Harvard researchers by the Rockefeller philanthropies. The impetus came not from Mayo and Henderson, but from David L. Edsall, dean of the Harvard Medical School. As a newly appointed trustee of the Rockefeller Foundation, Edsall had participated in the reorganization of the philanthropies in 1927–8, which saw the Laura Spelman Rockefeller Memorial and the International Health Board absorbed into the Rockefeller Foundation. The foundation was now dedicated to the "advancement and application of knowledge," with divisions encompassing the medical sciences, natural sciences, social sciences, and humanities. In 1929 Edsall submitted a proposal to the foundation that would have consolidated the Rockefeller philanthropies' funding of medical and related research at Harvard and expanded the funding to incorporate several other medical and public health researchers.[45]

In the event, Edsall's proposal did not meet with the approval of the Rockefeller officials, who correctly perceived it to be an attempt to win funding for a diverse array of quite unrelated projects. The Rockefeller Foundation did, however, agree in April 1930 to increase the funding to Mayo and Henderson so that they could appoint additional assistants, and it gave them a research fund that they could allocate to researchers working on projects relevant to their own. The foundation authorized the sum of $875,000 over seven years for "research in industrial hazards"; Mayo and Henderson would each receive roughly $50,000 per annum for their projects, while the remaining $25,000 per annum would go into the fluid research fund. While Edsall felt slighted because his proposal had been rejected, Mayo and Henderson were significantly better off because of Edsall's influence; they would now receive an annual sum three times that of the Memorial grant, and this at the outset of the Great Depression, which affected even the Rockefeller Foundation.[46]

Mayo's involvement with the Hawthorne experiments was attractive to the philanthropy officers for a number of reasons. The research promised a technology of social control that could confront problems of industrial unrest and individual maladjustment among workers. But just as important, any discoveries and techniques should be more generally applicable to so-

dustrial Research Division Program During 1929," HSCM/150, A2–7; "Plan for 1930 Activity of the Industrial Research Division," HSCM/104, E4–5. Information on the background and careers of Hawthorne managers is meager, especially those of division level or below; it has been gleaned from personnel files and organization charts at Western Electric and from the *Hawthorne Microphone*.

45 D. L. Edsall, "Memorandum," RF/200S/343/4081, sent to the Rockefeller Foundation in September 1929. On the reorganization of the Rockefeller philanthropies, see Robert E. Kohler, "A Policy for the Advancement of Science: The Rockefeller Foundation, 1924–1929," *Minerva*, 1978, 16: 480–515.

46 Rockefeller Foundation docket, "Harvard University: Research in Industrial Hazards," 16 Apr. 1930, RF/200S/342/4069; Edsall to Day, 3 Apr. 1930, RF/200S/342/4069.

ciety and to all individuals; industry simply provided a preferred arena of study, and one where implementation was more direct. Edsall had stressed this point in his discussions with the foundation officials, pointing out that whereas much of the research in psychology and psychiatry was conducted on the "mixed clientele of a hospital," industry consisted of relatively homogeneous groups of workers operating under similar and controllable conditions. "Industrial operatives are, therefore, more than other groups or the people at large, subject to deliberate changes in and control of conditions in ways that may clarify knowledge of both cause and control of disorders." The relay assembly test room was to stand as proxy for all problems of behavior and social control.[47]

The Rockefeller Foundation grant constituted the last major institutional link in the development of the network surrounding the Hawthorne experiments. Mayo and his Harvard colleagues were now able to expand their research, free of financial constraints during the depression, and the Hawthorne researchers were members of a rapidly expanding Industrial Research Division that enjoyed the personal support of New York executives. Meanwhile, Arthur Young of Industrial Relations Counselors glided behind the scenes in New York, ensuring that Rockefeller officials, Bell executives, and corporation personnel directors understood the importance of the research being conducted in Chicago.

Mayo moved easily through the network, articulating those elements of the experiments that would appeal to the various parties. He enjoyed and was skilled at this social interaction. Two or three times a year he would pay a visit to the Hawthorne plant for a few days, where he conferred with the researchers and managers and talked with foremen and workers. Mayo was both pleased and amused that Western Electric accorded him the status of company executive when he visited Chicago, putting him up at the luxurious Palmer House hotel and providing a limousine. He described the scene to his wife:

> Every morning at 8.30 the doorman clears the taxis away from the Wabash St. entrance of this hotel – and a large limousine with a uniformed chauffeur slides noiselessly in. The door is opened and Elton Mayo, formerly of South Australia, gets in and glides off to his alleged industrial researches.[48]

Frequently he would return via New York, where he would meet with Arthur Young, Western Electric personnel managers, and Rockefeller Foundation

---

[47] Edsall, "Memorandum," quotes on 4. For an overview of the organization of the social sciences in the United States in the 1920s and the role of the Rockefeller philanthropies, see Franz Samelson, "Organizing for the Kingdom of Behavior: Academic Battles and Organizational Policies in the Twenties," *Journal of the History of the Behavioral Sciences,* 1985, 21: 33–47; and Donald Fisher, "The Role of Philanthropic Foundations in the Reproduction and Production of Hegemony: Rockefeller Foundations and the Social Sciences," *Sociology,* 1983, 17: 206–33.

[48] Mayo to Dorothea Mayo, 3–7 Sept. [1929], EM/film.

Figure 7. Elton Mayo. The symbolism of the photo is revealing: Mayo is holding in his fingers some data from an industrial experiment; once it has passed through his head it becomes the "objective" knowledge in the books on the shelves behind. This photograph was taken in 1946, just before Mayo's retirement. From *Fortune*, November 1946.

officials to fill them in on the latest developments at Hawthorne. Back in Cambridge, Massachusetts, Henderson and Mayo's assistants in the research became his closest friends. Nearly every summer Mayo sailed to England, where he paid visits to his friends among British social scientists and industrial researchers and kept them informed on the progress of the Hawthorne research.

These institutional and personal connections formed a network that served as the foundation for the remainder of the research and was critical for the stabilization and dissemination of the Hawthorne experiments. But it was a network, not a single organism, and different participants had significantly varied opinions on the events at Hawthorne. In the following two chapters I will analyze the other major Hawthorne research projects. From 1928 to 1930 the researchers undertook a massive program of interviewing the entire Hawthorne workforce and developed a new supervisory training program based on insights drawn from the interviews. Then in late 1931 the researchers began a new test room, where they conducted an anthropological study of the social organization of the workplace. The structure of the research and the interpretations of the results reveal the tensions between the practical concerns of the company researchers and the intellectual commitments of the academics and also highlight the different disciplinary interests and political concerns of Mayo and his colleagues.

5

The psychopathology of industrial life

WHEN THE INDUSTRIAL RESEARCH DIVISION was established at Hawthorne in late 1928, most of its energies were directed at the development of two new personnel research programs. These were the interviewing program, in which all workers in the factory were asked to comment on every facet of their work at Hawthorne, and the supervisory training program, which attempted to probe supervisors' attitudes toward their work and inculcate a new style of supervision. In both programs the researchers were hoping to disseminate the findings and approaches developed in the relay assembly test room into the Hawthorne Works as a whole. The interviews were an extension of the interviews with the test room workers and the records of their conversations; the program was to provide a window for the researchers onto the attitudes and reactions of the workforce. The new forms of supervisory training were designed to create throughout the entire factory the friendly supervisor–employee relations that it was believed had developed in the test room. Interviewing and supervisory training symbolized the new status accorded personnel research at Hawthorne. They involved taking the work of the research division to every corner of the plant; the researchers hoped that in a short time they would reach every worker and supervisor. And the programs underscored the growing conviction of the researchers that only personnel managers trained in psychopathology and human relations could perceive the actual personal and social relations of the workplace.

Elton Mayo had a considerable influence on the interviewing and supervisory training programs as they developed, introducing the company researchers to his psychopathological techniques and theories. In the relay assembly test room, Mayo's role had been primarily that of commentator on the test reports, and the only application of his physiological and psychopathological model was to provide an explanation for Irene Rybacki's uncooperative behavior. But Mayo became an active collaborator in the new research programs, visiting regularly and keeping in touch through regular correspondence and exchange of documents. In addition, several of Mayo's assistants and colleagues were drawn into the research; in particular,

Fritz Roethlisberger would play a major role in transmitting Mayo's ideas to the company researchers. In Philadelphia and again in Boston, Mayo had been frustrated in his attempts to tap the personal situations and reveries of workers; but at Hawthorne an entire research division was soon adopting his interview techniques and sending him the resulting transcripts.

Interviewing the workers

The interviewing program at Hawthorne was a response to two developments, both of which suggested the need for closer attention to employee–supervisor relations and to the training of supervisors. First, the progress reports from the relay assembly test room emphasized that supervisory styles could have important effects on worker attitudes and hence on production. The third report of June 1928 in particular had implied that the aggressive style of supervisors could adversely affect the output of workers, many of whom were thought to be emotionally sensitive, and it had suggested that ways could be found to improve supervisory techniques. Second, the rapid expansion of the Hawthorne workforce in the late 1920s required the selection and training of a large number of supervisors. Employment at Hawthorne almost doubled between 1927 and 1929, from 21,929 to 40,272 workers. Supervisors were also being transferred from Hawthorne to establish departments at the plant in Kearny, New Jersey, opened in 1923, and more would soon be leaving when the company opened its third factory, in Baltimore. Surveying the situation in 1929, Western Electric president Edgar Bloom regarded the provision of "experienced supervisory personnel" as the company's largest problem.[1]

George Pennock, recently promoted to assistant works manager, elaborated on these problems in an evening address to supervisors of the Inspection Branch at Hawthorne in September 1928. Noting that the tenth commandment of the company's personnel policy was "to carry on the daily work in a spirit of friendliness," he suggested that this could be achieved only if each supervisor was able to "establish a condition of trust and friendly cooperation among his employees." For Pennock and his fellow managers, the factory was a large family, the supervisors parents and the workers children – indeed, the works manager, C. L. Rice, liked to be referred to as "Dad." Pennock argued that supervisors had to be more keenly aware of the emotional nature of their subordinates: "The average employee at the bottom of the industry is keenly sensitive in matters of human relationship. Emotions are stronger and minor matters of greater importance among these people, whose fields of vision are limited and whose interests are few." Citing the relay test results, he argued that it was possible to lead workers

[1] RATR, Progress Report No. 3, 30 June 1928, sec. VIII, 3, HSCM/5–6, D1; E. S. Bloom to C. P. Cooper, 1 April 1929, AT&T/45.

much further than it was possible to drive them; proper supervision would relieve workers of nervous tension and result in increased output. Pennock painted a rosy picture of the test room results: "We have succeeded in establishing a relationship of confidence and friendship with these operators to such an extent that practically no supervision is required and we can depend upon them to do their part in the absence of any drive or urge whatsoever." This was only eight months after the removal of two workers from the relay test room and demonstrates how the researchers were able to rationalize the episode as one of "noncooperation" in the experiment rather than a supervisory problem of who would control the pace of production.[2]

The interviewing program was introduced as a means of identifying existing problems in employee–supervisor relations and of gauging the effects of an expanded supervisory training program. It was expected that interviews with workers would provide a picture of the morale of the workers, their likes and dislikes, and their attitudes toward their bosses. Interviewing was to provide on a large scale the kind of window onto worker attitudes and responses that had been achieved on a more intimate scale in the relay test. Workers' comments were to be used in three ways. Consistently unfavorable comments about working conditions could be used as a basis for corrective action, where possible. Compilations of representative comments, favorable and unfavorable, would provide a "picture of the thoughts and feelings of workers." And comments on supervision would be discussed in conference groups of supervisors and used as the basis for a supervisory manual.[3]

The implication of the interviewing program was that the Hawthorne researchers were broadening their research to encompass the supervisor as well as the worker, and Pennock spent considerable time trying to allay supervisors' fears. After all, it was being proposed that interviewers from outside a department come in and talk to workers about the quality of their immediate supervisors, a situation that could potentially undermine their authority on the shop floor. Interviews, Pennock insisted, would be kept strictly confidential. This was necessary if workers were to be persuaded to open up to the interviewer, without fear of retribution from their boss; it was also essential in order to protect individual supervisors. Material taken from the interviews for use in training conferences would be carefully edited to remove any names or other identifying material. Nevertheless, there was a veiled threat in the program, for Pennock hinted that follow-up interviews

[2] G. A. Pennock, "Talk Introducing the Interviewing Program to Inspection Branch Supervisors," 13 Sept. 1928, quotes on 2–3, HSCM/107, F1–14; Pennock "Talk to Division Chief Conference, 27 November 1928," quote on 2, HSCM/145, G8–145A, A9.

[3] "Summary Outline of Employee Interviewing Program, Inspection Branch, September 1928 to February 1929," HSCM/109, A3–9.

might be used to establish whether supervisors had put lessons from the conferences into practice.

The interviewing program spread rapidly. Five interviewers, all supervisors, interviewed the 1,600 workers in the Inspection Branch between September 1928 and January 1929. The plan was then extended to the Operating Branch, which included the main manufacturing departments at Hawthorne, where there were some 12,000 nonsupervisory employees. With the establishment of the Industrial Research Division in January 1929, all aspects of interviewing were controlled by the Employee Relations Research Department, headed by Harold Wright. For the next two years, until blanket interviewing was suspended at the end of 1930, Wright and his colleagues, in collaboration with the Harvard academics, directed a huge enterprise. They grappled with problems of interviewing techniques, training of interviewers, as well as analysis and interpretation and tried to gauge the effect the interviews themselves were having on the workforce.

The initial form of the interview emerged after a process of trial and error by the early interviewers. An interviewer would normally contact a worker through the supervisor, then shift to a quiet place nearby or to the company restaurant. Here the interviewer would explain the program to the worker, emphasize the confidentiality of the material, and invite the worker to comment on anything relating to work; questions were often needed to get the worker talking. The worker's comments were noted at the time, then later organized by the interviewer into three categories: plantwide working conditions, the worker's particular job, and the supervisors. Each category was subdivided into likes and dislikes. Records of the names, numbers, and departments of workers interviewed were kept by each interviewer, but the typed interview itself had no identifying marks other than date, branch, and sex of the worker. The form of the interview transcript reflected the concerns of the researchers, who were interested in aggregate reactions of the workforce rather than the individual worker and sought material that could be used in supervisory training.[4]

The workers responded to the interviewing program with mixed feelings, surprised that management wanted to listen to their complaints, uncertain of the guarantees of confidentiality, and skeptical whether the company would act on their comments. In time this crystallized into either support for the program or cynicism about its purpose and likely outcomes, dutifully recorded by the interviewers as they listened to the workers:

> I would never think of going up to the office with the things I've told you, because I know I would be found out and this way I know that the Company is going to find out how many people are dissatisfied and

---

[4] "Resume of Methods and Practices, Employee Interviewing Program," [1929], HSCM/104, A2–7; A. Lemkau and J. R. White, "General Outline of Interviewing Methods Followed by the Interviewers in the Inspection Branch," [1929], HSCM/104, A9–B2.

why. I have a hunch that this man I had so much to say about is getting cold feet already, because he just hates to see the operators who are not his friends get called up to be interviewed for fear that he will be talked about, and every time one of us gets called, he gives us a dirty look, as if to try and scare us.

Say, does all this I am saying mean anything? Well, if you want my honest opinion, to me it seems like a lot of nonsense. Now I have told you about the rates, do you mean to tell me that they will be taken care of just because a few of us have kicked about them?

Well, sometimes if you tell somebody else what's on your mind it makes you feel good. It helps a lot. If you have anything that bothers you it gives you a chance to tell somebody.

You say this is confidential. Well, the way I understand it they take some of these interviews and discuss them. I relate to you a certain incident about a boss. He may recognize it and although he might not say so, he may hold it against me. A boss might even think he recognizes an interview and hold it against his help whether it is him or not.

I worked at several places but I never worked for any concern that tries to find out whether the help was satisfied or not. If you did not like what they had to offer you could quit. Here they consider the employees and try to make things nice for them.

When you first started to interview we thought the Company wanted to find out who was giving information to the Communist Paper, "The Hawthorne Worker," but as the program progressed we were convinced that the Company was really interested in finding out the actual conditions in the shop both as to the working conditions and supervision.

Our boss told me that one of these days I would be interviewed. He said I should tell the Interviewer that I get along all right with my bosses. It would not be necessary for me to tell him about the other things here.[5]

Whatever their doubts may have been, the workers were on the whole prepared to talk to the interviewers, telling them what they considered both good and bad about working at Hawthorne. When the interviewers had finished analyzing the 10,300 interviews with Operating Branch workers in 1929, they had a total of 86,426 comments from workers, consisting of favorable and unfavorable comments in almost equal numbers. Setting to one side the problems inherent in the data — such as the workers' distrust of the interviewing process, the interviewers' classification of comments, and the loss of subtleties due to the aggregation of the data — analysis of the comments gives some insight into the everyday concerns of the Hawthorne workers. The major topic the workers discussed was pay (including

---

[5] "Comments and Reactions on Interviewing Program," HSCM/122, B1–D8; "Substance Analysis of Comments on Interviewing Program," HSCM/125, F13–G11. The *Hawthorne Worker* was a radical news sheet, handed out at the factory gates, that commented on company policy, conditions of work, and even individual supervisors. Attempts to locate copies have been unsuccessful.

both wage levels and piece rates); almost 14 percent of all comments were about pay, or on average more than one comment for each worker. The other prominent topics were job placement (a broad category covering whether workers liked their job), making up 10 percent of comments, company savings plans (7 percent), supervision (5 percent), and hours of work (5 percent). The researchers were, of course, most interested in the percentage of favorable or unfavorable comments on any particular topic. Workers spoke most favorably about the company's personnel policies, including the savings plans (95 percent favorable), the Hawthorne Club's social, recreational, and educational activities (89 percent), and the company's welfare benefits (85 percent). Compared with other employers in Chicago, Western Electric was regarded by the workers as a good place to work. But there was room for improvement. Workers were especially critical of the amount of smoke and fumes in parts of the plant (95 percent of comments were unfavorable), the inadequate washrooms (one-quarter of all women commented unfavorably on this), and management's lack of concern for the health and safety of workers (almost one-third of all workers made unfavorable comments).[6]

Workers' comments on the organization of work at Hawthorne were more complex. They were moderately disapproving of working hours (53 percent unfavorable), payment (58 percent), supervision (60 percent), and the bogey system (66 percent). Nevertheless, workers considered these major issues, for they made up more than one-quarter of all comments made. Finer breakdowns of these large categories reveal the workers' views more clearly. In the case of pay, workers approved of the overall rates of pay offered at Hawthorne, which were higher than most workers could have got outside Western Electric. But they overwhelmingly disliked the predominant system of paying workers a piecework rate based on the earnings of the "gang," many workers feeling they could earn more on individual piecework. Many complained that the current piecework rates were set too low by the rating engineers, who tended to base the rates on the fastest worker and did not allow for slowdowns in production due to a delay in receiving parts or the time required to reset machines. Some reported that piece rates were lowered even when the job had not changed, requiring the workers to produce more to earn the same wage. Others complained that the bogey – a production quota set for each job by engineers, which served as the basis for calculating bonuses – was set too high or too low or was raised if workers consistently achieved it. Similarly, while workers approved of the rest periods that had been introduced following the relay assembly test, they generally disliked

[6] "A Substance Analysis of Employee Comments on Various Subjects Taken From 10,300 1929 Operating Branch Interviews," HSCM/124, B4–6; "Substance Analysis of Comments from Operating Branch Employee Interviews Taken During 1929," 2 parts, HSCM/124–30.

the large amount of night work and compulsory overtime that had been introduced to deal with the demand from the rapidly expanding Bell System. Some workers were being required by their supervisors to work a seven-day week.

In spite of elaborate personnel policies and a large personnel department, supervisors continued to have considerable power over their workers. They could shift them onto good or bad jobs, recommend them for wage increases or demote them, become friendly with them or make their working hours miserable. Comments on supervision were probably more likely to be influenced by workers' concerns that their statements might get back to their supervisor, yet 60 percent of workers who talked about their bosses made unfavorable comments. One worker complained: "These bosses don't rate very well with me. The foreman reminds me of some beast. He isn't human. When you ask him anything he grunts like a pig." Another reported: "Some time ago I was working for a Gang Boss and we got into an argument and he took me up to the old man, and when he found out that I was right he took me back and put me on all the dirty and hard jobs in the place." Other workers praised their supervisor: "I want you to put down that my foreman, Mr. X, is one of the best bosses that can be had in the Western today. He is what I call a real fellow. You will never see another fellow like him. He gets out and bowls with the boys or plays ball with them and doesn't think that he is too good to mingle with the boys. He is what I call a real honest-to-goodness foreman." But what comes out most strongly from the workers' comments about their bosses is not whether their particular foreman or gang boss was fair or unreasonable, but that the workers' experience at Hawthorne was dominated by their supervisors' extensive power and constant surveillance. One worker captured this succinctly: "No matter how much you argue with these bosses they always get their way whether it is right or wrong, and the sooner you learn that they are boss, the better off you are going to be."[7]

The researchers' use of this interviewing material changed considerably over time, especially under the impact of Mayo's increasing involvement in the research. The company researchers had initially seen interviewing as a means of compiling the collective attitudes of workers toward the organization of work at Hawthorne and toward company personnel policies. But Mayo was far more interested in the individual personalities of the workers and their individual adjustments to industrial conditions. Mayo applauded the interviewing program, seeing it as a step toward establishing the kind of "listening post" that he had attempted at Continental Mills in Philadelphia, but he exerted gentle pressure on Pennock and Wright to modify the interview so that it would capture more fully the personality of each worker.

---

[7] "Substance Analysis of Comments on Supervision," HSCM/123, C1–14, quotes from comments A-6, A-31, A-2, A-47.

During visits in 1929, Mayo lectured on interviewing techniques, taking great pains to explain that the interviewer should listen attentively, should not interrupt the worker, and should restate the workers' comments so as to elicit further material. On one memorable occasion, Mayo interviewed a worker while interviewers listened over a loudspeaker in another room, learning his technique by example. Mayo modeled his advice on his clinical experience as a psychopathologist, so much so that he sometimes assumed that the primary aim of the interview was to increase the workers' psychological self-awareness.[8]

Wright, the head of the interviewing program, was receptive to Mayo's guidance, and newly trained interviewers were soon drawing out more personal material from workers. This required a dramatic change in the format of the recorded interview. Now the interviewer tried to reproduce the interview verbatim, without editing and rearranging comments to fit the preconceived categories. Where previously the record of an interview averaged two and a half pages, it now expanded to ten pages, and the duration of the average interview leaped from thirty to ninety minutes.[9]

Mayo's major influence was to shift the interviewers' attention to what was taking place during the process of interviewing. Mayo introduced Wright and his colleagues to the work of Jean Piaget, the young Swiss psychologist who had recently published *The Child's Conception of the World* (1929). Mayo thought that Piaget's approach to the interviewing of normal children was applicable to workers at Hawthorne. Piaget used clinical interviewing to reveal to children their preoccupations, irrationalities, and subjective judgments; interviewing was a process that enabled children to reach a new understanding of their subjectivity and thus to reach a new synthesis between themselves and the environment. Mayo was attracted to Piaget because, unlike most research in psychiatry, his work was done with normal individuals and because, like Freud, Piaget held that the egocentricity of the child extended into adulthood, thereby causing continued maladjustments.[10]

The details of this approach were fleshed out by Fritz Roethlisberger, whom Mayo had sent to Hawthorne for the summer of 1930. Fritz Jules Roethlisberger, thirty-two years old, had led a life that challenged Mayo's in its diversity. Born in 1898 in New York to Swiss parents, Roethlisberger

---

[8] Mayo to Pennock, 29 Apr. 1929, HSCM/159, C6–10; Elton Mayo, "The Interview," in "A Plan for Improving Employee Relations on the Basis of Data Obtained from Employees," Project 2: Interviewing Techniques, HSCM/148–149, B1.

[9] "An Account of the Work of the Industrial Research Division, April 1931" (henceforth IRD Report, 1931), sec. 2, "Development and Use of the Employee Interview as a Research Tool," HSCM/152–3.

[10] "A Plan for Improving Employee Relations on the Basis of Data Obtained from Employees," Project 2: Interviewing Techniques, HSCM/148–9, B1; K. J. Kopplin, "The Egocentric Hypothesis," 1930, HSCM/106, D12–F5.

had studied science as an undergraduate at Columbia University before switching to MIT for a degree in engineering administration. To his dissatisfaction the MIT program consisted of the crudest form of scientific management; he later recalled that it offered little more than directions to keep the workers' toilets cold in winter and hot in summer so that they would not stay there long. By this time he regarded himself as a socialist, and after a few months of working as an engineer in Texas, he moved to Greenwich Village in New York to pursue the life of a Bohemian. At twenty-six he returned to the university, this time to pursue a Ph.D. in philosophy at Harvard, studying with Alfred North Whitehead and Etienne Gilson. But by 1927 Roethlisberger had lost interest in his dissertation on Descartes, and he spent an increasing amount of time working as a psychological counselor for Harvard students. The lack of direction in his own life took him to Mayo, probably at the suggestion of the Harvard student psychiatrist, Clifford Shaw. Roethlisberger's encounter with Mayo was a miracle; "never before had I had this kind of relation to a teacher and to an older man to whom I could state freely not only my intellectual questions but also my personal doubts, anxieties, and concerns." Soon he was employed as an instructor in industrial research at the business school, paid from the Rockefeller grant, where he worked as Mayo's assistant. Roethlisberger's debts to Mayo were personal, intellectual, and professional, and he felt a strong obligation to Mayo for having provided him with a career.[11]

Mayo intended that Roethlisberger's longer visit would consolidate his influence on the interviewing program, strengthening the psychiatric components of the interview. Roethlisberger proved to be adept at translating abstruse concepts into terms that could be grasped by Wright and his assistants. In clinical interviewing, he instructed them, it was unimportant whether the worker was telling the truth; what was important was what the individual believed to be the truth. The interviewer should treat everything the worker said as symptoms, not as facts. By grasping the "total situation" – the worker's subjective analysis as well as the objective situation – the interviewer could judge the extent to which the worker was properly adjusted to the environment. Furthermore, the process of interviewing was itself therapeutic, in the same way that the clinical methods of Piaget and Freud aided the adjustment of child or patient. The worker underwent an emotional release that diminished anxiety and even, perhaps, came to a clearer understanding of his or her subjectivity.[12]

No matter how skilled Roethlisberger and Mayo were at translating these

---

[11] Roethlisberger gives an engaging and self-effacing account of his career in Fritz Jules Roethlisberger, *The Elusive Phenomena: An Autobiographical Account of My Work in the Field of Organizational Behavior at the Harvard Business School*, Cambridge, Mass.: Harvard University, Graduate School of Business Administration, 1977; for his early life and career, see 11–44, quote on 30.

[12] F. J. Roethlisberger, "Method of Interviewing," 1930, HSCM/105, E3–G2.

concepts, a good proportion of their ideas were difficult to digest. Terms like "syncretistic formulations," "hedonistic judgments," and "egocentrism" were not readily absorbed by managers and interviewers; one interviewer later commented that when "Dr. Mayo talked I had to listen so hard and then he kind of talked over my head." Mayo sent books whose relevance to their task was not always apparent; thus, Putnam acknowledged the receipt of a book by Robert Yerkes on the social behavior of apes with the comment: "Received your book on Chim and Panzee. We don't quite see the connection as yet but we don't feel insulted about it." Humor played an important role as the Hawthorne researchers grappled with these concepts: One informal report was titled "Summary of Discussion Held This Morning as Conditioned by Having Been Verbalized Through a Transformer Called 'Howarth' – Tolerance Is Prayed for All Subjective Interpretations." The company researchers' attitude was summed up in the 1930 report on interviewing, which admitted that "some of our discussions have bordered upon the metaphysical" but suggested that "we have been kept within bounds by the necessity of eventually relating our thoughts to concrete human problems as viewed from industrial management's point of view." For his part, Mayo was well aware of the danger of his analysis of the interviews becoming too elaborate. He reduced his initial emphasis on the active role of the interviewer in bringing the worker to a clearer self-awareness and reintegration of self and environment. It was, after all, impossible to suppose that a supervisor trained in rudimentary interviewing techniques could have such an effect in a single interview, when skilled psychiatrists took many sessions to achieve the same end.[13]

Nevertheless, Mayo's emphasis on the therapeutic effect of the interview was broadly accepted by the Hawthorne researchers. A report of the Industrial Research Division noted:

> Until Doctor Mayo came along the most important uses for the interview seemed to be in Supervisory Training and Research work. As we know, he revealed what seems to be the greatest use of all – emotional release. In other words, the employee is given greater freedom to unburden himself and a chance to express his thoughts.

Simply by describing their anxieties and problems to the interviewer, workers "talked out" their problems and gained relief. This was in addition to the value the interviewing program had in persuading the workers that the company was concerned about each individual.[14]

---

[13] Quotes from "Rotational Training as Practiced in the Industrial Research Division," Interview no. 10, HSCM/142, D13–14; M. Putnam to Mayo, 12 March 1930, EM/1.089; M. Howarth to F. J. Roethlisberger, 24 August 1931; "Developments in Interviewing: A Progress Report for the Year Ending Dec. 31, 1930," 1, HSCM/105, A1–D10.

[14] "A Plan for Improving Employee Relations on the Basis of Data Obtained from Employees," Project 13, D. D. Davisson, "Special Training Course for Interviewers," HSCM/148–9, B1.

Equally important, Wright and his assistants adopted Mayo's long-held belief that workers' views about their job were as much determined by their personal situation as they were by objective conditions. Wright described in a conference of interviewers the case of a worker who complained about pay rates throughout the interview. An analysis of the interview, he suggested, showed that "what apparently was a real cause of complaint or discouragement was really not the cause at all"; the fundamental cause of the complaint was the worker's home life, specifically family sickness and debts. Much was also made of a lengthy, twenty-page interview with a woman described by her supervisor as a "chronic kicker." The worker complained repeatedly that her supervisor was stern and reprimanded the workers for the slightest error, unlike her previous, more understanding supervisors. She also talked at some length of her stepfather, who mistreated her mother and family. Given the researchers' interest in changing supervisors' behavior, it might be expected that they would accept her complaints at face value. But Wright and his assistant William Dickson were particularly taken by her comment that her supervisor reminded her of her stepfather and believed that they had found the source of her discontent at work in her home life. They concluded that "although scarcely anything escapes her condemnation, it is obvious that our problem would not be eliminated were we to consider her remarks at face value and attempt to 'correct' those things she complains about." They did not consider that the young woman might simply be describing how her life was dominated by two tyrannical men.[15]

Of course, as Dickson admitted, it was not exactly clear what was the cause and what the effect; for example, the worker who complained about low rates of pay may have been in debt precisely because his wages were low. (Bill Dickson was particularly sensitive to these issues; he had taken a summer job as an interviewer in 1929 to support himself through the Ph.D. in economics he had started at the University of Chicago the previous year. In the event, he liked the work, abandoned his studies, and stayed with the company until his retirement.) Dickson was relieved that interviewers were not explaining every complaint about pay and piece rates in terms of the worker's personal situation and that in most cases they felt that the worker had a legitimate grievance. While the company researchers were reluctant to use the psychopathological approach to undermine all worker complaints, Mayo consistently dismissed worker unrest as manifestations of psychological disturbance.

An unresolved tension existed within the interviewing program, brought about by the different perspectives of the company researchers and the

[15] "A Plan for Improving Employee Relations on the Basis of Data Obtained from Employees," Project 1, W. J. Dickson, "Evaluation of Interviews," 13–14, HSCM/148–9, B1; IRD Report, 1931, Sample Interview, HSCM/152, F5–G11.

academics. On the one hand, the interviews were intended to be a technique for identifying legitimate worker complaints, which would then be used to change personnel policies and to train supervisors. On the other hand, the interviews apparently opened a window onto the seething personal life of the individual worker, whose complaints were perhaps determined by irrational drives and unconscious associations. The Hawthorne researchers had to balance these approaches, for the interviewers often found it difficult to determine what type of analysis they should use. The solution was essentially administrative: Discussion of the psychopathological approach was increasingly confined to a small group of company researchers, primarily in Wright's Employee Relations Research Department, while the interviewers' task was regimented through training and manuals. Further, a separate Industrial Development Department was added in August 1929 to attend to the statistical analysis of employee comments; members of this department were not involved in thorny problems of interpretation or meaning – here comments were treated as facts.[16]

Analyzation, as it was called, was a massive clerical task. Each interview transcript was analyzed in detail, and every comment, whether favorable or unfavorable, was extracted and entered on three-inch by five-inch slips of paper. These were then categorized by subject matter and by the department and branch from which the comment came. In 1930 almost 13,000 interviews were analyzed and 86,300 comments were extracted. With the exception of comments on supervision, which were used solely in supervisory training, copies of the comments were sent to the investigation organizations of the various branches, where it was expected that managers would follow up on complaints that could be remedied. Meanwhile, in the Analyzation Department, detailed consideration of comments on a particular subject was expected to reveal worker attitudes on any topic, while taken together they would form a picture of employee morale throughout the plant.[17]

In the first instance, the interviews served as a conduit for worker complaints to managers, circumventing the first two or three levels of supervisors. For example, the Safety and Health Division was directed by workers' comments to several cases of unsafe working conditions; in all, the safety division investigated seventy-two departments during 1930. Managers and supervisors did not always respond in the manner expected. When the supervisors of the Hospital Division gathered to discuss the complaints addressed at the hospital and its staff – notably that doctors gave too little credence to workers' descriptions of their illnesses and were too keen to get

---

[16] On the confusion among interviewers regarding the direction to be taken in interview analysis and the need to keep the two functions separate, see Roethlisberger to H. A. Wright, 11 Sept. 1930, HSCM/159, F2–5.

[17] "The Growth of Analyzation," HSCM/133, E1–8; IRD Report, 1931, 13–18, HSCM/152, D1–6.

them back on the job – the researchers noted caustically that "all discussion was of a defensive nature. Little or nothing constructive came from this meeting."[18]

The second aspect of analyzation consisted of the preparation of reports that provided a statistical account of comments on a single subject, a sample of favorable and unfavorable comments, and a discussion of the employee attitudes revealed by these figures and comments. Whereas the individual branches and divisions were addressing specific complaints, these reports were intended to provide the basis for setting factory policy. On rare occasions these reports could be critical of existing company practices. The bogey system attracted special criticism; the researchers concluded that the interviews showed that bogeys had been established in an arbitrary manner and that supervisors had done a poor job of explaining and selling the system. But, taken overall, the interview analyses concentrated on ways of increasing worker acceptance of existing policies; they never presented comments in a form which conceded that workers might have a coherent alternative view.[19]

Conclusions that undermined workers' comments were especially evident when the complaints were directed not at the conditions of work or personnel policies, but at the job itself. The report on fatigue suggested that fatigue was as much a mental attitude as a physical condition attributable to long hours; echoing Mayo, it played down the problem by stressing the complexity of factors involved. The report on worker comments concerning monotony went even further. It argued that since workers differed over whether repetitive work was monotonous, it was impossible to say that any particular kind of work induced monotony. Because only a small percentage of workers complained about monotonous jobs, one could assume that such comments were attributable to the mental attitude of individual workers, not to the work itself. At any rate, it concluded, workers fell into the jobs that suited them; in particular, "women by nature can work and dream of other things and be perfectly satisfied on the job, thus we find them employed in the types of work which permit this condition."[20]

The limitations of existing analyzation soon became apparent to the researchers, especially Roethlisberger and Dickson, one of the most research-

---

[18] "Results Obtained from the Study and Use of Employee Complaints," HSCM/131, A1–B5; "Safety and Health Division, Meetings of Supervisors," 1930–1, HSCM/133, A1–C10, "Summary of Conclusions Drawn from a Study of 2195 Comments on Hospital," HSCM/134, C14–D7; "Minutes of Meetings with Supervisors of the Hospital Division," HSCM/133.

[19] "Substance Analysis of Comments from Operating Branch Employee Interviews taken during 1929," HSCM/124–30; "Summary of Conclusions Drawn from a Study of 2133 Comments on Bogey," HSCM/133, G1–6.

[20] "Summary of Employee Comments on Fatigue," HSCM/134, A4–C10; "Conclusions Drawn from a Study of 571 Comments on Monotony," quote on 4, HSCM/134, E9–13.

oriented members of the research division. Complaints amenable to direct action could be investigated and remedied, worker attitudes toward a particular issue could be reconstructed, and material could be used in supervisory training. But the analysis was limited in that it did not permit the correlation of an individual worker's comments on different issues or relate these comments to the worker's personal situation. In the summer of 1932 Roethlisberger attempted to remedy this by tabulating 522 interviews so that the degree of dissatisfaction with work (none, mild, or extreme) could be correlated with other variables, including the worker's department, age, sex, working hours, payment system, home responsibilities, education, average earnings, type of work, nationality, nativity, dominant posture at work, and the interviewer. Mayo and Roethlisberger obviously expected that the personal situation of the worker would correlate highly with degree of dissatisfaction. Instead, the highest correlation with dissatisfaction was the worker's department (0.301 for women); the coefficients of correlation for personal situation were very low (0.138 for women). The results tended to undermine the assumption that the workers' psychological states were the major determinant of their attitudes toward work. It is notable that this study was not reported in *Management and the Worker* nor in any other published accounts of the experiments.[21]

Workers on the whole seem to have approved of the interviewing program, if we accept the researchers' assessment of workers' attitudes toward interviewing. It seemed to have a salutary effect on supervisors' behavior; in combination with supervisory training, it provided a channel for worker complaints, which were remedied in at least some instances; it allowed workers to "get things off their chests," as the researchers liked to express it; and the program demonstrated that the company cared about its workforce. The researchers were encouraged when comments showed that workers accepted that it was better to direct complaints to the interviewer than to take collective action against management. As one worker put it:

> I think interviewing is a good idea. It helps some people get a lot of things off their chest. I think my supervisor is much better since they are interviewing. When they first started to interview in my sister's department, somebody said this Company wanted to find out who puts those articles in the *Hawthorne Worker*. I don't think there is any sense to that stuff that they write in that paper. I think if anybody has anything to say they would advantage more by it if they would tell everything to the interviewer than by putting it in that paper.[22]

Thus, although the interviewing program actively sought workers' complaints, it did so in a way that encouraged workers to see themselves as

[21] F. J. Roethlisberger, "A Statistical Analysis of Employee Interviews," 1 June 1932, EM/3.090. For private criticisms of the work of Byron's department, see Dickson to Roethlisberger, 16 Feb. 1931, FJR/1, and Roethlisberger to Mayo, 20 July 1931, EM/1.090.
[22] "Comments and Reactions on Interviewing Program."

isolated individuals who could influence their work environment only by making complaints through the system, whether to the interviewer or to their supervisor. Moreover, worker complaints were collected individually, and the researchers were then free to compile the data and construct what they believed were workers' attitudes.

Many workers saw interviewing as a positive step because they lacked any experience of formal collective action, either through trade unions or even employee representation plans. With the exception of a small number of skilled male workers, the factory workers were not unionized; unlike the rest of the Bell System, Western Electric had not even introduced an employee representation plan. Many of the young women and men who took unskilled jobs at Western Electric during its expansion in the middle and late 1920s were the children of immigrants from Europe. They lived in Chicago's ethnically segregated working-class communities – conservative, inward-looking communities in which people worked hard to buy a house and achieve individual success in their new country. Meanwhile, as in the rest of the United States, Chicago's trade unions were on the defensive in the 1920s, their membership declining in the face of "open-shop" campaigns. When in 1929 the craft-based unions did begin to regroup, they sought first to build membership in their traditional trades. More radical workers at Hawthorne produced the *Hawthorne Worker* – the Communist Party in Chicago encouraged the publication of plant newspapers as a means of organizing rank-and-file groups – but they seem to have had little success.[23]

Some workers were openly cynical about the interviewing program, expressing doubt that there would be any permanent change in the attitudes of supervisors or that the company would address any but the simplest complaints. In the latter instance they were clearly correct. Managers were prepared to act on complaints, especially about the working environment, that required simple ameliorative action. But they ignored complaints about wage scales and actively attacked the idea that many of the jobs were monotonous. Nevertheless, although many workers might remain skeptical about the program, only the most committed would risk their jobs by joining those handing out the *Hawthorne Worker* at the factory gates. And the workers could have no influence on the interpretations developed by the researchers and thus on the image of the typical worker fed back into the supervisory training program.

An industrial psychologist at the University of Chicago, Arthur Kornhauser, shared the concerns of workers who doubted that interviewing

[23] On the Chicago labor movement in the 1920s, see Lizabeth Ann Cohen, "Learning to Live in the Welfare State: Industrial Workers in Chicago Between the Wars, 1919–1939," Ph.D. dissertation, University of California, Berkeley, 1986; Barbara Warne Newell, *Chicago and the Labor Movement: Metropolitan Unionism in the 1930s*, Urbana: University of Illinois Press, 1961.

would result in any significant changes in the organization of work at Hawthorne. Kornhauser was invited to comment on a talk by Mark Putnam to the Industrial Relations Association of Chicago in March 1930; Kornhauser was qualified for the task because he had visited the Hawthorne Works several times during the course of the experiments and talked to the company researchers. Kornhauser praised the research as "extremely valuable," but he spelled out what he saw as some major weaknesses in the interviewing program. He doubted that interviewing would make workers feel that the company had a personal interest in them, when the whole system of work at Hawthorne was so large and impersonal. At any rate, he wondered, was interviewing as effective as a system in which workers were always at liberty to make complaints and suggestions? Interviewing might help workers get things off their chests, but he doubted that this feeling would last more than a few weeks:

> What is needed is an actual change in conditions: If it is a matter of my being dissatisfied with promotional possibilities, the fact I have not been promoted, or with my wage or my working conditions, the arrangement of my work or the way my tools are kept, how good my tools are, the kind of chair I have to sit on, merely getting those things off my mind, I fancy, is not going to help me very much.

If their complaints were not addressed by the company, what would be the workers' attitudes toward interviewing by the time of their third or fourth annual interview?[24]

The Hawthorne researchers did not have to face this last problem, because the worsening effects of the depression brought an end to the interviewing program. Plans to interview the entire workforce in 1930 were never achieved, primarily because the lengthening of interviews and the preparation of more detailed transcripts undermined initial targets. For 1931 the Industrial Research Division proposed to dispense with the mass interviewing program, both because of its cost and because the researchers had come to realize that a single interview told them little about each worker. As a personnel program, interviewing was declared a success: It provided information that could guide personnel policy and supervisory training, it made workers feel that their needs were recognized by management and that they were participating fully in the company, and it permitted the release of irrational and emotional elements that might otherwise disturb production. As a research program, interviewing was seen by 1931 as a useful beginning in the analysis of worker attitudes, but limited in that it dispersed research resources across the factory rather than concentrating them on small groups of workers, who could then be studied more intensively. The senior researchers in the Industrial Research Division focused on the establishment

[24] Arthur Kornhauser, comments on M. L. Putnam's "Improving Employee Relations," Industrial Relations Association of Chicago, 10 Mar. 1930, quote on 4, HSCM/162, A3–8.

of the bank wiring test room, where workers would be closely observed and regularly interviewed.[25]

The role of the supervisor

Both the interviewing program and supervisory training program were designed to deal with perceived weaknesses in employee relations at Hawthorne. Interviewing provided a mechanism for middle- and upper-level managers to learn of workers' attitudes toward work and supervision without having to rely on immediate supervisors for the information. It was based on the assumption that the functions of organizing and motivating workers could not be left entirely to shop floor supervisors, but must become an executive function. Supervisory training reinforced this shift in responsibility for employee relations. A new group of personnel managers now focused attention on the social relationships between workers and their supervisors, convinced that a change in supervisors' treatment of subordinates would improve employee morale, and hence production. As they saw it, the most practical way to intervene in the employee–supervisor relationship was to concentrate on redefining the role of supervisors and then to inculcate that role through a rigorous supervisory training program. The Industrial Research Division at Hawthorne was established to study supervisors as well as workers.

The emerging interest in the social role of supervisors was due to two major, long-term changes at Hawthorne. First, as the factory expanded dramatically in the late 1920s, the higher plant managers, especially works manager C. L. Rice and the eight branch superintendents, felt increasingly distanced from the workplace. Between Rice and the Hawthorne worker at the bottom of the organization were a branch superintendent, an assistant superintendent, a general foreman in charge of a division, a department foreman, assistant foremen, a section chief, and a gang boss. Addressing the workers through the *Hawthorne Microphone*, Rice lamented that "as the nominal head of our big family, I am handicapped at times by my inability to discuss our problems, our plans and our progress with each of you." The sheer number of supervisors at Hawthorne exacerbated this alienation; in 1929 there were more than 2,500 supervisors of the rank of foreman or below.[26]

The second major change had occurred in the supervisor's job. The func-

[25] IRD Report, 1931, II, 11–19, HSCM/152–3; "Developments in Interviewing: A Progress Report for the Year Ending Dec. 31, 1930," III, Plans for 1931, HSCM/105, A1–D10.

[26] C. L. Rice, *Hawthorne Microphone*, 27 Feb. 1928. The estimate of the number of supervisors is based on figures for supervisory training programs in 1929 and 1930 in IRD Report, 1931, III, 4–6, HSCM/152, D10–F3, and on a visitor's estimation of supervisor–employee ratios, in C. A. Cole, "Report on Industrial Relations Experiments," Apr. 1930, 15, HSCM/161, F7–162, A1.

tional specialization of supervision had been under way since the 1890s, when Western Electric managers took over control of the work process from skilled workers. By the late 1920s many of the original functions of a supervisor – hiring and firing of workers, purchasing and storekeeping, inspection of finished products, rates and pay, and employee welfare – had been taken over by special divisions. Supervisors retained responsibility for reporting to these organizations, a task that had become increasingly bureaucratic. A list of typical activities for a section chief identified eighty-eight separate tasks. (The very preparation of such a list is a measure of the extent to which scientific management was being applied to supervisors as well as workers.) The one central responsibility that supervisors retained was to ensure that their workers reached production goals. Until now, the day-to-day interactions between supervisors and their workers had remained the one area where higher managers were willing to leave matters up to the individual supervisor. They would intervene only if a grievance escalated into organized action by workers or if a worker found a way to take a complaint over the head of the supervisor, typically to the foreman or the personnel division. Now managers were proposing to intervene in this last major task of the supervisor, "the organization of the will of his employees."[27]

Mark Putnam, soon to be made chief of the Industrial Research Division, explained his views on the function of the supervisor to a meeting of Inspection Branch supervisors in November 1928, in a talk entitled "Selling Yourself to Your Subordinates." The supervisor's job should consist of leading workers, not driving them; he should be a salesman who sold the workers on the company. It was not sufficient for workers simply to get the assigned job done; the supervisor should ensure that they were interested in their work, were loyal to the company, were interested in the savings plans, and felt that Hawthorne was a good place to work. Finally, to underscore his message, Putnam gave notice that from now on "our superiors are going to measure our performance and our value by our ability to secure voluntary and interested effort from our subordinates rather than by our ability to secure the effort they can be forced to give."[28]

Both a moral vision and a practical concern with production fueled this emerging interest in supervision. Works manager C. L. Rice drew on both strands of the argument in an address to senior supervisors in October 1929. He pointed out that the relay assembly test results had shown that "correct

---

[27] On the decline of the power of the foreman, see Daniel Nelson, *Managers and Workers: Origins of the New Factory System in the United States, 1880–1920,* Madison: University of Wisconsin Press, 1975, passim; "Typical Activities of a Section Chief," 21 Apr. 1925, WVB/11/WECo-Kearny; "Employee Development Conferences – Text Material #2, The Supervisor and His Job," 1930, quote, EM/5.018.

[28] M. L. Putnam, "Selling Yourself to Your Subordinates," 15 Nov. 1928, 2, HSCM/145a, A11–B14.

and understanding supervision is a greater aid to production than constant surveillance." But most of his address concentrated on the social and moral role of industry. He acknowledged that mechanization had removed some of the incentives for individual achievement, resulting in soldiering and a "holocaust of wastefulness and lost motion." Workers who wasted even a small amount of time were on a slippery slope; soon they would be taking still more time off, until finally they would lose their self-respect. The problem was one of saving the soul of the individual worker as much as one of saving the company money. Supervisors had to help workers direct their energies efficiently, by considering how each worker "can work with a maximum of zest and pride of accomplishment, and of how you can make it possible for him to find some way of expressing his own thought, personality, or ideas in the performance of the task to which he is assigned." Rice assumed that such self-realization was possible even in the endless assembly of relays, because workers would identify with the success of Western Electric and the Bell System.[29]

Supervisory training was intended to inculcate in supervisors this new vision, along with an understanding of how to perform their new role. A training program had been introduced at Hawthorne in 1926 and formalized the following year with the establishment of a Supervisory Training Department in the Works Training Division. Conferences were held with the division chiefs and foremen, who in turn acted as conference leaders for lower-level supervisors in their own divisions. These early conferences discussed the full range of supervisors' responsibilities, from rating employees to promoting the company's stock purchase plan; only four of the seventeen conferences were specifically devoted to supervisor–employee relations. In its outline and approach the program was similar to the hundreds of programs being conducted by companies around the country.[30]

This program was transformed in 1929. The Supervisory Training Department was shifted to the new Industrial Research Division, where it was headed by Max Howarth, a young personnel manager. Conferences were made a permanent fixture for supervisors, with a two-hour session every two weeks. Most important, the material for discussion was now drawn from the interviewing program. At each session the conference leader, normally a supervisor with interviewing experience, would hand out a mimeographed sheet of employee comments on a subject. These would be used to draw out the supervisors to talk about their own views and practices and enable the leader to direct the conference toward an understanding of supervision in keeping with the new approach. Within a few months more

[29] C. L. Rice, "Soldiering in Industry," 30 Oct. 1929, quotes on 13 and 19, HSCM/145, B9–D4; see also C. L. Rice, "Know Your Job," *Hawthorne Microphone*, 25 May 1925.
[30] "Conference Leaders' Course," 1928, HSCM/141, A1–14; D. D. Davisson, "Supervisory Training," HSCM/149, C8–10. For a brief discussion of foreman training, see Nelson, *Managers and Workers*, 151–2.

than 1,400 supervisors in the inspection and operating branches were participating in conferences, and in 1930 an additional 1,075 supervisors in the remaining branches joined the program.[31]

The conferences evolved under the impact of changes in the interviewing program and feedback from supervisors. As the interviews became longer and more psychopathological in their approach, they formed the basis for lengthy discussions of individual workers' motivations and attitudes and provided a mechanism for the dissemination of research findings. Supervisors in turn found these sessions too abstract and inconclusive, and complained that too much time was being spent understanding the workers' side of employee–supervisor relations, without taking into account the views of supervisors. With the aid of Richard S. Meriam, a young economist and assistant to Mayo who worked on the preparation of teaching materials at the Harvard Business School, Howarth introduced Harvard's "case method" into supervisory training. Specific supervisory problems were presented along with workers' and supervisors' comments, and conference participants worked through the problems to an acceptable resolution.

The results of supervisory training were admittedly hard to judge. Both workers and supervisors claimed that the conferences did change supervisory behavior and improve workplace relations, but this was impossible to measure in any convincing way. Indeed, former interviewers who had returned to their regular departments told the researchers that many supervisors continued to drive their workers – this was true even of supervisors who in conferences were eloquent in their praise of the new approach. Supervisors were often suspicious of the new techniques, especially as the pressure on them to reach production goals was as great as before. A questionnaire sent by a superintendent to his supervisors in February 1931 showed that 96.5 percent believed that supervisory training gave superintendents a clearer understanding of their duties, and 92.2 percent agreed that they were better supervisors as a result of the conferences. The positive results of this confidential questionnaire were tempered somewhat by the discovery that several supervisors had held the sheet to the light to see if there were concealed identification marks, and others discussed what answers the superintendent expected. Still others replied positively to ensure that friends who were interviewers or members of the research division would not lose their jobs in the worsening depression. Howarth and the conference leaders suspected that the approval was closer to 70 percent. Even so, the researchers were persuaded of the value of the program. Especially gratifying were the changes in the tone of the conferences; supervisors were less dogmatic, analyzed the material more deeply, and were readier to enter into the spirit of company personnel policy.[32]

[31] For an overview of the supervisory training program, see IRD Report, 1931, III, HSCM/152, D10–F3.
[32] "Substance Analysis of Comments on Supervision," HSCM/130, C14–E3; "Rotational

As a next step, Putnam proposed that a group of supervisors be interviewed. If interviewing increased workers' effectiveness and aided researchers in their understanding of workers' attitudes, surely it would also work on supervisors. In 1931, two of Mayo's assistants, Osgood "Steve" Lovekin and Fritz Roethlisberger, spent the summer at Hawthorne to conduct the interviews. Lovekin's report was a dull affair that merely tallied comments on a variety of issues, but Roethlisberger was a skilled interviewer who had thoroughly absorbed Mayo's psychopathological views. This would be Roethlisberger's first real opportunity to prove himself as an industrial researcher, for Mayo had gone to Europe, leaving his protégé free to work independently. Roethlisberger interviewed 256 supervisors over the course of the summer, ranging from gang bosses to foremen. Several refused to speak or muttered only "yes" or "no" to his questions; "many of these interviews were spent by both parties in staring vacantly in space and devouring cigarettes." But the majority did respond to Roethlisberger's clinical interviewing techniques, talking for as long as two and a half hours. In a series of memoranda to Putnam during the summer and in the final report, Roethlisberger tried to analyze the supervisors' attitudes. He insisted that he was not in a position to judge the objective complaints made by supervisors in the course of the interviews; to do so he would need to investigate every department and situation mentioned. What he tried to achieve was an understanding of the subjective meaning of the supervisors' attitudes, what they revealed about the supervisors themselves.[33]

Roethlisberger used Mayo's psychopathological approach to argue that supervisors had infantile and primitive attitudes and that the existing supervisory training program had failed to change supervisors' behavior in a fundamental way. For example, supervisors often resented the fact that their superiors demanded total agreement with their decisions. This, Roethlisberger observed, was the classic infantile conflict of outward submission to one's parents combined with inner rebellion. The relationship of child to parent was particularly evident in supervisors' attitudes toward the company, for their greatest demand of the company was that it be fair and just. In conclusion, Roethlisberger advocated that supervisors become aware of the infantile drives that were the basis of their complaints; once they realized that they were projecting personal needs onto supervisory relationships, they could begin to deal with those relationships more clearly and collaboration with the company would improve. He also explored what he saw as the "primitive" side of supervisors' thinking about their job. Much of

Training as Practiced in the Industrial Research Division," 1930, HSCM/142, A1–G8; H. C. Beal to Pennock, 12 Mar. 1931, HSCM/153, C8–10; Putnam to Pennock, 24 Mar. 1931, HSCM/160, A5–7; IRD Report, 1931, App. 9, HSCM/153, C8–D8.
[33] Putnam to Pennock, 24 Mar. 1931, HSCM/160, A5–7; F. J. Roethlisberger, "A Report Based on Interviewing 256 Supervisors in the Operating Branch," 1 Nov. 1931, quote on 2, HSCM/121, D10–122, A5; Roethlisberger to Putnam, 14 July 1931, HSCM/159, C7–10.

the rhetoric of the supervisory training program about the need for supervisors who lead rather than drive, for soft-boiled rather than hard-boiled foremen, was a kind of "word magic":

> They have substituted a new for an old bag of tricks by means of which the ills of supervision are to be corrected. A frown takes the place of a "bawling out"; a cheery "good morning" takes the place of a frown; interviewing takes the place of "good morning"; and tact and diplomacy become more important than clearness.

Roethlisberger suggested tactfully that too much emphasis had been placed in the supervisory training programs on the need for the supervisor to sell himself to his workers, which had encouraged empty rituals. Superficial changes could not substitute for what he called the "experimental attitude" toward supervision in which supervisors adopted a flexible and creative approach and saw themselves as part of the human relations problems with which they had to deal. The company somehow had to find a way to increase its supervisors' self-awareness if it was to expect employee relations to improve.[34]

The difficulty lay in defining exactly what the ideal supervisor should be like. Implicit in Roethlisberger's reports was the view that a supervisor should be a kind of a lay psychiatrist, a person capable of analyzing the subjective side of supervisory relationships. His views of the ideal supervisor drew strongly on his experience as a student counselor and echoed the views of his mentor. The company researchers differed, however, over the question of whether they could delineate the concept of "ideal supervision" and remained uncertain as to just what the test rooms and interviewing program did tell them about supervision. But they were sufficiently persuaded to agree to present the new round of supervisory training conferences as a "personal improvement" series in which supervisors were taught to analyze the "total situation" in their department. Because of the depression, the new program was confined to a small group of excess supervisors, who were turned over full time to the research division; there they studied several of Roethlisberger's papers and reports on all phases of the research at Hawthorne. It was hoped that by the time production picked up and the supervisors returned to their departments, they would have been converted to the human relations approach of the research division. To be a successful supervisor, one now needed training in the latest scientific knowledge of human relations.[35]

[34] Roethlisberger, "Animism Among Supervisors," 18 June 1931, quote on 2, HSCM/144, A13–B1; Roethlisberger, "Concerning the Experimental Attitude," HSCM/143, B10–C2; Roethlisberger to Putnam, 8 July 1931, HSCM/159, E11–12.

[35] Howarth to Roethlisberger, 24 Aug. 1931, EM/3.090; Roethlisberger to Putnam, 7 Aug. 1931, HSCM/159, E2–6; "Special Research Group in Supervisory Training Methods, 1932," HSCM/143–4, B1.

Could the supervisor be transformed into an amalgam of psychopathologist and scientist? Howarth was aware that the average first-level supervisor and many foremen could not absorb the material in its present form. But he and his fellow researchers embraced it wholeheartedly, sure that in Mayo's and Roethlisberger's ideas lay "our philosophy of supervisory development in the field of human relations." The members of the Industrial Research Division had by now absorbed a great deal of the scientific, especially psychopathological, approach advocated by Mayo and Roethlisberger. They had become a close-knit team, and while they were fully aware of the need to develop practical supervisory training programs, their sense of having undergone a conversion experience made them somewhat impervious to the more mundane requirements of supervisors.[36]

But in practice there was an implicit admission that supervisors did need to be trained in the very rituals and tricks that Roethlisberger frowned upon. Training material suggested that supervisors address a worker's grievance not by criticizing the complaint, which would only produce a defensive reaction, but by repeating the worker's complaint as a question:

> The thing for the supervisor to accomplish is to get the employee to analyze the case himself instead of the supervisor attempting to point out just where the employee is wrong. This can be done by questions and repetitions of statements already made by the employee. The supervisor should remember that free expression will go a long way toward relieving emotional pressure.... The fact that the supervisor is viewing the matter calmly will strengthen the employee's belief that he is repressing personal bias or prejudice in a sincere effort to act upon facts.

Relationships of power and subordination were thus to be transformed, wherever possible, into relationships of patient to psychopathologist, in which power was concealed behind a veneer of paternal concern. Of course, if this relationship was challenged, power had to be wielded more openly. The same training material directed supervisors to deal with deliberate stubbornness by telling the employee "that it is not your personal pride, but the necessity of discipline which causes you to demand obedience."[37]

This vision of the new supervisor remained a theoretical one, confined to the research division. Like the interviewing program, supervisory training halted as the depression cut into budgets. The need for training had also declined, for as Hawthorne's workforce fell from a peak of 40,272 workers in 1929 to 7,463 workers in 1933, the remaining supervisors were experienced men who had been gradually demoted from fairly high supervisory positions, while the mass of section chiefs and gang bosses, if still employed, were once more working as operators. The Hawthorne researchers would

[36] Howarth to Roethlisberger, 25 Apr. 1932, FJR/1.
[37] "Employee Development Conferences – Text Material," 1930, no. 9, quotes on 5–6, 7–8, EM/5.018.

have to wait until economic recovery and the threat of unions prompted the development of a "personnel counseling" program in 1936, when a team of industrial psychopathologists attempted to defuse the Hawthorne workers' personal and collective maladjustments.

In the meantime, Mayo was satisfied that the interviewing and supervisory training programs, along with the test rooms, had demonstrated the importance of the worker's personal adjustment. The interviewing program, Mayo argued, provided evidence that almost all workers' complaints could be dismissed as irrational constructions:

> At no time as I see it, did the research imply a direct criticism of existing [supervisory] methods, except perhaps in a few isolated and negligible instances. The interviews increasingly have shown that an attitude of hostility towards a "boss" includes always something of falsification and has small value as a critique, in the ordinary sense, of supervision.

Proper individual adjustment to work entailed an unquestioning acceptance of authority. Workers, Mayo explained to Pennock, "suffer" an apprehension of authority that leads them to restrict output, either consciously or as an unconscious reaction. The illness metaphor is revealing of the medical and psychopathological model that was central to Mayo's style of human relations; most workers were sick and could be made healthy only through the imposition of an understanding, paternalistic authority.[38]

Mayo's theories of personal adjustment came to life in the "clinical cases" that he used repeatedly in his correspondence with company researchers and executives. Irene Rybacki, the "Bolshevik" and "anaemic" relay test worker remained Mayo's favorite case, but he also often cited the cases of two of the mica splitting test room workers. Interviews with the mica splitters in 1930 and 1931 revealed, Mayo believed, that the women with the widest fluctuations in production were also the ones with the greatest psychological problems. In particular, one worker was a moody young woman of eighteen whose mother apparently disliked and mistreated her and took all her pay. Mayo made much of the fact that when she left home for a time her production increased significantly, only to decline when she returned home. Here was a dramatic example of how conditions outside the workplace could affect production. It was in these individual cases, in which the worker's complaints about supposedly objective conditions could be shown to be nothing more than an expression of the individual's psychiatric maladjustment, that Mayo knew his ideas were most original and effective.

Mayo was convinced that interviewing was the best existing antidote for these "industrial 'falsifications' of situations." The positive responses of workers to the interviewing program and the improved morale were indications that workers were talking out their anxieties. Clearly this was hard to establish on the basis of the material gathered by the interviewers, and

---

[38] Mayo to Pennock, 9 Feb. 1931, quote on 6, HSCM/159, A10–14, B1–6.

Mayo relied on the test rooms for more detailed evidence. Indeed, he attributed the majority of the improvement in production in the relay test room to the fact that normal supervision had been replaced by what he called "continuous interviewing." Supervisory training should therefore concentrate on instilling interviewing skills; when this was achieved, "industry will enter upon a new and undreamed of era of active collaboration, that will make possible an almost incredible human advance." Thus, in Mayo's eyes, clinical cases of workers, the interviewing program, supervisory training, and the test room results all blended into a resounding victory for the psychopathological approach to industrial relations.[39]

By the time the interviewing program, supervisory training, and the mica splitting test had come to an end, victims of the depression, Mayo had succeeded in planting his ideas among the Hawthorne researchers. Wright and Dickson in the interviewing department had converted completely to the psychopathological approach; a two-week visit to Harvard in April 1930 and their close collaboration with Roethlisberger strengthened their commitment. Hibarger and Chipman in the test rooms had also come to look more closely at the role of personal factors in the workers' attitudes and production, especially after closer attention was paid to these areas in the mica splitting test. Meanwhile, Howarth in supervisory training had worked closely with Roethlisberger and was using his material as a basis for the new training course for supervisors transferred to the research division.

But just as the Hawthorne–Harvard collaboration was working smoothly, the depression killed off the major programs. Interviewing and supervisory training ceased at the end of 1930, while the mica splitting test room limped into 1931, with all of its experimental controls abandoned. Surprisingly, however, the disintegration of these programs aided the development of the Hawthorne experiments. As the temporary members of the Industrial Research Division were laid off or returned to their regular departments, a core of the experienced and committed researchers remained. With the responsibilities of running large interviewing and training programs gone, the researchers were able to redirect the experiments along fresh lines.

[39] Quotes from Mayo to Pennock, 29 Apr. 1929, HSCM/159, C6–10; Mayo to Pennock, 28 Oct. 1929, EM/1.088; Mayo to Pennock, 9 Feb. 1931.

6

The anthropology of work

THE HAWTHORNE RESEARCHERS were able to conduct one major new experiment during 1931–2 before the depression slowly but inexorably brought research to a standstill. The bank wiring test room brought significant shifts in experimental approach. In the relay assembly and mica splitting tests the major method had been to introduce a variable in each test period and observe its effect on production. Other approaches had been added – Mayo's and Turner's physiological studies of fatigue, Mayo's analysis of the personal situation of the worker – but output had continued to be used as the major index of change. In the bank wiring room, the focus shifted to a study of the social structures and social relationships in the test room and their influence on production. The new research involved the adaptation of two of the previous research techniques. The role of the observer was made more rigorous than it had been in the relay assembly test room, through the application of techniques from social anthropology, and the study of the workers was intensified through the use of repeated interviewing. The result was a far more intensive observation of individual workers and shop floor organization than had been hitherto attempted.

As in the previous experiments, the researchers formulated quite different interpretations of the events in the bank wiring test room. This was exacerbated by the participation of two new members of the research team, each of whom brought a new disciplinary perspective to the experiments. William Dickson, the observer in the bank wiring room, had trained as an economist and tended to emphasize how the workers were making rational decisions about their level of output. Lloyd Warner, an anthropologist colleague of Mayo's, emphasized the significance of informal social structures in the test room and recognized that the workers had a collective interest that conflicted with that of management. Both of these new perspectives contrasted significantly with Mayo and Roethlisberger's emphasis on the emotional aspects of worker behavior and attitudes. Where Mayo's psychopathological approach encouraged a focus on the maladjustment of the individual worker to the industrial environment, Warner's anthropological approach suggested that workers created their own shop floor culture and that this was as legitimate as the social structures created by management.

From primitive society to Hawthorne

By the end of 1930 the outlook for the experiments was bleak indeed. The interviewing and supervisory training programs had been brought to a halt, victims of the cost cutting that accompanied curtailments in production. The mica splitting test room was still in existence, but all attempts to gather fresh data had ceased, and the test would be halted completely in March 1931. Only the relay assembly test room continued, partly because the workers had sufficient seniority to avoid being laid off, partly because it was a small program compared with the costly interviewing and training programs, but primarily because of its symbolic importance for the researchers. However, the relay test had become totally routinized, its new test periods determined by the incessant reductions in working hours rather than by any research plan, and its researchers, Homer Hibarger and Don Chipman, were at an intellectual standstill. The clearest indication of the relay test's decay was the fact that no report had been compiled in eighteen months.

The Industrial Research Division continued to enjoy political and financial support from senior company executives, nevertheless. George Pennock at Hawthorne maintained his close interest, and Mayo impressed upon the New York executives the importance of the research. This support was crucial as the layoffs bit deeper and branch superintendents at Hawthorne tried to save positions in their departments by questioning the value of continuing the research. And in June 1931 the division could enjoy a symbolic measure of its importance and visibility when Mark Putnam, chief of the division, was chosen president of the Hawthorne Club in the annual election among all Hawthorne workers. (In a congratulatory letter to Putnam, Mayo observed that his election by the plant's workers indicated "that there is far more understanding than suspicion of what you are doing." Mayo's criticism that elections were subject to emotional and irrational persuasion seemed to subside when they produced a result of which he approved.) Thus, although its large research programs were gone, the Industrial Research Division survived the first cuts of the depression, emerging with a reduced budget and personnel.[1]

The reductions brought about a significant restructuring of personnel and resulted in a reorientation of the research. During 1929 and 1930 the departments in charge of interviewing and supervisory training had clearly been on the ascendancy. They oversaw the exciting aspects of research and

[1] E. Mayo to M. L. Putnam, 20 Oct. 1931, HSCM/159, A6.

were in close collaboration with Mayo and his colleagues. By comparison, Hibarger's Research Studies Department limped along with Turner's assistance, and the Analyzation Department, with its routine tallying of employee comments, was held in contempt by the leading researchers. A small core of key company researchers had emerged in these years, in particular Mark Putnam, Harold Wright, who was in charge of interviewing, and his assistant, William Dickson. All three were in their middle to late twenties, were college educated, and had worked exclusively as personnel managers for Western Electric. Young, enthusiastic, and seeking ideas and techniques that would establish their careers and the importance of personnel management in the company, they had been particularly receptive to the Harvard researchers, readily absorbing Mayo's and Roethlisberger's guidance. Now, with interviewing and supervisory training gone, they sought ways to maintain their position in the division.

Vague plans for another test room had circulated on numerous occasions. As far back as 1928 there had been discussions about establishing a test room of male workers, but interviewing and supervisory training eventually absorbed all the division's energies. In 1929 there had been a proposal to interview a group of workers repeatedly in order to measure the effect of interviewing on productivity. The idea resurfaced in Dickson's report on the interviewing program in 1930, which had admitted the shortcomings of the existing interviewing program. What was needed, Dickson proposed, was to develop interviewing as a method of research, over and above its uses as a means of eliciting employee grievances and as a therapeutic tool for worker dissatisfaction. Interviewing could be used in a far more intensive way than it had been to date – for example, to study individual cases of maladjustment, to examine the relationship between preoccupational thinking and "accident-proneness," or to understand how workers assimilate and attach meaning to experiences. Dickson proposed that the division "establish study groups in the plant and endeavor to keep a continuous record of and correlate production and mental attitudes, at the same time recording any changes in the individual's physical condition or social situation and relating these to production and mental attitudes." The expression was imprecise, but the central idea was clear enough: The time had come to concentrate the various resources and talents of the researchers in a single test room, in which production, the personal attitudes of the workers, the physical environment, and the social relationships would be studied and interrelated. Dickson and Wright were confident that they could develop the interviewing side of such a study, relying on their experience and the assistance of Mayo and Roethlisberger. But for the social analysis of the proposed test room they turned to W. Lloyd Warner, another of Mayo's Harvard colleagues.[2]

---

[2] RATR Daily History Record, 21 Aug. 1928, HSCM/11–15; "A Plan for Improving Employee

Lloyd Warner was one of the first anthropologists to apply his techniques to modern society. He had trained at the University of California, then spent three years in Australia, on Rockefeller funding, conducting fieldwork among the Arnhem Land aborigines. As a student he had come under the influence of several of the leading social anthropologists: Robert Lowie, Malinowski, who visited California while Warner was there, and A. R. Radcliffe-Brown, then professor of anthropology at the University of Sydney, who guided Warner's Australian research. On his return to the United States in 1929, he took up an instructorship at Harvard, hoping to find support for an anthropological study of an American city. The idea was not new: Sociologists Robert S. Lynd and Helen Merrell Lynd had loosely adopted an anthropological approach in their famous study of Middletown; the first volume of their work was published in 1929 and may have spurred Warner to conduct a similar study.[3]

Mayo was receptive to Warner's interests. Back in 1925 he had wondered "what would happen if one took a young anthropologist, fresh from investigation of a Pacific island culture, and set him down in a modern city with instructions to follow the same anthropological method." Warner learned of Mayo, and probably of his large Rockefeller grant, and was soon outlining to Mayo his plans for a large-scale study of U.S. society. At this stage it was little more than an idea, for he lacked funds and had not yet determined an appropriate city. Mayo sent Warner off to visit Hawthorne in May 1930 with a letter of introduction to Putnam: "I think you will all be interested to hear of his wild experiences with other Australian savages. I think that you will also find that his inquiries unquestionably possess significance for us even if they cannot be directly or immediately applied in the Hawthorne Works." Putnam was impressed with Warner's perspective, and he quickly became convinced that the next research should be of the home and social life of the Hawthorne workers. Other projects of a similar nature were also being floated. Beardsley Ruml, now dean of social sciences at the University of Chicago, was trying to tie some of the Chicago sociologists into the Hawthorne research, and the urban sociologist Ernest Burgess had approached the company with a proposal to conduct research in the vicinity of the works. Warner seems to have persuaded Putnam that the sociologists' proposals were unsound, for Putnam wrote to Mayo declaring

Relations on the Basis of Data Obtained from Employees," Project 10: "An Experiment to Determine the Results of Repeatedly Interviewing a Shop Group," 1929, HSCM/149, A12–13; "Developments in Interviewing: A Progress Report for the Year Ended Dec. 31, 1930," Part III, quote on 3, HSCM/105, A1–D10.
[3] Warner's Australian research was eventually published in W. Lloyd Warner, *A Black Civilization: A Social Study of an Australian Tribe*, New York: Harper, 1937. The Lynds discuss their anthropological approach in Robert S. Lynd and Helen Merrell Lynd, *Middletown: A Study in American Culture*, New York: Harcourt, Brace, 1929, 3–5.

that the Chicago sociologists "have not gone sufficiently far into the field of social organization and structure to suit our purposes" – a sophisticated critique that could only have come from Warner.[4]

Negotiations and discussions continued for some time, but eventually Warner decided to conduct his research in Newburyport, Connecticut. The industrial communities of Chicago, Warner felt, were too disintegrated for meaningful comparison with social anthropological studies of other communities. Certainly the areas adjacent to the Hawthorne plant must have seemed unpromising for a community study. The gangster Al Capone had set himself up in Cicero in the 1920s, established his headquarters in a hotel near the Hawthorne plant, and organized a "chain of speak-easies, honky-tonks and gambling houses" along the streets on two sides of the factory; Cicero retained its reputation as a wild town into the 1950s. Behind the main thoroughfares, a diverse range of ethnic communities of Czechoslo-vakians, Poles, Italians, and Greeks lived in the local residential streets of semidetached houses. Newburyport, by comparison, was a stable community with strong social traditions, more like the traditional societies studied by anthropologists. Nevertheless, Warner became a part-time member of Mayo's Industrial Research Department at the Harvard Business School, and by 1931 Mayo and Henderson's Rockefeller grant was providing four-fifths of Warner's salary and all of his research expenses at Newburyport, and the following year it was supporting an additional anthropological study of a community in the South. The Newburyport study would eventually be known as the Yankee City Series, one of the most significant community studies ever undertaken, and was published in five volumes between 1941 and 1959.[5]

The possibility of a Chicago community study abandoned, Warner took a greater interest in the factory research, especially Dickson's proposal for a new test room. In visits to the plant he stressed the importance of studying not only the individual workers, but also the social relationships in the test room and the relationships between those in the test room and other groups in the factory. The way to do this was to combine interviewing with careful observation in the test room; Warner explicitly commended the fieldwork techniques of anthropologists. In any such study, Warner lectured Dickson,

[4] Mayo to C. E. Merriam, 16 Mar. 1925, quote on 2, CEM/35/17; Mayo to Putnam, 12 May 1930, EM/1.089; Putnam to Mayo, 28 May 1930, EM/1.089; W. L. Warner to Putnam, 3 July 1930, HSCM/159, F11–12; Putnam to Mayo, 5 Mar. 1931, EM/1.090.

[5] E. Osborne to A. H. Young, report for Nov. and Dec. 1930, EM/3.073; quote on Cicero from American Guide Series, *Illinois*, Chicago: McClurg, 1939, 585. For an account of the development of the Newburyport study, see W. Lloyd Warner and Paul S. Lunt, *The Social Life of a Modern Community*, New Haven, Conn.: Yale University Press, 1941, 1–5. The southern study was reported in Allison Davis, Burleigh B. Gardner, and Mary R. Gardner, *Deep South: A Social Anthropological Study of Caste and Class*, Chicago: University of Chicago Press, 1941.

the central task was to discover the solidarities and antagonisms within and among groups and relate these to the social structure: "The same is true, Dickson, no matter whether you study the Australian totemic clans, the gangs of Chicago, or your departmental groups."[6]

The proposal to study social relationships and social structure was a significant shift from Mayo and Roethlisberger's psychopathological approach, with its emphasis on the individual's adjustment to a relatively undifferentiated social environment. Although Mayo perceived the value of social anthropology, he had never really absorbed its emphasis on understanding behavior and attitudes through the analysis of social structure; he always felt more comfortable with the individual and drew instinctively on clinical studies of personal adjustment. Mayo's choice of the term "total situation" to describe his approach was misleading, for it seemed to suggest that the psychopathological level of analysis subsumed all the other levels of social analysis. A disparity between Warner's and Mayo's research methods and interpretative schemes surfaced briefly in correspondence on the proposed test room. Roethlisberger, clearly echoing Mayo's views, expressed some concern at the direction in which Dickson and Warner were taking the research. He questioned whether Dickson could use the interviewing technique to discover facts about the workers, citing as evidence Mayo's favorite example of the worker who hated her supervisor because he resembled her stepfather. Roethlisberger insisted that interviews could reveal only one kind of fact and that was the psychological adjustment of the individual worker.[7]

Warner did not believe that personal beliefs could be so easily explained away or that they held no significance for the analysis of social structure. Writing to Dickson, he defended his approach against Roethlisberger's criticisms:

> The big thing to look for is the attitudes of the person or group being observed. [Their] attitudes are very frequently unconscious; they are usually what might be called prejudices. Psychologically they would fall into what the psychoanalysts call latent content, but what the sociologists would describe as social structure if they were found among all, or the greater part, of the people in the group.

Warner's entry into the experiments was a sharp reminder that collective behavior and attitudes also had legitimacy; unlike Mayo, Warner did not quickly dismiss the political views of radicals and unionists. Whatever the differences between Warner, Mayo, and Roethlisberger (and it seems likely that the debate continued privately at Harvard), Dickson and his fellow company researchers were clearly receptive to Warner's fieldwork approach.

[6] W. J. Dickson to F. J. Roethlisberger, 16 Feb. 1931, FJR/1; Warner to Dickson, 27 Feb. 1931, HSCM/159, F7–8.
[7] Roethlisberger to Dickson, 20 Feb. 1931, HSCM/159, E13–F1.

The new bank wiring test room drew on the techniques of social anthropology, although as with all of the Hawthorne research, the techniques were adapted to industrial conditions.[8]

The bank wiring test room

The transition to a social anthropological analysis of the workplace was a gradual process, dependent as much on the exigencies of research as on Warner's guidance. Indeed, the research design of the bank wiring test was shaped in a quite accidental fashion by two individuals outside the group of researchers: the foreman of the Bank Wiring Department and an engineer who had conducted a fatigue study in the department earlier that year. The resulting research was significantly different from that in the previous test rooms, and the theoretical approach reflected that advocated by Warner. Although Dickson could later rationalize the changes in terms of the researchers' realization that it was necessary to analyze the social system of the test room, the research design emerged more erratically.

The resistance of the Bank Wiring Department foreman to the initial research proposal forced the researchers to establish a test room that closely paralleled the regular department and did not introduce new variables. Putnam, Wright, and Hibarger had met with the foreman and proposed a study almost identical to those carried out in the other test rooms: "We will keep records which will assist in determining the kinds and degrees of reactions and adjustments the man makes towards his working situation and toward his outside situations as these are reflected in his production, attendance, and in his physical and mental status." They were interested primarily in the individual's relationship to work and the causes of maladjustment, rather than the social structure of the test room. Because the researchers planned to get at the root of each worker's personal problems, it was proposed that the supervisor in the test room would not have the authority to reprimand or even admonish the workers; an active supervisor in the test room would interfere by reacting to the symptoms of maladjustment rather than searching for the underlying cause. In essence, the plan consisted of grafting Mayo's psychopathological approach onto the test room model developed in the relay test; the presence at the discussions of Wright, formerly in charge of interviewing, and Hibarger, in charge of the relay test, and the absence of Dickson underscore the fact that the researchers were proceeding according to prevailing assumptions.[9]

The foreman, H. S. Wolff, resisted these proposals. He was willing for research to be conducted with some of his men, but was wary of the research design. Wolff objected to any aspect of the test room that would involve a

---

[8] Warner to Dickson, 27 Feb. 1931.
[9] Putnam to H. S. Wolff, 11 May 1931, HSCM/73, C2–4.

noticeable departure from the practices in the regular department, insisting that supervisors be permitted to exercise their normal power, that the workers be kept on the department's group rate, that the job layout be identical to that in the regular department, and that the test room not be protected from the disruptions of changing work schedules that normally attended production. The reason for his objections gradually became apparent to the researchers. Wolff was concerned that his department and the quality of its supervision would be shown up if production increased substantially in the test room. Like many other supervisors, he felt that the increase in production in the relay assembly test room was due to the many small but significant changes made in the organization of production rather than to the fact that there was little or no supervision, as the researchers often claimed. The researchers admitted that Wolff's views were widely shared:

> [Supervisors] felt that those girls had been given special inducements in the form of a special gang rate, that ordinary production difficulties had been carefully eliminated, and that the operators had been petted and babied along from the start. "Of course," they said, "anybody could get production that way, only we can't get away with things like that."

By trying to keep the test room as similar as possible to the regular department, the foreman could hope to obviate these problems; if production did go up, at least it could not be attributed to the absence of supervision.[10]

The researchers had little choice but to accede to the foreman's requests. They were already committed to using workers from the department in the test room, for they had begun a program of preliminary observation and interviewing in the regular department in June 1931, three months before final arrangements with Wolff were agreed upon. But the researchers were also willing to move in the directions he suggested. Responsibility for the test had passed to Dickson and Moore, the interviewer and observer in the study, and both readily accepted requirements that would lessen the differences between the test room and the regular department.

The bank wiring test began on 13 November 1931, its working conditions only marginally different from those of the regular job. Nine wirers, three solderers, and two inspectors were set up in a test room in a building adjacent to the regular department. Because of reduced production, it was possible to move an entire job, the wiring of connector banks, into the room. The regular supervisor, or group chief, accompanied the workers into the test room and was directed to supervise them in the same way as he would in the regular department. The workers were not placed on a special group rate, but shared in the group earnings of a department of 175 workers, thus removing the pay incentive that had been so important in the relay test. And no elaborate system of measuring production was adopted, for the

[10] "Procedure in Establishing Bank Wiring Test Room," quote on 3, HSCM/73, A1–8.

researchers decided that introducing a measuring mechanism would interfere with the work; instead, morning and afternoon production figures were supplemented with occasional surreptitious timings by stopwatch. The only significant changes, then, consisted of shifting the workers to the test room, introducing an observer into the work group, and interviewing the workers.[11]

The observer, Art Moore, and the interviewer, Bill Dickson, quickly established constructive relationships with the workers. The young men – all except one were between twenty and twenty-five years old – were at first apprehensive about Moore, suspecting that his role was to force an increased pace of production. But Moore's daily activities of recording conversations and activities in the test room seemed innocuous enough, especially since his assurances that the records would not be seen by the department foreman seemed with time to be genuine. It became apparent that Moore would not supervise them in the absence of the group chief or prevent them from gambling or drinking in the back of the test room, and soon several of the workers talked openly with him about their work and personal lives. Moore's scrupulousness in not informing on the workers, even under direct questioning from the foreman, prompted the foreman to comment, with a tinge of sarcasm, that Moore was "getting to be a regular father to these fellows." But only twenty-seven years old himself, Moore was more friend than father. Dickson also proved remarkably capable of drawing out the workers in interviews; for the most part the workers did not feel threatened by this gentle and unassuming man.[12]

The bank wirers seem to have accepted the researchers to a greater degree than the relay assemblers had, for a number of reasons. Whereas Hibarger was both supervisor and researcher in the relay test, Moore's nonsupervisory role was clearly demarcated by the presence of a supervisor in the bank wiring test. Hibarger was considerably older than the relay assemblers, and as a man was simply excluded from a large part of the women's conversation and concerns. Because the bank wiring job required the workers to coordinate their work and move around the shop floor, the men had far greater control of their work environment than had the relay assemblers, each of whom had performed an individual task at a bench. Confident of their power, the bank wirers never felt as threatened by the test room environment and could incorporate a friendly observer into their world.

Bank wiring was a repetitive and monotonous task, lightened only by the social interactions among the workers. Banks were a major component of

---

[11] "Procedure in Establishing Bank Wiring Test Room," HSCM/73, A1–8; "Report of Search for Test Room Group of Men," HSCM/73, B6–14.

[12] "Bank Wiring Test Room, Record of Observations" (13 Nov. 1931 to 19 May 1932), HSCM/75–78, quote on 28 Jan. 1932; "Record of Interviews, 1931–1932," EM/5.013–014; W. J. Dickson, personal histories of Bank Wiring Test Room workers, constructed from interviews, in WJD/1/19.

Figure 8. Manually wiring and soldering step-by-step banks. Courtesy of AT&T Archives.

automatic telephone exchanges; mechanical selectors moved across the banks to establish contact between two telephone numbers. Each bank consisted of one or two hundred terminals on a convex face, each of which had to be wired and soldered to the terminals of ten other banks; another level of banks was placed on top, and the process of wiring and soldering continued. Depending on the equipment, a set of banks would require the wiring of between three thousand and six thousand terminals. Lengths of wire were supplied with the insulation stripped off at the proper intervals; the wirer's task was to move down the six-foot-long set of banks, hooking the exposed wire over each terminal, and then start the process over again. If the wirer missed a terminal, he would have to undo his work and restart the row. Each wirer had two sets of banks to work on, allowing the solderer, who could cover the work of three wirers, to work without hindrance on a completed bank (Figure 8). The banks were then inspected to ensure that the connections were sound and that there were no "reverses" in the set. The work was also tiring, especially for the wirers: It required them to stand in the same position all day, their heads and necks straining forward, their arms held up to jerk the wire around the terminal, using the resistance of the wire to balance their bodies as they rhythmically worked along the bank. After several hours of wiring, their hands would become habituated to the action, and even after work was over they would continue to twitch. The bank wirers countered the boredom and fatigue by talking, playing around, and taking as many breaks from work as they could contrive. Indeed, the workers went further and deliberately restricted their output, a fact that provided the main focus of analysis in the bank wiring test.[13]

The detailed account of the workers' restriction of output became one of the most famous aspects of the Hawthorne experiments. Soldiering, as it was commonly called, had been widely discussed in the past by managers and engineers; F. W. Taylor's scientific management had been designed to prevent soldiering by scientifically determining a proper day's work. By the 1920s managers tended to assume that modern personnel practices, including time study, bonus payment systems, and the dilution or elimination of union control of production, had squeezed out the more serious elements of the problem. A study of output restriction funded by Walter Bingham's Personnel Research Federation and published in 1931 noted that four-fifths of managers surveyed believed that restriction had never been or was not now a problem in their company. Yet when the researcher examined work practices in the same managers' companies, he found that output restriction was widespread among unorganized workers and that time studies and incentive schemes could actually encourage workers to restrict their output. Workers knew from bitter experience that if they consistently produced more than 30 or 40 percent above the level at which bonuses began to be paid, their job would be rerated and they would have to work harder to make the same wage. The trick was to work at a level that would maximize earnings without attracting the attention of piece-rate engineers. The interview program indicated that Hawthorne workers had identical concerns about the setting of piece rates and the bogey (the daily output expected of each worker).[14]

The decision by Dickson and Moore to study the restriction of output among the bank wirers was shaped by two previous studies. Although there is no direct evidence, it is probable that the researchers were aware of the Personnel Research Federation report before they began their study of bank wiring; the federation was, after all, a primary reference group for the Hawthorne researchers. The second influence was more concrete: An en-

---

[13] "An Engineering Study of Human Fatigue" contains a Hawthorne piece-rate engineer's description of the bank wiring task in January 1931, HSCM/73, C8–11. Solderer no. 1 observed the wirers' work closely and described it to Dickson; see interview with "S1," 10 Dec. 1931, EM/5.013–014.

[14] See, e.g., Whiting Williams, *What's on the Worker's Mind*, New York: Scribner's, 1920, esp. 15; Charles S. Myers, *Mind and Work*, New York: Putnam's, 1921, esp. chap. 4; Stanley B. Mathewson, *Restriction of Output Among Unorganized Workers*, New York: Viking Press, 1931.

gineer conducting a study of fatigue in the bank wiring department in January 1931 had specifically noted that the workers controlled their output. He observed that "the workers obviously plan to do certain amounts of work per day, and this is considerably less than the bogey requirement." When two faster workers were encouraged to undertake a speed test for a day, they had no trouble making the bogey in the morning and early afternoon, but under unspoken pressure from their fellow workers were forced to slow down as the afternoon wore on, thus bringing their output down to a level commensurate with that of the group. The negotiations with the foreman over the design of the test room also encouraged a study of restriction, for the foreman had vetoed the introduction of experimental conditions, such as a special group rate, that might remove some of the factors that encouraged workers to limit their work.[15]

What was original about the account of restriction among the bank wirers was not the discovery that workers deliberately slowed down production, but rather the form of explanation given for their behavior. Drawing on Warner's advice, Dickson used restriction as a means of analyzing the system of social relations on the shop floor. The importance of Warner's social anthropological model for the bank wiring study is illustrated by the fact that Dickson prepared an eleven-page memorandum on the social meaning of output restriction *before* the bank wiring test room was started, based only on preliminary interviews with twenty-four workers in the regular department and on the engineer's observations. The test room study simply provided further evidence for an already well developed hypothesis.

Restriction of output, Dickson suggested, was a reflection of group solidarity among the workers, an indication that workers shared common purposes, ideas, and sentiments. Individual workers, even those who complained that restricting production resulted in lower wages, were prepared to accept the group norm, even though this might mean sacrificing individual interests to the group. The most admired workers in the department were those who managed to produce the least, because they symbolized resistance to management authority. Individual differences in output could also be explained in social terms. Workers who produced at or below the group norm were well socialized into the group, while those who tried to produce more in order to meet the bogey tended to be the introverted members of the department, not sharing their fellows' social norms.

Dickson argued that, in such a context, management intervention to increase production backfired, for it served only to increase group solidarity and hence restriction. Rate setting and cost reduction investigations simply made workers apprehensive and encouraged them to band together in the face of pressure from management. Particularly ironic was the practice of posting each worker's production on a bulletin board in the department:

[15] "An Engineering Study of Human Fatigue," quote on 3, HSCM/73, C8–11.

"The ostensible purpose of these charts is to foster competition. As a matter of fact they serve a further function. They inform everyone where each person stands in relation to everyone else and if anyone is out of line he can be checked by the group." The practice of choosing supervisors from the highest producers in a department was also counterproductive; on Dickson's theory management was selecting the least socialized member of the group, who would drive workers and thereby increase solidarity and restriction of output. In many cases, however, Dickson thought that immediate supervisors (gang bosses, group chiefs, section chiefs) sided with their workers in the restriction of output – "unconsciously, perhaps." After all, the supervisors' earnings depended on the group's production and they therefore also had an interest in protecting rates.[16]

Restriction of output was thus a function of existing industrial organization, beyond the control of individual workers or supervisors:

> *The function of restriction of output, to sum up, is to protect the worker from management's schemes.* It galvanizes the worker's apprehensions into action. Management, failing to understand the problem, feels that the worker is lying down on the job, trying to get something for nothing. It therefore concocts new schemes or applies old ones with renewed vigor. Mutual distrust is intensified and production is controlled more than before.

Dickson was skeptical that the workers' apprehension of authority could be dissipated through interviewing, as Mayo supposed. He believed the solution instead lay in guaranteeing that rates would not be reduced and in stopping driving forms of supervision; if these changes were made it was likely that output would increase 20 to 30 percent. Looking back at the relay assembly test room, he suggested that a major reason for the increased production was the "fundamental reform" of the small-group payment system in the test room and the related assurance by managers that rates would not be lowered if production increased.[17]

Moore's close observation in the bank wiring test room and Dickson's interviews with the workers provided ample evidence for his thesis. Although the bogey was 8,000 connections per day, the workers ignored this standard, substituting their own norm of what they considered a fair day's work, which was two bank sets, or between 6,000 and 6,600 connections. Moreover, the group chief, their immediate supervisor, acquiesced in this unofficial norm and never forced the workers to produce more. This standard had become so firmly established that several of the workers were actually under the impression that 6,600 connections was the official bogey. Both workers and the supervisor consciously balanced their desire for higher wages with the knowledge that rates would be cut if they consistently pro-

---

[16] Dickson to Wright, 28 Oct. 1931, quote on 6, HSCM/74, C1–11.
[17] Ibid., 8–11, quote on 10.

duced at a high rate; the unofficial norm was a result of these conflicting pressures. Much attention was therefore devoted to ensuring that production records "looked right" – if individual workers made more than 6,600 connections in a day, they would not declare the surplus, saving them for tomorrow's production report. Time spent waiting for solderers, inspectors, or parts could also be claimed, allowing further manipulation of the records. Indeed, considerable skill was required to coordinate one's production figures with work actually performed. Hoarding of production, when combined with the collusion of the group chief, enabled the workers to structure their day, working hard in spurts, easing up as the day wore on, and leaving time for conversation and games.[18]

The group chief was caught between his workers and his superiors, constantly trying to balance the need to enforce his foreman's orders while at the same time protecting his workers and keeping them content. Practices that the foreman did not allow – such as wirers and solderers swapping their jobs for variety, workers helping one another out, or workers ignoring safety regulations – the group chief permitted, explaining to Moore that "maybe I am a little too easy on my fellows, but I'd rather be that way than have them all down on me."[19]

Dickson also found some support for his thesis that the fastest workers would be the least socialized into the group, whereas the slower workers would be well adjusted. The fastest worker, who averaged more than 7,000 connections a day, was contemptuous of his fellow workers, considering them lazy; he was, Dickson observed, a "lone wolf," eccentric in dress and manner. Through his interviews Dickson attempted to comprehend the social and psychological meaning of work for each of the workers, relating their behavior on the shop floor to their personal lives. But where Mayo all too readily passed superficial judgments of psychiatric maladjustment on workers who did not conform to management's expectations, Dickson emphasized the personal and social meaning of work for the individual. The slowest worker in the test room, a twenty-one-year-old who managed only 3,400 connections a day and was regarded by supervisors as a "problem case," turned out to be a cheerful and intelligent youth who had been forced to assume responsibility for the family upon the death of his father, undermining his hopes of going to college. Dickson could sympathize with him, for he felt that he understood why the worker resisted managerial authority. Although he still used Mayo's psychopathological techniques,

[18] See, e.g., "Record of Observations," 11 Dec. 1931, 27 Jan. 1932, 24 Feb. 1932; "Personal Histories," Wireman 1, 6–8, Wireman 3, 7–11, WJD/1/19. The payment scheme was hideously complicated, comprising group payment based on output, individual rates for each worker, with some work calculated on a piece-rate basis and other on an hourly basis. Roethlisberger and Dickson take four pages to give a simplified explanation in *Management and the Worker*, Cambridge, Mass.: Harvard University Press, 1939, see 409–12.
[19] "Record of Observations," 14 Dec. 1931, 22 Dec. 1931, 8 Feb. 1932.

Dickson did not follow Mayo in equating low production with maladjustment. What was most important was how well the worker was integrated with his work group, even if this meant low production.[20]

The report by Dickson and Moore on the bank wiring test was a shattering condemnation of the existing social structure of the test room and, by implication, of the entire industrial organization at Hawthorne. Dickson and Moore did not pull any punches, because they hoped that the report would shock the top Hawthorne managers into continuing the test room. By March 1932 layoffs were gathering momentum; every day rumors of further layoffs swept through the plant. Although little research could be conducted in such circumstances, the researchers hoped that a symbolic continuation of the experiments would ensure rapid growth when economic recovery finally arrived. The report first pointed out that the researchers had been able to discover things that were concealed from supervisors, noting that the workers had been "unbelievably frank," drawing the observer into conversations from which supervisors were excluded. A series of numbered sections set out their view of the chasm between the organizational structure and actual behavior:

> 1.1 The employees do not recognize the group or section chief as possessing authority...
>
> 1.2 The Group Chief, in order to defend his reputation, has had to align himself with the group against the rest of the supervisory hierarchy...
>
> 1.3 The Foreman and his assistant have inaccurate knowledge of how the group in the test room functions or of how it might function. Such information is kept from them.
>
> 1.4 The Foreman and his assistant feel that information passed along to them by their subordinates is not always reliable...
>
> 1.5 The supervisors have a definite idea as to what the maximum output should be. It is their belief that the group has now reached this level. The employees have concealed their real abilities from them. The Group Chief feels that the group is producing below capacity but he does not tell this to anyone above him.

Production, the report concluded, was at least 30 percent below what it might be. However, little could be expected to change under the existing production and wage system, for output records were highly inaccurate and the incentive payment scheme had ceased to have any effect on individual or group production. Nor was the situation in the test room unusual; evidence from the interviewing program suggested rather that it was "symptomatic of a disintegrate industrial situation."[21]

---

[20] "Record of Interviews, 1931–1932," EM/5.013–014; "Personal Histories," esp. Wireman 2 and Wireman 9, WJD/1/19.

[21] A. C. Moore and W. J. Dickson, "Report on Bank Wiring Test Group for the Period Nov. 9, 1931 to Mar. 18, 1932," 21 Mar. 1932, quotes on 2–3, 9, HSCM/74, A1–B1; Dickson to Roethlisberger, 15 Apr. 1932, FJR/1.

The report exploded through the upper levels of management, although only at Hawthorne, for George Pennock had agreed with the researchers that it should not be forwarded to New York – thereby exemplifying precisely the kind of defensive behavior among subordinates that the report condemned. Operating superintendent H. C. Beal, the manager directly responsible for production at Hawthorne, reacted by calling the bank wiring foreman and the test room group chief to his office on the pretense that he had received a complaint from the Inspection Branch about the quality of work in the test room. Just what transpired in his office is unclear; probably not much, since Beal was unable to confront the supervisors directly with the report because to do so would undermine the research project. What was clear was that Dickson and Moore's findings had touched a raw nerve, for they undermined management's confidence in the ability of the industrial organization to control production or even to know what was occurring on the shop floor.

The bank wiring test also highlighted the tensions between Warner's anthropological and Mayo's psychopathological approaches. In the initial report on restriction of output and in the most recent report, Warner's emphasis on the conflict between formal industrial structures and informal shop floor organizations had been the central element of the analysis. But after conversations with Mayo, who was visiting Hawthorne at the time, Dickson and Moore prepared a supplement to the report, partly to assuage managers' feelings by stressing that they had been describing fundamental problems and were not trying to fix responsibility on individual supervisors and partly to incorporate some of Mayo's views. The shift was subtle but revealing. Where the two earlier reports had seen restriction of output as a collective response by workers to managerial authority and the pay system, the supplementary report suggested that restriction of output was a misleading term. Workers, they argued, were not consciously doing something wrong, but rather were effecting a compromise within the system, adapting to the fact that there was no incentive for them to work harder. What was needed was further research on the workers' attitudes, judgments, and demands and the development of an industrial system that would meet these needs.[22]

Throughout the supplementary report, the emphasis shifted to the individual worker and away from the analysis of the informal organizations developed by workers on the shop floor. In his report on restriction of output, Dickson had argued that the logic of management and the logic of the employee were antithetical. This was a radical view for a manager in a

---

[22] Dickson to Roethlisberger, 15 Apr. 1932; "Supplement to Report on Bank Wiring Test Group," HSCM/74, A1–B1; W. L. Warner, "Suggested Methods for Studying the Social Situation in the Two Test Rooms," 8 Jan. 1932, EM/1.081; Dickson to Wright, 28 Oct. 1931, HSCM/74, C1–11.

paternalistic, nonunionized company and was attributable to Warner's influence and probably also to Dickson's training in economics, with its emphasis on the rational choices of individuals and groups. Dickson also had little to lose; he had worked for the company for only two and a half years, exclusively in the research division, and when he wrote the report he had every reason to believe that given his short service, he would be laid off within the next few months. But under the influence of Mayo and the explosive response of their superiors, Dickson and Moore adopted a more mainstream position, promising optimistically that industrial organization could meet the needs of the individual worker.

The depression removed any opportunities for further interpretive accommodations. In March 1932 the entire plant began working only seven days a month, and in April this was reduced to five days. A massive layoff was planned in April, but fearful of demonstrations outside the factory, management decided instead to reduce the workforce gradually. As layoffs continued, supervisors were pushed back onto bench jobs; finally, on 19 May 1932, the bank wiring test was terminated and all the workers laid off. The test room finished on a futile note of hope: The day before it closed, the horse on which the test room workers had often bet won for the first time.

Collaborative research in the Hawthorne experiments

Even though the researchers might not be able to agree on interpretations of the experimental results, they worked together closely and convivially, company managers and Harvard academics collaborating in a lengthy research program. Indeed, much of the success of the Hawthorne experiments should be attributed to the organization of a network of collaborative research in which each group and individual made a distinctive contribution. The influence of the Harvard academics on the development of the interviewing and supervisory training programs and the bank wiring test was clearly far greater than it had been in the first four years of the relay assembly test room. Mayo and his colleagues slowly became equal partners with the company researchers, although the relationships between the Harvard and Hawthorne researchers varied considerably according to the individuals concerned. Specific roles emerged, especially for Mayo and Roethlisberger, who became important actors within the social and political hierarchy of Western Electric. At the same time, the meanings drawn from the experiments varied among the participants, under the influence of individual, political, and professional commitments.

Mayo at first enjoyed his visits to Hawthorne; taking the overnight train to Chicago, staying at a luxury hotel at company expense, collaborating with managers who took his ideas seriously, and exploiting this unprecedented opportunity to examine the workers. In 1929 he made five visits, each of roughly one week's duration, primarily to consult on the interviewing program. But his enthusiasm for the visits soon began to pall, and the trip to Chicago seemed increasingly onerous; from 1930 to 1932 Mayo made the trek only when it seemed absolutely necessary, roughly twice a year, and even less after that. In his place he sent his colleagues and assistants, especially Steve Lovekin, Richard Meriam, Fritz Roethlisberger, Lloyd Warner, and "North" Whitehead. He confided to his wife in 1931 that "my absence this year won't be noticed as much as last year – several visits from Warner, Fritz there for four months, Meriam going again and Lovekin probably two visits."[23]

The contributions of the Harvard researchers were coordinated in only the loosest fashion by Mayo. He felt that he imparted all he knew to his young men through reading seminars and personal discussion. In addition, Mayo arranged for them to attend a Boston psychopathological clinic, where they would pose as doctors by putting on white coats and practice their interviewing skills on patients. After that it was up to them to make their way individually at Hawthorne, collaborating with the company researchers rather than carrying out Mayo's directions. This was a highly successful strategy, for it permitted the Harvard researchers to adjust to the circumstances at Hawthorne. It was also a necessary strategy, for the lengthiest stays at Hawthorne by the Harvard researchers occurred during summer, when Mayo was with his family in Europe and effectively out of touch with the research. This casual organization also had its disadvantages. When Roethlisberger visited Hawthorne in the summer of 1931 he discovered that differences between him and Warner had surfaced at Hawthorne and were confusing Wright and the interviewers. Roethlisberger realized that he had only a vague conception of Warner's anthropological point of view and proposed tentatively to Mayo that it might be useful if the Harvard group had occasional meetings to outline their research and approaches for one another. That Roethlisberger was proposing this as late as 1931 is a measure of how loosely Mayo held the reins.

The Harvard academics had to be careful to behave in a manner that would be acceptable to the company researchers. Mayo was always heedful of where responsibility for the experiments lay, and in his writings and talks he invariably stressed that the research was conducted by Hawthorne managers. The behavior of visiting academics at Hawthorne was an equally sensitive issue. Roethlisberger wrote to Mayo describing the problems that Meriam had brought upon himself at Hawthorne by undiplomatic behavior: "Meriam, I feel, made the unfortunate mistake of being a bit too patronizing with regard to the scientific and intellectual capacities of the people out here. This was not said directly, as you know, but I think it showed itself indirectly in many ways. There were too frequent references by first names

---

[23] Mayo to Dorothea Mayo, 10 Apr. [1931], EM/film.

to the vice presidents in New York. He was a bit too anxious to contribute something to research with the net result that he had some of them out here on their back haunches." It was important to act in a way commensurate with one's position: as a consultant and not as research director.[24]

The Hawthorne managers welcomed the Harvard participation. They soon came to depend on Mayo's visits, for they became occasions to hold conferences, reflect on the direction of research, discuss problems, and harvest approval. The company researchers could often be swayed by whoever was visiting at the time. Members of the Interviewing Department described to Roethlisberger how Hal Wright, their department chief, was influenced by the academics: When Warner was visiting, Wright talked of sociological forms and group solidarity; when Roethlisberger was at Hawthorne, Wright emphasized schemas and syncretisms. Dickson similarly moved between anthropological and psychopathological explanations, moderating his sociological analysis of the bank wirers after a visit by Mayo. Wright and Dickson were even more responsive to Mayo's ideas after spending two weeks at the business school in April 1930, where they were put through an intensive session of seminars and informal discussion. They returned to Hawthorne enthusiastic converts; they had received, Putnam told Mayo, "a concentrated dose of the thing all of us feel we have gotten in this work but which does not lend itself to any adequate means of expression."[25]

The difficulty of expressing the accomplishments of the experiments troubled the company researchers. They knew that they had benefited immeasurably from the research and the Harvard collaboration, but remained unsettled by the lack of certainty in the test results and the differences of opinion and approach. Roethlisberger, who spent more time at Hawthorne than any other Harvard researcher and was most in touch with the attitudes of the company researchers, tried to reassure them. He emphasized that they were doing scientific research, not simply carrying out some project with a definite goal; research was characterized by precisely the kind of reformulations that had occurred in the Hawthorne experiments. A certain amount of confusion was healthy, for it prompted new questions and further research: "It may take several years to find out that you are not asking the right question. But one need not grow morbidly pessimistic about that." This was justifiable scientific method (albeit a method that conveniently excused the lack of coherence in the research), but it was not necessarily good politics, for the managers of the Industrial Research Division were required to justify their existence to company executives. At the same time that Roethlisberger was reassuring the company researchers, Mayo advised

---

[24] Roethlisberger to Mayo, 20 July 1931, EM/1.090.
[25] Putnam to Mayo, 14 Jan. 1930, EM/1.089; Putnam to Mayo, 6 May 1930, EM/1.089 (quote); Roethlisberger to Mayo, 20 July 1931, EM/1.090.

Putnam that the time had come "for making an extensive claim in order that your work shall get the attention it deserves."[26]

Mayo's role as public relations officer for the Hawthorne experiments constituted a major part of his contribution. This was most notably the case in the series of publications on the research in the 1930s and 1940s, but also important during the research itself, when the audience was primarily the Western Electric executives and the circle of corporate personnel executives in New York. Mayo's assessments were clearly an important factor when company executives such as Vice-President Clarence Stoll and Thomas K. Stevenson evaluated their investment in the research. When Pennock and Putnam presented papers to a meeting of the Personnel Research Federation in New York in November 1929, the first public airing of the experiments, Mayo was there to underscore their general significance for management and the control of human behavior, and in July 1930 he addressed the Western Electric executives on the contributions of the Hawthorne experiments to industrial psychology. Mayo and George Pennock, who as assistant works manager was the highest Hawthorne manager involved in the research, cooperated closely to maintain the interest and support of the New York executives. Mayo had several conferences with Stoll in 1930 and 1931, impressing upon him the importance of the research and its growing reputation in both America and Europe. The two also collaborated in heading off attacks on the research. At Pennock's request, for example, Mayo wrote a letter defending the experiments from criticism by some New York executives that the interviewing program undermined supervisory functions; his letter dismissing this complaint was duly incorporated into the 1931 report of the research division. Mayo had become integrated into the corporate hierarchy.

The success of the collaborative research at Hawthorne contrasts starkly with the difficulties that Mayo faced in Philadelphia. Several differences in the industrial environment were crucial. First, Western Electric and its parent AT&T were two of the largest corporations in the world, able to invest huge sums in personnel research with little concern for the cost, especially as the Bell System enjoyed phenomenal growth in the 1920s. The textile companies in Philadelphia were small, often family, concerns, caught in an expensive labor market and facing larger competitors with lower costs. For these companies, increasing productivity was a pressing need, one demanding immediate measures; they could not afford to engage in long-range research.

Second, Western Electric had developed an industrial relations and personnel organization that encompassed all levels of the company, from a

[26] Roethlisberger to Wright, 11 Sept. 1930, HSCM/159, F2–5; Wright to Roethlisberger, 9 Oct. 1930, FJR/1; Mayo to Putnam, 18 Dec. 1930, EM/1.089.

vice-president to representatives in every factory branch. The existence of
a large corps of young, enthusiastic personnel managers was essential for
the success of the experiments at Hawthorne. True, the lighting tests and
relay assembly test had been conducted by piece-rate engineers, not personnel managers. But it was the establishment of the Industrial Research
Division, as part of the Industrial Relations Branch, that institutionalized
the research and made its continuation possible. The senior members of the
division were a new breed of middle-level manager; they were recent college
graduates whose careers depended on the success of the experiments. The
careers of most of them at Western Electric would be in this one specialization: Mark Putnam was superintendent of Personnel Service at the Kearny
factory when he left the company in 1945; Hal Wright continued as a
supervisor of personnel research at Hawthorne and New York, finally leaving the company in 1944; Art Moore held various personnel administration
positions in the company, finishing his career in the 1960s back at Hawthorne as director of labor relations; and Bill Dickson worked until his
retirement in 1969 as assistant superintendent for personnel research at
New York headquarters. Max Howarth had the most successful career, first
as superintendent of labor relations and personnel administration for several
Western Electric plants and subsidiaries during the 1930s and 1940s, and
finally as general manager of Sandia Corporation, the Bell subsidiary that
managed nuclear weapons production for the U.S. government. No such
management level existed in the Philadelphia textile mills.

Third, the Hawthorne workers for the most part cooperated with the
research, not an inconsiderable factor when one recalls the resistance Mayo
faced at Continental Mills and Masland in Philadelphia. Several differences
between the Philadelphia textile workers and the Hawthorne workers stand
out. The textile workers, even if they were not presently members of a
union, were part of an established culture of skilled workers in which unionization and resistance to textile owners were deeply ingrained. The Hawthorne workers, at least the large mass of unskilled and semiskilled
operators, were immigrants or the children of immigrants, ethnically frag-
mented, with little or no experience of worker organizations. Their primary
identification was with the company – an attitude fostered by Western
Electric's extensive personnel and welfare programs – and not with their
job or fellow workers. Yet it would be incorrect to assume from this that
the Hawthorne workers were passive experimental subjects; as we have
seen, they cooperated with the research in part because they believed they
could benefit from it, whether by influencing the results in the relay test
room or expressing their complaints in the interviewing program.

Finally, the Hawthorne experiments were perhaps unique among all the
personnel research conducted between the wars in that the researchers were
able to protect the experiments from disruption by the exigencies of industrial production. Mayo's research had been disrupted in Philadelphia by

fluctuations in the business cycle of the textile trade, and the researchers of the British Industrial Fatigue Research Board complained repeatedly of the difficulties of conducting research when production varied so greatly. In contrast, the Hawthorne test rooms were provided with a constant supply of work and parts, ensuring that comparable data could be gathered over significant periods of time.[27]

But in the end the Great Depression caught up with the experiments. The Industrial Research Division was subject to endless rumors of imminent layoffs or disbandment, but significantly its research budget was reduced in line with budgets of production divisions, an indication of its status in the company. By August 1932, however, the researchers realized that while the research organization might continue, several of the key researchers were likely to be laid off. Wright returned from spending the summer at Harvard, where he was analyzing data with Roethlisberger and Whitehead, to find that the situation at Hawthorne had become critical. Dickson was to be laid off, the research was to be placed under the control of a manager who knew nothing of its development, and Wright's own job was in jeopardy. Wright proposed that he and Dickson try to arrange employment at Harvard under Mayo's grant, where they could continue working up the experimental results and prepare them for publication. His experience that summer had made it clear that the research materials were not always self-explanatory and that it was necessary to have one of the company researchers present when the academics were working up the results. If he and Dickson were lost, he pointed out, a good deal of the intimate knowledge of the experiments would disappear with them, especially of the interviewing program and the bank wiring study. His arguments were persuasive, and Pennock and Rice at Hawthorne gave him permission to seek Mayo's approval.[28]

The decision was delayed until late September, when Mayo returned from his European trip. Mayo agreed immediately to Wright's proposal – he had begun himself to work on a series of lectures on the experiments and was acutely aware that the publication of a full and detailed report was sorely needed. Salaries for Wright and Dickson could come out of the ample Rockefeller Foundation grant, whose annual appropriation Mayo never managed to spend completely (a fact that attracted some criticism within the foundation). The final hurdle was to gain the approval of Vice-President Stoll in New York, who was being asked not only to release two of his managers, but also, in effect, to hand the Hawthorne experiments over to Mayo and his Harvard colleagues. Mayo had already been talking with

[27] Industrial Fatigue Research Board, *Third Annual Report*, London, 1923, 4–7; *Sixth Annual Report*, 1926, 47–51.
[28] Wright to Mayo, 22 Feb. 1932, EM/1.091; Dickson to Roethlisberger, 15 Apr. 1932, FJR/1; Wright to Roethlisberger, 25 [Aug.] 1932, EM/1.091.

Stoll for some time about the need to publish an account of the experiments, but this had always been in terms of a collaborative effort between researchers at Hawthorne and Harvard. Stoll needed little persuasion, however, and gave his instant approval. Nevertheless, he was obviously concerned that Pennock and Rice might feel that they were losing their experiments and spent some time trying to sell the idea to them, unaware that they had already agreed. The readiness of the company executives and researchers to entrust the experimental material and publication to Mayo indicates the degree to which he had won their admiration and approval.[29]

The shift of location of the Hawthorne experiments was more than a geographical move from Chicago to Boston. It entailed a transfer of the control of the experiments from Western Electric managers to the Harvard academics. While the experiments were under way it had always been clear that the members of the Industrial Research Division had control of the research, drawing on the talents of their academic consultants, but doing so selectively. It was the academics who had visited Hawthorne, absorbing the industrial environment that shaped the company researchers' attitudes and responses. When Dickson and Wright moved to Harvard, it was their turn to adapt to the atmosphere of the business school. The change in physical environment underscored the move, from the grime and clamor of the Hawthorne Works to the almost rustic serenity of the business school, stretched along the banks of the Charles River. Here the Hawthorne experiments, their publication and dissemination would be controlled by Mayo and his academic colleagues. At Harvard the conflicting approaches and interpretations would gradually be homogenized into a narrative of scientific discovery.

[29] Mayo to Pennock, 7 Dec. 1931, HSCM/159, 2–5; T. N. Whitehead to Mayo, 6 Sept. 1932, EM/1.097; Mayo to Dorothea Mayo, 2–3 Oct. [1932], EM/film.

7

Manufacturing the Hawthorne experiments

BETWEEN 1929 AND 1939 the Hawthorne researchers produced some thirty-three articles and three monographs describing the experiments and their implications for industrial relations; the final work of this series, Fritz Roethlisberger and William Dickson's massive *Management and the Worker*, published in 1939, soon acquired the status of a classic in the social sciences. In their published form, the Hawthorne experiments would have a major impact on the social sciences, on industrial relations practice, and on the elaboration of corporate ideology. The Hawthorne experiments in the official accounts are the logical and unambiguous experiments of the printed page, not the ambivalent research we have been following, the meaning of which could not even be agreed upon by the various participants. Readers of these works were presented with a story of scientific discovery and claims of an increasingly sophisticated understanding of the social relations of work. Disagreements between the researchers over interpretation and meaning were disregarded as the authors sought to construct the authoritative account of the experiments. The workers' views on the experiments were either ignored or explicitly rejected.

The factory site for this production process was not the Hawthorne plant of Western Electric, but Elton Mayo's Industrial Research Department at the Harvard Business School; all the monographs and twenty-five of the thirty-three articles up to 1939 were written at Harvard. Mayo was able to orchestrate the writing of the official accounts and the popularization of the experiments by drawing on the institutional and academic resources of Harvard and the financial resources of his Rockefeller grant. Whereas the development of the research had always been under the control of the company researchers, with the academics only advising the researchers, publication came under the control of Mayo and his Harvard colleagues, a shift that had a significant impact on the type of knowledge produced and on its subsequent influence.

Reflecting in his autobiography on the process of writing *Management and the Worker*, Roethlisberger commented that "the consumer of knowledge can never know what a dicky thing knowledge is until he has tried to produce it."[1] The production of scientific knowledge entails the generation of theories, selection of data, and imposition of meaning, all essentially social activities and subject to the social, political, and disciplinary commitments and personal idiosyncrasies of the scientist. This chapter analyzes the manufacture of the "Hawthorne experiments" out of the raw materials gathered at Hawthorne between 1924 and 1933. It compares the official publications produced in the 1930s with the experimental data and interpretations generated at Hawthorne and Harvard during the research; and it contrasts the different genres published, showing how the researchers produced a variety of publications that reflected their own agendas.

Early dissemination

Mayo was associated with the dissemination and publication of reports of the research from the very start. The New York executives of Western Electric had been attracted to Mayo because he appeared to possess the qualities that would ensure a measured release of the company's research to a wider audience: He was skilled at communicating complex ideas succinctly and clearly; he was sensitive to executives' concerns that reports of the research not reflect unfavorably on company policies; and he was always diplomatic in stressing that the research was being conducted by company managers. From the beginning of Mayo's association with the company, it was probable that he would be responsible for the presentation of the research to the academic community, although at that stage no decisions had been made regarding publication.

The first steps toward releasing information on the experiments came in late 1929. By that time the second relay assembly test had been completed, the mica splitting test had been through its major experimental periods, and the interviewing and supervisory training programs had been operating for a year. With the approval of New York, the Industrial Research Division sent out more than one hundred copies of the fourth progress report of the relay test, in which the results of the first thirteen test periods were described and tentative conclusions were developed about the importance of supervision on morale and production. Some copies were intended for company executives and managers at the other Western Electric plants, but the majority went to industrial relations experts in industry, government, and universities. Mayo provided a list of his American and European contacts, and soon the report was landing on the desks of Piaget, Janet, and Malinowski. Accompanying the report were three papers by George Pennock, Mark Putnam, and Mayo, delivered at the Personnel Research Federation

[1] F. J. Roethlisberger, *The Elusive Phenomena*, Boston: Harvard University, Graduate School of Business Administration, 1977, 53.

in New York in November 1929 and subsequently published in the federation's *Personnel Journal*.

The three articles stressed the scientific nature of the research being conducted at Hawthorne. Pennock contrasted the intuitive and speculative character of most managerial decisions on personnel matters with the experimental approach adopted by the Hawthorne managers. Mayo dismissed previous attempts to conduct human and biological inquiries in industry: "Rags and tatters of physiology and psychology coupled with oddments of techniques have been expected to yield increased production or diminished labor turnover or some other rather obvious justification of the so-called experiment." The researchers argued that the experiments constituted a qualitative leap in personnel research; it seemed that the utopian hopes of the founders of the Personnel Research Federation at the start of the decade were now being realized.[2]

Two themes ran through the articles, and they would be repeated, with variations, through all the writings on the experiments. First, the researchers emphasized that the experiments had entailed a series of major changes in the scientific method of personnel research and that these had been forced upon the researchers as the limitations of existing research methods became apparent. In his paper, Mayo sketched a highly stylized history of the experiments, in which the failure of the lighting tests to isolate a single variable led to the establishment of the relay assembly test room, where there was no attempt to measure the effects of single variables. This history misrepresented both tests, for the lighting tests had tried to take into account the effects of other variables, such as supervision and pay, while the relay test had most definitely tried to gauge the effects of rests, hours of work, and the like. The most significant development in the test room, Mayo felt, was that the supervisor had adopted a "sympathetic and careful technique of listening," which had enabled the researchers to detect the impact of the workers' personal situation on production. But this reorientation to a psychopathological model was by no means as strong as Mayo made out and, to the extent that it had occurred, was because of Mayo's growing influence on the company researchers, and not, as he implied, a necessary outcome of the scientific development of the research.

---

[2] G. A. Pennock, "Industrial Research at Hawthorne," *Personnel Journal*, 1929–30, 8: 296–313; M. L. Putnam, "Improving Employee Relations: A Plan Which Uses Data Obtained From Employees," *Personnel Journal*, 1929–30, 8: 314–25; Elton Mayo, "Changing Methods in Industry," *Personnel Journal*, 1929–30, 8: 326–32, quote on 326–7. These three articles were also produced as a pamphlet for distribution by the company: Western Electric Co., *Research Studies in Employee Effectiveness and Industrial Relations*, 1929. Pennock's and Putnam's speeches and articles were written, at least in the first instance, by R. H. Frazier, the MIT engineer assisting Turner and Hibarger in the relay test; see RATR Daily History Record, 9 Aug. 1929, 20 Aug. 1929, 7 Sep. 1929, HSCM/11–15.

Second, the articles stressed that the experiments had resulted in an extraordinary increase in production. Pennock noted that "from these tests have come some startling results, startling because they were unexpected as well as because they were sometimes contrary to accepted opinion." The overturning of existing conceptions of fatigue, the breakthrough in scientific method, and the adoption of a psychopathological model were all taken to have been scientifically demonstrated by the increase in production. It was as if the increased production had forced particular interpretations on the researchers.[3]

The company researchers differed with Mayo over the importance of increased production, and this reflected their different professional interests. Pennock and Putnam were interested in the practical outcome of the research, in terms of increased production and improved supervision. But Mayo was a social scientist trying to use the factory research as the empirical basis of his social theories. Mayo seemed concerned that the impact of the research would be lessened if it were seen as primarily an attempt to raise productivity. He went to great lengths to argue that increased output had "never been the end or intention of the inquiry"; rather, "the intention of the inquiry from the beginning has been the advancement of our understanding of human situations, the development of a more precise and biological knowledge of what is happening in industry, knowledge of the general conditions that affect human capacity for work." This formulation underscored the unexpectedness of the rise in output, ascribing it to the disinterested application of scientific research. The implication, which Mayo never spelled out and had probably not even consciously recognized, was that management needed to draw on the disinterested research of social scientists; the Hawthorne managers, it seemed, had succeeded only because they had adopted social scientific methods. The tensions between the company's emphasis on practical results and the academics' interest in using the experiments as grounding for their social theory would continue throughout the 1930s.[4]

The success of the Personnel Research Federation meeting encouraged the researchers to present their results to a variety of audiences. Putnam spoke in 1930 and 1931 to the Industrial Relations Association of Chicago, the annual convention of the National Association of Foremen, the YMCA's annual Silver Bay Industrial Conference, and the Pittsburgh Personnel Association, while G. A. Holmes of the Supervisory Training Department spoke to the American Vocational Association and the National Metal Trades Association – an indication of the variety of organizations that

---

[3] Pennock, "Industrial Research at Hawthorne," quote on 303–4.
[4] Mayo, "Changing Methods in Industry," quote on 327. For a further example of the company researchers' more modest interpretation, see M. L. Putnam, "An Experiment in a Scientific Approach to Industrial Relations," Silver Bay Industrial Conference, *Report*, 1930, 30–4.

existed to disseminate research and practical programs to personnel managers in industry. Mayo took the academic road, talking to the annual meeting of the American Economic Association on the "human effects of mechanization," to the British Association for the Advancement of Science and to British industrialists during his 1930 summer trip to Europe, and to the American Neurological Association; these were balanced by a popular talk in an NBC radio series on psychology. Articles by Mayo, Pennock, Putnam, Steve Lovekin, and Richard Meriam spread through the industrial relations and social science journals, Arthur Young of Industrial Relations Counselors distributed reprints of one of Mayo's articles through his industrial relations network, and the International Management Institute in Geneva, closely allied with Arthur Young and for a time funded by John D. Rockefeller, Jr., published translations of the Personnel Research Federation papers into French, German, and Italian. The publicity had its intended effect: By 1931 Mayo could report to Stoll and Pennock that the experiments were widely known throughout Europe and were being cited as a major contribution to personnel research.[5]

Mayo now began to speak to the company researchers and executives about publishing a complete account of the research. Publication at this point was attractive for several reasons. By 1931 the company researchers were beginning to sense that the lack of analysis of the research material already gathered was holding back their research. With the depression biting into the ranks of the Industrial Research Division, a major publication would also demonstrate the valuable work the division had performed and contribute to its chances of survival. Western Electric was receiving many requests from other companies for assistance in establishing interviewing and supervisory training programs, but the absence of a detailed account made it difficult to provide such advice. The New York executives were particularly concerned in this regard that the company's personnel programs might suffer from bad publicity if they were mishandled by other companies. Once Mayo secured Pennock and Putnam's agreement to publish, he went to

---

[5] Mayo to C. G. Stoll, 20 Oct. 1931, EM/1.090. The major papers published at this time were Elton Mayo, "The Western Electric Company Experiment," *Human Factor,* 1930, 6(1): 1–2; idem, "The Human Effect of Mechanization," 42nd Annual Meeting, American Economic Association, *Papers and Proceedings,* 1930, 20(1): 156–76; idem, "Supervision and Morale," *Journal of National Institute of Industrial Psychology,* 1931, 5: 248–60; idem, "Psychopathologic Aspects of Industry," *Transactions American Neurological Association,* 1931, 468–75; idem, "The Problem of Working Together" (NBC radio broadcast, 30 Apr. 1932) in Walter V. Bingham, ed., *Psychology Today,* Chicago: University of Chicago Press, 1932, 231–9; G. A. Pennock and M. L. Putnam, "Growth of an Employee Relations Research Study," *Personnel Journal,* 1930–1, 9: 82–5; Putnam, "An Experiment in a Scientific Approach to Industrial Relations,"; O. S. Lovekin, "The Quantitative Measurement of Human Efficiency under Factory Conditions," *Journal of Industrial Hygiene,* 1930, 12: 99–120, 153–67; and R. S. Meriam, "Employee Interviewing and Employee Representation," *Personnel Journal,* 1931, 10: 95–101.

broach the subject with Vice-President Clarence Stoll in New York. In December 1931 Stoll gave his permission for a narrative of the experiments, which Mayo would prepare from the various reports and experimental records; the title page of the book would simply state that it was written by the Industrial Research Division of Western Electric. At Putnam and Pennock's insistence, the book would be an "account of the actual happenings rather than a discussion of implications" and contain detailed appendixes of the experimental data. The company researchers apparently wanted to deal with the interpretative differences and confusions by confining publication to a descriptive account.[6]

The single collaborative book planned by Mayo never eventuated in its original form. Mayo ended up following his own interests and wrote a semipopular account of the experiments and their social and political implications, delivered in eight Lowell Lectures and published in 1933 as *The Human Problems of an Industrial Civilization*. The task of preparing an account of the development of the experiments and a detailed analysis of the data was passed on to Roethlisberger, Dickson, and Harold Wright, the latter two having arrived at Harvard in November 1932; completed in 1936, *Management and the Worker* would not appear until 1939. Meanwhile, Thomas North Whitehead at Harvard undertook an intensive statistical analysis of five years of data from the relay assembly test, the results of which appeared in *The Industrial Worker*, published in 1938. Each of these works, and the related articles published during the course of their preparation, took different approaches to the presentation of the Hawthorne experiments, reflecting the disciplinary, ideological, and practical concerns of their authors. Yet at the same time the works shared a large common ground of theoretical schemas and ideological orientations, arising from the shared values of the group forming at Harvard.

The Human Problems of an Industrial Civilization

The form of Mayo's *Human Problems of an Industrial Civilization* (1933) reflected fully both his personality and his ideological commitments. Mayo had never enjoyed writing, especially anything of an extended nature; his favorite genre was the essay rather than the academic article or monograph, for the essay came closest to the conversation at which he excelled, at once informal, wide ranging, intimate, and speculative. The eight chapters of the book, originally delivered as Lowell Lectures, form a collection of essays rather than the closely reasoned chapters of an academic monograph. The breadth of Mayo's interests and reading leaps off the page; the theories and research findings of psychiatry, psychology, physiology, political theory, social anthropology, biochemistry, economics, and sociology are jammed

---

[6] Mayo to Putnam, 18 Dec. 1930, EM/1.089; Mayo to Pennock, 7 Dec. 1931, quote on 1, HSCM/159, A2–5; Wright to Mayo, 11 Dec. 1931, EM/1.090.

into its 180 pages. If at times rather bewildering, the overall effect is exhilarating, and the book has attained the status of a minor classic.

That this work was something more than a report of the Hawthorne experiments was clearly signaled in the title and in the placement of chapters. The book opened with a discussion of industrial fatigue, criticizing the physiological concept and rejecting the view that industrial work was fatiguing. The final two chapters consisted of a major attack on existing political theory, a condemnation of the reliance on government intervention to solve social problems, and a call for the establishment of a new "administrative elite" that would promote true human and social collaboration. Strategically placed in the middle of the work were three chapters reporting the Hawthorne research, or at least as much as could fit into this confined space and would support Mayo's thesis. In Mayo's hands, the Hawthorne experiments provided the experimental data on which he could base his political and social theory.

The first two chapters of the book were carefully argued attempts to discount the popular conception of modern industrial work as inherently fatiguing and monotonous. Surveying the research on industrial fatigue since the First World War, Mayo noted that the researchers' hopes of isolating a single cause of fatigue had not been realized. As more research was conducted, in particular by the British Industrial Fatigue Research Board, the less clear did the concept of fatigue become; the physiological changes associated with fatigue – such as oxygen debt and the accumulation of lactic acid in muscles – did not correlate well with actual feelings of fatigue, and attempts to develop a fatigue test had failed. The research of Henderson and his colleagues in the Harvard Fatigue Laboratory had undermined further the concept of fatigue as a single entity. It was rather a term applied loosely to a collection of mutually dependent physiological states, including oxygen consumption, pulse rate, and chemical changes in the blood. What was more, the individual's ability to conduct muscular work before feeling the effects of fatigue varied widely, depending greatly on physical training. "One begins to wonder at this point," Mayo concluded, "whether the word 'fatigue' is not itself in serious danger of being over-worked; it seems to be used to describe a wide variety of situations."[7]

What were the implications of this research for industrial work? Mayo noted first that the kind of fatigue produced at the Fatigue Lab (the researchers, experimenting upon themselves, would often exercise until exhaustion set in) was very rare in industry. Hard physical labor was increasingly being assumed by machines, and where it still existed, there was a process of natural selection through labor turnover whereby only those workers fit enough would remain at the job. (This acceptance of

---

[7] Elton Mayo, *The Human Problems of an Industrial Civilization*, New York: Macmillan, 1933, quote on 8.

turnover and physically demanding labor contrasts starkly with Mayo's views during his Philadelphia research, when he was highly critical of managers who used turnover for this purpose. It is a measure of the extent to which Mayo had accepted management's view of work.) Fatigue was a complex organic imbalance, involving many factors, and a person was forced to stop exercise or work once it set in. But Mayo believed that his studies of workers' pulse pressures and heart rates had demonstrated that the vast majority of manual workers maintained an organic equilibrium and did not become fatigued.

If industrial work was no longer fatiguing, neither was it monotonous in the way often implied by critics. Drawing extensively on the research of the Industrial Fatigue Research Board, Mayo suggested that monotony and boredom were also hypothetical entities; they were inferred from low output and labor turnover and were not experimentally verifiable. Indeed, the British research showed that workers reacted in quite different ways to repetitive work and that the individual temperament of the worker, which itself varied from day to day, and the nature of the work group were as important as the work itself in determining the experience of monotony. Thus, the main effect of the rest periods introduced at Continental Mills in Philadelphia was not that they reduced fatigue but that they altered the workers' psychological response to the repetitive work and permitted greater social cohesion among the workers. Monotony was not located in industrial work, then, but was the result of a "disequilibrium within the individual and between him and his work."[8]

Mayo argued that the results of the relay assembly test provided irrefutable evidence of the importance of the worker's psychological adjustment. In the process of creating the test room and ensuring the cooperation of the workers, the researchers had constructed a more cohesive industrial environment, and thereby transformed the attitudes of the workers. This "novel industrial milieu" was so established by period 12 that the removal of rests and morning meal had little effect on output: "By strengthening the 'temperamental' inner equilibrium of the workers, the company enabled them to achieve a mental 'steady state' which offered a high degree of resistance to a variety of external conditions."[9]

Such a description of the first thirteen periods of the relay test involved a considerable degree of creative interpretation. First, although least important, was Mayo's rather cavalier use of the research data. In describing period 12 (in which rest periods and shorter hours were removed but production remained 19 percent higher than in period 3) Mayo reported that the "daily and weekly output rose to a point higher than at any other time." This was true, but it was also the case that average hourly output had

---

[8] Ibid., quote on 52.
[9] Ibid., quotes on 71 and 72.

declined 3.5 percent; the discrepancy arose because the women were now working a full forty-eight-hour week, compared with less than forty-two hours in the preceding test period. The company researchers had always used average hourly output as the measure of production changes. Indeed, nine pages further on, while discussing a different issue, he noted that hourly output in period 12 had diminished, but dismissed it as being of "minor consequence." In this respect he was correct; a rise or decline of 3.5 percent in a single test period was not crucial one way or another to the interpretation of the experiment. What is revealing is that Mayo felt at liberty to select and shape the data to fit his narrative of scientific discovery and conceptual development.[10]

Second, Mayo sought to discount the test room workers' interpretations of the data by demonstrating that the women's statements were emotional responses rather than objective assessments. In both conversation and questionnaires the women had mentioned the improved work flow, absence of driving supervision, and small-group wage incentive. But, Mayo insisted, the working conditions at Hawthorne were excellent, and the women's comments on the superior conditions in the test room should not be taken as an objective critique of the regular department: "This is simply a type of statement almost inevitably made when a not very articulate group of workers tries to express an indefinable feeling of relief from constraint."[11]

The same was true of the comments gathered in the interviewing program. Mayo regarded workers' comments as merely prejudiced judgments that revealed more about the workers' personal situations than about actual workplace conditions. This was especially true of complaints about supervisors, which had far less validity than complaints about material situations. How Mayo arrived at this distinction is not at all clear, for unlike all other complaints, those about supervisors were never investigated by the Industrial Research Division, but were used only in the preparation of supervisory training materials. Thus, in both the test rooms and the interviewing program, Mayo dismissed the workers' view of events and their environment as prejudiced, emotional, and irrational. In so doing he wrested from the workers the basis for claiming any significant say in the control and direction of their work. In Mayo's view, before the workers' comments could be of any use they had to be reinterpreted by managers trained in the techniques of psychopathology.

In this first half of the book Mayo had stayed fairly close to the literature on industrial fatigue and the experiments in Philadelphia and at Hawthorne.

[10] Ibid., 62–3, 71. Mayo was still more cavalier in articles on the relay test, reporting weekly output without a caveat; see, e.g., Elton Mayo, "The Human Effect of Mechanization," 159–61; and idem, "The Blind Spot in Scientific Management," *Sixth International Management Congress, London, 1935*, London: King, 1935, Development Volume, 214–18, esp. 215.

[11] Mayo, *Human Problems*, quote on 78–9.

But in the final four chapters he drew increasingly on writings in psycho-pathology, sociology, and anthropology, mixing general diagnoses of personal and social maladjustment with the Hawthorne material and his own political observations. Citing the examples of two of the workers in the mica splitting test room, Mayo suggested that their maladjustment was indicative of the widespread mental instabilities that permeated industry and modern society. They were preoccupied with their personal problems and brought these to work; the result was low production and irrational responses to difficulties at work. Their cases were typical of the obsessions and mild neuroses that permeated the "whole fabric of our civilization," and here Mayo referred the reader to the writings of Freud and Janet. Otherwise normal people might be triggered into obsessive thinking by some event that disturbed their personal equilibrium; they would then be less capable of adapting to social situations, including those at work. Thus, Irene Rybacki – who, Mayo informed his readers, had been "permitted to with-draw" from the relay test – had become unbalanced as a result of her anemic condition and therefore responded inappropriately to the company re-searchers.[12]

Not all personal and social maladjustment could be analyzed in terms of individual irrationalities; the problem often lay in group relationships and routines. Mayo turned to the bank wiring test room, where social anthro-pological techniques had enabled the researchers to study the workers' ad-aptation to a specific situation. Despite the fact that there was no conflict between the workers and their supervisor and the work was not monoto-nous, the relationship between the workers and their work was poor: "The group failed to establish an integrate activity and fell into a degree of discord which no one could understand or control." The restriction of output ob-served in the test room was not the result of deliberate collective action by the workers; rather, it was an exasperated response to a poor work sit-uation.[13]

This was a dramatic reinterpretation of the bank wiring test. Dickson and Moore, with Warner's assistance, had viewed restriction of output as the result of a clash between the logic of management and the logic of the workers, or between the technical and social organization of the factory. They had considerable respect and admiration for the way the bank wirers had created their informal group within the formal industrial structure. But Mayo showed no such interest in the workers' perspective; he reported that the workers "expressed their dislike for a situation which imposed upon them a constraint and a disloyalty." This constituted a considerable mis-reading of the workers' attitudes, but then Mayo had never spoken to the bank wirers, for the research protocol had excluded any visitors from the

---

[12] Ibid., quotes on 103, 110.
[13] Ibid., quote on 114.

test room. Sitting at Harvard, Mayo read the research data in the light of his own, primarily psychopathological perspective.[14]

The social disorganization evident in the bank wiring room, Mayo concluded, was symptomatic of a general social disintegration. Sociologists at the University of Chicago had conducted many studies of the effects of this disintegration: Clifford Shaw had observed the higher frequency of juvenile delinquency in the migrant neighborhoods of Chicago, where the traditional cultural patterns and social control of immigrant groups were being broken down; Ruth Cavan had shown a similar statistical pattern for suicides in Chicago. The central problem had been diagnosed by Durkheim: As modern societies underwent rapid industrial development, they lost the solidarity of smaller societies and suffered from anomie – the individual no longer enjoyed a clear social function in the community. The neuroses described by Freud were maladjustments of the individual in the face of this social disintegration; however, Mayo rejected Freud's sexual theory, arguing that sexual obsessions were just one manifestation of more basic social changes. Nevertheless, Mayo believed that it was possible for societies to maintain or regain their social integration; he cited Warner's study of Newburyport as evidence of a community where migrants had become integrated and social classes recognized their community responsibilities.[15]

All of these problems could be confronted if we ceased to rely on political intervention as the only method of social control and turned instead to the insights to be drawn from anthropology, psychology, and sociology. Governments around the world, whether capitalist, socialist, or fascist, were increasing their political control of all social functions in an attempt to enforce order and stability; but such measures were doomed to failure, for they ignored the true causes of social disequilibrium. What, then, was the solution? Mayo paused before providing the answer to that question to consider the findings of anthropologists and psychologists on the problem of social integration. Drawing on the work of Malinowski on the Trobriand Islanders and that of A. R. Radcliffe-Brown on the Andaman Islanders – some of the leading works in the functionalist school of social anthropology – and Warner's research on Australian Aborigines, Mayo argued that primitive societies were stable because the individual was subordinated to the community's social functions:

[14] Ibid., quote on 115.
[15] For the Chicago studies, see Clifford R. Shaw, *Delinquency Areas*, Chicago: University Of Chicago Press, 1929; and Ruth Shonle Cavan, *Suicide*, Chicago: University of Chicago Press, 1928. Mayo perhaps overestimated the degree of social integration in Newburyport. Warner's series discussed in detail how immigration, the depression, and the absentee ownership of factories were combining to split the traditional dependence among the social classes; see, e.g., W. Lloyd Warner and J. O. Low, *The Social System of the Modern Factory*, New Haven, Conn.: Yale University Press, 1947.

> In these primitive communities there is room for an individual to develop skill, but there is no latitude for the development of radical or intelligent opinions.... The unit is, in a sense, the group or commune, and not the separate individuals; the development of anything in the nature of personal capacity must be subordinate to the whole. With us it is quite otherwise; the intent of education in a complex society is to develop intelligence and independence of judgment in the individual. The primitive community develops a social intelligence and not individual intelligences.... This is a very restricted method of living, but it is highly integrate and "functional"; in addition to this it is very comfortable for the individual, who does not need to "wrestle with a solitary problem."

This was not to say that education and intelligence were not important in modern society, but Mayo felt that their importance had been exaggerated. Few individuals in any society were able to arrive at independent judgments; the majority were compelled to live by the "social code."[16]

The work of Jean Piaget on the mental development of children provided Mayo with a further example. Piaget had concluded that children's logical capacity developed in step with their social experience. At one major stage children reached a point where they could respond appropriately to social signals, but still lacked the ability to understand or judge those social situations fully. Mayo believed that most members of society remained in this stage: "Understanding and adequate judgment are acquired late and by many people are not acquired at all, except within some limited area of achieved skill and logic." Individuals made three types of response to their surroundings: logical, in which they had the ability to make independent judgments; nonlogical, in which the logic was socially derived and individuals learned simply to respond to situations without understanding them; and irrational, which indicated social maladjustment and obsession.[17]

By combining these findings from psychology and anthropology, Mayo forged his personal critique of modern society. Social collaboration and integration, especially in primitive societies and small communities, derived from the predominantly nonlogical responses of individuals. But the rapid social change of modern societies had broken down traditional social codes and thus occasioned irrational responses and social maladjustment. In industry, new methods of production had destroyed existing craft traditions; as a consequence nonlogical social organization had been transformed into irrational social disorganization: "The belief of the individual in his social function and solidarity with the group – his capacity for collaboration in work – these are disappearing, destroyed in part by rapid scientific and

---

[16] Mayo, *Human Problems*, quote on 149–50. Mayo drew explicitly on the following works: Bronislaw Malinowski, *Argonauts of the Western Pacific*, New York: Dutton, 1922; and A. R. [Radcliffe-]Brown, *The Andaman Islanders*, Cambridge University Press, 1922. Warner's research in Australia was subsequently published as W. Lloyd Warner, *A Black Civilization: A Social Study of an Australian Tribe*, New York: Harper, 1937.

[17] Mayo, *Human Problems*, quote on 157.

technical advance." The problems in the bank wiring test room were the problems of modern industrial society.[18]

The solution lay in the development of an administrative elite that would look beyond simplistic political intervention to the careful application of scientific knowledge of social organization and control. As the nonlogic of traditional social codes disappeared, it must be replaced by the "logic of understanding" of the administrator. Mayo pointed to the observations by American social philosopher Brooks Adams and Italian sociologist Vilfredo Pareto that revolutions occurred when the ruling class failed to administer society effectively; such would be the fate of the United States and Europe unless a new elite of administrators arose, trained by the universities in the methods of promoting human collaboration: "Better methods for the discovery of an administrative *élite,* better methods of maintaining working morale. The country that first solves these problems will infallibly outstrip the others in the race for stability, security, and development."[19]

The book finished on this note, a mixture of dire warning, guarded optimism, and vague prescription. After the diagnosis of social disintegration and the rosy picture of social collaboration in traditional societies, Mayo's solution seemed terribly imprecise and inadequate. He could identify in a general way the need for a new social code and an administrative elite – in government, business, and the community – that would understand the problems of social collaboration. But he had less interest in the details of building the future, for he was at heart a conservative man who identified more strongly with the Victorian values of his childhood. Writing to his wife, he admitted, "I support 'modern change,' whatever it is, and work for it as faithfully as I can – but in my private self I don't have to like it, and I don't." By 1935 Mayo was forecasting the "breakdown of civilization" within three years, and he placed much of the blame on revolutionaries, whom he believed controlled Hollywood and were using entertainment to disaffect the public, and on Jews, against whom Mayo railed in his letters to his wife: "One is staggered by the effective destruction that the Jew is unwittingly accomplishing – one cannot talk about this topic because one is instantly classified with the 'antis.' "[20]

This political pessimism and conservatism was accompanied by recurring depression and an acute boredom with his work at Harvard. His commitments to Western Electric and the Rockefeller Foundation having been fulfilled by the publication of *Human Problems,* Mayo could not find other work to absorb him. In addition, Dorothea Mayo had moved to England in 1934, where their two daughters were attending school. Mayo contem-

[18] Ibid., quote on 159.
[19] Ibid., quote on 171.
[20] Quotes from Mayo to Dorothea Mayo, 3–5 Nov. [1934], EM/film; Mayo to Dorothea Mayo, 5–6 May [1935], EM/film. See also Mayo to Patricia Mayo, 19 Oct. [1932], EM/ film; Mayo to Dorothea Mayo, 9–11 Apr. [1935], EM/film.

plated quitting Harvard, and he instructed his wife to sound out the possibility of a job in England. But English academic jobs paid little compared with his handsome Rockefeller salary, and no other opportunities were forthcoming in the middle of the depression. Wallace Donham, dean of the business school, and L. J. Henderson persuaded Mayo that he was needed at Harvard, especially since the publication of his book and other articles on the Hawthorne experiments had awakened interest in Mayo's ideas. So Mayo remained, lonely and often depressed in his rented apartment, waiting for the summer when he could join his family for a European vacation; in all these years at Harvard Mayo formed a close friendship with only one person, Henderson, an egotistical and irascible man with whom Mayo had to exercise his considerable clinical skills of tact and patience. The articles he produced during the rest of the decade bear the marks of his boredom. They were for the most part repetitive and rambling, even erratic, and to the extent that they discussed the Hawthorne experiments they simply paraphrased the articles being prepared by Whitehead, Roethlisberger, and Dickson.[21]

Mayo's major work received generally favorable reviews; Chicago sociologist Robert Park wrote an especially laudatory essay review in the *American Journal of Sociology,* and many reviewers praised the interdisciplinary nature of the research, although some noted that the research hardly supported the generalizations of the later chapters. Chicago industrial psychologist Arthur Kornhauser, who had followed the experiments closely and visited Hawthorne on several occasions, described the problems forcefully: "The author, in his search for answers, delightfully ignores the fences separating academic fields of knowledge ... and uses what bricks lie at hand in each. Even so, only a few shaky columns are erected. The need for vastly better building blocks is only too apparent." Bill Dickson astutely commented to Roethlisberger that Mayo had been unable to capture in his writing the clarity and graphic illustrations that made his conversation so effective – a testament perhaps to Mayo's conversational abilities rather than a criticism of the book.[22]

In the process of embedding the Hawthorne experiments in his ideological matrix, Mayo crystallized certain interpretative constructs of the Hawthorne experiments that would, to various degrees, influence his colleagues' writing on the experiments and the assumptions of generations of readers. First,

[21] For observations on Mayo's and Henderson's personalities in this period by a student, see George Caspar Homans, *Coming to My Senses: The Autobiography of a Sociologist,* New Brunswick, N.J.: Transaction Books, 1984, 90, 139–40.
[22] Dickson to Roethlisberger, 25 Oct. 1939, FJR/1. Reviews of Mayo's *Human Problems* include Robert E. Park, "Industrial Fatigue and Group Morale," *American Journal of Sociology,* 1934–5, 40: 349–56; Edward S. Cowdrick, *Personnel Journal,* 1934, 12: 362–3; and Arthur Kornhauser, *Annals of the American Academy of Political and Social Science,* 1934, 172: 171.

Mayo, as had previous researchers, took changes in production as a measure of fatigue, monotony, and morale. He was always careful to insist in his writings that production was used as a measure simply because it was the only objective measure readily available; it was a useful index of the worker's adaptation to the industrial environment. At times he went so far as to claim that the Hawthorne researchers had no interest in increasing production. But by operationalizing workers' adaptation and morale in terms of their output, Mayo was building an identity of interest between managers and workers right into his measures: Increased production not only pleased managers but was an indication of the workers' happiness with their job. Low production was not only less profitable to employers, but the sign of a dispirited workforce that would welcome managerial intervention.

Second, Mayo placed the relay assembly and bank wiring test rooms at opposite poles of industrial organization and worker adaptation. In his writings the relay test room became an industrial utopia in which the workers were content and well adapted to their environment and, of course, production rose:

> They have constituted themselves a social group and associate together outside the factory. They have developed a positive preference for the surroundings of the "test room" and their work, formerly perfunctory, perhaps even deliberately restricted, is now done with wholehearted interest and zest. One can fairly claim that in each instance the whole personality has emerged in action, and that the major increment in production records this rather than the effect of any item of the experimental change of conditions.

The bank wiring test room, in contrast, was an industrial disutopia, its workers discontented and maladjusted, and the restriction of output the result of mental conflict. In the relay test, a nonlogical social code had been inadvertently established by the researchers, whereas the bank wirers continued to be dominated by irrational responses to their environment. Each of these test rooms were, in turn, microcosms of social organization at large.[23]

Finally, Mayo consistently rejected the view that workers had any contribution to make to the organization of their work. Mayo denied that workers' comments in the test rooms and interviewing had any validity as descriptions of actual problems; workers' complaints reflected for the most part their personal and social maladjustment. Workers were able only to adopt a nonlogical relationship to their work and society, accepting unquestioningly the existing social code. Workers who did question that code, who became radicals and "destroyers," did so because they had overintellectualized their situation, probably as a result of some personal psychic trauma. (Mayo still liked to use the example of a Brisbane radical whose

[23] Mayo, "Psychopathologic Aspects of Industry," quote on 475.

politics stemmed from his mistreatment by his drunken and brutal father. Mayo's attacks on radicals strengthened during the 1930s, as the Communists gained influence in American working-class politics.)[24] A logical understanding of the workplace and society was reserved for only a few – the managers and administrators who would work to ensure that the social code was adapted to scientific and technical change. Frederick Winslow Taylor had advocated that knowledge of the technical organization of production be consolidated in management, leaving workers to perform on command a series of discrete, unskilled tasks. Mayo was now advocating that management take charge of the social relations of production, and he seemed to offer scientific proof that workers could achieve happiness and their full productive potential only if managers recognized that workers were emotional children who needed firm parental guidance.

The interaction between Mayo's version of the Hawthorne experiments and his social and political ideology was therefore dialectical. The experiments became Mayo's major evidence for his ideological position, by providing examples of the need for nonlogical social codes and enlightened administrators and by providing experimental proof of his theories. For Mayo the increase in production in the relay test room proved that his theories, if applied throughout society, would promote human happiness and well-being. In turn, Mayo's ideological framework permeated the Hawthorne experiments, reinterpreting and reshaping the events in fundamental ways.

A statistical analysis

Where Mayo was cavalier in his use of the experimental data, using it as illustrative material rather than as rigorous evidence for his hypotheses, Thomas North Whitehead presented a painstaking analysis of the data in an attempt to prove statistically that personal and social relationships had been the dominant factors in the relay assembly test room. Whitehead, the son of the famous British philosopher Alfred North Whitehead, had trained as an economist and engineer in Britain, worked as a science officer for the British Admiralty in the 1920s, then taken an assistant professorship at the Harvard Business School in 1931, at the age of forty. He accompanied Mayo on his next trip to Hawthorne and was soon participating in the experiments, bringing his statistical skills to bear on the extraordinary array of detailed production data that had been collected in the relay assembly test. The expensive analyzing machines were purchased with Rockefeller funds, and by the end of 1932 Whitehead was employing six women to analyze the test room output tapes, all funded by Mayo's grant. The pro-

---

[24] Mayo, "The Blind Spot in Scientific Management," 217; idem, "Routine Interaction and the Problem of Collaboration," *ASR*, 1939, 4: 335–40.

duction of scientific knowledge involved the same sexual division of labor that obtained in the relay assembly test room itself.

Whitehead produced an impressive amount on the Hawthorne experiments – five articles and two books between 1934 and 1938; yet they have slipped into obscurity, while Mayo's *Human Problems* and Roethlisberger and Dickson's *Management and the Worker* continue to be read and cited. The reasons are not difficult to ascertain. Whitehead's statistical analysis was complex and poorly presented, and his ideas were unoriginal and expressed in infuriatingly vague prose. Nevertheless, Whitehead's work remains important for understanding the history of the experiments. It was the only attempt by the researchers to undertake a statistical analysis of the relay test data, and because Roethlisberger and Dickson covered only the first thirteen periods, it provided the only account of the entire six years of the relay test.

Whitehead's research culminated in *The Industrial Worker*, published in 1938, one year before *Management and the Worker*. It is a daunting book, consisting of two quarto volumes, one of text and one of tables, graphs, and figures. Much of the statistical material is presented in diagrammatic form, and while Whitehead had hoped that this would make his work more accessible, the effect is often to remove the reader still further from the statistical analysis on which the diagrams are based. In arriving at particular conclusions, Whitehead sometimes inundates the reader with superfluous information; at other places, sophisticated statistical constructs are explained so briefly that they remain quite impenetrable.[25]

If the evidence was at times confusing, the basic argument of the book was clear enough. Following the introduction, Part 2 comprised an analysis of the effect on production of the test room's "material environment." Much of this repeated, if more thoroughly, the calculations done by Turner and his assistants at MIT back in 1928. No significant correlation could be found between changes in quantity or quality of output and hours of work, hours of rest, temperature and humidity, or other changes in experimental conditions. In other cases, Whitehead managed to find support for conclusions already made by the researchers. For example, by comparing output in the first hour after changing a relay type with output on the succeeding day on that same type, he could show that the women did not have to go through a learning curve each time they changed relays; as experienced workers they were capable of shifting among a variety of work patterns without slowing their output. On the basis of these statistical findings, Whitehead concluded, as had the other researchers, that physical changes were not in themselves important factors in the test room, for they varied

[25] T. N. Whitehead, *The Industrial Worker: A Statistical Study of Human Relations in a Group of Manual Workers,* 2 vols., Cambridge, Mass.: Harvard University Press, 1938. See the bibliography of Hawthorne publications for Whitehead's other writings.

within a range that did not disturb the ability of the workers to maintain
a constant rate of production; they were important only inasmuch as they
were bound up with the personal and social situations.

In Part 3 Whitehead turned to a description of the social organization of
the test room and the relationships of the workers, based on the Daily
History Record, interviews, reports, and recollections of the workers and
researchers. His account concentrated on the constantly changing social
dynamics among the workers, both in terms of their group cohesiveness
and the relations among individual workers. The removal of the two workers
from the test room provided a key example of the importance of social
relations. Whitehead argued that the workers were removed because they
"failed to respond to the developing purpose of the group":

> The difficulty with Ops. 1a and 2a did not originate with their "low
> output." The group had a conscious purpose, a raison d'être, and in
> this purpose Ops. 1a and 2a had failed to take an interest. The result
> was a bifurcation of motive which split the residents into opposing
> camps, and ended in the rejection of the obstructive minority. The lead
> in this final act was taken by the other operators rather than by the
> supervisor.

Whereas Mayo had explained the event in terms of the psychiatric and
physiological problems of Irene Rybacki, Whitehead saw the women's behavior as being dysfunctional for the emerging group and claimed that this
was the reason for the women's expulsion. In both interpretations, however,
any notion that the women were trying to exert deliberate control over the
test room was rejected in favor of the view that the women's behavior was
unconscious and emotional.[26]

Finally, in Part 4 Whitehead attempted to show that one could detect the
changing social relations in the test room by a statistical analysis of changes
in output. Elaborate measures were developed to prove this point. Whitehead first constructed running averages of output for each worker and the
group, then created curves that measured fluctuations in output over different time spans – one day to one week, one to four weeks, and four to
twelve weeks. He then calculated, for each of the time spans, the relationships between the fluctuations of output of two workers; these were presented as coefficients of determination (r^2) in diagrams for several chosen
moments. Thus, in Figure 9, the numbers indicate the coefficient of determination for fluctuations in output between each of the workers. A high
positive coefficient indicates that the pair of workers is tending to speed up
and slow down its work in unison; a low coefficient indicates that there is
no measurable relationship between fluctuations in output of a pair of
workers.

These diagrams of the pair relationships of workers reflected, Whitehead

[26] Ibid., 1: 115–19, quotes on 131, 119.

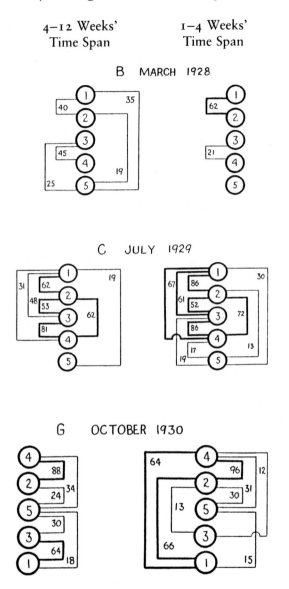

Figure 9. Pair relationships in the relay assembly test room. From Thomas North Whitehead, *The Industrial Worker*, Cambridge, Mass.: Harvard University Press, 1938, 2:D-23. Reprinted by permission.

claimed, the influence on production of such variables as personal friendships and the changing social sentiments of the group. For example, the friendship of Mary Volango (Op. 1) and Jennie Sirchio (Op. 2) was reflected in high coefficients of determination between the two workers (see March 1928); when Lottie Blazejak (Op. 4) challenged Sirchio for leadership of the test room, the coefficient between these two women increased dramatically (see July 1929). The effect of the rearrangement of seating from April 1930 to February 1931 resulted in a reduction in group solidarity, as revealed by a general decline in pair relationships (see October 1930). Changes in the coefficients of pair relationship or of individual workers to the other four workers coincided with important social events in the test room to a far greater extent than could be accounted for by chance. Whitehead concluded that the coefficients in each time span reflected different aspects of the personal and social situation of the test room: The one day to one week span reflected personal relations, the one to four week span related to the social process of the group, and the four to twelve week span recorded the more general sentiments of the group.

The results of Whitehead's years of statistical analysis were not that impressive. The pair relationships could be used too selectively to be very persuasive, and even Whitehead was forced to admit that the conclusions were qualitative rather than quantitative. Still, his work gave the Hawthorne experiments a patina of statistical rigor to back up the interpretations of the other researchers.

Whitehead's writings were also important for applying a new model, derived from the writings of Italian sociologist Vilfredo Pareto, to the interpretation of the experiments. The idea of using Pareto reflected theoretical shifts in the Harvard group and the ascendancy of Henderson to the position of intellectual leader of the group, replacing the increasingly dispirited Mayo. Henderson had begun reading Pareto in the late 1920s and became a zealous convert. As a physiologist who had devoted his scientific career to studying the body as a physicochemical system, measuring simultaneous changes in mutually dependent variables, Henderson was attracted to Pareto's view that society was also a system and that social phenomena had to be explained in terms of the whole system. Societies, like physiological systems, were in a state of equilibrium, and any disturbance in the system would result in a reaction that served to restore the system to equilibrium. For Pareto, social systems comprised two major elements: "residues," or the sentiments that drove individual and collective behavior; and "derivations," or the rationalizations that people used to explain their behavior. Historians and social scientists, Henderson observed, rarely analyzed the nonlogical basis of actions; and he felt that Pareto had revolutionized sociology by emphasizing the role of sentiments in social action.[27]

[27] L. J. Henderson, *Pareto's General Sociology: A Physiologist's Interpretation*, Cambridge,

Henderson overestimated Pareto's originality, primarily because, as Roethlisberger noted sardonically, he was "a one-book sociologist." Nevertheless, Henderson's enthusiasm for Pareto influenced a significant group of young sociologists. For two years commencing in the fall of 1932 Henderson ran a seminar on Pareto in which he tried to convert a group of colleagues and graduate students. In addition to Mayo, Roethlisberger, Whitehead, and Warner, the seminar included Talcott Parsons and Robert Merton, who would soon become two of the leading sociologists of their generation, and George Homans, a young sociologist studying with Henderson and Mayo. Henderson's zeal and energy (Homans said of Henderson that "his manner in conversation was feebly imitated by a pile-driver") influenced Whitehead, Roethlisberger, and Dickson, who began to view Henderson as the leader of the group and applied the Paretan scheme to the Hawthorne data. Mayo always remained less enthusiastic about Pareto; he confessed to his wife that he was bored by the seminars, and although he referred to Pareto in his writings, he preferred Janet and Freud on the importance of nonlogical action and relied on social anthropology for insights into social systems.[28]

Adopting Pareto's model and language, Whitehead argued that the relay test room had all the characteristics of a social system. The workers were always reacting to changes in the entire system of social and technical factors rather than to any experimentally induced change. Once the social system of the workers in the test room had been formed and reached equilibrium, the collection of sentiments and activities — Pareto's term for this was the "persistence of aggregates" — would resist any disturbances, until finally the system would suddenly disintegrate and establish a new equilibrium. Thus, Whitehead's figures of pair relationships were interpreted as snapshots of the social system of the test room.

Further, the relay test room became a model for all social systems, for it showed how leaders could build new patterns of social activity in the face of established social routine. In his *Leadership in a Free Society*, published in 1936, Whitehead recast, in Paretan terminology, many of Mayo's criticisms of the excessive reliance in industry and government on formal organizations. Modern administrators had to take into account the sentiments

Mass.: Harvard University Press, 1935; L. J. Henderson, *On the Social System: Selected Writings*, Chicago: University of Chicago Press, 1970; Vilfredo Pareto, *The Mind and Society: A Treatise on General Sociology*, 4 vols., New York: Harcourt Brace, 1935. For a discussion of Henderson's organicist views, see Stephen J. Cross and William R. Albury, "Walter B. Cannon, L. J. Henderson, and the Organic Analogy," *Osiris*, 1987, 2d ser., 3: 165–92.

[28] On the Pareto seminar, see Barbara S. Heyl, "The Harvard 'Pareto Circle,' " *Journal of the History of the Behavioral Sciences*, 1968, 4: 316–34; for the accounts of two participants, see Roethlisberger, *The Elusive Phenomena*, 60–71, quote on 61; and Homans, *Coming to My Senses*, 104–18, quote on 91. Other members of the seminar included Joseph Schumpeter, Crane Brinton, Bernard De Voto, Hans Zinsser, Pitirim Sorokin, and Edwin Cohn.

and social routines of organizations if they were to be effective leaders. If managers did not do so, then other organizations such as the informal organization in the bank wiring test room, unions, or political organizations would arise to fulfill workers' needs for social activity; these groups were "not always desirable or easy to control." The warning was clear: Unless industrial and government leaders concerned themselves more with the human relations of industry and society, they would be replaced by other groups more capable of constructing a social equilibrium.[29]

Management and the Worker

By the time Roethlisberger and Dickson's *Management and the Worker* appeared in 1939, the audience had been well prepared. The writings of Mayo, Whitehead, and the company researchers, as well as earlier articles by Roethlisberger and Dickson, had made the Hawthorne experiments widely known among social scientists and personnel managers. But these publications had reported the experiments in piecemeal fashion or, in the case of Mayo's writings, left the reader hungry for further details. *Management and the Worker* addressed that need; here was the comprehensive and definitive account of the Hawthorne experiments, coauthored by researchers from Harvard and Western Electric.

The size and the presentation of the book seem to guarantee its authority. The reader is confronted by more than six hundred pages of text and more than eighty tables and figures, organized in twenty-six chapters. A foreword by Western Electric vice-president C. G. Stoll and a preface by Mayo underscore the significance of the publication. In the introductory chapter the authors stress that in addition to reporting the experimental results, theoretical conclusions, and practical applications, they are presenting a chronological report of the experiments – a history of the process of discovery. Here, the reader is assured, is an objective history of the experiments, a narrative made all the more authentic because it reports the "trials and tribulations of a research investigator" and bears the "stamp of human imperfection."[30]

This modesty is misleading, for although it has a certain beguiling charm and is in keeping with Roethlisberger's and Dickson's personalities, it masks the extent to which the authors imposed particular interpretations on the experimental data. The patterns of interpretation developed in the earlier writings are present throughout *Management and the Worker:* the dismissal of workers' comments and beliefs as irrational, or at least nonlogical; the

[29] T. N. Whitehead, *Leadership in a Free Society*, Cambridge, Mass.: Harvard University Press, 1936, quote on 119.

[30] F. J. Roethlisberger and William J. Dickson, *Management and the Worker: An Account of a Research Program Conducted by the Western Electric Company, Hawthorne Works, Chicago*, Cambridge, Mass: Harvard University Press, 1939, quote on 4.

brisk rejection of economic motives as an explanation for workers' behavior; the attention to the supposed emotional needs of the individual worker; and the assumption that workers themselves could be satisfied only if managers extended their control over the social organization of the workplace. The ideological message was all the more potent because it was presented in conclusions that were apparently the unbiased result of scientific research.

The structure and style of the book were influenced by several converging factors. Roethlisberger felt an obligation to Mayo and the Rockefeller Foundation to write up the experiments as a whole; he felt guilty that instead of producing the definitive volume of experimental results, Mayo seemed interested only in wining and dining the Rockefeller officials. Roethlisberger was also the one Harvard researcher who had spent extended periods of time at Hawthorne, and he had absorbed the concerns of managers to a greater degree than Mayo, Whitehead, or Warner. When Roethlisberger sat down with Dickson and Wright to plan the book in late 1932, the group's center of gravity leaned toward the problems that had motivated the Industrial Research Division at Hawthorne rather than the Industrial Research Department at Harvard. However, Roethlisberger and Dickson had been associated with only parts of the research, notably the interviewing program and bank wiring test, and knew the other research only secondhand. In writing up all of the research they were obliged to make sense out of a diverse set of experiments that had been guided by a variety of perceptions and motivations. They adopted a historical approach that emphasized the gradual evolution of the experiments, in which each new piece of research addressed issues raised in the previous experiment. *Management and the Worker* was designed to be at once comprehensive, historical, and a record of the research from the viewpoint of the company researchers.[31]

The writing of the book turned out to be a far more arduous task than anyone had envisaged. When Dickson and Wright joined Roethlisberger at Harvard in November 1932, the three optimistically planned that they would have a draft within eight months: Wright would report on the relay assembly test, Dickson on the bank wiring test, and Roethlisberger on interviewing. Eight months later, with a new division of labor, each of them was still writing the chapters on the relay test; one in particular, that on the fatigue hypothesis, required extensive reading and research and occupied Dickson for ten months. In August 1933 Wright returned to Hawthorne, leaving the other two to complete the bulk of the manuscript. (The title page of the book would record his contribution by noting, beneath Roethlisberger and Dickson's names, "the assistance and collaboration of Harold A. Wright.") For the next two and a half years, Roethlisberger prepared the chapters on the interviewing program and Dickson those on the bank

[31] For Roethlisberger's revealing recollections of writing *Management and the Worker,* see his *Elusive Phenomena,* 51–4.

wiring test. They had also planned to return in the final part of the book to the new developments in the relay assembly test – the interviewing and observation program as well as the statistical analysis – but this was dropped in favor of Whitehead's separate volume on the relay tests. Finally, in February 1936 Bill Dickson returned to Hawthorne and the completed manuscript was sent to Stoll at Western Electric headquarters.[32]

Management and the Worker is, despite its length and exhaustiveness, an eminently readable book. The authors had the Hawthorne supervisors and managers in mind as their potential readers, and consequently the book is written in clear and accessible prose, eschews lengthy theoretical discussions, and presents the material entertainingly and at times humorously. Narrative interest is maintained by the presentation of the practical and theoretical difficulties of conducting the research and the gradual changes in the researchers' understanding; indeed, the drama of scientific discovery provides the very structure of the book.

Yet for all the emphasis on providing a realistic account of the research, the book is a highly stylized rendering of the Hawthorne experiments and one that has misled generations of social scientists. The authors constructed an unfolding chronology of discovery in which the results of one part of the experiments brought insights that transformed the research and pushed the researchers along a new path. The authors emphasized the moments of insight by dividing the book into four parts, each of which presented a particular experimental approach and marked the transition to the next. "Chronologically," the authors argued, "the inquiry divided itself naturally into four stages, each stage representing a major change in working hypothesis and method." Thus, according to Roethlisberger and Dickson, the early test room studies – the relay assembly test, second relay test, and mica splitting test – concentrated on the effects of working conditions on employee efficiency. But the growing realization that the factors being studied were all interrelated and could not be measured independently led to the implementation of the interviewing program, which aimed to collect and analyze workers' comments throughout the plant. Eventually the researchers recognized that the comments could not be taken as indicative of the objective conditions in the workers' departments; complaints reflected the workers' personal situations and maladjustment more than they did actual conditions. When in turn the researchers' attention was directed to the adjustment of a group of bank wirers to their work, it was discovered that the informal social organization of the workers had a major influence on the structuring of their work and behavior.[33]

Two examples will suffice to demonstrate the ways in which this chro-

[32] "Book Log," FJR/3; Mayo to Stoll, 21 Feb. 1936, EM/1.092; Roethlisberger to Wright, 27 Feb. 1934, HSCM/159, D14–E1.
[33] Roethlisberger and Dickson, *Management and the Worker*, 3–5, quote on 5.

nology differed from the dynamics of the experiments presented in the earlier chapters of this book. First, the authors suggest that the dramatic events of period 12 of the relay test, in which production remained high despite the removal of rest periods and shorter working hours, brought a transformation in the research:

> No longer were the investigators interested in testing for the effects of a single variable. In the place of a controlled experiment, they substituted the notion of a social situation which needed to be described and understood as a system of interdependent elements.

This is a post facto reinterpretation of the researchers' views at the time: The progress report of May 1929 did not arrive at such a firm conclusion, but continued to emphasize the effects of changed supervision. Roethlisberger and Dickson also imply that the interviewing program arose out of the recent insights of period 12; however, interviewing commenced before that moment of revelation. Second, in their description of the transition from the interviewing program to the bank wiring test, the authors claim that the investigators had become dissatisfied with the program of interviewing individuals, for although it captured the workers' personal situations it missed the social relations within the plant, and that the bank wiring room was established as a place to observe these social relations without disturbing the work environment. Missing are the more pragmatic reasons for the bank wiring test: the abandonment of interviewing because of the depression; the influence of the foreman in ensuring that the bank wiring test room was no different from the regular department; the practical concern with restriction of output, previously noted in the department; and Warner's considerable influence on the approach taken by the researchers over the objections of Roethlisberger and Mayo. (Although the bank wiring room was referred to in the original experimental records as the "bank wiring test room," Roethlisberger and Dickson renamed it the "bank wiring observation room" in the book to highlight the social anthropological approach taken.) In both of these examples, a transition in the experiments caused by a variety of factors was presented as a purely logical development arising out of the dynamics of scientific research.[34]

The book suppressed the significant differences among the researchers, describing the many participants simply as "the investigators" or "the experimenters," terms that expressed their scientific status. No attempt was made to identify the company and academic researchers who participated in any particular experiment. Although footnotes recorded the assistance of Turner in the relay test, Mayo in interviewing, and Warner in the bank wiring test, the reader cannot gain any sense of the degree or importance of that participation. In keeping with the chronological account, the term

[34] Ibid., 182–6, quote on 183, 373–91.

"the investigators" was intended to describe those researchers actually participating in any particular test, but from our perspective it seems to refer to what the opinions of Roethlisberger and Dickson would have been had they been involved in that part of the research.

The confusion of chronological narrative and authorial interpretation was probably inevitable, but it undermined the authors' claim that they had carefully separated experimental facts and the theories used to order and interpret those facts. True, they did try to split material into descriptive and analytical chapters, and they avoided abstruse theoretical discussions in the text, confining to footnotes their references to social scientists such as Pareto and Radcliffe-Brown. But in practice the descriptions of the relay and mica tests were infused with notions of group solidarity and sentiment, even if the authors avoided the use of those terms. This is not to argue that the authors had a simplistic notion of scientific method; Roethlisberger believed that there was a continual interplay between theories and observations. But there was a clear sense in *Management and the Worker*, highlighted by its narrative structure, that the experimental facts had forced the final conceptual scheme upon the investigators. This feeling is reinforced by the book's failure to discuss other personnel research that made similar observations or arguments and that had in some cases influenced the Hawthorne researchers – for example, the work of the Industrial Fatigue Research Board on fatigue and industrial neuroses, of Stanley Mathewson on the restriction of output, or of Arthur Kornhauser on worker attitudes. The Hawthorne experiments stood alone, their facts incontrovertible, their conceptual scheme unchallenged.[35]

The theoretical framework of the book came out most clearly in the discussions of the interviewing of supervisors and the bank wiring test, the experiments with which the authors had been directly involved. They argued that the attitudes and complaints of workers and supervisors had to be analyzed in the same way that Radcliffe-Brown had studied the beliefs and sentiments of the Andaman Islanders: "Their meaning, or function, can be discovered by understanding, first, the sentiments which these attitudes express and, secondly, the social interaction to which the sentiments can be related." And they insisted that the existing social organization, whether in the bank wiring room or in the factory as a whole, was best viewed as a Paretan social system: "We conceive the chief character of a social organization to be an interaction of sentiments and interests in a relation of

---

[35] The absence of references to the work of other industrial researchers is striking; of the forty-six references that could be described as industrial research, nineteen are to research by those at Harvard, including the Fatigue Laboratory, and of the remaining twenty-seven references to work by others, the vast majority occur in the chapter on fatigue and are highly critical of the research.

mutual dependence, resulting in a state of equilibrium such that if that state is altered, forces leading to re-establish it come into play."[36]

A detailed analysis of social participation in the bank wiring room provided the evidence for this framework. By studying the interactions among the workers – such as their games, the controversies over whether the windows should be open, and their job trading and assisting of one another – Roethlisberger and Dickson measured the informal organization of the group. Graphic representations of these relationships (which were clear and accessible in comparison with Whitehead's confusing diagrams) showed that there were two cliques in the test room (Figure 10). These were based on a combination of occupational status of the different jobs in the test room, physical location, and individual personalities. The work behavior of individuals, including their level of output, was related closely to membership in these cliques. The authors suggested that Clique B, consisting primarily of lower-status connector wiremen, produced less than Clique A of selector wiremen because, in part, the lower production of Clique B expressed their opposition to the other clique. But there was also social solidarity in the bank wiring group as a whole, especially in relation to external forces and outside interference. The group protected itself from interference by enforcing certain sentiments and behavior; thus, the activities associated with the restriction of output "represent attempts at social control and discipline and as such are important integrating processes."[37]

Workers behaved in this way because the factory had a human organization as well as a technical organization. They demanded personal satisfaction and social meaning from their work, not just an economic wage; the workplace was a social system with two interrelated functions, the production of goods and the creation and distribution of satisfaction among the members of the organization. Yet companies were judged only in terms of their economic success and never in terms of their internal social equilibrium:

> A great deal of attention has been given to the economic function of industrial organization. Scientific controls have been introduced to further the economic purposes of the concern and of the individuals within it. Much of this advance has gone on in the name of efficiency or rationalization. Nothing comparable to this advance has gone on in the development of skills and techniques for securing co-operation, that is, for getting individuals and groups of individuals working together effectively and with satisfaction to themselves. The slight advances which have been made in this area have been overshadowed by the new and powerful technological developments of modern industry.

[36] Roethlisberger and Dickson, *Management and the Worker*, quotes on 358, 365n. The authors thanked Warner, rather than Mayo, for drawing their attention to the works of Durkheim, Malinowski, Radcliffe-Brown, and Simmel; see 389n.
[37] Ibid., quote on 523.

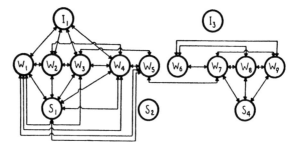

Participation in Games

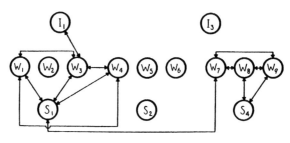

Friendships

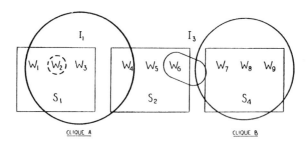

The Internal Organization of the Group

Figure 10. Social groups in the bank wiring test room (W, wirer; S, solderer; I, inspector). From F. J. Roethlisberger and William J. Dickson, *Management and the Worker*, Cambridge, Mass.: Harvard University Press, 1939, 501, 507, 509. Reprinted by permission.

Thus, the authors warned, the goals of the formal, technical organization would never be reached if managers ignored the informal, social organization. The informal organization of the bank wirers had succeeded in undermining the wage incentive scheme and supervisory control precisely because the managers viewed the job only in terms of a "logic of efficiency."[38]

[38] Ibid., quote on 552–3.

The task of managers was to satisfy both functions of an industrial organization. Roethlisberger and Dickson believed that the inadvertent changes in the supervision of the relay test workers demonstrated how the informal organization could be integrated with the formal organization:

> What the Relay Assembly Test Room experiment showed was that when innovations are introduced carefully and with regard to the actual sentiments of the workers, the workers are likely to develop a spontaneous type of informal organization which will not only express more adequately their own value and significances but also is more likely to be in harmony with the aims of management.

Management needed to take into account the impact of technical changes on the social organization of work and to explain the changes in ways that the workers would be likely to accept. Similarly, they needed to take more care to learn the actual situation on the shop floor; managers were operating in ignorance of workers' sentiments and informal organization, primarily because the supervisory structure prevented the transmission of information from the shop floor to higher management levels. Finally, management had to devote more attention to the problem of adjusting the individual worker to the industrial structure. Workers' needs and expectations varied, and they changed with the job and with the workers' ages; supposedly rational policies would fail if they ignored the subtle interrelations of different parts of the human and social organization.[39]

Management and the Worker is an extended argument for the increased involvement of management, and particularly personnel managers, in shop floor organization and in the lives of their workers. For too long managers had left the organization of work to engineers who, driven by the logic of efficiency, ignored the nonlogical consequences of their actions; left to their own devices, engineers had become a source of interference in the organization. Influenced by the engineers, supervisors forced workers to act according to the rules of the technical organization, with little regard for the social organization of the factory. The only way to address the problem was to broaden the activities and power of personnel managers. Roethlisberger and Dickson admitted that personnel managers lacked the scientific knowledge and techniques that would place them on an equal footing with scientists or engineers, but argued that this actually increased their role. The Hawthorne experiments had shown that there were no universal solutions to such problems as fatigue and monotony; personnel managers had to study problems in the context of the specific work situations, on a case-by-case basis. Using such techniques as interviewing and observation, they could diagnose the imbalances in the social system and develop methods to return it to equilibrium. The book was a manifesto, which, at the practical level, reflected the career interests of the personnel managers in the Hawthorne

---

[39] Ibid., quote on 561–2.

Industrial Research Division but at the ideological level saw the personnel manager playing a critical role in the maintenance of social stability and progress.

The Hawthorne experiments seemed to provide irrefutable evidence that workers should not have any control over their jobs or their working environment. Two scientific discoveries ran through the experiments: Economic incentives were not the major motivation for workers, and workers' comments about their work could not be taken at face value. For example, Roethlisberger and Dickson dismissed the assumption that the bank wirers restricted their output because they were motivated by economic interest and feared a reduction in piece rates if they actually achieved the bogey. The authors pointed out that none of the bank wirers had experienced a rate reduction; nor was their extensive use of daywork consistent with the assumption that they only wished to increase their wages: "The ideology expressed by the employees was not based upon a logical appraisal of their situation and . . . they were not acting strictly in accordance with their economic interests." The economic argument was simply an unconvincing rationalization of behavior actually driven by sentiments.[40]

This critique was itself revealing for its ideological assumptions. The only form of economic behavior that Roethlisberger and Dickson considered was the individual behavior of each worker; they simply ignored the possibility of collective action by the workers. They denied that workers' restriction of output symbolized their resistance to managerial control – something they had been prepared to concede in their initial report on the bank wirers back in 1931. The authors suggested that if workers were truly motivated by economic values, they would demand individual pay scales that reflected their individual output. But it seems equally possible that the workers were acting collectively to ensure that piece rates were not lowered; there was little sense in increasing production if wages were then reduced accordingly. In a factory the size of the Hawthorne Works, with a large department of dedicated piece-rate engineers, it is most unlikely that there had not been cases of piece-rate reduction, and knowledge of these reductions would spread rapidly through the factory. Indeed, the bank wirers could have replied to Roethlisberger and Dickson that the reason they had not experienced a piece-rate reduction was precisely because of their defensive practice of restricting output.[41]

Workers' complaints derived from the interviewing program were similarly individualized and dismissed. Many of the workers' complaints were analyzed as expressions of sentiments or rationalizations of sentiments and consequently not a reliable guide to workplace conditions. For example,

[40] Ibid., 531–5, 575–7, quote on 534.
[41] Ibid., 331–8; Dickson to Wright, 28 Oct. 1931, HSCM/74, C1–11.

complaints about low piece rates were more likely to be due to a worker being less efficient than a fellow worker and were not a reflection of low rates in the company. The latent content of complaints was more important than their manifest content: "The same underlying complaining attitude might be present, even though the employee might on one occasion be complaining about smoke and fumes and on another occasion about his supervisor." The authors denied that this continuity might be justified, that the worker might indeed see an economic and political pattern behind poor working conditions and the behavior of the foreman; personal maladjustment, and not political consciousness, was the reason for these complaints. "The important consideration was not whether his complaint was justified but why he felt the way he did." The very title of the book, *Management and the Worker*, with its imbalance between the terms for managers and workers, captured this ideological vision of an impersonal and collective authority controlling the individual worker.[42]

When the Western Electric executives and Hawthorne managers read Roethlisberger and Dickson's manuscript, they were deeply troubled by its revelations of the lack of managerial control over workers' behavior. New York executives Clarence Stoll and William Hosford, vice-presidents, respectively, of operations and manufacturing, gave their approval for publication in early 1936. Mayo and Roethlisberger sent the manuscript to several publishers and after being rejected by Macmillan and Oxford University Press (Macmillan thought the book would cost too much to produce and Oxford explained that it was already committed to "other projects of equal magnitude that seem to have prior call"), the book was accepted by Harvard University Press, although only after Mayo had offered to subsidize publication from his Rockefeller grant. Then toward the end of May, when it appears that the executives actually sat down to read the manuscript closely, they began to criticize the presentation of the experiments, suggest revisions, and even question the wisdom of publishing the book.[43]

They objected most strenuously to the description of the bank wiring room, which they felt constituted a damning criticism of the quality of supervision at Hawthorne. They found it hard to believe that the group chief had been present in the bank wiring room all the time, were most upset by the inverse correlation between output and earnings among the bank wirers, and were simply amazed by the assumption at Hawthorne that a worker's hourly rates should not be lowered even if the worker's efficiency had fallen. Stoll quickly shot a letter off to Pennock at Hawthorne, directing

---

[42] Ibid., 255–69, quotes on 266, 269.
[43] Roethlisberger to Dickson, 1 May 1936, FJR/1; Roethlisberger to Dickson, 8 Apr. 1936, FJR/1; H. F. Lowry (general editor, Oxford University Press) to Roethlisberger, 11 Apr. 1936, FJR/1; Mayo to Stoll, 18 May 1936, EM/1.092.

that "something be done about such situations." After a conference with Stoll in New York, Roethlisberger wrote to Dickson explaining the problem: "Stoll feels quite strongly that the Bank Wiring story gives a very bad picture of management. If the situation is as we describe it, he feels that management is at fault, and he feels that management needs to be protected."[44]

The majority of the other objections were also directed at the parts of the manuscript dealing with supervisors, especially the account of interviews with supervisors, which revealed the communication bottlenecks in the supervisory structure. Further, the Hawthorne managers had no trouble identifying several of the supervisors on the basis of quotations in the text. The New York executives objected to the use of the phrase "supervisory hierarchy" because they felt that it was "uncomplimentary and liable to create an undesirable impression of our supervisory organization." By September the mounting paranoia had spread to Hawthorne, where Pennock and Wright began to demand the deletion or revision of whole chapters, especially those on the bank wirers, and objections to particular phrases came from several sources. Roethlisberger did his best to hold the line, arguing that while the company clearly had the right to determine what could go into the book, the actual text was the responsibility of the authors; comments were welcome, but the authors would use them as they saw fit. But by early 1937 he began to doubt that the book would ever be published.[45]

These problems paled into insignificance when compared with the major stumbling block to publication: the company's concern that the book would be used as evidence in a major congressional investigation of the Bell System. In March 1935, as part of New Deal concerns over the influence of monopolies on the U.S. economy, Congress had authorized the Federal Communications Commission (FCC) to conduct a thorough investigation of AT&T, intending that this would provide the basis for future regulation of the telephone industry. The ensuing inquiry was a mammoth affair, costing $1.5 million and producing sixty volumes of transcript and seventy volumes of staff reports. The investigators delved into all aspects of AT&T's operations, including its corporate, financial, and managerial structure, earnings, scientific and technical research, public relations, and labor policies. The final report of the commission, while critical of a number of company practices, concluded that the FCC had sufficient powers to regulate the monopoly.[46]

---

[44] Dickson to Roethlisberger, 21 May 1936, FJR/1, Roethlisberger to Dickson, 29 May 1936, FJR/1.

[45] Dickson to Roethlisberger, 21 May 1936, FJR/1; Dickson to Roethlisberger, 10 July 1936, FJR/1; Roethlisberger to Mayo, 11 Aug. 1936, FJR/1; Roethlisberger to Dickson, 1 Sept. 1936, FJR/1; Pennock to Hosford, 23 Oct. 1936, FJR/3.

[46] U.S. Federal Communications Commission, *Investigation of the Telephone Industry in the United States*, Washington D.C.: U.S. Government Printing Office, 1939. On the place of the FCC inquiry in the regulation of the U.S. telecommunications industry, see Gerald W.

Nevertheless, AT&T was subjected to systematic criticism throughout the course of the inquiry. One of the commissioners issued a report which argued that AT&T was boosting its profits by allowing Western Electric, the one part of the system currently not under state or federal regulation, to overcharge the operating companies, and he recommended the regulation of Western Electric and the severance of its ties with the operating companies. (This was the first of several antitrust efforts to split the Bell System, which would finally be achieved in 1985.) Many of the accusations were gathered by N. R. Danielian, one of the FCC researchers, and published in *A.T.&T.: The Story of Industrial Conquest*. The book is a classic among the New Deal attacks on corporations, Danielian concluding:

> In a true sense, this organism is a state within a state, exhibiting all the economic and political propensities of a national state in its most imperialistic moods. Reared upon a foundation of private property, governed by a hereditary oligarchy, and motivated by a singular desire for profits, this economic state is dictatorial in control, disciplined in behavior, aggressive in its single-minded purpose. And like its larger counterpart, it must curry favor with its equals, caress and cajole its followers, win public favor through propaganda.

Danielian accused the company of making excessive profits, of causing technological unemployment by the introduction of automatic exchanges, of manipulating the shareholders, and of using advertising and public relations techniques to ensure that government regulation was minimized. One of his examples was the close relationship that had evolved between AT&T and the Harvard Business School: The AT&T general counsel frequently gave lectures at the school, and business school professor Philip Cabot gave public speeches praising the Bell System and defending its rate increases. The FCC investigators also noted that ten officers and directors of Bell companies held positions at Harvard; three were university overseers. Given this environment, Western Electric decided that it would be foolhardy to publish a book that described collaboration between the company and the Harvard Business School in the politically charged area of labor relations.[47]

But by 1939 the political storm had subsided, and the final FCC report dropped proposals that the ties between Western Electric and AT&T be cut

---

Brock, *The Telecommunications Industry: The Dynamics of Market Structure*, Cambridge, Mass.: Harvard University Press, 1981, 178–80.

[47] N. R. Danielian, *A.T.&T.: The Story of Industrial Conquest*, New York: Vanguard Press, 1939, quote on 379. AT&T prepared a defense of the Bell System, written in an anodyne style by one of its vice-presidents; see Arthur W. Page, *The Bell Telephone System*, New York: Harper Bros., 1941. On the Harvard–AT&T connection, see Danielian, *A.T.&T.*, 297–302, 480–1. On the Western Electric decision to withhold publication, see Roethlisberger to Dickson, 29 May 1936, FJR/1; Roethlisberger to Dickson, 20 Mar. 1937, FJR/1; Dickson to Wright, 19 Nov. 1937, FJR/1.

and that Western Electric be subject to FCC control. *Management and the Worker* was finally released for publication in May 1939, shortly before the release of the final FCC report. The only concessions to the objections raised by executives three years earlier were occasional paragraphs or footnotes stressing that the research findings did not reflect poorly on the workers, supervisors, or company; for example, the authors pointed out that the bank wirers had turned out a tremendous amount of work, even as they joked and played. As the book was sent out to reviewers and bookstores in October 1939, Roethlisberger cautioned his coauthor and friend from expecting too much: "I would not be discouraged, Bill, if this book does not have a wide sale. The more I think about it the less likely, in my opinion, will this book appeal to any large number of people."[48]

Roethlisberger was being excessively cautious. As with most books, the reviews were mixed and at times contradictory, yet most applauded the scientific nature of the research, the measured conclusions, and the interdisciplinary approach. The most critical review appeared in the *American Journal of Sociology*, where sociologist Mary Gilson dismissed the work as unoriginal and a waste of money and suggested that the researchers were "in the kindergarten stage of industrial knowledge." (Gilson had spent a few frustrating years working for Industrial Relations Counselors and, aware of Mayo's close links to the Rockefeller interests, apparently saw this as a way of getting even with this circle of conservative industrial relations executives.) The most important and positive reviews came from the industrial research network to which the Hawthorne researchers belonged. In the *Personnel Journal*, Charles Slocombe, who had replaced Walter Bingham as director of the Personnel Research Federation, hailed the work as the "most outstanding book on industrial relations that has yet been published anywhere, anytime." And the book gained unexpected public attention when liberal journalist and social thinker Stuart Chase acclaimed the book in the pages of *Reader's Digest* in February 1941, informing millions of readers that "there is an idea here so big that it leaves one gasping" – an assessment that sent sales soaring and pushed the book into its fourth printing.[49]

But perhaps the most significant praise came in a private letter from Chester Barnard to Roethlisberger. Barnard personified the network that

---

[48] Roethlisberger to Dickson, 5 Oct. 1939, HSCM/157, C4–5. The relevant passages in *Management and the Worker* are 331n, 459–60.   .
[49] Reviews of *Management and the Worker* include James A. Campbell, *American Economic Review*, 1940, 30: 177; Stuart Chase, "What Makes the Worker Like to Work?" *Reader's Digest*, Feb. 1941, 38: 15–20, quote on 20; Paul A. Dodd, *Annals of the American Academy of Political and Social Science*, 1940, 208: 230–1; Mary B. Gilson, *American Journal of Sociology*, 1940, 46: 98–101; John G. Jenkins, *Psychological Bulletin*, 1940, 37: 319–21; H. S. Person, *Survey Graphic*, 1940, 29: 37–9; Murray Ross, *Political Science Quarterly*,

had funded the research and provided the institutional and ideological context for its development: He was president of New Jersey Bell Telephone Company (1927–48), friend of Wallace Donham and Philip Cabot at the business school, and author of *The Functions of the Executive* (1938), a classic work in the theory of administration and organization; in due course he would become president of the Rockefeller Foundation (1948–52) and chairman of the National Science Foundation (1952–4). *Management and the Worker*, he told Roethlisberger in his measured style, confirmed his own research and experience:

> Both in detail and as a whole it seemed to me that the presentation was sound both because it checked with my personal judgment based on experience, but more particularly because the important statements were based upon, and illustrated by, factual information as to the concrete behavior. At last we have something that really is a basis for scientific management.[50]

With the publication of *Management and the Worker* the Hawthorne experiments were finally rendered in fine detail and in an accessible form, in what seemed to be a definitive account of every step of the research. The next challenge would be to ensure that the experiments had a lasting effect on the social scientific study of work and on the practice of industrial management.

1940, 55: 629–30; C. L. Shartle, *Management Review*, 1940, 29: 157–8; Charles S. Slocombe, "Million Dollar Research," *Personnel Journal*, 1940, 18: 162–72; and Ordway Tead, *Advanced Management*, 1940, 5: 92–3.
[50] Chester Barnard to Roethlisberger, 10 Oct. 1939, FJR/1.

8

Human relations in industry

MANAGEMENT AND THE WORKER was released into an industrial and political world significantly different from that in which the Hawthorne experiments had been conducted. During the 1920s employers had been successful in restricting union influence, particularly in the large mass production industries, and the early years of the depression had further undermined union membership. But this trend was soon reversed by the militancy of new industrial unions of mass production workers in the middle to late 1930s, strengthened by New Deal legislation that protected workers' rights to organize and bargain collectively with their employers. Personnel management flourished in this environment, and a function that had previously been the responsibility of middle managers was transformed almost overnight into the province of high executives; henceforth, no managerial decisions could be made without considering their impact on labor relations. A newly unionized workforce increasingly challenged working practices and personnel arrangements at the shop floor level, forcing senior management to recognize that the supervisor played a critical role as management's representative to the workers. Industrial relations, from shop floor politics to labor contracts and government intervention, was being transformed, and by 1950 a new system of labor relations was in place in the majority of U.S. industries.

The Hawthorne experiments and the human relations approach derived from them appealed greatly to personnel managers for two reasons. First, they codified a managerial perspective that recognized the necessity of gaining the active support and participation of workers, while retaining all the key elements of managerial control – that is, they provided a powerful managerial ideology. Second, human relations focused management's attention on the supervisor–worker relationship and offered strategies for improving the practice of industrial relations on the shop floor, especially through the techniques of personnel counseling and supervisory training.

This chapter sketches the reception of the Hawthorne experiments in industry and attempts to assess their impact on industrial management. The first section analyzes the impact of the experiments on industrial relations in the Bell System, so as to assess the practical achievements as well as the ideological functions of the human relations approach. This section focuses on the development of personnel counseling and its effects on union organization. The second section surveys the single most significant contribution of human relations to industrial management in the 1940s and 1950s – the development of a new conception of the role of the supervisor. Social scientists during this period conducted an extraordinary range of research on the tasks of the foreman, and personnel managers implemented supervisory training programs designed to teach foremen the skills of human relations.

Unions and counseling in the Bell System

In *Management and the Worker*, Roethlisberger and Dickson had proposed a framework for analyzing the human problems of management based on the insights and techniques of the Hawthorne experiments. But granted that managers might put down the book more enlightened about the social structure of their factory and the personal situation of their workforce, what practical guidance could they find there? When the first version of the manuscript was completed in early 1936, there was perhaps not much, but by the time the manuscript was released for publication by AT&T in 1939, the authors were able to add a final chapter entitled "Implications for Personnel Practice." They stressed the need for a program of continual research by trained personnel managers in which the factory and its constituent parts would be analyzed as an intricate social system. And, more concretely, they reported briefly on a new program of "personnel counseling" at the Hawthorne Works in which counselors combined the techniques of interviewing and observation to study the personal and social situations of the work group and thereby aided the individual worker's adjustment to the industrial structure. The program, they stressed, was still in its experimental stages and not easily transferred to other settings; nevertheless, there was a clear implication that a major new personnel technique had developed out of the Hawthorne experiments.[1]

Personnel counseling quickly became the most visible aspect of the experiments and came to be regarded by the management community as the practical conclusion of the research and the program that embodied and applied all of its discoveries. Counseling spread rapidly during the 1940s, both in the Bell System and in other large manufacturing corporations, especially during the industrial expansion of the war years. By the mid-1950s, however, counseling was in decline, caught between criticisms from managers that it was an expensive and impractical method of managerial

---

[1] F. J. Roethlisberger and William J. Dickson, *Management and the Worker*, Cambridge, Mass.: Harvard University Press, 1939, 590–604.

control and concerns expressed by unionists and liberal industrial sociologists that, far from trying to improve human relations in the factory, its sole purpose was to turn workers into "contented cows." The impression that counseling was the major practical outcome of the Hawthorne experiments was subsequently strengthened in 1966 when Roethlisberger and Dickson collaborated to produce a second book, *Counseling in an Organization: A Sequel to the Hawthorne Researches*, in which they defended the program from its critics. While affirming that counseling was clearly a technique of managerial control of its workers, they argued that it had not been intended to be an antiunion device and indeed had been accepted by the Hawthorne unions.[2]

To ascertain the role played by personnel counseling at Hawthorne and in U.S. industry we must look beyond the intentions, however honorable, of managers and academics like William Dickson and Fritz Roethlisberger and consider the structural changes in industrial relations that promoted this new managerial technique. Counseling flourished during a tumultuous period in industrial relations and must be understood in that political context; for example, it is notable that counseling at Hawthorne commenced soon after Western Electric was forced by the government to implement an employee representation plan in 1933, only to be phased out shortly after a more powerful AFL union succeeded in organizing its workers in 1954.

Western Electric executives had always hoped that the Hawthorne experiments would produce new labor relations techniques. When the interviewing program was expanded in early 1929 there had been considerable discussion between Hawthorne and New York managers regarding the comparative value of interviewing and employee representation as means of handling employee grievances. Western Electric had been the one part of the Bell System that had not introduced an employee representation plan in the early 1920s, a decision that had been criticized by Bell System personnel managers. Personnel director F. W. Willard therefore welcomed interviewing as an answer to those critics, and he pressed the Hawthorne researchers to develop a way to handle the workers' comments administratively, suggesting, in contravention of the researchers' guarantees to supervisors, that even complaints about supervisors be investigated. Another New York manager wanted to know if the researchers were keeping detailed records of the actions taken to correct conditions reported in the interviews. While the company researchers recognized the validity of such concerns, they resisted this pressure, for they were more interested in interviewing for the purposes of research and as a means of relieving workers' emotional reveries.[3]

---

[2] William J. Dickson and F. J. Roethlisberger, *Counseling in an Organization: A Sequel to the Hawthorne Researches*, Boston: Harvard University, Graduate School of Business Administration, 1966.
[3] F. W. Willard to G. A. Pennock, 28 Feb. 1929, HSCM/160, C11–13; R. S. Meriam to M.

The researchers were always aware that interviewing offered a particularly useful method of addressing worker grievances without encouraging any form of collective action by the workers. In 1931 Mayo's colleague, economist R.S. Meriam, following discussions with Western Electric personnel managers at Hawthorne and New York, published an article in the *Personnel Journal* in which he compared the effectiveness of employee representation and interviewing. He concluded that employee representation was a fast and inexpensive way to discover workers' major concerns, but that interviewing provided a more reliable guide to workers' underlying worries and could deal with "irrational human nature." With representation, there was also a danger that "group loyalty may be aroused" and that workers would collectively oppose management. In comparison, the "absence of political machinery is the chief advantage of the interview plan. The employee is interviewed as an individual.... He is not required to propose remedies or to listen to counter arguments or counter proposals."[4]

Within two years Western Electric had introduced an employee representation plan, but as a result of government edict rather than as a deliberate choice. On 13 June 1933 Congress passed the National Industrial Recovery Act (NRA), one of Franklin Delano Roosevelt's early attempts to pull the nation out of the depression. The act in effect put the country on a war footing by suspending antitrust legislation so as to permit companies to form industrial cartels, through which it was hoped national planning would halt the spiral of unemployment and a contracting economy. Among the measures was a requirement that echoed the provisions of the War Labor Board of the First World War and President Wilson's industrial conference of 1919; under section 7(a) of the NRA, workers gained the right "to organize and bargain collectively through representatives of their own choosing." Business leaders interpreted this to mean only that they were required to establish some form of employee representation, and indeed the NRA lacked any of the teeth that would have enforced employers' acceptance of organized labor.[5]

The corporate leaders in the Special Conference Committee (SCC), whose companies had introduced employee representation plans or works councils after the First World War, worked closely with the government to support the cartelization of industry and the dissemination of employee representation. Edward S. Cowdrick, secretary of the SCC, became secretary of the Industrial Relations Committee of the Business Advisory and Planning

L. Putnam, 2 Sept. 1930, HSCM/159, F6; J. W. Skinkle to Pennock, 19 Dec. 1930, HSCM/160, B1; H. A Wright to F. J. Roethlisberger, 19 Oct. 1931, FJR/1.

[4] R. S. Meriam, "Employee Interviewing and Employee Representation," *Personnel Journal*, 1931, 10: 95–101, quotes on 98, 99.

[5] On the complex relationships between corporations and the New Deal, see Ellis Hawley, *The New Deal and the Problem of Monopoly: A Study in Economic Ambivalence*, Princeton, N.J.: Princeton University Press, 1966; and Kim McQuaid, "Corporate Liberalism in the American Business Community, 1920–1940," *Business History Review*, 1978, 52: 342–68.

Council of the Department of Commerce, a focal point for corporate participation in the early stages of the New Deal. In a related move, Arthur Young left Industrial Relations Counselors to become vice-president of industrial relations at U.S. Steel, where he oversaw the introduction of a representation plan and brought the company into membership of the SCC. The aim of these corporate accommodations to the New Deal was to try and restrict more independent forms of labor organization; Cyrus McCormick, president of International Harvester, wrote to Raymond Fosdick, chairman of Industrial Relations Counselors and a director of the Rockefeller Foundation, explaining that "my belief that the future of industrial happiness lies in the Works Counsel [*sic*] method of doing business is stronger than ever. I see a storm of labor trouble sweeping over the country but as far as I can hear the companies which are represented in the Special Conference Committee are more free from them than are any others."[6]

AT&T acted speedily to ensure that its subsidiaries were in compliance with the NRA. Operating companies were directed to make sure that the plans were in full operation and that any offending practices, such as requiring workers to sign an agreement that they would not join a union, be speedily removed. Western Electric executives mobilized to establish a representation plan; at Hawthorne the task was handed to Mark Putnam, who, Roethlisberger informed Mayo, "has been given charge of looking over the possibilities of starting a company union or some sort of employee representation plan which will meet the requirements of the government." Some skill was required to ensure that workers accepted the plan – unions everywhere were trying to persuade workers that the NRA actually required them to join a more independent union than that offered by representation plans. However, while some of those in the smaller Western Electric plants initially turned down the plan, it was approved at Hawthorne by 92 percent of the voting workers. When Harold Wright returned to Hawthorne in August 1933, after collaborating on *Management and the Worker,* he joined Putnam in implementing the new plan.[7]

Putnam and his fellow company researchers threw themselves into the representation plan, hopeful that it would provide a fresh avenue for industrial research. But they were implementing a bureaucratic plan conceived by New York executives, and they soon discovered that they had little room

[6] Cyrus McCormick to Raymond Fosdick, 21 June 1934, OMR/2F/16/127. On corporate labor policy in the New Deal, see Stephen J. Scheinberg, "The Development of Corporation Labor Policy, 1900–1940," Ph.D. dissertation, University of Wisconsin, 1966, 162–86. On the Special Conference Committee, see U.S. Senate, Committee on Education and Labor, *Violations of Free Speech and Rights of Labor. Hearings. Part 45,* "The Special Conference Committee," Washington, D.C.: U.S. Government Printing Office, 1939, 16798–812.

[7] Memorandum, AT&T to Operating Company Presidents, 30 June 1933, AT&T/46; "Bell System Resolutions, National Industrial Recovery Act, 1933–1935," AT&T/1142; Roethlisberger to Mayo, 11 July 1933, (quote) FJR/1.

to maneuver. Wright's time was occupied trying to explain to headquarters why the representation plan was still turning up the same complaints that had been prevalent in the interviews. Howarth resisted a proposal that he run conferences to help supervisors adjust to working with employee representatives and was transferred to the Teletype Corporation, a Bell subsidiary; Wright took Howarth's place and within a few months was contemplating asking Arthur Young for a job at U.S. Steel. The Company researchers were frustrated, Wright explained to Roethlisberger, because they were being prevented from undertaking any research:

> It is astonishing to me to see how much we have gained in understanding the various current problems, but at the same time pretty discouraging in the sense that we must keep most of it to ourselves, for the job of communicating any of this is still ahead of us. The tendency now is to label everything we turn out as theoretical instead of practical. I am tempted to chew nails every time I hear the dichotomy mentioned.

One of the issues requiring closer study was the emerging organization of the workers: Wright reported that the present leaders were "political types" who used the representation plan "as a means of social climbing"; however, there were promising indications that the more conservative workers were "offering some resistance to left wing activities in the group."[8]

Finally, in January 1936 a series of conferences on employee relations policies at Hawthorne provided an opportunity for Wright and his colleagues to propose the revival of personnel research. The representation plan, he pointed out to his superiors, was not what they would have designed if they had had the choice. Wright and his fellow personnel managers were particularly concerned that too many "minor irritations" among workers, their supervisors, and the industrial relations organization were being transformed into grievances to be handled by employee representatives in meetings with management. Wright was also concerned that bureaucratic red tape and organizational barriers were preventing the proper utilization of many personnel services, such as the hospital, thrift counselors, and personnel placement. The previous research had demonstrated the necessity of creating a specialized manager who would concentrate on human relations in the workplace in the same way that other specialists had responsibility for planning, scheduling, and maintenance. What was needed, he suggested, was a "Personnel Man" who would "study human problems existing in the groups, ... institute corrective procedures and make available to management better information regarding the human aspects of the existing problems." The personnel man's approach would be to combine the techniques of interviewing and observation, and as in the bank wiring test room, he

---

[8] Wright to Roethlisberger, 7 Nov. 1933, Wright to Roethlisberger, 10 May 1934 (quotes), FJR/1.

would have no authority other than the right to study the work situation. The personal problems of workers would be corrected through a mixture of interviewing, counseling, and consultation with the supervisor, while group problems would be tackled through consultation with management and supervisors.[9]

In the following month the researchers began an experiment in what was now called "personnel counseling," the first step in the application of the findings of the Hawthorne experiments. Arthur Moore, who had previously been the observer in the bank wiring room, was assigned to the Panel Apparatus Department, where he interviewed, observed, and counseled 150 workers. The researchers were particularly concerned with the reactions of supervisors and employee representatives, for Moore's responsibilities clearly overlapped with theirs. Moore was permitted to take workers off the job to interview them only after obtaining permission from the supervisor, and any problems that Moore identified had to be referred back to the supervisor for action; thus, after discovering the extent of discontent over recent wage cuts, Moore recommended to the supervisors that they explain the reasons for the cuts more fully to their workers. The supervisors quickly accepted Moore's position and were soon recommending their "difficult" workers for interviews, including complainers, slow workers, and, predictably, the worker representatives in the employee representation plan. Somewhat unexpectedly, the employee representatives proved as willing as the supervisors to accept Moore's assistance. One representative was in an extraordinarily difficult position; a former supervisor who had been demoted during the depression, he was under pressure from workers to take action over rate cuts at the next worker–management meeting, but still identified sufficiently with management to accept its reasons for the decreases in piece rates. Indeed, according to Moore and Dickson, the employee representatives "feel that a good part of this demand for action is emotional, but as representatives they cannot oppose it openly as they will lose their jobs as representatives" – this, at least, was the way employee representatives chose to present the situation to Moore. Whether representatives and counselor were in as close agreement as Moore suggested is questionable, but what is certain is that managers accepted Moore's argument that representatives supported the counselor and that both could function to defuse worker complaints. From the beginning, personnel counseling was seen as performing a function parallel to employee representation.[10]

[9] H. A. Wright, memorandum, 17 Jan. 1936, (quote), HSC/vol. 24; "Record of Observation – Personnel Experiment," HSC/vol. 25; A. C. Moore, memorandum, 23 Feb. 1937, HSC/vol. 25.
[10] Dickson to Roethlisberger, 10 Mar. 1936, FJR/1; G. S. Rutherford to Pennock, 19 Feb. 1936, HSC/vol. 25; "Record of Observation – Personnel Experiment," HSC/vol. 25; W. J. Dickson and A. C. Moore, "Preliminary Report on the Experiment in Personnel Counseling," 8 Apr. 1936, HSC/6.

Counseling expanded steadily thereafter, from five counselors covering 600 workers in 1936 to a peak of fifty-five counselors covering some 21,000 workers in 1948. The ascendancy of counseling was marked in 1941 by the renaming of Wright's Personnel Research and Training Division as the Personnel Counseling and Research Division; Moore now headed a Personnel Counseling Department within the division, while Dickson was in charge of the Employee Relations Research Department. After a series of conferences at Hawthorne and New York, higher management agreed that counseling and research should be conducted in all major plants and appointed Walter Dietz, personnel relations manager in New York, to oversee the program. The Harvard researchers were also drawn into the program: Mayo paid two visits to Hawthorne during 1936 and 1937 to give his imprimatur to counseling, and Roethlisberger worked half-time as a consultant to Western Electric during 1937–8, primarily to train counselors in interviewing techniques. The expansion to other parts of the company was a slow process, despite the enthusiasm of company executives in New York. Roethlisberger was used to introduce the idea at the Kearny and Point Breeze works in 1941 since it was felt that managers would accept the plan more readily from an outsider than from their rivals at Hawthorne.[11]

The company researchers believed that counseling constituted the ideal balance between their desire for long-term research and their superiors' demands for a practical program to improve personnel relations. Each counselor was assigned a particular territory consisting of two hundred to four hundred workers and their supervisors; his or her task (female workers were given a female counselor) was to understand everything about those departments – the technical and formal organizations, payment systems, and gradually, through interviews and daily interactions, the personal situations and interpersonal relations of workers and supervisors. With no formal authority in the line organization, the counselor's power lay in listening to problems and in acting as a catalyst, quietly encouraging workers and supervisors to talk to one another and, through skillful questioning, suggesting certain courses of action. Confidentiality and discretion were essential to the task; counselors were not meant to pass on to supervisors information acquired in an interview with a worker, nor were they to take sides in disputes. The relationship between counselor and worker was intended to be analogous to the doctor–patient relationship, both in terms of the counselor's professional responsibility and because the counselor's role was essentially therapeutic, helping workers adjust to their work, aiding communication between workers and supervisors, and improving managerial control. This eminently practical program would, however, provide

[11] Roethlisberger to Dickson, 20 Sept. 1937, WJD/1/26; Mayo to Patricia Mayo, 24 Sept., 2 Dec. [1937], EM/film; Wright to Dickson, 24 Nov. 1937, WJD/1/26; Wright to Roethlisberger, 18 Jan. 1938, FJR/1; Dickson, handwritten notes on counseling, 1937, WJD/1/26.

the basis for research on more general problems of worker–management relations: Personnel managers would be able to combine the information and insights of individual counselors with supplementary research, thereby providing managers with the kind of information about employee attitudes that was not passed up the normal line organization.[12]

How successful was the counseling? The issue is too complex and the information too fragmentary for a definitive answer to be given; it is next to impossible to gauge the effect of counseling on the incidence of workers' grievances or on union organization. But in many respects this is the wrong question, for the strength of counseling lay in the coherence of its ideology – in the framework of explanation and guidance for practical intervention that it provided to managers, counselors, and supervisors faced with a difficult worker or a union grievance. It is also important to recognize that counseling at Western Electric, although unusual in some of its specific mechanisms, was broadly representative of a widespread shift in the behavior expected of supervisors in U.S. industry, in large measure due to the impact of the Hawthorne experiments and the human relations approach to personnel management. In effect, the counselor was charged with concentrating on those functions of the supervisor concerned with the human relations and social organization of the work group; but the supervisor continued to be responsible for these problems, and counseling material was used in supervisory training. The successes and difficulties of counselors at Hawthorne are therefore indicative of the problems faced by supervisors in other firms; the major difference lies in the extent to which worker–supervisor relations at Hawthorne were recorded and analyzed.

The primary function of counseling was the adjustment of the individual worker to the work organization and to managerial imperatives – in short, persuading workers to submit to managerial authority. Putnam and his colleagues never addressed the power relationships implicit in counseling, however, and talked only of its clinical and therapeutic role by referring to counseling as the "diagnosis and treatment of employee complaints and grievances." Drawing on the analysis in *Management and the Worker,* the researchers instructed counselors and supervisors to make a clear distinction between complaints and grievances. Complaints, Putnam explained, are "symptoms rather than statements of fact or statements of the real cause of dissatisfaction.... Not every employee who complains is expressing a real grievance. The situation is usually too complex for him to make an accurate diagnosis without assistance." It was the counselor's task to bring about a "more adequate orientation of the employee," primarily by revealing to the worker, through nondirective interviewing, the personal problem that

[12] "Report of Personnel Counseling Activity, January 1936 to March 1937," HSC/6; Wright to J. W. Dietz, 22 Nov. 1937, FJR/1; Roethlisberger and Dickson, *Management and the Worker,* 593–604.

lay at the bottom of the complaint. Thus, workers who complained about the lack of opportunity for advancement were shown that their complaints stemmed not from the job hierarchy of the company, but rather from the unrealistic demands placed on them by their families. It is striking that while the researchers did note that in some cases the job or work environment might need changing, they never cited instances of a legitimate grievance; the impression they gave was that such occurrences were rare.[13]

On occasions the counselor would be called upon to mediate between worker and supervisor. For example, a counselor wrote up a case in which a new foreman upset the social equilibrium of a work group by changing the accepted rules. The foreman had reprimanded a worker for talking, an activity previously allowed, and when she continued to talk, as punishment he placed her on a physically demanding job normally given to a man, thereby raising the concern of male workers that women would henceforth be given the job. The counselor intervened by encouraging the lower supervisors to explain to the foreman that the woman was an efficient and reliable worker and by encouraging the worker to approach the foreman, who eventually agreed to allow the woman to return to her previous job – if she promised not to talk. The counselor's lack of authority, combined with the ideology of human relations, ensured that it was the worker, and not the supervisor, who made the adjustment.[14]

Another counselor described coming upon a small group of workers in heated discussion about labor grades and the unwillingness of the union representatives to pursue the issue with management. The counselor's description of his response to the workers illuminates the role of counseling:

> The counselor expressed his interest briefly and they spoke on. It wasn't very long before other workmen in the area joined the conversation. The counselor became concerned in having too many people taking part in the discussion and expressed his desire to hear more about the subject only in a place where they would not cause too much distraction among the rest of the group. He directed his question of going to a conference room for privacy to the individual who had made the opening remarks. The man accepted the suggestion very willingly. After the counselor got permission to take the employee off the job they proceeded to the conference room.

Having succeeded in breaking up the group discussion, the counselor then listened to the worker's complaints, which centered on the unduly low rating

[13] M. L. Putnam, "Diagnosis and Treatment of Employee Complaints and Grievances," *Bell System Personnel Conference, Oct. 29 – Nov. 2, 1940*, AT&T, 1940, quote on 13; H. A. Wright, "Personal Adjustment in Industry," *Occupations*, 1940, 18: 500–5, quote on 502; Western Electric Co., *Complaints and Grievances: Supervisory Training Conference Material*, n.p., 1938.

[14] "The Girl Who Talked Too Much," 23 May 1939, HSC/6/Personnel Counseling – Results and Contributions.

of the work, inadequate tools, and an unsupportive supervisor. The group of workers were also critical of the union for agreeing to a contract that did away with merit pay raises, and that morning they had refused to pay their union dues. When at the end of the interview the worker asked the counselor, "Do you think there's a chance for a change to the better in our outfit some day?" the counselor replied with vague optimism, "We see changes all over the plant from time to time." But in the typed report the counselor concluded with the observation that "it is evident that the man likes his work and has no serious complaint to offer concerning the company and its policies." The very technique of counseling, whether the counselor was aware of it or not, effectively transformed the grievance of a group of workers into the personal and therefore misplaced complaint of an individual worker.[15]

Counseling had been operating at Hawthorne for only one year when in April 1937 the employee representation plan was discontinued and a more independent union took its place. The impetus had come from forces outside Hawthorne and outside the Bell System. Ever since the enactment of the NRA, union leaders in the AFL had been pressing Congress for legislation that would provide more than the vague directives of section 7(a); the result was the National Labor Relations Act, or Wagner Act, passed in June 1935 despite the opposition of corporate leaders and organizations. The act was unenforceable until April 1937 due to court battles over its constitutionality, orchestrated in part by the SCC, but when finally declared constitutional it was a powerful weapon for organized labor. The act gave workers the right to organize in independent unions and specified what actions would constitute an "unfair labor practice" on the part of employers; company-dominated representation plans were among the practices made illegal. The Wagner Act gave teeth to the legislation by establishing the National Labor Relations Board (NLRB), which had the power to enforce and interpret the act and recognize unions as bargaining agents in each factory. Meanwhile, the labor movement had expanded dramatically, rank-and-file militancy combining with the organizational skills of the Congress of Industrial Organizations (CIO), formed in November 1935 by union leaders frustrated by the unwillingness of the AFL craft unions to organize mass production unions. Labor relations in 1936 and 1937 were characterized by sit-down strikes, powerful union leaders such as John L. Lewis and the Reuther brothers, and the capitulation of the giant General Motors, which in March 1937 signed a contract with the United Auto Workers.[16]

[15] "Counseling in Relation to Grievance about Supervisor," quotes on 1, 4, in "Information Regarding Personnel Counseling Activity, Hawthorne Works, November 1949," HSC/6.
[16] On New Deal labor legislation and the rise of mass production unions, see David Brody, *Workers in Industrial America*, New York: Oxford University Press, 1980, chaps. 3 and 4; and James R. Green, *The World of the Worker: Labor in Twentieth-Century America*, New York: Hill & Wang, 1980, chap. 5.

Unionization in the Bell System took a much less explosive course. Management moved quickly to disband employee representation upon the declaration of the constitutionality of the Wagner Act and encouraged the establishment of local unions in its place. Hawthorne workers were organized in May 1937 into the Western Electric Independent Labor Association, and the workers at other Western Electric plants were organized into similar local associations. In November 1938 the National Federation of Telephone Workers (NFTW) was created to coordinate the activities of member affiliates, but local unions maintained complete control of their bargaining powers, a situation favored by AT&T, which refused to bargain with the NFTW. The first significant strikes did not occur until 1945, and only in 1949 did the federal union, renamed the Communication Workers of America (CWA), join the CIO.[17]

The establishment of unions independent of management influence and the development of union consciousness were a gradual process; in most cases union leaders had been representatives under the old plan and took time to assume a more powerful role. Reflecting in 1950 on this process, CWA president Joseph Beirne commented:

> Somewhere along in the NFTW's history, and where I can't put my finger, although I was an officer of that organization, whether it was a feeling of self-respect coming to the leaders of the telephone workers, a conscientious effort was made to throw off the influence and domination of the management in the Bell System, particularly. In the NFTW you would begin to hear trade-union discussions.

Revealingly, leaders and members of the Hawthorne union seem to have resisted this process: In 1942 the union ceased its affiliation with the NFTW, apparently because the local union objected to moves to centralize power in the NFTW as part of an attempt to establish national bargaining. Although Hawthorne workers participated in a four-hour walkout in 1945, they did not join the first national strike in 1947. Only in 1954 did the Hawthorne union join a national union, and then it was the International Brotherhood of Electrical Workers (IBEW), a more conservative organization than the CWA. The IBEW offered a significant degree of local autonomy and was openly preferred by Western Electric management. Other Western Electric manufacturing workers also felt outnumbered in the CWA, which

---

[17] On unionization in the telephone industry, see John N. Schacht, *The Making of Telephone Unionism, 1920–1947*, New Brunswick, N.J.: Rutgers University Press, 1985; Jack Barbash, *Unions and Telephones: The Story of the Communications Workers of America*, New York: Harper Bros., 1952; Thomas R. Brooks, *Communications Workers of America: The Story of a Union*, New York: Mason/Charles, 1977; Melvyn K. Bers, "Unionism and Collective Bargaining in the Telephone Industry," Ph.D. dissertation, University of California, 1956; and U.S. Senate, Labor and Public Welfare Committee, Subcommittee on Labor–Management Relations, *Labor–Management Relations in the Bell Telephone System*, Washington, D.C.: U.S. Government Printing Office, 1950.

was dominated by the more militant women telephone operators and was organized in regional districts that swamped the factory workers; thus, several other plants, including Kearny, left the CWA for the IBEW in 1948–9, while others, including Point Breeze, reverted to independent unions. By 1954 the majority of Western Electric workers were organized outside the CWA.[18]

When compared with the mass production workers of the automobile or steel industry, or even other parts of the electrical industry, Western Electric manufacturing workers were relatively docile. With the notable exception of a sixty-five-day strike at Kearny in 1946, there was little of the militant rank-and-file activity that was the core of industrial unionism in other industries, and local union leaders seemed more concerned with protecting local autonomy than forging a national organization. The predominantly female telephone operators, and not the manufacturing workers, were the militants of the telephone industry.

The counseling organization and management at Hawthorne did not doubt that counseling had played a part in restraining union activity. When in 1941 workers at Kearny, which had not yet introduced counseling, implemented an overtime ban to underscore a demand for wage increases, Wright told Roethlisberger, "I must confess we would enjoy the credit to counseling that such a comparison would bring." By the late 1940s, when Hawthorne workers were still in an independent and very cooperative union, counseling enjoyed its peak, regarded favorably by managers as a major contributor to this state of affairs. Whether counseling did in fact play such a role is impossible to answer definitively and should not detain us; nevertheless, it is important to consider the mechanisms through which counseling may have dampened union militancy.[19]

Unions and counseling were in direct competition on the shop floor because they provided workers alternative mechanisms for adjusting grievances without going to the supervisor. Two separate studies of Bell System unions in the early 1950s agreed that telephone workers saw the union first and foremost as a protection against supervisors:

> Interviews with union officials at both the local and higher levels revealed a general agreement that unions in the telephone industry rest

[18] Joseph Beirne made his comment to the U.S. Senate's Labor and Public Welfare Committee, Subcommittee on Labor–Management Relations, *Labor–Management Relations in the Bell Telephone System*, 49. The process of transformation of the representation plan into an independent union is fully documented in an NLRB hearing on charges that the Kearny union was company-dominated; see *Western Electric Co. and United Electrical, Radio & Machine Workers of America*, 72 N.L.R.B., no. 134.

[19] Wright to Roethlisberger, 12 June 1941, FJR/1. The views of Hawthorne managers on the effectiveness of counseling are reported in Jeanne L. Wilensky and Harold L. Wilensky, "Personnel Counseling: The Hawthorne Case," *American Journal of Sociology*, 1951, 57: 265–80, esp. 275.

upon a substantial base of member loyalties. The consensus was that a great deal of allegiance to the unions stems from what appears to be an inexhaustible supply of relatively small grievances – perhaps an inevitable phenomenon in an organization of the size of the Bell System. Union officers report that a large fraction of these grievances arise from the response of the work force to the behavior of first-line supervisors.

As an AT&T technician explained: "If the union wasn't there they would be pretty tough on the men. The supervisors had to take a little more human approach to the employees in general. Today you get your own choice about hours on the basis of seniority. They can't throw you back on a dirty job and forget you. They can't keep on picking for the same men in the premium-pay jobs. It has forced them to give a bit more human thought to the employees."[20]

The major tasks of counseling were the adjustment of grievances before they reached the shop steward and the training of supervisors to be a "little more human." The Hawthorne researchers were well aware of the competition between unions and counseling. In their annual "Appraisal of the Labor Situation at Hawthorne" for 1939, Dickson and Moore noted that whereas under the representation plan workers were taking their complaints to their supervisors, they were now taking their problems to the steward, for they had discovered that management was far more responsive to the union than it was to its lower-level supervisors. Indeed, there were many instances in which workers and their supervisors had cooperated to use the union grievance procedure as a way of bringing their problem to higher management. Counseling provided a means of dealing with complaints before they escalated into union grievances.

In more public forums, Dickson denied that counseling posed a threat to unions. In a chapter on counseling contributed to a 1948 book entitled *The New Industrial Relations,* Dickson argued that "since the counselor does not transmit information to supervisors or management, his activity in no sense undercuts the union. Also, since he gives no advice or direction to the individual it cannot be said that he seeks to divert complaints or grievances away from union channels." Yet counseling was intended to do precisely that; the techniques and psychopathological approach of counseling encouraged the worker to see the complaint as a personal rather than a structural problem, and when the problem stemmed from relations between the worker and a supervisor, counselors subtly directed the worker toward a rapprochement with the supervisor, not toward filing a grievance with the union. After three years as a counselor at Hawthorne from 1947 to 1950, Jeanne Wilensky concluded that "counseling has helped protect management's freedom to promote, downgrade, transfer, train, discipline, lay off,

[20] Bers, "Unionism and Collective Bargaining," 76; the technician was interviewed in 1953 by Joel Seidman, a University of Chicago sociologist, whose study of an AT&T local is reported in Brooks, *Communications Workers of America,* 193–5.

apply a variety of rewards and sanctions (with a minimum of interference from a relatively cooperative union) – in short, it has helped the company retain its control over the worker." This listing of managerial activities is a useful reminder that counseling was but one of many forms of control.[21]

Counseling was less successful as a means of research into the social organization of the factory. The researchers had seen counseling as a generator of raw material that could be compiled by their division into reports addressed to higher management, and it was expected that counselors would unearth problems requiring more focused research. The early years of the program saw some success in this respect. Dickson, Moore, and several other personnel managers conducted research and wrote reports on general personnel problems; the most notable were the annual surveys of the labor situation in the plant. By 1941, however, Putnam noted that "research is much talked about – and generally left at that level." Several reasons for this decline can be adduced. The influx of new employees to work on war production (the workforce grew from 13,007 in 1939 to 26,689 in 1943) and a postwar domestic boom (when the workforce reached a peak of 36,757 in 1947) required a parallel expansion in counseling and supervisory training, as the company sought to help inexperienced workers, including a large number of women and blacks, adjust to the discipline of the factory. The experienced members of the division found that their time was fully occupied by the training and supervising of counselors. Moreover, Pennock, Putnam, and Moore were transferred from Hawthorne between 1938 and 1943, leaving only Dickson and Wright out of the original cadre of researchers. Dickson reported many years later that higher management at Hawthorne had accepted the researchers' reports for a few years, but had come to regard the counseling division as being in league with the workers and low-level supervisors. Managers did not particularly like having to deal with so many shop-level grievances and problems, whether they came from the union or from the counseling and research division. Finally, it seems apparent that the union usurped the role of the counseling division as the organization that brought these problems to the attention of management, both through collective bargaining and grievance procedures and, during the war, through the labor–management committees established by the National War Labor Board.[22]

[21] W. J. Dickson and A. C. Moore, "An Appraisal of the Labor Situation at Hawthorne, March 1939," 5 Apr. 1939, EM/1.096; W. J. Dickson, "An Approach to the Human Factor in Work Relations," *The New Industrial Relations*, Ithaca, N.Y.: Cornell University Press, 1948, 95–122, quote on 116; W. J. Dickson, "Employee Counseling," transcript of address at a Reconversion Problems School of the Chicago Association of Commerce, 2 May 1946, WE/Personnel/Counseling; Wilensky and Wilensky, "Personnel Counseling," 279.
[22] "Outline and Suggestions for Discussing the Labor Situation at Hawthorne," app. E of "Report on Personnel Counseling Activity, January 1936 to March 1937," HSC/6; Dickson and Moore, "An Appraisal of the Labor Situation at Hawthorne, March 1939"; idem,

The annual reports of the labor situation at Hawthorne bore the unmistakable mark of the Hawthorne experiments, and especially of *Management and the Worker*. Dickson and Moore argued that the labor situation comprised all of the personal and social relations in the factory, and they sought to identify the social processes that contributed to conflict or integration. The aim of management should be to manipulate these processes so as to reduce social distance and promote integration:

> It is our belief that marked opposition to management cannot develop without 1. Strong horizontal solidarity within employee groups, 2. Strong solidarity within management groups, and, 3. Marked social distance or opposition between group 1 and group 2. From the standpoint of labor relations the important thing is to see that no gap develops between these two groups. Ideally it is preferable that groups 1 and 2 merge into one another through infinite gradations of social distinctions and that a vertical solidarity is developed which will keep the horizontal solidarities in equilibrium.

From this perspective it is possible to see how counseling was always intended to be part of a broader strategy; other approaches were needed to cover all aspects of the social organization. The function of counseling was to reduce solidarity among workers by preventing complaints from becoming generalized grievances and to reduce tensions between workers and their immediate supervisors; supervisory training, by sensitizing supervisors to the personal and social needs of their workers, would ensure that the social distance between workers and their supervisors was kept to a minimum; and management should develop a "social ladder" of "infinite gradations" through the sensitive application of labor grading, wage scales, placement, and promotion: "The danger is that if [the workers] are not given adequate opportunity to differentiate themselves they may develop a strong horizontal solidarity and attempt to satisfy their demands through the exercise of power." The unionists' view of industrial relations as class conflict had to be replaced by the corporate vision of human relations.[23]

There is no evidence that the research division had any significant effect on management decisions in these areas at Hawthorne. The problem was that Dickson and his colleagues were trying to influence decisions made for the most part in New York at the highest levels of management. Human relations, defined and given a scientific basis by the Hawthorne researchers, had passed out of their control; ironically, managers could now turn to

"Appraisal of the Labor Situation at Hawthorne, April 1940," EM/1.096. It is possible that further annual reports were written and have not survived; Wright and Dickson's comments suggest, however, that they continued for only the first few years of the counseling program. On the decline in research, see Putnam to Roethlisberger, 9 May 1941, FJR/1; Dickson and Roethlisberger, *Counseling in an Organization*, 396–409, 468.

23 "Outline and Suggestions for Discussing the Labor Situation at Hawthorne," quotes on 2 and sec. 1, 2.

Management and the Worker and the other publications of the Harvard group and rely less on internal reports from their own researchers. Where the researchers regarded constant research of the changing social system as intrinsic to human relations, higher managers were generally content to distill a few general principles. The ideology of human relations permeated the Bell System and informed managerial practice, but the personnel managers and researchers at Hawthorne never realized their hopes for making themselves a court of human relations that would judge each proposed technical change in terms of its impact on the social organization.

Counseling spread into other parts of the Bell System in the 1940s. In 1941 it was introduced to the Kearny and Point Breeze plants of Western Electric, and over the next few years to Indiana Bell, Chesapeake & Potomac Bell, Ohio Bell, Bell Telephone Company of Canada, and finally, in 1948, to the New York headquarters of AT&T. The counseling programs in these companies were considerably smaller, however, and did not involve any research. Even though the programs were established with the assistance of the Hawthorne researchers, the counselors never seem to have attained anything more than a marginal position in the workplace; for example, Dickson was later told by a former manager that the Kearny counselors had been a largely untrained group of housewives and ballet dancers who had talked among themselves about their interviews, thereby incurring the suspicion and hostility of workers and supervisors alike. By the late 1950s these programs had been disbanded or allowed to dwindle away; this was illustrated at Hawthorne, where a Personnel Counseling Research Section still existed in 1961, but had lacked members since 1956.[24]

The reasons for the abandonment of counseling were numerous and overdetermined its demise. First, higher management increasingly questioned the cost of a program whose benefits were very difficult to demonstrate in a report. Counseling at Hawthorne cost $356,000 in 1949, or more than $13 per employee covered by the program. Second, there is ample evidence that even at Hawthorne the counseling program became bureaucratized and aimless. Without the research component to orient it toward management's needs, the organization turned in on itself, and counselors became concerned mainly with writing reports that would please their supervisor. Third, Western Electric began to decentralize its operations after the war, following the trend toward smaller, specialized plants instead of the massive integrated factories of the first half of the century. By 1954 Hawthorne accounted for only 35 percent and Kearny for 20 percent of the nonsupervisory employees

---

[24] Putnam to Roethlisberger, 28 Oct. 1941, FJR/1; Bell Telephone Company of Canada, "Summary of Experiment in Industrial Counselling," WJD/3/13; W. J. Dickson, "Record of Discussion with Jerry Arnold," *Business Week*, 16 May 1963, WJD/3/13; J. L. O'Marra (Superintendent of Personnel Administration, Western Electric, New York) to E. W. Hertenstein, 19 Dec. 1960, HSC/vol. 27; E. C. Tessman (Supervisory Training & Counseling Research Department, Hawthorne Works) to Dickson, 21 Mar. 1961, HSC/vol. 27.

in Western Electric's manufacturing plants; the remaining 45 percent were in plants of five thousand or fewer employees. Managers felt that they were able to establish a closer relationship with their workers and supervisors, obviating the need for counseling. Fourth, as we have already seen, the unions appropriated many of the functions of counseling. Higher managers might grant that counseling would help weaken the base of union support on the shop floor, but as labor relations steadied in the 1950s, managers became accustomed to dealing with a responsible union leadership and counseling seemed redundant. Finally, many of the components of counseling were incorporated into the regular supervisory structure, primarily by training supervisors in the techniques and ideology of human relations. Surveying this change in 1961, the Western Electric personnel superintendent observed that "while we never thought that the supervisor could fully replace the counselor, we did feel that with proper training he could achieve considerable success with the ordinary run of problems brought to our counselor's attention."[25]

The supervisor and personnel management

What impact did the Hawthorne experiments have on industrial relations practice in the 1940s and 1950s? Historians of management and the social sciences have generally avoided the question, preferring discussions of the lineage of ideas to the knottier problem of the impact of those ideas. Those willing to risk an assessment have done so on little evidence and have arrived at remarkably dissimilar conclusions. Thus, Loren Baritz, in *The Servants of Power* (1960), the only historical survey of the social sciences in American industry, concludes that the human relations approach is a successful manipulative technique and that counseling is "one of the most seductive levers of social control that the ingenuity of man has ever invented." At the other extreme, Harry Braverman, in his classic work *Labor and Monopoly Capital* (1974), criticizes Mayo and the Hawthorne experiments for trying to habituate the worker to industrial capitalism, but believes that the "natural resistance" of the worker will always be able to break through the mythologies of management. He therefore concludes that the human relations and similar managerial schools of thought have had "little real impact upon the management of worker or work." In most of the histories of managerial thought, the rise of industrial unions in the 1930s and 1940s is presumed to have undermined the essentially antiunion approach of human relations, the collective action of workers making nonsense of its emphasis on individual adjustment. Indeed, the failure of counseling to gain widespread

[25] O'Marra to H. A. Black, 20 June 1961, (quote) WJD/1/8; "Information Regarding Personnel Counseling Activity, Hawthorne Works, November 1949," HSC/6.

support as a personnel technique, along with its eventual demise in the Bell System, seems to provide some evidence to support this view.[26]

To provide a definitive answer to the question would require a detailed exploration of the interrelations among management theory, supervisory practices, and shop floor industrial relations. Part of the problem with the assessments of Baritz and Braverman is that they draw broad conclusions on little evidence; Baritz tends to assume that the rhetoric of managers and social scientists reflects shop floor reality, while Braverman adopts a static view of human relations, equating it with Mayo's ideological writings and not taking into account that the human relations approach adjusted easily to unions and collective bargaining. Nevertheless, it is possible to come to a tentative conclusion if we consider the parallel developments of industrial relations, the human relations literature, and personnel management from the New Deal to the 1950s. In this context, we can see that human relations provided a particularly powerful ideology for managers as they sought to *adapt* to the demands of collective bargaining. Further, personnel managers, government agencies, and even union leaders implemented human relations programs in a concerted effort to alter industrial relations at the bargaining table and on the shop floor.

The rise of industrial unionism in the 1930s, the New Deal labor legislation, and the Second World War combined to transform U.S. industrial relations. Historian Arthur M. Schlesinger listed in 1950 the "upsurge of labor" as one of the great events of the first half of the twentieth century, second only to the world wars in its impact. Fifteen million U.S. workers belonged to unions at the end of the war, five times the membership in 1933. Equally important, the majority of large employers recognized the rights of their workers to organize and bargain, and while they wished to limit the issues on which bargaining could take place, they did not attempt a replay of the open-shop drives and employee representation plans that had sliced into union membership at the end of the First World War. By 1950 a system of industrial relations was firmly established, based on contractual relations between employers and unions, with grievance procedures to ensure that the contract was enforced, and with the rights of each side protected and limited by government legislation.[27]

[26] Loren Baritz, *The Servants of Power: A History of the Use of Social Science in American Industry*, Middletown, Conn.: Wesleyan University Press, 1960, chaps. 5 and 6, quote on 116; Harry Braverman, *Labor and Monopoly Capital: The Degradation of Work in the Twentieth Century*, New York: Monthly Review Press, 1974, 139–52, quote on 145.

[27] The survey of industrial relations in this and the following paragraphs draws on Brody, *Workers in Industrial America*, esp. chaps. 3–5, reference to Schlesinger on 173; Christopher L. Tomlins, *The State and the Unions: Labor Relations, Law, and the Organized Labor Movement in America, 1880–1960*, Cambridge University Press, 1985; Nelson Lichtenstein, *Labor's War at Home: The CIO in World War II*, Cambridge University Press, 1982; Howell John Harris, *The Right to Manage: Industrial Relations Policies of American Business in the 1940s*, Madison: University of Wisconsin Press, 1982; Bryce M. Stewart and

The war was the crucible in which this new system of industrial relations was forged. Union leaders in the AFL and CIO alike found themselves increasingly bound to a framework of legislation that both protected and constrained their activities. In return for recognition, maintenance of membership, and the participation of organized labor in government war agencies, unions were required to forgo strike action for the duration of the war; indeed, union leaders often found themselves disciplining those workers who were perceived to be threatening the war effort through unauthorized strikes. The National Defense Mediation Board and its successor, the National War Labor Board (NWLB), played as significant a role as the Wagner Act and the NLRB in setting the new ground rules of labor relations; critical developments such as the introduction of industry-wide wage patterns and a legalistic system of grievance procedures were introduced by these government boards and shaped the future structure of collective bargaining. Industrial relations executives from major corporations played a major role in shaping the ideology of these agencies; for example, Walter Teagle of Standard Oil of New Jersey and Cyrus Ching of U.S. Rubber, both representatives on the SCC in the 1930s, were particularly influential. After the war some CIO leaders hoped to move past collective bargaining to some form of labor–management partnership; thus, United Auto Workers' president Walter Reuther challenged General Motors to "open the books" to prove that it could not meet the union's demand for wage increases with no increase in prices. But the National Association of Manfacturers and U.S. Chamber of Commerce, guided by the reports and staff of Industrial Relations Counselors, worked hard to undermine this assault on "management's prerogatives," and the Taft–Hartley Act of 1947 severely curtailed union power and institutionalized many of the industrial relations practices of the war. By 1950 unions were confining their activities to collective bargaining over wages, hours, conditions, and, to a lesser extent, promotion and discipline; their participation in such areas as product design, production methods, and prices was nonexistent.

Two effects of this transformation in industrial relations concern us here: the increased importance of personnel management and the impact on the foreman's authority. As companies responded to the changing climate of labor relations, personnel management became a major executive function, equal in importance to production or marketing. Industrial relations departments expanded their authority over other parts of the company, ensuring that industrial relations was being conducted in accordance with union contract and government edict. Personnel managers who were previously powerless to control the behavior of supervisors now determined whether union grievances against a supervisor were legitimate. Where in

Walter J. Couper, *Reconversion in Industrial Relations*, New York: Industrial Relations Counselors, 1946; and Green, *The World of the Worker*, chap. 6.

the 1920s industrial relations was an afterthought, the province of middle management, by the 1940s no major company decision could be made without the consideration and active participation of industrial relations executives.

The second change was closely related to the first. On the factory floor, supervisors now found that they were being squeezed from both sides: From above, personnel managers were assuming more and more of the supervisor's authority, while at the same time increasing the supervisor's responsibility for compliance with the union contract; from below, workers and union stewards were restricting the supervisor's right to discipline workers, determine production methods, and make promotions. Workers soon found that problems on the shop floor could be more easily resolved by ignoring the supervisor and filing a grievance under the contract, which enabled the shop steward to negotiate directly with personnel managers. These problems had been exacerbated during the war by a decline in wage differentials between supervisors and their workers and by the huge increase in supervisors, drawn mainly from the shop floor, to cope with war production. The result was an unexpected efflorescence of "foremen's unions"; by 1947 the largest of these, the Foreman's Association of America, had 33,000 members. They did not last long: The Taft–Hartley Act of 1947 included a provision that removed the right of supervisors to organize under the protection of the Wagner Act. But management had learned its lesson, and it began to consider how supervisors could be integrated into management and trained to be effective representatives of management on the shop floor. A report by Industrial Relations Counselors spelled out clearly what had to be done:

> In industry generally it will be necessary to give better pay and working conditions to the lower levels of supervision, to integrate them more closely with the entire supervisory group, to encourage them to contribute to the formulation of company policy and to inculcate in them a greater consciousness of managerial status. Success in this area will improve management's direction of the operation of the enterprise and will strengthen its title to the right of direction.[28]

While most participants in the new industrial relations – managers, union leaders, government officials, and academics – concentrated on the legal structures and everyday problems of collective bargaining, a significant minority turned to the social sciences for a philosophy that made sense of

[28] See Industrial Relations Counselors, *Reconversion in Industrial Relations*, 27. On the changing position of supervisors and foremen's unions, see Robert David Leiter, *The Foreman in Industrial Relations*, New York: Columbia University Press, 1948; and Herbert R. Northrup, "The Foreman's Association of America," *Harvard Business Review*, 1944–5, 23: 187–202. The NWLB commissioned a panel to report on the problem; for a summary of the report, see Sumner Slichter, Robert Calkins, and William Spohn, "The Changing Position of Foremen in American Industry," *Advanced Management*, 1945, 10: 155–61.

these developments and for techniques to deal with them. The Harvard researchers were not slow to claim that their human relations approach provided an ideal framework. Fritz Roethlisberger argued that the findings of the Hawthorne experiments offered the "road back to sanity" in industrial relations and pressed this point in *Management and Morale* (1941), a collection of talks and essays that did much to popularize the experiments. Roethlisberger claimed that by ignoring the importance of human relations in their company, managers had contributed directly to the current turmoil in industry. In industry, many personnel managers agreed with J. Walter Dietz, vice-president of the Personnel Division of the American Management Association (AMA), who outlined a more powerful role for personnel management and, citing *Management and the Worker*, declared that "this newer concept of the personnel function is based upon the growing conviction that we must look upon our organizations as social structures." As personnel relations manager of Western Electric, Dietz had special reasons for citing the Hawthorne experiments, and he played a significant role in spreading the gospel through the personnel management community. For both Roethlisberger and Dietz, however, human relations was essentially a management function; workers, whether unorganized or organized, remained passive recipients of this more human form of management.[29]

A handful of union leaders also saw value in presenting their political arguments in the language of human relations. Perhaps the most dramatic example was *The Dynamics of Industrial Democracy* (1942), by Clinton S. Golden and Harold J. Ruttenberg, regional director and research director, respectively, of the CIO's Steel Workers' Organizing Committee, who used the Hawthorne experiments as scientific evidence that worker participation in all levels of management would increase productivity and aid the war effort. In the first of their principles of union–management relations, they stated that "workers organize into labor unions not alone for economic motives but also for equally compelling psychological and social ones, so that they can participate in making the decisions that vitally affect them in their work and community life." The bank wiring test room, they argued, showed that the same motives could be found among unorganized workers; it was up to management to decide whether informal and formal worker organizations were to be used defensively or constructively. Likewise, the relay assembly test room provided powerful evidence that if workers were able to participate collectively in decisions respecting their

[29] F. J. Roethlisberger, *Management and Morale*, Cambridge: Harvard University Press, 1941, quote on 9. J. Walter Dietz's statements include "New Trends in Personnel Policies," *Personnel*, 1940, 16: 97–106, quote on 98; "This Thing Called Personnel Relations," American Management Association, *Personnel Series*, no. 45, 1940, 3–8; and "Organizing the Personnel Function of Management," *Proceedings of the Seventh International Management Congress, Washington, DC, 1938*, Baltimore: Waverly Press, 1938, Personnel Volume, 3–6.

work, then management, workers, and the public stood to gain from increased productivity. Those unions with research officers prepared to read the expanding social scientific literature on industrial work could find considerable evidence to support their views.[30]

A new breed of labor relations experts, located in both universities and government, perceived that human relations could be made complementary to the contractual and legal aspects of collective bargaining. The arguments were marshaled most effectively by Benjamin Selekman, professor of labor relations at the Harvard Business School, who recorded his debt to Donham, Mayo, Roethlisberger, and Whitehead in the preface to his influential *Labor Relations and Human Relations* (1947). Selekman's acceptance is especially notable because he had long championed collective bargaining and in the early 1920s had researched and coauthored a scathing attack on the employee representation plan established by Rockefeller at Colorado Fuel and Iron Company. The thesis was in the title. Collective bargaining and organized unions were only the first step toward building industrial cooperation; it was also necessary to establish new human relations on the basis of that legal framework. Grievances, whether legitimate or not, were disputes between workers and supervisors on the shop floor; they were problems arising from a whole network of human relations, and their resolution required human as much as legalistic solutions. The whole structure of industrial relations thus pivoted on the relations between supervisors and union stewards, and industrial coooperation could be established only when employers and unions trained their agents in the skills of human relations. Throughout the book Selekman insisted that supervisors should be trained in the skills of human relations, and especially in the clinical approach developed in the Hawthorne experiments; the introduction of clinical skills to the shop floor would "modify and expand prevailing procedures until orderly handling utilizes not only the law of the agreement but every instrument of control that psychological and social insights make available."[31]

Personnel managers and social scientists agreed that the supervisor was the key figure in industrial management, and this new realization spurred the growth of an enormous literature on the role of the supervisor as the

---

[30] Clinton S. Golden and Harold J. Ruttenberg, *The Dynamics of Industrial Democracy*, New York: Harper Bros., 1942, quote on xxiii–xxiv; on the Hawthorne experiments, see 178–83, 250–2. This book echoed the arguments for industrial democracy in Morris L. Cooke and Philip Murray, *Organized Labor and Production: New Steps in Industrial Democracy*, New York: Harper Bros., 1940.

[31] Benjamin M. Selekman, *Labor Relations and Human Relations*, New York: McGraw-Hill, 1947, quote on 88; Benjamin M. Selekman and Mary Van Kleeck, *Employee Representation in Coal Mines: A Study of the Industrial Representation Plan of the Colorado Fuel & Iron Company*, New York: Russell Sage Foundation, 1924. For similar arguments by members of the Industrial Relations Section at MIT, see Douglas McGregor and Irving Knickerbocker, "Industrial Relations and National Defense: A Challenge to Management," *Personnel*, 1941, 18: 49–63.

human relations expert on the factory floor. Roethlisberger contributed to the discussion with an article entitled "The Foreman: Master and Victim of Double Talk," a piece that became a classic of the human relations literature, appearing frequently in collections and sold in huge numbers as a reprint to be used in management training programs. In a racy and entertaining style Roethlisberger described the foreman as "management's contribution to the social pathology of American culture," for the foreman had been given an impossibly complex task: "He has to be a manager, a cost accountant, an engineer, a lawyer, a teacher, a leader, an inspector, a disciplinarian, a counselor, a friend, and, above all, an 'example.'" While foremen would give lip service to all these roles in supervisory training classes, they knew well enough that they were functions over which they no longer held authority; accordingly, they worried only about the task they knew their superiors would hold them responsible for – getting the job finished on time. Foremen were masters of double talk, conveying to their superiors only that information they expected to hear and effectively concealing the true conditions of the shop floor. Hemmed in by the actions of managers, technical specialists, unions, and workers, the foreman was "victim, not monarch, of all he surveys." Roethlisberger warned that the supervisor responded by succumbing to one or more of the "three major ills of our industrial civilization" – becoming obsessive, joining a union, or seeking a "political solution to his social void."[32]

The human relations advocates believed that the solution lay in convincing higher management of the importance of the supervisor's role, ensuring that managers were receptive to communications from supervisors on the social organization of the workplace, and training supervisors more effectively in the skills of human relations. Burleigh Gardner and William Foote Whyte, of the Committee on Human Relations in Industry at the University of Chicago, described the supervisor's role in terms similar to those used to delineate the task of the personnel counselor – Gardner had in fact been a section head in the Personnel Counseling and Research Division at Hawthorne from 1937 to 1942. The supervisor was the leader of a team who by using leadership skills could gain the cooperation of the workers; the supervisor should be able to utilize the informal groups on the shop floor and be able to identify and gain the cooperation of informal leaders. By consulting workers over proposed changes and by listening to their complaints, the supervisor could reduce their resistance to the technical organization of work and could obligate the workers through ties of personal loyalty. But Gardner and Whyte hastened to reassure managers that "this does not mean that the supervisor must always be able to do something

[32] F. J. Roethlisberger, "The Foreman: Master and Victim of Double Talk" (*Harvard Business Review*, 1945), reprinted in idem, *Man-in-Organization*, Cambridge, Mass.: Harvard University Press, 1968, 35–56, quotes on 35, 37, 49, 50.

concrete to meet a complaint. Perhaps he is powerless to make the desired change, but, if he gives the worker a chance to express himself fully before explaining his own position, he has a good chance of keeping that line of communication open." If management trained the foreman in this new role and consulted him on proposed changes so that he could make suggestions about how to reduce worker resistance, then the foreman would be more capable of leading his work group, thereby increasing morale and productivity.[33]

Supervisory training programs in human relations flourished during and after the Second World War, initially through government programs to increase war production, but increasingly through the efforts of personnel managers who sought to develop the leadership and human relations skills of their supervisors. The war provided an extraordinary opportunity for the dissemination of the human relations approach to foremen and personnel managers throughout the country. In July 1940 the National Defense Advisory Commission established a Training within Industry (TWI) program to assist industrial mobilization efforts. Personnel and industrial relations managers from major corporations were appointed to run the program – the director of TWI was C. R. Dooley, industrial relations manager of Socony–Vacuum Oil Company, who was assisted by J. Walter Dietz, personnel relations manager at Western Electric. They chose to concentrate on supervisory training, for the rapid expansion of industry, combined with the loss of supervisors to the military, had resulted in a shortage of experienced supervisors. They also decided that the program would be most effective if it selected problems that were common across all of industry, leaving to factory managers the responsibility for training supervisors for specific jobs. Three major TWI programs were established during the war: Job Instruction, which trained supervisors to teach new workers; Job Methods, which provided techniques in production supervision; and Job Relations, which trained supervisors in the basics of human relations. During the course of the war, 1,750,650 TWI certificates were issued to supervisors who had taken one or more of the courses; Job Relations training was given to 490,022 supervisors in war factories and to a further 138,800 supervisors in the military and government and in Canadian and British factories.[34]

[33] Burleigh B. Gardner and William F. Whyte, "The Man in the Middle: Position and Problems of the Foreman," *Applied Anthropology*, 1945, 4(2): 1–28, quote on 11; Roethlisberger, "The Foreman," 53–6. Similar arguments were made by Abraham Zaleznik, a student of Roethlisberger, in his *Foreman Training in a Growing Enterprise*, Boston: Harvard University, Graduate School of Business Administration, 1951, esp. chap. 12.

[34] War Manpower Commission, Training within Industry Service, *The Training within Industry Report, 1940–1945*, Washington, D.C.: U.S. Government Printing Office, 1945; J. Walter Dietz, *Learn by Doing – The Story of Training within Industry, 1940–1970*, Summit, N.J.: J. Walter Dietz, 1970. TWI was placed under the authority of a series of wartime agencies: the Office of Production Management, the War Production Board, and finally the War Manpower Commission.

The TWI Job Relations program was a direct outgrowth of the Hawthorne experiments. Walter Dietz of TWI was already committed to the human relations approach, based on his knowledge of the experiments and experience at Western Electric. In designing the program he was able to draw on the assistance of Roethlisberger, Hal Wright from Hawthorne, and John Fox, a new student of Mayo's. The Job Relations program was designed to give supervisors a brief but intense training in human relations. It consisted of five two-hour conferences in which a TWI trainer, normally a local personnel manager who had taken a special course for TWI trainers, led discussions with approximately ten supervisors. The essence of the program was that of the Hawthorne experiments; the central tenet was that "it is important to know the kind of person who has a problem – rather than what kind of problem that person has." Supervisors talked through concrete examples prepared for discussion or taken from their own experience, referring to the "textbook" for guidance – a small blue card containing the principles of human relations:

Foundations for Good Relations
Let each worker know how he is getting along.
Give credit when due.
Tell people in advance about changes that will affect them.
Make best use of each person's ability.
People must be treated as individuals.

As with personnel counseling, the program taught the supervisors the importance of developing their skills of interviewing and listening to their workers, which could be applied whether or not the workers were unionized. Just what the impact of Job Relations was on supervisory practice is impossible to determine; more important was that managers throughout the country had been exposed to these training techniques and to the human relations approach. Many would have agreed with Stuart Chase's verdict, given in an article on Job Relations in the *Reader's Digest,* that "it is now being proved in thousands of war plants that *the human approach is also the approach which results in maximum production."* When in 1945 the Society for the Advancement of Management presented its first award in human relations to Dooley and Dietz for their work in TWI, it was a sign of the widespread acceptance among industrial managers of the need for supervisory training in human relations.[35]

Supervisory training gathered pace after the war, spurred on by continuing industrial unrest and concern with the position of the foreman. The AMA

[35] Stuart Chase, "Teaching Foremen That Workers Are People," *Reader's Digest,* Sept. 1943, 43: 17–21, quote on 21; War Manpower Commission, Training within Industry Service, *The Training within Industry Report, 1940–1945,* 204–22, quote on 207; Frances Kirkpatrick, "What TWI Has Learned about Developing Training Programs," *Personnel,* 1945–6, 22: 114–20.

played a significant role in the dissemination of human relations, through surveys of the best practices of major corporations, handbooks for personnel managers, conferences, and its journal and pamphlet series. Association president Lawrence A. Appleby introduced the association's *Supervisor's Management Guide* by declaring:

> While the manager on the front line deals with two major resources – physical and human – effective handling of the latter is by far his more important job. The degree to which the supervisor's job is pervaded by the human factor may be gauged by the finding of a recent survey that fully 60 per cent of the average foreman's responsibilities involve personnel and human relations problems.

The "Human Relations Reading List" at the end of the guide was dominated by the literature on the Hawthorne experiments and subsequent human relations research.[36]

At the same time social scientists and personnel managers experimented with other techniques for inculcating human relations in supervisors. The Research Center for Group Dynamics, first at MIT and then at the University of Michigan, developed role-playing methods for supervisory training, arguing that supervisors learned the human relations approach much more effectively when they could actually practice it rather than simply talk about it in conferences. By the 1950s supervisors around the country, especially those in the larger companies, were being put through an endless stream of training conferences and role-playing sessions from which they were expected to take away skills in nondirective interviewing or counseling, leadership, human relations, and even "democratic supervision."[37]

Whether this barrage of human relations training paid off is difficult to assess. Several of the social scientists committed to supervisory training expressed considerable skepticism about the efficacy of many programs. Roethlisberger noted that too often the supervisors only learned the appropriate verbal responses to give in the conference session, and University of Michigan psychologist Norman Maier reflected that human relations was too often "sugar coating" that did little to alter basic attitudes. However, these criticisms were often simply attacks on existing practices, preparatory to the social scientist's discussion of a technique that would supposedly overcome these difficulties. Other research suggested that even where train-

[36] M. Joseph Dooher and Vivienne Marquis, eds., *The Supervisor's Management Guide*, New York: American Management Association, 1949, quote on 5; see also American Management Association, *The Foreman's Basic Reading Kit*, New York, 1944; idem, *The Development of Foremen in Management*, New York, 1945.

[37] Alex Bavelas, "Role Playing and Management Training," *Sociatry*, 1947, 1: 183–91. A major textbook of this period is Norman R. F. Maier, *The Principles of Human Relations*, New York: Wiley, 1952; Maier was professor of psychology at the University of Michigan, associated with the Research Center for Group Dynamics, and a consultant to Michigan Bell Telephone Company.

ing programs were successful in changing supervisors' attitudes, the pressure of the job would overwhelm their best intentions. Yale University researchers analyzed the daily activity of foremen and showed that the supervisor's job consisted of dealing with an endless stream of small problems, four hundred to six hundred each day, that had to be solved with little time for reflection or discussion. They concluded that the "foreman who has to jump from one operating emergency to another every 45 seconds has neither the time nor the inclination to practice the fine precepts he is exposed to in human relations training programs." Nevertheless, they concluded along with other researchers that the most effective supervisor was one who could lead the workers and shape them into a social group. However many constraints the industrial environment and managerial hierarchy might place on the supervisor's ability to create a socially cohesive informal group of well-adjusted workers, personnel managers and social scientists alike remained convinced that human relations training provided useful supervisory skills.[38]

The Hawthorne experiments therefore had a considerable impact on the practice of industrial management. Commentators who focus on Mayo's conservative antiunion rhetoric and on the abandonment of the counseling program in the Bell System assume that the experiments were ineffectual because they could not address the advent of industrial unions and collective bargaining and because they offered no practical managerial technique. But the antiunion rhetoric quickly disappeared from the human relations literature in the face of the extraordinary successes of industrial unions during the New Deal and the Second World War. The human relations techniques deriving from the Hawthorne experiments were adapted to the new industrial relations environment. Indeed, the existence of a union contract and the presence of union representatives in the factory made skilled supervision even more critical, for collective bargaining was most successful in constraining managerial authority in personnel matters and on the shop floor, and in many cases rank-and-file action forced managers to give way on even more than was formally conceded in the contract.

Company executives and personnel managers embraced human relations because it seemed to offer a way of reestablishing managerial authority on the shop floor by reducing the number of everyday conflicts that might become union grievances. Counseling at Hawthorne and elsewhere in the Bell System was a highly visible version of human relations techniques in use on the shop floor, but the same techniques and managerial ideology suffused the majority of supervisory training programs. The function of

---

[38] F. J. Roethlisberger, "Training Supervisors in Human Relations" (*Harvard Business Review*, 1951), reprinted in Roethlisberger, *Man-in-Organization*, 125–44; Maier, *Principles of Human Relations*, 2–14; Zaleznik, *Foreman Training in a Growing Enterprise*, 215–32; Robert H. Guest, "Of Time and the Foreman," *Personnel*, 1955–6, 32: 478–86, quote on 484; Charles R. Walker, Robert H. Guest, and Arthur N. Turner, *The Foreman on the Assembly Line*, Cambridge, Mass.: Harvard University Press, 1956.

counseling and the human relations aspects of supervision was to counteract the increasing tendency for a worker's complaint to be elevated to the status of a union grievance; workers' problems were individualized and thereby rendered politically neutral, and the worker was adjusted to the existing industrial system.

But human relations was more than a collection of supervisory techniques; it had become a professional ideology for personnel managers, giving them a coherent philosophy that underscored the central importance of their managerial function in production and industrial relations. By the 1950s personnel managers and social scientists could point to a body of research and industrial practice that established the importance of human relations in increasing productivity, improving morale, and reducing industrial unrest. Indeed, long after the human relations approach had become unpopular among academic social scientists, personnel managers and management consultants continued to use its techniques and embrace its comfortable ideology. Human relations told managers that no matter how much they might be forced to bargain with unions over wages and conditions, workers' basic understanding of the workplace was flawed by their specific psychological needs and their personal situation. It sought to create among supervisors a managerial ethos that discouraged them from identifying too closely with their subordinates. Human relations confirmed managerial assumptions that only management was able to assess what was best for both the company and its workforce. Learning of the Hawthorne experiments in training programs and in the ever-expanding management literature, personnel managers could manage with self-assurance, knowing that the Hawthorne experiments had established the scientific foundations of their field.

It should be stressed that supervisory training and the human relations approach to personnel management were only part of a broader battle over managerial authority in the United States after the war. The "right to manage" became enshrined in legislation such as the Taft–Hartley Act and was written into union contracts. The unions themselves supervised their agreements: The more radical union locals were forced to abide by national contracts, and left-wing union activists were purged during the cold war. So successful were these tactics that when in the late 1940s and early 1950s the U.S. government gave economic aid to help rebuild the European capitalist economies and ensure the long-term stability of U.S. cold war allies, U.S. management experts and union officials worked side by side in an effort to replicate the system of industrial relations in the United States. Here, among funding for non-Communist unions and national productivity councils, the Marshall administrators arranged for the TWI programs to be run for German and Italian supervisors, European union leaders were funded to attend three-month training programs at the Harvard Business School, and funds were provided for British academic research on the influence of human relations on productivity. The Hawthorne experiments and human relations had been mobilized in a contest that Paul Hoffman, the administrator of the Marshall Plan, liked to call a contest between the U.S. assembly line and the Communist party line.[39]

[39] Anthony Carew, *Labour under the Marshall Plan: The Politics of Productivity and the Marketing of Management Science,* Manchester: Manchester University Press, 1987. The appreciation of the Hawthorne experiments in Great Britain was assisted by Mayo's daughter, Patricia Elton Mayo, who after the war was a researcher for the British Institute of Management; her publications included "Scientific Management and Shop Discipline," *Industry Illustrated,* Mar. 1945, 45–6, 25, and "The Work of Elton Mayo," *Occupational Psychology,* 1950, 24: 1–6.

9

Human relations in the social sciences

THE HAWTHORNE EXPERIMENTS and human relations school flourished in an environment conducive to the social scientific study of organizations and management. The New Deal and the Second World War provided social scientists with singular opportunities to expand their influence in government, industry, and the military, where their specialized knowledge and techniques were applied to problems of planning and administration. The experiments had been the first large-scale, experimental, interdisciplinary study of an industrial organization and had revealed the importance of informal groups within larger formal structures. Such insights, social scientists contended, were applicable to any organization, whether it be a factory, a government office, a school, or a warship. Further research, encompassing both laboratory experiments and detailed observations of organizations, seemed to confirm the importance of the social structure of the organization and the crucial role played by the leader of a group. Sociologists, social psychologists, and social anthropologists in particular saw in the Hawthorne experiments a new approach to the study of organizations. And for social scientists the experiments stood as a model for the combination of basic research and applied science that delineated an expanded role for the social scientist as scientific arbiter of social problems.

Though sometimes used to embrace all the social sciences, the term "human relations" always retained an identification with the particular methodological techniques and ideological vision of the Hawthorne researchers. Close observation of the workplace combined with interviewing characterized the future research of Mayo and his colleagues at the Harvard Business School and spread to other groups of industrial researchers, most notably the Committee on Human Relations in Industry at the University of Chicago. Here, as in the Hawthorne experiments, the researchers were concerned predominantly, although by no means exclusively, with establishing the importance of informal human relations in the social organization of the workplace and consequently on production, turnover, and strikes. To critics, the human relations philosophy expressed an ideology and technique of manipulation inappropriate in a democratic society. Debates over human relations and the function of the social sciences in industry were at the center of discussions in the 1950s on the professional role of the social scientist.

This chapter examines the mechanisms by which human relations permeated the upper levels of management, focusing on the incorporation of human relations into business education at Harvard and into influential writings on management theory. And it surveys the reception of the experiments by social scientists, in particular by tracing their influence on industrial research. By the 1940s the experiments were taken to exemplify the recent achievements of the social sciences, although some critics regarded them as an illustration of subservience by social scientists to the dictates of management. Just as with the original research at Hawthorne, the published versions of the Hawthorne experiments were adapted and assimilated into a variety of disciplinary and political contexts, thereby ensuring their survival in an industrial and social scientific world markedly different from that in which they had been conducted.

Human relations at Harvard:
business education and administration

One avenue for the dissemination of the Hawthorne experiments lay at the very feet of the Harvard researchers – the Harvard Business School itself, with its prestigious faculty, students, and close ties to business executives. Mayo and his colleagues were for many years on the edge of the business school community, however, and the incorporation of the human relations approach was a slow process, resisted by many members of the faculty. A combination of factors assisted the gradual acceptance of human relations into the school: an increased concern among business executives and social critics alike with the social responsibility of business; an emerging consensus that increased attention to the social sciences was necessary if business schools were to achieve their goal of becoming key institutions for the professionalization of management; and the steadily growing prestige of the Hawthorne experiments in management circles. Mayo played only a nominal role in these changes, confining himself to his writings and to training a handful of students; the institutional task of building human relations at Harvard and among industrial executives passed to Mayo's colleagues, notably Wallace Donham, Philip Cabot, and Fritz Roethlisberger.

Mayo's position at the Harvard Business School had been marginal from the start. Brought to Harvard by Donham and funded by the Rockefeller philanthropies, Mayo remained separate from the rest of the business school faculty; the Industrial Research Department was itself unusual, for there were no other departments at the school, the faculty being organized into course groups that reported directly to the dean. After a decade at Harvard, Mayo could still describe his position in the school in the following terms: "There is no hostility so far as I know...but I am permitted to be a privileged eccentric who never attends meetings." Because he and his assistants held research positions, they were not required to teach any courses, an arrangement that distanced them from their fellow faculty members, whose work revolved around the classroom and whose primary research focus was the preparation of case materials for teaching. Mayo's working habits contributed to his marginality: Where the faculty mimicked the behavior and working hours of the business executive, Mayo rarely appeared before eleven in the morning, held court with his colleagues and students, then returned home after lunch. Fritz Roethlisberger echoed the predominant business school assessment when he reflected on his early work with Mayo:

> Even to my then organizationally and scientifically untutored eyes, what Henderson and the Fatigue Laboratory would do on Monday morning at 9 a.m. was clearer to me than what Mayo would be up to. Henderson and his colleagues, Bruce Dill and Arlie Bock, could set up their treadmills, and they could measure the physiological effects (on dogs and men) of different simulated conditions of work. Mayo, on the other hand, seemed to be sitting in his office and practicing his charisma or doing his research on me.[1]

Mayo and Henderson remained almost totally dependent on the Rockefeller Foundation for support. On each occasion that the Rockefeller grant was scheduled to finish, a flurry of correspondence and meetings would take place between Mayo, Henderson, business school dean Wallace Donham, Harvard president James B. Conant, and philanthropy officers. A distinct pattern emerged. Rockefeller officers would suggest that the time had come for Harvard to assume the financial commitment, given the foundation's generosity in the past; the Harvard administration would reply craftily that the program had been initiated at the suggestion of the foundation, and that, besides, Harvard provided a valuable institutional milieu for the research; and Donham would emphasize his total commitment to the program, but point to the business school's chronic lack of funds. The foundation's normal practice was to fund such large programs for five or at most ten years, then insist that the university assume responsibility – but Mayo and Henderson's grant proved an exception. In 1937, upon completion of the seven-year grant of $875,000, a five-year grant of $360,000 was appropriated by the Medical Sciences Division of the Rockefeller Foundation, starting at $100,000 and tapering to $50,000 in the fifth year; in 1940 Mayo was given an additional $30,000 over two years to enable him to

---

[1] Mayo to Dorothea Mayo, 14–17 Mar. [1936], EM/film. Mayo's working habits are described in George Caspar Homans, *Coming to My Senses: The Autobiography of a Sociologist*, New Brunswick, N.J.: Transaction Books, 1984, 138–9; on the anomalous position of the Industrial Research Department, see F. J. Roethlisberger, *The Elusive Phenomena*, Boston: Harvard University, Graduate School of Business Administration, 1977, 184–5, description of Mayo's research habits on 32.

provide further fellowships; and in 1942 Mayo received $40,000 to support his research for the following year. Between 1923 and 1943 Mayo and his colleagues received from the Rockefeller philanthropies grants totaling $1,520,000 – a huge commitment even by the foundation's standards. Without the Rockefeller funding, the Hawthorne experiments would not have been expanded from the initial lighting and relay assembly tests and would certainly not have been transformed into social scientific knowledge by Mayo and his colleagues.

Several reasons can be adduced for the foundation's willingness to continue the funding. The director of the Medical Sciences Division, Alan Gregg, was an old friend of Henderson and became quite friendly with Mayo; Gregg clearly felt a personal commitment to the support of their research. But more important, Gregg believed that Mayo and Henderson's research could play the same role at the business school that preclinical sciences did in medical education, forming a scientific foundation for professional practice. Further, during a period of explosive industrial unrest in the late 1930s, the foundation officers appear to have accepted Donham's argument that such research was the "principal basis for the avoidance of social disruption" and could serve as the basis for changing business executives' understanding of human behavior. Moreover, the foundation officials were well aware that John D. Rockefeller, Jr., and his eldest son John D. Rockefeller III maintained their interest in industrial relations and that they continued to provide private support for academic research in the field. Rockefeller funding finally ended in 1943 due to a combination of circumstances: Henderson had died in 1942, lessening the ties to Gregg; Donham retired the same year and the new dean, Donald K. David, made it clear to Gregg that he had no particular commitment to supporting Mayo and would be pleased if Mayo could find another institution; and Gregg felt that the Medical Sciences Division was no longer in a position to fund social scientific research. Until Mayo retired in 1947 the business school was obliged to pay his salary out of its regular funds.[2]

Mayo's institutional position reflected his preference for spreading his ideas through his publications and by training the handful of students referred to him. Mayo's pedagogical methods were highly personalized; instead of establishing formal courses that might reach a large number of students, he preferred to impart his various interests and skills to a few promising individuals. In addition to Fritz Roethlisberger and Thomas North Whitehead, Mayo drew into his group Graham Eyres-Monsell, a young English peer visiting Harvard, and George Homans, who was strongly

[2] Discussions are recorded in Alan Gregg's diary for 4 Feb. 1936, 10 Mar. 1937, 12 Mar. 1937, 2 Dec. 1938, 2 Feb. 1942, 16 Nov. 1942, 9 Apr. 1943, RF/200S/342/4071–9, quote from 4 Feb. 1936. The three appropriations are RF 37055, 7 Apr. 1937, RF 40064, 14 June 1940, RF 42019, 20 Feb. 1942, in RF/200S/342/4069, 4078.

influenced by Mayo and Henderson and became an eminent sociologist at Harvard after the war. When Whitehead and Eyres-Monsell returned to England at the start of the war, Mayo obtained a special grant from the Rockefeller Foundation to provide fellowships for a few new students and took on, among others, John B. Fox and George F. F. Lombard, both of whom gained permanent positions at the business school. Several other young men established looser ties with Mayo, relying on him for guidance in reading or research; they included the social anthropologists Eliot Chapple and Conrad Arensberg, both students of Lloyd Warner, and the sociologists William F. Whyte and Talcott Parsons. The most structured teaching Mayo gave was an informal reading seminar, held in his rooms over tea, at which they would discuss Mayo's favorite works in psychology, psychiatry, anthropology, and sociology. As mentioned earlier, for a time in the mid-1930s Mayo arranged for his students to attend a psychiatric clinic at the Boston Dispensary, where they put on doctors' white coats and practiced their interviewing skills on the patients – a highly irregular practice even then. But Mayo was convinced that such firsthand experience was essential if his students were to acquire clinical skills; the dispensary, like industry, was a "sort of observation post [and] a method of training individuals for effective observation and action in our modern world." He was, he felt, training the new breed of administrators he had called for in *Human Problems*.[3]

This is not to say that Mayo's ideological perspective and political concerns were marginal to the business school. Indeed, Mayo's growing interest in the problems of administration reflected a general awareness among business leaders in the 1930s that government planning was an essential part of any plan for economic recovery. In his *Business Adrift* (1931), Wallace Donham called upon businessmen to assume the task of rebuilding the society:

> To a large extent in this industrial civilization of ours the potential leadership of the country is concentrated in industry.... How can we as business men, within the areas for which we are responsible, best meet the needs of the American people,... maintain profits, handle problems of unemployment, face the Russian challenge, and at the same time aid Europe and contribute most to or disturb least the cause of International Peace?

Businessmen, Donham continued, had for far too long been concerned only with narrow economic concerns and had ignored the destruction of social routine and stability that had accompanied economic progress. The new administrator, whether in business, government, or the university, must take

---

[3] Mayo to Dorothea Mayo, 27–30 Oct. [1935], quote, EM/film; Mayo to Dorothea Mayo, 4 Dec. [1935], EM/film. For Homans's account of his contact with Mayo, including descriptions of the seminar and the Boston Dispensary, see Homans, *Coming to My Senses*, 135–66.

into account the whole social organism. Donham and Beardsley Ruml encouraged Mayo to develop the ideas he had sketched out in the final chapters of *Human Problems* and show how the clinical method could inform this new conception of administration.[4]

The results did not appear until 1945, when Mayo published *Social Problems of an Industrial Civilization*. The book was a pale imitation of his earlier *Human Problems*. A short work, only 120 pages long, it consisted of a rambling critique of economic rationality; a condemnation of the tendency to seek political and legalistic solutions to social problems (the work was full of trite statements such as "If our social skills had advanced step by step with our technical skills, there would not have been another European war"); and an extended argument, using examples from Mayo's industrial research, that only administrators skilled in human relations could encourage spontaneous social collaboration and bring social order. The relay assembly test room, with the group cohesion brought about by sensitive supervision, became the model for all society, and the interviewing program showed the value of clinical skills for administrators. Only a new social elite trained in the skills of human relations could save civilization; the threat to civilization did not come from the atom bomb, Mayo asserted, but because leaders had not yet learned how to secure cooperation.[5]

Mayo's tract may not have been argued rigorously, but it was nevertheless effective, for it reflected the ideological values of business leaders hoping to rebuild the world after a major depression and world war. Donald K. David, who had replaced Donham as dean of the business school in 1942, echoed the views of many businessmen in his 1949 address "Business Responsibilities in an Uncertain World." Cold war rhetoric infused his speech: America was engaged in a war between democracy and totalitarianism, a conflict of "social systems — of methods through which society makes its decisions in social, political, and economic affairs." The business leader was engaged in an ideological battle that required a range of weapons:

> At the moment there seem to be discernible three important qualities of a business leader. The first of these is competence in the management of his business activity. The second is the development and application of social skill so as to make his business enterprise a "good society." The third is the willingness to participate constructively in the broader affairs of the community and nation.... A business is more than an economic unit; it is a social unit as well — or, rather, a group of interrelated social units of varying sizes. Thus each business executive — each foreman and supervisor — is within certain limits guiding a small society.

[4] Wallace Brett Donham, *Business Adrift*, New York: Whittlesey House, 1931, quotes on 106, 38.
[5] Elton Mayo, *The Social Problems of an Industrial Civilization*, Boston: Harvard University, Graduate School of Business Administration, 1945, passim, quote on 23.

David concluded that business leaders needed to develop a "tough-minded humility" (a phrase intended to convey the necessary combination of authority and human relations) and pay attention to developments in the social scientific study of organizations. Donham concurred, and in the foreword to Mayo's book he too emphasized the importance of social skills in administration, concluding that "Mayo shows us for the first time in the form of specific instances that it is within the power of industrial administrators to create within industry itself a partially effective substitute for the old stabilizing effect of the neighborhood." Human relations, in the form of skills taught to business leaders and administrators, could ensure social collaboration in the factory and in society at large and win the war against Communism.[6]

Under Donham's direction the Harvard Business School began to spread the gospel of human relations to business executives. The most notable mechanism was the "Cabot Weekends," discussion groups of executives held every two or three months from 1935 to 1941, led by Philip Cabot, professor of public utilities at the school. The participants, an extensive cross section of business leaders from manufacturing, public utilities, and the financial world, were fed the Hawthorne experiments and human relations approach during a two-day seminar. Mayo quickly became the star attraction at these events; sitting on the edge of the table, he would lead discussions, illustrating his philosophy with memorable clinical examples. Mayo summarized for his daughter the gist of his presentation: "Its thesis was – you may not approve or understand entirely what has been offered by the W.E. [Western Electric researches] – we cannot go back to old conventional methods – if you don't like this you must contribute something better – if so, do it soon – because-we-haven't-much-time." Roethlisberger was also a regular participant, and it was in these seminars that he honed his popular presentations of the experiments; in 1941 he gathered many of his Cabot talks and published them as *Management and Morale*, which quickly went through several printings. On one notable occasion the importance of the Hawthorne experiments and informal organization was stressed in talks by Chester Barnard, president of New Jersey Bell, and Harold Ruttenberg, research director of the CIO's Steel Workers' Organizing Committee; Roethlisberger wrote enthusiastically to Bill Dickson that "to have the CIO on one hand and the president of New Jersey Bell Telephone Company on the other, both acknowledging our work as 'fact,' appeals to me greatly."[7]

[6] Donald K. David, "Business Responsibilities in an Uncertain World," supplement to *Harvard Business Review*, May 1949, 27, quotes on 1, 3–4, 5; Donham, in Mayo, *Social Problems*, ix.

[7] On the Cabot Weekends, see Roethlisberger, *The Elusive Phenomena*, 86–7; Melvin Thomas Copeland, *And Mark an Era: The Story of the Harvard Business School*, Boston: Little, Brown, 1958, 328–9; Mayo to Patricia Mayo, 7 Feb. [1938], quote, EM/film; and Roeth-

The executives who attended Cabot Weekends were impressed with what they heard. In response to a letter from Alan Gregg at the Rockefeller Foundation, who was collecting evidence on Mayo and Henderson's work before making a decision on refunding, Chester Barnard praised their research and the conferences:

> I spent ... one week-end conference with this group and I saw a number of the industrial fellows under easy conditions, i.e., at table and over a highball, etc. Several of these men, including some of my own business, I have known for some time. There isn't the slightest doubt that the reaction of some of these men to the doctrine being preached is very enthusiastic. I think this rather gratifying evidence that the Business School is doing really progressive work, showing the rare combination of getting well underneath the surface, at the same time focused on practical problems that are crying for attention.[8]

Barnard played an even more significant role in disseminating human relations among executives. Educated at Harvard, Barnard had joined AT&T as a statistician in 1909 and witnessed Vail's reorganization of the Bell System; he was himself responsible for restructuring the commercial organization of the system. Moving steadily up the Bell hierarchy, he had become fascinated with the problems of organization and administration, and when appointed director of New Jersey's emergency relief organization during the depression, he had been struck by the similarity of administrative problems, regardless of the type of organization. Then, by his own account, he read Mayo's *Human Problems* and immediately recognized the parallels between informal organization on the shop floor and that in the central office, between the task of the supervisor and that of the executive. In 1938 he published *The Functions of the Executive,* a book that quickly became a classic in management theory. In the preface of the work he acknowledged his debt to Donham, Cabot, Henderson, Mayo, and Whitehead for their contributions to his ideas. The influence is indeed striking.

The task of the executive, Barnard explained, was to administer a complex cooperative system, balancing social, biological, and physical factors so as to maintain equilibrium. The system could survive only if it was both effective, achieving its goals in the context of the outside environment, and efficient, by which Barnard meant the capacity of the organization to achieve cooperation and a common purpose among the individuals and groups making up the system. Emphasizing the importance of informal organizations in motivating the behavior of the group, he argued that the executive must find ways to persuade individuals to cooperate; coercion through the

---

lisberger to Dickson, 11 Mar. 1940, FJR/1. One weekend was devoted entirely to the Hawthorne experiments, with Pennock, Putnam, Dickson, and Wright all giving presentations; see Mayo to Patricia Mayo, 7 Feb. [1938], EM/film.

[8] Chester Barnard to JVS (Rockefeller Foundation), 24 Mar. 1937, RF/200S/342/4072; the file contains letters of endorsement from other conference participants.

formal organization was ineffective. Indeed, Barnard's influential theory of authority postulated that "the decision as to whether an order has authority or not lies with the persons to whom it is addressed, and does not reside in 'persons of authority' or those who issue these orders." Just as Mayo emphasized that true social stability must come from administrators able to induce spontaneous social collaboration, so Barnard asserted that "authority is another name for the willingness and capacity of individuals to submit to the necessities of coöperative systems." Only through careful attention to the human relations of their organization could executives, including supervisors, persuade their subordinates to "submit" to authority. In both men's writings, and in the human relations approach in general, power was concealed behind discussions of cooperation and communication.[9]

Barnard's work therefore extended the lessons of the Hawthorne experiments into all areas of organization, from the shop floor to the executive office. By 1950 any leading businessman wanting to read a book on management and administration turned almost automatically to the publications that had come out of the human relations group at the Harvard Business School. A 1949 survey of subscribers to *Harvard Business Review* – itself a major conduit for the dissemination of human relations – asked executives what books they were reading; of the top nine books in the field of industrial relations and management theory, six were from the human relations school: Mayo's *Human Problems* came first, followed by Roethlisberger and Dickson's *Management and the Worker*, Barnard's *Organization and Management* (1948) and *Functions of the Executive*, Roethlisberger's *Management and Morale*, and Selekman's *Labor Relations and Human Relations* (1947).[10]

The responsibility for training the next generation of executives in human relations fell to Roethlisberger and Whitehead. In 1938 they commenced teaching Human Problems of Administration, a one-semester elective in the second year of the Masters of Business Administration (MBA) program; the previous year they had established a similar course at Radcliffe College, primarily with the plan of training women for personnel work in industry. But it was only in 1943 that Roethlisberger began to take teaching seriously; concerned that Mayo's group was still peripheral to the regular business

[9] Chester I. Barnard, *The Functions of the Executive*, Cambridge, Mass.: Harvard University Press, 1938, quotes on 163, 184; see also his *Organization and Management: Selected Papers*, Cambridge, Mass.: Harvard University Press, 1948. Barnard gave an account of the development of his ideas in "Corporate Management and Morals," a presentation before the National Research Council, Conference on a Scientific Study of Industrial Labor Conditions, 13 Nov. 1937; the transcript is in NAS–NRC/Exec. Bd./CSSILC/Transcript, 91–9.

[10] Edward C. Bursk and Donald T. Clark, "Reading Habits of Business Executives," *Harvard Business Review*, 1949, 27: 330–45.

school faculty, Roethlisberger dedicated himself to establishing human relations as part of the core of the MBA program. He succeeded when the curriculum was redesigned in 1946; a required course, Administrative Practices, presented the human relations approach to the seven hundred first-year students. In 1948 Roethlisberger established a second-year elective, Human Relations, in which he taught students counseling techniques, using for the most part counseling cases from Hawthorne.[11]

The introduction of the social sciences, of the human relations variety or otherwise, into business education was a gradual process, at Harvard and elsewhere. The whole philosophy of the Harvard Business School was to train the business administrator through the study of cases; the social sciences were not taught in separate courses but were subsumed into courses oriented to the requirements of the business world. The human relations group at Harvard in the 1950s – including Roethlisberger, George Lombard, Kenneth Andrews, and Abraham Zaleznik – were often attacked for being too social scientific and insufficiently administrative; nevertheless, their commitment to teaching basic social sciences as well as administrative skills was part of a growing trend in business education. Executives like Barnard and social scientists like Lloyd Warner were in agreement after the war that the social sciences were the key to the professionalization of business; they argued that business schools must accept responsibility for teaching and research in the social sciences and singled out human relations as the most important area of study. From 1953 to 1961 the Ford Foundation poured $20,000,000 into business education, trying especially to encourage basic research and the application of the social sciences to business administration. Harvard received $2,000,000 under this program, and $100,000 of this went to Roethlisberger to prepare human relations practitioners for work in industry. When in 1959 the Carnegie Corporation and Ford Foundation funded two major studies of business education, both could point to progress in the professionalization of business education, especially through MBA programs, and to a growing acceptance of the need for research and training in the social sciences as an essential part of the education of business leaders.[12]

[11] Copeland, *And Mark an Era*, 169–70; Roethlisberger, *The Elusive Phenomena*, 107–16, 197. The Administrative Practices cases were published as a textbook; see John Desmond Glover and Ralph M. Hower, *The Administrator: Cases in Human Relations in Business*, Chicago: Irwin, 1949.

[12] Chester I. Barnard, "Education for Executives" (1945), in idem, *Organization and Management*, 194–206; W. Lloyd Warner, "Social Science in Business Education," in *The Challenge of Business Education*, Chicago: University of Chicago, Graduate School of Business, 1949, 20–9. On the teaching philosophy at Harvard, see Copeland, *And Mark an Era*, 176–7; Roethlisberger, *The Elusive Phenomena*, 257–303; Ford Foundation, *Annual Report*, 1951–62; and F. J. Roethlisberger, George F. F. Lombard, and Harriet O. Ronken, *Training for Human Relations: An Interim Report*, Boston: Harvard University, Graduate

Human relations thus served as an important conduit for bringing the social sciences into business education and management theory, although as the disciplines of management science and organization theory expanded rapidly in the 1950s and 1960s, the human relations school was subsumed into more elaborate theoretical frameworks.

Human relations in the social sciences

In 1939, the year that *Management and the Worker* was published, sociologist Robert S. Lynd published a critical assessment of the role of the social sciences in American culture. *Knowledge for What?* confronted social scientists with what Lynd regarded as their inadequate response to the requirements of society. Like many other social observers, Lynd argued that the Great Depression had arisen because the technical progress derived from the natural sciences had outstripped social progress; the term "cultural lag" was widely used to describe this perceived imbalance. Social scientists realized they had a golden opportunity to raise the status of their professions because politicians seemed increasingly prepared to support investigations of the capacity of the economic and social system to satisfy human needs and might even welcome more direct intervention by social scientists in economic and political administration. However, Lynd observed that the social sciences were organized in such a way as to militate against social utility: There was little contact between the two blocs of social scientists – "the scholar becoming remote from and even disregarding immediate relevancies, and the technician too often accepting the definition of his problems too narrowly in terms of the emphases of the institutional environment of the moment." At the same time, the specialization of social scientists into inward-looking disciplines (such as economics, sociology, psychology, political science, and anthropology) had prevented interdisciplinary integration and resulted in studies abstracted from the real world. The study of labor was a case in point. Economists dominated the field with statistical studies and discussions of the role of legislation; consequently, there was little analysis of "labor actually on the job and at home, of labor's motivations and frustrations." Lynd was particularly critical of the mass of social scientists who claimed that their findings were objective because they were empirically based; this blind empiricism did not result in neutrality and objectivity, he argued, only an unthinking acceptance of the status quo and of melioristic change. *Knowledge for What?* was an impassioned call for a

School of Business Administration, 1954. The two foundation reports are Frank C. Pierson et al., *The Education of American Businessmen*, New York: McGraw-Hill, 1959; and Robert Aaron Gordon and James Edwin Howell, *Higher Education for Business*, New York: Columbia University Press, 1959.

critical, interdisciplinary social science that could become an important tool for the rebuilding of U.S. culture.[13]

Although written as a critique of the field, Lynd's manifesto reflects some of the major concerns of social scientists in the 1930s and 1940s and identifies several of the criteria by which the Hawthorne experiments would be received and judged. The experiments exemplified many, though by no means all, of Lynd's ideals: They had achieved a striking fusion of academic research and practical application; and they were aggressively interdisciplinary, bringing a wide range of methods and theoretical perspectives to a common problem. This conception of the field echoed the agenda for the social sciences planned by Beardsley Ruml for the Laura Spelman Rockefeller Memorial in the 1920s, and it can in large measure be seen as the fruition of the seeds planted by the Memorial and academic entrepreneurs like Charles Merriam. The ideological perspectives of the Hawthorne researchers was less likely to appeal to Lynd, although it should be noted that Lynd's political position was more radical than that of most social scientists. Each of these issues – applied research, interdisciplinary study, research methods, and the ideological role of social scientists – assumed central importance in debates in the 1930s and 1940s and shaped the reception of the Hawthorne experiments in the social science community.

The New Deal and the Second World War provided a propitious environment for the growth of the social sciences and their increased application to social problems. Social scientists were among those drawn into government to serve in the agencies and programs of the New Deal – among them Ruml, who became head of the New York Federal Reserve Bank, and Merriam, who played a crucial role in convincing Franklin Delano Roosevelt of the need to introduce social sciences and the skills of the industrial executive into the administration of government. The Second World War accelerated this trend, as social scientists were mobilized to apply their skills to everything from the national planning of industry, to surveys of the attitudes and morale of soldiers, to the management of internment camps for Japanese Americans. Economists had the greatest success in maintaining their professional power in peacetime – the Employment Act of 1946 established a Council of Economic Advisors that had considerable influence over government administration and management of the economy – and the other social scientists also organized to retain some of their wartime influence. After the war, funds poured into the social sciences from several sources: funding of research in universities, especially by the Naval Research Laboratory and the federal government's National Science Foundation; consulting work, most notably in industry; philanthropic foundations, espe-

[13] Robert S. Lynd, *Knowledge for What? The Place of Social Science in American Culture,* Princeton, N.J.: Princeton University Press, 1939, quotes on 1, 35.

cially during the early 1950s by the Ford Foundation's program in behavioral sciences; and the expansion of higher education, which provided a larger institutional base for social scientists and ensured the dissemination of their ideas.[14]

In the process of analyzing their wartime experiences and sketching out a continued role for the social sciences in administration, social scientists turned in large number to the study of organizations, seeing now essential similarities between the management of all organizations, whether in industry, government, or the military. At the same time, the dramatic rise of industrial unionism and the increasing government involvement in industrial relations attracted social scientists to the study of labor problems and industrial organization. In this context the Hawthorne experiments and human relations took on special significance as a prime example of the application of social science to industrial problems. Disciplinary, theoretical, and political orientations shaped each social scientist's response to the experiments, creating a complicated patchwork of opinion. Indeed, the interpretation of the Hawthorne experiments did not stop with publication, but continued with their assimilation into the postwar social sciences.

The area in which the Hawthorne experiments and the human relations approach had the greatest impact was the study of industrial organization and labor relations. Problems that had previously been of concern only to managers were now subjected to close study at universities, where researchers dissected industrial relations in individual plants and throughout the nation. By 1948 there were centers for research in industrial relations in more than thirty colleges and universities, nearly all of them established in the previous decade. By the end of the same year the Industrial Relations Research Association, established only twelve months previously, had attracted more than one thousand members. For social scientists trying to

[14] On social sciences and the administration of the New Deal, see Barry D. Karl, *Executive Reorganization and Reform in the New Deal: The Genesis of Administrative Management, 1900–1939*, Cambridge, Mass.: Harvard University Press, 1963. On the social sciences in the 1930s and 1940s, see Gene M. Lyons, *The Uneasy Partnership: Social Science and the Federal Government in the Twentieth Century*, New York: Russell Sage Foundation, 1969, chaps. 3 and 4; Talcott Parsons and Bernard Barber, "Sociology, 1941–46," *American Journal of Sociology*, 1948, 53: 245–57; and an excellent popular survey, Stuart Chase, *The Proper Study of Mankind*, New York: Harper, 1948. For a discussion of the wartime experiences of the social sciences, see James H. Capshew, "Psychologists on the March: American Psychologists and World War II," Ph.D. dissertation, University of Pennsylvania, 1986; Peter Buck, "Adjusting to Military Life: The Social Sciences Go to War, 1941–1950," in Merritt Roe Smith, ed., *Military Enterprise and Technological Change*, Cambridge, Mass.: MIT Press, 1987, 203–52; and the entertaining personal account of economics by John Kenneth Galbraith, *A History of Economics*, London: Hamilton, 1987, 237–50. On the social scientific study of industry and labor, see Baritz, *The Servants of Power*, chaps. 7 and 8; and Lorenz J. Finison, "An Aspect of the Early History of the Society of the Psychological Study of Social Issues: Psychology and Labor," *Journal of the History of the Behavioral Sciences*, 1979, 15: 29–37.

establish the importance of this new area of study in their intellectual disciplines, the Hawthorne experiments constituted a major example, to many *the* example, of the theoretical insights to be gained from industrial research. Just as important, the apparent success of the experiments in increasing productivity and worker satisfaction was a powerful argument for those social scientists trying to persuade managers to permit research in their factories or organizations.[15]

As we have seen, the Harvard researchers had concentrated in the 1930s on publishing the Hawthorne experiments; the small amount of additional industrial research conducted in the 1930s was exploratory and remained unpublished. But beginning in 1943 Mayo's group conducted several small studies that supplemented and reaffirmed the findings at Hawthorne. A study for the War Production Board of three brass mills in Waterbury, Connecticut, demonstrated that absenteeism varied considerably among the companies and argued that the mill with the lowest absenteeism had foremen attentive to the social organization of the factory and able to encourage self-discipline among the workers. Another project studied turnover among workers in aircraft factories in southern California; here too, it was claimed, those plants where supervisors had forged work groups with high social solidarity had much lower turnover. George Homans, who had returned from his wartime navy service, joined Jerome Scott in a brief visit to Detroit in June 1946, where they talked with managers, union officials, and workers about the causes of the frequent "wildcat" strikes (i.e., strikes not authorized by the union office). They concluded that the wildcats stemmed from the legalistic and bureaucratic organization of industrial relations; managers and unions alike relied too much on government intervention, while foremen and rank-and-file workers were cut off from their respective organizations by a lack of communication. Many wildcat strikes could be avoided if managers concentrated on promoting social collaboration, and here the authors pointed to a specific case in which the close ties between a foreman and his workers prevented a threatened strike. Each of these studies served to underscore the claim that the Hawthorne findings were representative of the social organization of industry.[16]

The organization and argument of these three studies were remarkably

[15] "The Formation and Development of IRRA," Industrial Relations Research Association, *Proceedings of the First Annual Meeting, Cleveland, Ohio, December 29–30, 1948*, Champaign, Ill., 1949, 2–4; Edwin E. Witte, "Where Are We in Industrial Relations," ibid., 6–20.

[16] John B. Fox and Jerome F. Scott, *Absenteeism: Management's Problem*, Boston: Harvard University, Graduate School of Business Administration, Bureau of Business Research, 1943; Elton Mayo and George F. F. Lombard, *Teamwork and Labor Turnover in the Aircraft Industry of Southern California*, Boston: Harvard University, Graduate School of Business Administration, Bureau of Business Research, 1944; Mayo, *Social Problems*, chap. 5; J. F. Scott and G. C. Homans, "Reflections on the Wildcat Strikes," *ASR*, 1947, 12: 278–87. On the unpublished research of the 1930s, see Roethlisberger, *Elusive Phenomena*, 75–86.

similar and capture well the clinical emphasis in the Harvard approach to the study of human relations. In each study the authors demonstrated, preferably with statistical material, that a particular industrial problem – absenteeism, turnover, strikes – varied within the industry and community being studied; the implication here was that economic, political, or structural factors could not be the cause of the problem because they could not account for the local variation. The authors then switched gear to examine the social organization of those plants with the best industrial relations record and found that managers and foremen were more skilled in human relations and leadership than they were in plants with poorer industrial relations. Therefore, they concluded, the administrator in industry could reduce a particular industrial problem, and by implication all industrial relations problems, by ensuring that supervisors knew how to gain the collaboration of the work group. These articles, it should be noted, were no less problematic than the Hawthorne experiments themselves. In particular, the researchers' information on the social organization of the shop floor was highly impressionistic, and it was an easy matter for the researchers to perceive positive supervisory behavior only in plants with the least problems. In the study of wildcat strikes, for example, a description of a single foreman preventing a walkout was intended to serve as an example of how all industrial unrest could be prevented. This clinical, case-study approach to industrial relations remained dominant in the work of Roethlisberger and his colleagues in the 1950s.

The lack of detailed research at Harvard compared unfavorably with the impressive research program of members of the Committee on Human Relations in Industry at the University of Chicago, and by the late 1940s the Chicago group had become the leaders of the human relations approach. Established in 1943 by members of several departments, the Chicago committee included researchers who became major figures in sociology in the postwar decades: Lloyd Warner, William Foote Whyte, and Everett C. Hughes. Executive secretary of the committee from 1943 to 1946 was Burleigh Gardner, who had previously worked in the counseling program at Hawthorne, was coauthor of an influential textbook, *Human Relations in Industry* (1950), and subsequently established a successful management consulting firm, Social Research, Inc. But Whyte was the key figure in the group. Trained as an economist, he had switched to sociology while a junior fellow at Harvard's Society of Fellows, primarily under the influence of Conrad Arensberg, but also that of Mayo and Henderson. Following his study of the social interactions of members of a street gang, *Street Corner Society* (1943), he shifted to industrial research on arriving at Chicago in 1944, and from 1948 held a chair at the School of Industrial and Labor Relations at Cornell University.[17]

---

[17] On the Committee of Human Relations in Industry, see William Foote Whyte, ed., *Industry*

Whyte regarded his work as an extension of the Hawthorne experiments. They were, he and Gardner declared, "perhaps the first major social science experiment... and we feel that continued efforts in this direction will yield rich returns in the development of the social sciences." Whyte held that the research method of the bank wiring test, with its combination of anthropological observation and nondirective interviewing, was especially suited to industrial research, although, like many other researchers, Whyte perceived interviewing as a research tool rather than a therapeutic technique and conducted directed interviews that focused on the research topics. In two major books, *Human Relations in the Restaurant Business* (1948) and *Pattern for Industrial Peace* (1951), he demonstrated the importance of personal interactions and informal groups in shaping workplace organization. He also proposed a theory of human relations, based on the mutual dependence of four categories – interaction, symbols, activities, and sentiments – which he believed could form a basis for the prediction and control of human behavior. *Pattern for Industrial Peace* was especially notable because it involved a study of the process of collective bargaining in a unionized steel factory. Collective bargaining, Whyte argued, was permeated by social and emotional processes as much as any other aspect of industry, and industrial peace would be achieved only when managers and union leaders grasped that negotiation had to be based on an understanding of the other side's feelings and assumptions – both sides needed improved social skills. It is a measure of the postwar enthusiasm for human relations programs that Whyte felt it necessary to warn that human relations was by itself not sufficient; cooperation could come only through attention to both the design of organizations and their daily operation. For example, formal organizations should be designed to reduce the levels of authority and to encourage delegation of responsibility. Yet while he more readily accepted the values of collective bargaining than the Harvard researchers, Whyte accepted the limits placed on worker participation by existing industrial relations legislation and practices; the task of human relations was to improve the operation of a system of managerial control already in place.[18]

Lloyd Warner's view of industrial relations was less optimistic, for he detected structural changes in industrial organization and the U.S. com-

and Society, New York: McGraw-Hill, 1946, v–vi. The updated text by Gardner, first published in 1945, is Burleigh B. Gardner and David G. Moore, *Human Relations in Industry,* Chicago: Irwin, 1950. On Whyte, see Homans, *Coming to My Senses,* 162; and William Foote Whyte, *Street Corner Society,* Chicago: University of Chicago Press, 1943.

[18] Burleigh B. Gardner and William Foote Whyte, "Methods for the Study of Human Relations in Industry," *ASR,* 1946, 11: 506–12, quote on 512; William Foote Whyte, *Human Relations in the Restaurant Business,* New York: McGraw-Hill, 1948; idem, *Pattern for Industrial Peace,* New York: Harper Bros., 1951; idem, "Small Groups and Large Organizations," in John H. Rohrer and Muzafer Sherif, eds., *Social Psychology at the Crossroads,* New York: Harper Bros., 1951, 297–312; idem, "Human Relations Theory – A Progress Report," *Harvard Business Review,* 1956, 34(5): 125–32.

munity that questioned Whyte's vision of cooperation. The fourth volume of the Yankee City series, *The Social System of the Modern Factory* (1947), examined the reasons for a strike in the shoe factories of Newburyport during 1933. It was insufficient, Warner argued, to ascribe the strike solely to economic factors, when wage cuts had been imposed on many other occasions in the town's history without causing a strike. He pointed instead to long-term changes in the organization of the industry: Mechanization and the division of labor were increasing management control over work, and unskilled workers could no longer hope to work their way up a ladder of skill and responsibility. Workers turned to mass action because individual attainment of the American Dream was no longer possible. At the same time, ownership of the factories had passed from the local elite to large, out-of-town companies; whereas workers had respected, even idealized, the local owners, they reviled the absentee capitalists and their local managers. The lower classes in Newburyport were, Warner concluded, being shaped into an industrial working class, its increasing solidarity a measure of the lack of economic and social opportunity; thus, subordination in the factory and low status in the community reinforced one another. Unions were successful because they gave workers bargaining power, a feeling of solidarity, and the opportunity for status and advancement within the union. Yet in the conclusion, Warner backed away from the radical implications of his analysis, calling only for planning that took account of human needs and championing the role of the government as a political and industrial referee between workers and management. Human relations entailed a tinkering with the social system to improve its equilibrium, not a radical reordering of society.[19]

Human relations research in the late 1940s and 1950s demonstrated considerable theoretical and methodological pluralism combined with a striking ideological consistency. In a 1954 survey of research in human relations in industry, Chris Argyris detailed the work of twenty groups and a further seven individual researchers. Probably the most notable group was the Research Center for Group Dynamics at the University of Michigan, founded by social psychologist Kurt Lewin. Grounding their work in Lewin's field theory and experimental studies on the effects of authoritarian and democratic leadership styles, Dorwin Cartwright and his colleagues studied leadership behavior in industry and promoted the use of role playing for training supervisors in human relations. At a related organization at Michigan, the Survey Research Center, Rensis Likert and others studied the organizational factors and leadership style associated with high morale and productivity. Other major research groups included Whyte's Human Relations Group at Cornell, Yale University's Labor and Management Center

[19] W. Lloyd Warner and J. O. Low, *The Social System of the Modern Factory – The Strike: A Social Analysis*, New Haven, Conn.: Yale University Press, 1947.

and Technology Research Project, the Organizational Behavior Project at Princeton, MIT's Industrial Relations Center, and the Institute of Labor and Human Relations at the University of Illinois. Research methods varied from observation and interviewing, to controlled experiments on small groups, to sociometric techniques involving the measurement of social interactions. Theoretical orientations came from a variety of fields, especially from social anthropology, social psychology, clinical psychology, psychiatry, and sociology; the disciplinary training of the researcher was the main factor here. Human relations in industry had become a diverse subject of research; while Roethlisberger continued to emphasize human needs and the importance of clinical skills for managers, Herbert Simon at Carnegie Institute of Technology was trying to build a highly rational theory of administration that would separate facts and values in managerial decisions. Yet for all of the researchers, the study of human relations was intended at most to ameliorate the harshness of industrial capitalism; as in the Hawthorne experiments, social scientists continued to study the effects of management action, leadership, and organization *on* the workers and persisted in equating worker satisfaction with increased productivity.[20]

Human relations had become so successful that by the late 1940s it was starting to attract a steady stream of criticism. The opening shot by sociologist Daniel Bell presaged many of the subsequent attacks. In a 1947 *Commentary* article entitled "Adjusting Men to Machines," Bell singled out Mayo, Warner, Whyte, and Gardner and criticized them for accepting the present system of industrial production, for psychologizing the worker while ignoring the institutional and power relationships of industry, and for seeing industrial relations as a problem of communication and leadership rather than the accommodation of conflicting interests:

> The gravest charge that can be leveled against these researches is that they uncritically adopt industry's own conception of workers as *means* to be manipulated or adjusted to impersonal ends. The belief in man as an end in himself has been ground under by the machine, and the social science of the factory researchers is not a science of man, but a cow-sociology.

---

[20] Chris Argyris, *The Present State of Research in Labor Relations in Industry,* New Haven, Conn.: Yale University, Labor and Management Center, 1954; Herbert A. Simon, *Administrative Behavior,* New York: Macmillan, 1947. For discussions of the social psychology of industry, see Conrad Arensberg, "Behavior and Organization: Industrial Studies," in Rohrer and Sherif, eds., *Social Psychology at the Crossroads,* 324–52; Mason Haire, "Industrial Social Psychology," in Gardner Lindzey, ed., *Handbook of Social Psychology,* Reading, Mass.: Addison-Wesley, 1954, 2: 1104–23; and Dorwin Cartwright, "Some Things Learned: An Evaluative History of the Research Center for Group Dynamics," *Journal of Social Issues,* 1958, suppl. no. 12, 3–19. On applied anthropology in industry, see Michael Burawoy, "The Anthropology of Industrial Work," *Annual Review of Anthropology,* 1979, 8: 231–66.

Radical sociologist C. Wright Mills agreed, telling members of the Industrial Relations Research Association that human relations studies amounted to nothing more than advice to personnel managers that they could more effectively exploit their workers by being less authoritative and more manipulative. Other social scientists also voiced the concern that industrial researchers were too readily accepting and reifying existing industrial organization – although it should be emphasized that with the possible exception of Mills these critics were not radicals, but liberals identifying a promanagement bias in their disciplines.[21]

Some of the criticism stemmed from the transformation in industrial relations that separated readers in the late 1940s and 1950s from research conducted before the New Deal. Several writers, including Bell, chastised the Hawthorne researchers for excluding unions from their study, unaware that union activity was nonexistent among the semiskilled workers studied at Hawthorne.[22] When Reinhard Bendix and Lloyd Fisher quoted at length from Mayo's Australian essay of 1919, which attacked unions and government intervention in industrial relations, they could rest assured that the majority of readers in 1949 would be shocked by Mayo's political conservatism. The implication was that Mayo's antiunion views had tainted the findings of the Hawthorne experiments. Certainly Mayo himself had changed little in this respect; his *Social Problems* of 1945 barely mentioned unions, and then with distaste. Yet as we have seen, researchers in human relations such as Roethlisberger and Whyte adapted readily enough to collective bargaining and industrial unions, and liberal critics shared more of the ideology of the human relations practitioners than they might care to admit.

With the exception of the few radical critiques, many of the attacks had more to do with defending disciplinary turf than any other factor. The most vocal critics were economists and sociologists, while social psychologists and applied anthropologists were almost unanimous in their praise. The economists clearly had good reason for their criticism: Ever since Mayo, the human relations school had used the economists' conception of economic and rational man as a convenient symbol for all that was wrong in the industrial system, including the engineer's sole concern with efficiency,

[21] Daniel Bell, "Adjusting Men to Machines," *Commentary*, 1947, 3: 79–88, quote on 88; C. Wright Mills, "The Contribution of Sociology to Studies of Industrial Relations," Industrial Relations Research Association, *Proceedings of the First Annual Meeting, 1948*, 199–222; Reinhard Bendix and Lloyd H. Fisher, "The Perspectives of Elton Mayo," *Review of Economics and Statistics*, 1949, 31: 312–19; Robert K. Merton, "The Machine, the Worker, and the Engineer," *Science*, 1947, 105: 79–84; Wilbert E. Moore, "Current Issues in Industrial Sociology," *ASR*, 1947, 12: 651–61.

[22] See, e.g., Mills, "The Contribution of Sociology to Studies of Industrial Relations"; C. W. M. Hart, "Industrial Relations Research and Social Theory," *Canadian Journal of Economics and Political Science*, 1949, 15: 53–73; Harold L. Sheppard, "The Treatment of Unionism in 'Managerial Sociology,' " *ASR*, 1949, 14: 310–13.

the manager's belief that workers were motivated only by money, and legalistic solutions to industrial relations. Economist Clark Kerr and political scientist Lloyd Fisher retorted that such attacks were simply the "most modern episode in the attack on reason in the name of harmony, cohesion and a traditional culture."[23]

Mayo and his colleagues, it must be admitted, did not make the Hawthorne experiments very accessible to social scientists, and the way in which the experiments were presented clearly influenced their reception by different disciplines. Most social scientists knew of the experiments primarily through the published accounts of the research, especially *Management and the Worker* and Mayo's *Human Problems* and *Social Problems*. Yet these works were distinctly unfriendly to the established disciplines. Both of Mayo's works consisted in large degree of attacks on the economists' conception of rational man and the psychologists' preference for the measurement of individual abilities. Although his criticism was legitimate, it was directed at highly stylized positions and ignored the more subtle works in these fields; nor did his work reflect an intimate knowledge of the current works and theories. Mayo's writings were therefore not likely to endear him to economists or psychologists. Nor did Mayo attempt to interest sociologists in his work, privately believing that "the sociologists of today in universities are the most incredible asses, who know nothing of the world about them [and] take no responsibility for others." *Management and the Worker* adopted a different approach, although the underlying attitude and the effect on social scientists were the same: Roethlisberger and Dickson had simply ignored the majority of work in the social sciences, with the notable exceptions of social anthropology and Pareto. Moreover, the researchers were institutionally marginal, albeit in a prestigious business school, and had few institutional contacts with mainstream social scientists. Where in the 1920s Mayo had been tied into the social science community through Ruml and Merriam, in the 1930s he became increasingly isolated, confining his work to the training of a handful of students.[24]

L. J. Henderson played a more significant role than Mayo in pursuing the relevance of the Hawthorne experiments to sociology. By the mid-1930s Henderson was devoting nearly all of his energies to propagandizing for his particular conception of social science. In his Pareto seminar Henderson tried to persuade, or failing that bully, graduate students and faculty to adopt Pareto's system; in this he was partially successful, influencing Talcott Parsons and George Homans in particular. The Hawthorne experiments served as the major example of Henderson's conception of the social sciences

[23] Clark Kerr and Lloyd H. Fisher, "Plant Sociology: The Elite and the Aborigines," in Mirra Komarovsky, ed., *Common Frontiers of the Social Sciences*, Glencoe, Ill.: Free Press, 1957, 281–309, quote on 282.

[24] For Mayo's scathing (and private) assessments of sociology, see Mayo to Patricia Mayo, 27 June [1943], quote, EM/film; Mayo to Gregg, 18 Apr. 1943, RF/200S/342/4079.

– at once practical, based on close observation, eschewing unnecessarily complex statistics, and framed by a general theory of social systems. But Henderson's influence extended to only a handful of Harvard sociologists and social psychologists, and the Hawthorne experiments would not receive a more general sociological treatment until Homans used them as a major case study in his sociological analysis of small groups, *The Human Group* (1950).[25]

The result of the relative isolation of the human relations school from sociology was that by the late 1940s sociologists found anthropologists and social psychologists occupying a field they could reasonably have expected to dominate. In this period sociologists wrote a series of articles disparaging human relations as repetitive, methodologically primitive, and theoretically naive; Princeton sociologist Wilbert Moore commented that "it is not wholly surprising therefore to find the sociologically obvious reported with an air of breathless discovery, as in the case of the Western Electric researchers who took several years to find that the individual reacts selectively to his environment in terms of his definition of the situation." When in the 1950s sociologists gained a more substantial position in the social scientific study of industry, the human relations findings were incorporated readily enough into the corpus of industrial and organizational sociology.[26]

Observing the increased prestige of the social sciences and the closer links between academic research and the formulation of policy, social scientists

[25] Henderson's sociological writings are gathered in L. J. Henderson, *On the Social System*, Chicago: University of Chicago Press, 1970; see also the introduction by Bernard Barber, esp. 39–41. Henderson did not live to see the establishment after the war of the Department of Social Relations, which brought together sociologists, social psychologists, and social anthropologists in a single department – a development due partly to Henderson's influence on a generation of social scientists at Harvard. Indeed, the department came close to being called the Department of Human Relations. On the Department of Social Relations, see Homans, *Coming to My Senses*, 293–313.

[26] Moore, "Current Issues in Industrial Sociology," quote on 657; Herbert Blumer, "Sociological Theory in Industrial Relations," *ASR*, 1947, 12: 271–8; Wilbert Moore, "Industrial Sociology: Status and Prospects," *ASR*, 1948, 13: 382–400, with extended discussion by Robert Dubin, Delbert Miller, Alvin Gouldner, and Paul Meadows. For a monograph-length defense of the Hawthorne experiments by industrial sociologist Henry A. Landsberger, a member of the School of Labor and Industrial Relations at Cornell, see *Hawthorne Revisited: Management and the Worker, Its Critics, and Developments in Human Relations in Industry*, Ithaca, N.Y.: Cornell University Press, 1958. My assessment here of the relative isolation of the Hawthorne experiments from industrial sociology until the mid-1950s differs considerably from that of Steven Cohen, who asserts that Mayo was a sociologist and that the Hawthorne experiments marked the professionalization of industrial sociology; see Steven Cohen, "From Industrial Democracy to Professional Adjustment: The Development of Industrial Sociology in the United States, 1900–1955," *Theory and Society*, 1983, 12: 47–67. Equally mistaken is the recent description of Mayo as an archetypical industrial psychologist, a discipline that he consistently criticized; see Daniel J. Walkowitz and Peter R. Eisenstadt, "The Psychology of Work: Work and Mental Health in Historical Perspective," *Radical History Review*, 1986, no. 34, 7–31.

began hesitantly to ponder the proper relationships between scientific expertise and the political, military, and industrial structures that used their research. The experiences of atomic physicists served as a concrete example of the troubled relationship between scientists and the state. The atomic bomb had demonstrated the utility and power of basic research in the physical sciences, and after the war social scientists looked on jealously at the research funds poured into university science departments by the military. But at the same time it was apparent that in exchange for military support atomic scientists had relinquished effective control of the technology; at best they could continue to have an influence on policy only as long as their views accorded with those of their political and military masters.[27]

The wartime social psychological research on soldier attitudes and morale, published in 1949 as *The American Soldier,* provided a focus for the debate in the social sciences. Social scientists in the Research Branch of the army had conducted surveys of soldiers' attitudes on trivial subjects such as whether they preferred Coke to Pepsi, to more substantial research on the factors that determined how they performed in battle; in the process the researchers pioneered many of the survey techniques used in the field of attitude research. In his review of the volumes, pointedly entitled "The Science of Inhuman Relations," Robert Lynd conceded the quality of the research, but questioned the morality of research "on how to turn frightened draftees into tough soldiers who will fight a war whose purposes they do not understand. With such socially extraneous purposes controlling the use of social science, each advance in its use tends to make it an instrument of mass control, and thereby a further threat to democracy." But the participants defended the research both as a useful contribution to the war effort and for its technical and theoretical accomplishments. In a 1950 review of his participation in the research, Samuel Stouffer conceded that there were tensions between academic research and the practical application of social science, but observed that "if social science is to be taken seriously and receive large financial support, its 'engineering' applications must visibly pay off."[28]

Industrial sociologists echoed these sentiments, and they argued that the fact that their research might be used to manipulate workers should not be

[27] The classic account of atomic scientists remains Robert Jungk, *Brighter Than a Thousand Suns,* Harmondsworth: Penguin, 1960; for a contemporary critique of the control of scientific research by the military–industrial complex, see C. Wright Mills, "The Military Ascendancy," in *The Power Elite,* chap. 9, New York: Oxford University Press, 1956.

[28] Samuel A. Stouffer et al., *The American Soldier,* 2 vols., Princeton, N.J.: Princeton University Press, 1949 (two further volumes were published on mass communication and survey techniques); Robert Lynd, "The Science of Inhuman Relations," *New Republic,* 29 Aug. 1949, 22–5, quote on 22; Robert K. Merton and Paul F. Lazarsfeld, eds., *Continuities in Social Research: Studies in the Scope and Method of "The American Soldier,"* Glencoe, Ill.: Free Press, 1950, esp. Samuel Stouffer's "Some Afterthoughts of a Contributor to 'The American Soldier,'" 197–211, quote on 198.

regarded as condemnation of the social scientific knowledge they had developed. Surveying the field of industrial sociology in 1957, Conrad Arensberg and Geoffrey Tootell concluded:

> Suffice it for us to say in closing that plant sociology is not merely an applied "manipulative" sociology. It is instead in the main line of our continuing efforts at building a scientific knowledge of man and his social action. If it opens Pandora's box, as all science does, we can only hope man is strong and brave enough to survive the self-knowledge.[29]

Even those social scientists troubled by the ideological perspective of the Hawthorne experiments and human relations reassured themselves of the significance and objectivity of the findings of human relations by drawing a line between scientific facts and the values of the researchers. Columbia University sociologist Robert K. Merton, one of the most eminent figures in postwar sociology, expressed concern that industrial research had been oriented toward the needs of management, but went on to argue that while this limited the type of research conducted, it did not negate the validity of the knowledge produced. Thus, Merton contentedly used the results of the relay assembly test as evidence for his theory of manifest and latent functions, but distanced himself from human relations by stressing, in a footnote, that "selection of the case for this purpose does not, of course, imply full acceptance of the *interpretations* which the authors give their findings."[30] The willingness of social scientists to draw such a strong line between facts and values stemmed in part from their desire to emulate what they perceived to be the scientific method of the physical sciences, but also because the social status of social scientists depended in large measure on their ability to present their knowledge as objective and value-free. It was unthinkable that social scientists should analyze their knowledge as a social product, for to do so would undermine their claims to expertise in a field in which the public was already quick to caricature social science as merely common sense masquerading as arcane knowledge. Only C. Wright Mills, one of the few radical voices in the profession, went so far as to argue that "the social context and ideological uses of this work have entered into its intellectual content," but even he seems to have wanted to confine the charge to human relations research.[31]

---

[29] Conrad M. Arensberg and Geoffrey Tootell, "Plant Sociology: Real Discoveries and New Problems," in Komarovsky, ed., *Common Frontiers of the Social Sciences*, 310–37, quote on 337. For similar arguments, see V. W. Bladen, "Economics and Human Relations," *Canadian Journal of Economics and Political Science*, 1948, 14: 301–11; and Donald Roy, "Quota Restriction and Goldbricking in a Machine Shop," *American Journal of Sociology*, 1952, 57: 427–42.

[30] Merton, "The Machine, the Worker, and the Engineer"; idem, "Manifest and Latent Functions" (1948), in his *Social Theory and Social Structure*, rev. ed., New York: Free Press, 1968, 73–138, quote on 120.

[31] Mills, "The Contribution of Sociology to Studies of Industrial Relations," 207.

The controversies over the Hawthorne experiments have persisted into the 1980s and 1990s, thereby ensuring that the experiments continue to have an existence other than as a distant historical event. Echoing Mills, radical critics have used the experiments to show how ideological assumptions perverted the social scientists' judgments and as a moral tale of how social scientists all too readily became "servants of power." At the same time, radicals and conservatives alike have reanalyzed the experiments to extract their "rational kernel," although not surprisingly they have come to strikingly different conclusions, some seeing the experiments as revealing the importance of pay systems and discipline, others stressing that the experiments long ago pointed the way toward more democratic forms of workplace organization. Textbook authors have adopted a more disciplinary-oriented approach reworking the experiments to fit into the progressive development of industrial psychology, or organization theory, or the sociology of occupations. These accounts relate how experimental findings forced the abandonment of the experimenters' preconceptions and proclaim a major and unproblematic scientific discovery in the social sciences. The process of reworking and reinterpreting the experiments that commenced during the experiments themselves and continued with the publications of the official accounts has continued ever since.[32]

The Hawthorne experiments, and in particular the relay assembly test, have therefore always been a flexible resource for supporting an impressive variety of theoretical, political, and disciplinary commitments. As early as 1948, Fritz Roethlisberger observed this phenomenon and wrote to Mayo, who was convalescing from a recent stroke, that he "was astonished to find the dent which our work has made in a number of circles. We were quoted, misquoted, assimilated, adapted to this and to that label. Only one thing held true: we were not ignored."[33]

[32] The phrase "servants of power" comes, of course, from Loren Baritz's *Servants of Power*, in which he argues that the social sciences in industry and especially the Hawthorne experiments are paradigmatic of the relationship of intellectuals to U.S. society. In his Marxist critiques of industrial sociology, Michael Burawoy argues persuasively that it is possible to extract the "rational kernel" of studies in industrial sociology, whatever their ideological bias; see Burawoy, *The Politics of Production*, London: Verso, 1985, 73.

[33] Roethlisberger to Mayo, 30 Jan. 1948, FJR/1. Roethlisberger reviewed the literature for the *Harvard Business Review* in 1948 in "Human Relations: Rare, Medium, or Well-Done?" reprinted in F. J. Roethlisberger, *Man-in-Organization*, Cambridge, Mass.: Harvard University Press, 1968, 59–84.

Conclusion: manufacturing knowledge

HOW DID THE ACTIVITIES of five women workers engaged in assembling intricate electrical components in a huge Chicago factory come to be seen as representative of the behavior and aspirations of all workers? That simple question captures the essential character of the Hawthorne experiments and has informed the historical analysis in this book. Providing a plausible answer has entailed following a large number of actors operating within complex networks of expertise and power. My central argument has been that we can make sense of the Hawthorne experiments, both as a historical event and as social scientific knowledge, only if we understand that scientific knowledge is manufactured rather than discovered and grasp the political character of experimentation and the acceptance of knowledge claims. This view of scientific knowledge is based in part on studies of the natural and human sciences by historians and sociologists of science. Drawing on the recent literature to develop a general account of the construction of scientific knowledge, Bruno Latour has observed that constructing a scientific fact is no different from constructing a technical artifact: "The problem of the builder of 'fact' is the same as that of the builder of 'objects': how to convince others, how to control their behaviour, how to gather sufficient resources in one place, how to have the claim or the object spread out in time and space."[1] Scientific facts and technological artifacts are not determined by "reality"; certainly the natural world constrains the kinds of facts and artifacts we construct, but the process of construction is an essentially social activity.

The very act of carrying out the experiments required a considerable mobilization of resources, including the physical infrastructure of the Hawthorne Works and the financial support of senior management. But the

---

[1] Bruno Latour, *Science in Action*, Milton Keynes: Open University Press, 1987, 131. Similar views have been expressed in the history of technology; e.g., Thomas Parke Hughes describes electric power systems as "sociotechnical systems" that "embody the physical, intellectual and symbolic resources of the society that constructs them"; see his *Networks of Power: Electrification in Western Society, 1880–1930*, Baltimore: Johns Hopkins University Press, 1983, 2.

experiments were also structured by a paternalistic management ideology that suffused the supervisors'/experimenters' perceptions of their workers/ subjects. Photographs of the relay assembly test room show a relatively simple scene: five workers at their bench, the boxes of parts and completed relays, a device for measuring production, and the desk of the supervisor. Missing from these pictures are the relationships of power that structured the participants' experiences during the course of the experiment and that shaped the kinds of facts "discovered" by the experimenters. The workers were young women accustomed to having little control over their working lives, bawled out by supervisors to increase their output, on the one hand, cajoled into identifying with the company through a company magazine, social club, and worker benefits, on the other. To the experimenters the workers were "girls" – immature, obedient, emotional – whose satisfaction with the new working conditions could be measured in terms of increased production. The experiment itself reflected the hierarchical relations between supervisors and workers. The power relations within the experiment oc- curred in innumerable ways, but were most dramatically revealed when Irene Rybacki took at face value the experimenters' suggestion that she work at her own pace, then was confronted by senior management for her low output. The worker's failure to increase production was taken as an indication of the subject's unwillingness to cooperate in the experiment, and her resistance to working harder became evidence of her disturbed physiological and emotional state and the effect of such psychopathological conditions on the level of output. The experimenters' power to transform workers into experimental subjects was the key to their ability to make scientific knowledge.

Further resources were required to stabilize the interpretations of the experimental results. In the early stages of the relay test, and again in the bank wiring test, the company researchers were able to formulate what to them were plausible explanations for the increased production, but their interpretations of the evidence and indeed the very "facts" of the experi- ments remained localized among the researchers and senior managers at the Hawthorne Works. The researchers were not even able to persuade the workers to adopt their interpretations, for the workers were more interested in using the test environment and results to argue for improvements in their working conditions. The decision to bring in academic collaborators was a critical one, not because the academics brought sudden clarity to the con- fusion by perceiving the true meaning of the relay test, but rather because the academics brought in additional resources that could help stabilize the researchers' interpretations. Elton Mayo played the pivotal role in this com- plicated process. He furnished powerful physiological and psychopatho- logical arguments as to why the researchers could discount the workers' interpretations, and he enabled the researchers to locate their work within existing academic research. A network of academic and corporate interests crystallized around Mayo, which gave him the power to develop an authoritative interpretation of the experiments at Hawthorne and ensured that the findings would exist not just at Hawthorne, but also at the AT&T head office in New York, at the Harvard Business School, and then rapidly in management and social science circles.

Facts are not discovered during experiments. Rather experimentation is one of the resources that can be mobilized by scientists to establish a fact. Ludwik Fleck, analyzing the development of a scientific fact, in this case Wasserman's development of a laboratory technique for the identification of syphilis, suggests that all "really valuable experiments" are "uncertain, incomplete, and unique." As with the Hawthorne experiments, establishing the facticity of the Wasserman reaction required an ongoing process of interpretation and experimentation stabilized within larger intellectual and institutional structures. The authoritative statements of the "facts" of the Hawthorne experiments only came several years after the experiments had halted, and then they emerged from the Harvard Business School, not the Hawthorne Works. With the publication of *Management and the Worker*, the activities of the five relay assemblers and other Hawthorne workers had been transformed into an account of all workers.[2]

The implications of the analysis presented in this book can be highlighted by considering the two main charges launched against the Hawthorne experiments by their critics: that they were "bad science" and that Mayo and his colleagues were "servants of power."[3] The charge that the experiments were bad science since they were tainted by Mayo's conservative ideological views has always been attractive to social scientists who disagree with the official interpretations of the experiments, because they are professionally committed to the view that the rigorous application of scientific method will produce a pure scientific knowledge untouched by personal, professional, and political interests. But if science is an inherently social activity,

---

[2] Ludwik Fleck, *Genesis and Development of a Scientific Fact*, Chicago: University of Chicago Press, 1979, 85. In his study of experimentation in twentieth-century physics, Peter Galison has similarly argued that experimentation is a complex social activity in which scientists with different perspectives and interests try to assemble persuasive arguments; see his *How Experiments End*, Chicago: University of Chicago Press, 1987. For a famous example of the expansion of laboratory experiments into society at large, see Bruno Latour's account of Pasteur's development of an anthrax vaccine, "Give Me a Laboratory and I Will Raise the World," in Karin Knorr-Cetina and Michael Mulkay, eds., *Science Observed*, Beverly Hills, Calif.: Sage, 1983, 141–70.

[3] For some of the classic criticisms of the Hawthorne experiments along these lines, see Reinhard Bendix, "The Perspectives of Elton Mayo," *Review of Economics and Statistics*, 1949, 31: 312–19; Loren Baritz, *The Servants of Power: A History of the Use of Social Science in American Industry*, Middletown, Conn.: Wesleyan University Press, 1960; Alex Carey, "The Hawthorne Studies: A Radical Criticism," *ASR*, 1967, 32: 403–16; and Dana Bramel and Ronald Friend, "Hawthorne, the Myth of the Docile Worker, and Class Bias in Psychology," *American Psychologist*, 1981, 36: 867–78.

whether it be knowledge of the natural or social world, then this conception of an asocial science is fundamentally misguided – all knowledge claims will bear the imprint of the social context in which they are constructed. It would, of course, be impractical to analyze the construction of each piece of scientific knowledge, but it is a mistake to assume that good science is that which is accepted by everyone, and bad science that which can be successfully challenged and overturned.[4]

Nor can Mayo and his colleagues so easily be dismissed as servants of powerful corporate interests, fashioning a transparent ideology and manipulative techniques for their masters. The relationship between Mayo, Western Electric and AT&T, the Rockefeller Foundation, Industrial Relations Counselors, and the Harvard Business School was not the relatively simple hierarchical one that the relay assemblers experienced at Hawthorne, but a mediated relationship of shared interests, negotiation, and accommodation. Mayo saw himself as a reformer setting out to ameliorate the harshness and conflict of industrial capitalism by changing the attitudes of workers and employers alike and reshaping the workplace culture. And by hanging his larger intellectual and political concerns on the activities and attitudes of Hawthorne workers, Mayo was able to gain an audience of academics and corporate managers who would otherwise have ignored him. Power flowed in all directions in the Hawthorne research network.

Nevertheless, the industrial and ideological context within which the Hawthorne experiments were manufactured did encourage a particular orientation toward the organization of industrial work and the role of management. In particular, the Hawthorne researchers consistently equated worker satisfaction with higher levels of production and used output as a measure of worker contentment with working conditions and management structures. Indeed, the notion that happier workers would work harder became one of the central tenets of the human relations school. Nor were Mayo and his colleagues prepared to concede that workers were able to organize collectively and deliberately reshape their work practices in positive ways. Instead, they believed that collective action would lead to a restriction of output, as in the bank wiring test room, and the increased production in the relay assembly test room was assumed to be due to management's skill in creating conditions that would lead to the spontaneous emergence of work groups that identified with management goals. There was also a tendency to concentrate on workplace cultures at the shop floor level and to set to one side the effects of larger economic forces and political structures on workers' and managers' beliefs and behavior. Although the human re-

---

[4] In his intricate analysis of an alleged case of scientific fraud, Jan Sapp argues that commentators have similarly seen fraud as simply bad science. Sapp argues that most cases of fraud should rather be seen as instances of failed knowledge claims that have been labeled fraud as part of the process of their rejection. See Jan Sapp, *Where the Truth Lies: Franz Moewus and the Origins of Molecular Biology*, Cambridge University Press, 1990.

lations school quickly adapted to the new industrial unions, it accepted the dominant management view that unions should be confined to collective bargaining and regarded union activity on the shop floor as an indication that supervisors had failed to defuse local grievances through appropriate human relations practices.

Finally, the Hawthorne researchers and the human relations school took for granted the necessity of complete managerial control of the workplace. Industrial unrest notwithstanding, managerial capitalism emerged triumphant in the 1940s, with engineers and managers celebrated for their success in mobilizing technical and human resources to secure an Allied victory in the Second World War and to establish the United States as the dominant industrial and political power in the postwar period. Human relations became an attractive ideology for a technocratic and managerial class trying to reconcile its expanded power with the principles of a liberal democracy. Experts and managers reassured themselves that the best administrator, whether a factory manager, army officer, government official, or school principal, was one that could fashion a cohesive group of subordinates who identified with the organization's goals and would spontaneously accept their superior's authority.

These assumptions continue to dominate management literature, particularly the influential popular management books of the 1980s, which have formed the basis of what could be called the new human relations. The stimulus for this recent literature has been the fragility of the U.S. economy in the 1980s, the stagnation of U.S. mass production industries, and the loss of export markets to Japan and the industrializing nations of Asia. Just as expert commissions were sent to the United States in the 1920s to discover the secrets of scientific management and mass production, so have the recent books advocated the adoption of Japanese management techniques, whether specific practices such as quality control and just-in-time manufacturing or general strategies aimed at encouraging workers to identify with corporate goals. Central to these arguments is the claim that Japanese businesses have achieved a corporate culture that more effectively motivates workers and managers, resulting in higher quality and less expensive products – and a happier workforce.[5]

---

[5] There is a historical irony in U.S. management's recent obsession with Japan. It has been noted that Japanese managers rebuilding their industries after the war relied on the U.S. human relations literature, believing that it provided an accurate depiction of management practices in the United States, and therefore went much further than their U.S. counterparts in involving workers in production design and quality control; see William Foote Whyte, "Worker Participation: International and Historical Perspectives," *Journal of Applied Behavioral Science*, 1983, 19: 395–407. Certainly several Japanese industrial relations managers visited Western Electric in the 1950s and assured William Dickson that *Management and the Worker* was widely read in Japanese management schools; see Alvin von Auw, *Heritage and Destiny: Reflections on the Bell System in Transition*, New York: Praeger, 1973, 355.

Little seems to have changed since Western Electric managers and Elton Mayo confronted similar problems of productivity and worker motivation at Hawthorne. At a general level, the same arguments surface criticizing the obsession with the technical organization of work and bemoaning the lack of attention to human needs. William G. Ouchi, author of the bestselling *Theory Z*, could be quoting Mayo when he writes:

> As a nation, we have developed a sense of the value of technology and of a scientific approach to it, but we have meanwhile taken people for granted. Our government appropriates hundreds of millions of dollars for research on new techniques in electrical engineering, physics, and astronomy. It supports the development of complex economic ideas. But almost no funds go to develop our understanding of how to manage and organize people at work, and that is what we have to do by studying the Japanese. . . . Up to now American managers have assumed that technology makes for increased productivity. What Theory Z calls for instead is a redirection of attention to *human* relations in the corporate world.[6]

Thomas J. Peters and Robert H. Waterman, Jr., are explicit about the relevance of the Hawthorne experiments in their influential book *In Search of Excellence*:

> The stream that today's researchers are tapping is an old one, started in the late 1930s by Elton Mayo and Chester Barnard. . . . For us, the very important message of the research . . . is that it is *attention to employees*, not work conditions per se, that has the dominant impact on productivity. (Many of our best companies, one friend observed, seem to reduce management to merely creating "an endless stream of Hawthorne effects.")[7]

Peters and Waterman combine accounts of the Hawthorne experiments with descriptions of the "best" management practices currently being used by U.S. companies to stress the importance of creating a workplace culture that will encourage innovation and commitment from the workers. The facts "discovered" in the relay assembly test room, reimported from Japan, are now applied not just to industrial workers but to all levels of the workforce, including senior managers.

Despite their rhetoric of "breathless discovery," the recent literature echoes many of the basic assumptions made by the old human relations school. There is the same tenet that worker satisfaction will automatically lead to higher production (or, as Ouchi puts it, "involved workers are the

---

[6] William G. Ouchi, *Theory Z: How American Business Can Meet the Japanese Challenge*, Reading, Mass.: Addison-Wesley, 1981, 4, 165.

[7] Thomas J. Peters and Robert H. Waterman, Jr., *In Search of Excellence: Lessons from America's Best-Run Companies*, New York: Harper & Row, 1982, 5–6. For a critical review of recent management books, many of which build upon Peters and Waterman's arguments, see Stephen J. Wood, "New Wave Management?" *Work, Employment & Society*, 1989, 3: 379–402.

key to increased productivity")[8] and that all that management has to do is find ways of unleashing this latent energy. To be sure, there are also differences; in particular, the new literature pays little attention to the psychological needs of the workers, in contrast to Mayo's explicitly psychopathological approach. The reason for this may well be that the industrial workforce of the 1980s has been quiescent compared with the militant workers of the 1940s, and managers can elaborate a management theory that assumes a relatively passive workforce. Overall, the new human relations literature tends to reinforce managerial authority and confine the subordinate's role to that of highly motivated obedience and greater productivity.

Of course, not all contemporary social scientific research on the organization of work operates with these assumptions. The career of William Foote Whyte is an instructive story of the emergence of different views of industrial management and the development of alternative forms of social scientific research. Influenced by Mayo and his associates while at Harvard in the late 1930s, Whyte joined the Committee on Human Relations in Industry at the University of Chicago in 1944 and conducted a workplace study, modeled on the Hawthorne experiments, for the restaurant industry. But as he pursued human relations research at Cornell in the 1950s, Whyte soon discovered that managers were not prepared to listen to anything that challenged their authority:

> The question that they frequently asked revealed the nature of their interest: "How can we make the workers *feel* that they are participating?" We sought to explain that, in the long run, workers would not *feel* that they were participating unless they had some real impact upon decisions important to management as well as to workers. This generally ended the conversations.

Only in the 1960s did Whyte begin to realize the extent to which U.S. researchers "acted as if private ownership and control of a company were *constants* rather than *variables*," and inspired by European research on industrial democracy, he began to undertake international studies of various forms of worker participation, ownership, and control. At the same time Whyte began to adopt different research methods, shifting from what he calls the "professional expert model," in which researchers conduct experiments and observations on relatively passive subjects, to a form of "participatory action research," in which researchers, managers, and workers collaborate in directing and interpreting the research.[9]

This is not the place to analyze the strengths and weaknesses of either

[8] Ouchi, *Theory Z*, 4.
[9] Whyte, "Worker Participation," quote on 396–7; see also idem, *Learning from the Field*, Beverly Hills, Calif.: Sage, 1984, esp. chap. 10; and idem, "On the Uses of Social Science Research," *ASR*, 1986, 51: 555–63.

the research on worker participation (which requires a detailed historical analysis similar to that attempted here on the Hawthorne experiments) or participatory action research, but Whyte's arguments do highlight two final aspects of the manufacture of knowledge in the social sciences. First, as we have seen in the case of the Hawthorne experiments, the knowledge produced will reflect the power relations within which the research was conducted. If workers' views about the nature of work are to be taken seriously rather than used as "facts" and experimental evidence, the institutional mechanisms for conducting social scientific research in the workplace must be changed. It is a whimsical but challenging thought to consider how the relay assembly test room would have been presented in the official accounts if the workers had attained an equal role in constructing and interpreting the experiment. Second, it is inevitable that social and natural scientists will embed political, professional, and personal values in their apparently objective knowledge claims. Since it is not possible to separate facts and values when manufacturing knowledge, it is critical that researchers try to make their own values clear, both to themselves as part of the reflexive act of constructing their knowledge and to their colleagues and the public.

Acknowledgments

IT IS A PLEASURE to record the debts I have incurred in writing this book. The contributions of two people have been critical. Henrika Kuklick inspired me to undertake research in the history of the social sciences and supervised the dissertation on which this book is based. Her knowledge and insights permeate the book, to an extent that I only dimly recognize. Belinda Probert was the consummate critical reader, constantly querying passages that I had thought quite clear and encouraging me to make the book more relevant to contemporary sociologists of work.

The arguments in this book are themselves a social product, constructed in large measure while I was a graduate student in the Department of History and Sociology of Science at the University of Pennsylvania. I am grateful to Walter Licht for guiding me through the literature on American labor history, to Robert Kohler and Charles Rosenberg for their knowledge of American science, and to Arnold Thackray and Alexander Vucinich for their advice and criticism. I am indebted to my fellow graduate students for their camaraderie, references, insights, and demanding standards, especially Thomas Broman, James Capshew, Deborah Fitzgerald, Alejandra Laszlo, Lynn Nyhart, Jack Pressman, and David Shearer, all of whom commented on various chapters. I have also benefited from the comments of Judy Wajcman and John Matthews, both of whom read the entire manuscript, and from conversations with Jan Sapp. Louis Galambos and Jeffrey Sturchio provided encouragement and support at a critical moment. The manuscript was edited expertly by Mary Racine.

I am acutely aware of the amount of intellectual labor performed by archivists and librarians that is so casually appropriated by historians. I gratefully acknowledge the guidance of Florence B. Lathrop, director of Special Collections, Baker Library, Graduate School of Business Administration, Harvard University. Young Hi Quick, librarian of the Corporate Library and Archives of Western Electric (now AT&T Technologies), gave me considerable assistance, not least by finding the papers of William J. Dickson, and sat me at a desk with a dramatic view up Broadway in Manhattan. Millie Ettlinger, Alan Gardner, Robert Garnet, Robert Lewis, and

Ralph Swinburne of the Historical Archives and Publications Division of AT&T gave me their full assistance as we perched almost alone in the old headquarters of AT&T and surveyed the breakup of the Bell System. The records of Western Electric and AT&T are now located in the Archives of AT&T Bell Laboratories in Warren, New Jersey, and I thank Linda Straub for her assistance there.

I also thank the librarians and archivists of the following institutions: Rockefeller Archive Center; Institute Archives and Special Collections, Massachusetts Institute of Technology; National Academy of Sciences; Thomas Alva Edison Papers, Edison National Historic Site; Special Collections, Carnegie-Mellon University; Sterling Memorial Library, Yale University; and Joseph Regenstein Library, University of Chicago. The librarians of the University of Pennsylvania and University of Melbourne libraries have handled innumerable requests.

The archival research and writing of the first draft were expedited by the financial assistance of American Telephone and Telegraph Company, which kindly supported me for a year with its fellowship in telephone history, Australian–American Educational Foundation, Andrew W. Mellon Foundation, and Rockefeller Archive Center. I am grateful to the University of Melbourne for providing research and travel grants while I was Dyason Research Fellow and then lecturer in the Department of History and Philosophy of Science.

Bibliography of the Hawthorne experiments

The following is, to the best of my knowledge, a complete list of publications by the Hawthorne researchers that report on the experiments. Publications by researchers such as Mayo and Roethlisberger that do not report on the experiments in an original way have not been included.

Barker, J. W., "Technique of Economic Studies of Lighting in Industry," *Transactions of the Illuminating Engineering Society*, 1928, 23: 174–88.

Dickson, William J., "Incentives and Wage Plans," *Personnel Journal*, 1935, 13: 324–30.

"Executive Leadership in Morale-Building," Proceedings of the Second Personnel Institute, Nov. 17–18, 1939, *Ohio State Univ. Publications – College of Commerce Conference Series*, no. 9, 25–45.

"The Hawthorne Plan of Personnel Counseling," *American Journal of Orthopsychiatry*, 1945, 15: 343–7.

"An Approach to the Human Factor in Work Relations," in *The New Industrial Relations*, Ithaca, N.Y.: Cornell University Press, 1948, 95–122.

Dickson, William J., and F. J. Roethlisberger, *Counseling in an Organization: A Sequel to the Hawthorne Researches*, Boston: Harvard University, Graduate School of Business Administration, 1966.

Dickson, William J., et al., "Understanding and Training Employees," *American Management Association Personnel Series*, no. 35, 1938.

Hayes, Elinor G., "Selecting Women for Shop Work," *Personnel Journal*, 1932–3, 11: 69–85.

Henderson, L. J., and Elton Mayo, "The Effects of Social Environment," *Journal of Industrial Hygiene*, 1936, 18: 401–16.

[Homans, George C.,] *Fatigue of Workers: Its Relation to Industrial Production* (Report of the Committee on Work in Industry of the National Research Council), New York: Reinhold, 1941.

The Human Group, New York: Harcourt, Brace, 1950.

Jackson, Dugald C., "Lighting in Industry," *Journal of the Franklin Institute*, 1928, 205: 285–303.

Lovekin, O. S., "The Quantitative Measurement of Human Efficiency under Factory Conditions," *Journal of Industrial Hygiene*, 1930, 12: 99–120, 153–67.

Mayo, Elton, "Changing Methods in Industry," *Personnel Journal*, 1929–30, 8: 326–32.

"The Western Electric Company Experiment," *Human Factor*, 1930, 6(1): 1–2.

"The Human Effect of Mechanization," 42nd Annual Meeting, American Economic Association, *Papers and Proceedings*, 1930, 20(1): 156–76.

"Supervision and Morale," *Journal of the National Institute of Industrial Psychology*, 1931, 5: 248–60.

"Psychopathologic Aspects of Industry," *Transactions of the American Neurological Association*, 1931, 468–75.

"The Problem of Working Together," in *Psychology Today*, ed. Walter V. Bingham, Chicago: University of Chicago Press, 1932, 231–9.

The Human Problems of an Industrial Civilization, New York: Macmillan, 1933.

"The Blind Spot in Scientific Management," *Sixth International Management Congress, London, 1935*, London: King, 1935, Development Volume, 214–18.

"Security, Personal and Social," *New England Journal of Medicine*, 1937, 217: 38–9.

"What Every Village Knows," *Survey Graphic*, 1937, 26: 695–8.

"Research in Human Relations," *Personnel*, 1941, 17: 264–9.

The Social Problems of an Industrial Civilization, Boston: Harvard University, Graduate School of Business Administration, 1945.

Meriam, R. S., "Employee Interviewing and Employee Representation," *Personnel Journal*, 1931, 10: 95–101.

Nichols, E. F., "Report of the Committee on Research," *Transactions of the Illuminating Engineering Society*, 1924, 19: 125–30.

Osborne, Emily P., "The Industrial Nurse and Fatigue," *Public Health Nurse*, 1930, 22: 555–7.

Pennock, G. A., "Industrial Research at Hawthorne," *Personnel Journal*, 1929–30, 8: 296–313.

Pennock, G. A., and M. L. Putnam, "Growth of an Employee Relations Research Study," *Personnel Journal*, 1930–1, 9: 82–5.

Putnam, M. L., "Improving Employee Relations: A Plan Which Uses Data Obtained from Employees," *Personnel Journal*, 1929–30, 8: 314–25.

"An Experiment in a Scientific Approach to Industrial Relations," Silver Bay Industrial Conference, *Report*, 1930, 30–4.

"Development of More Scientific Points of View in the Hawthorne Experiments," in AT&T, Personnel Relations Department, *Possibilities of Applying Scientific Method to Personnel Relations in a Business Organization*, New York, July 1940.

"A Useful Way of Looking at Problems of Individual Adjustment in a Business Organization," in AT&T, Personnel Relations Department, *Possibilities of Applying Scientific Method to Personnel Relations in a Business Organization*, New York, July 1940.

"Diagnosis and Treatment of Employee Complaints and Grievances," *Bell System Personnel Conference, Oct. 29 – Nov. 2 1940*, AT&T, 1940.

"Evolution of a Concept in Personnel Relations," *Bell System Personnel Conference, Oct. 29 – Nov. 2 1940*, AT&T, 1940.

Roethlisberger, F. J., "Understanding: A Prerequisite of Leadership," address to Professor Cabot's Business Executives' Group, 9 February 1936.

"Leadership to Ensure Collaboration," *Personnel Journal*, 1936, 14: 311–19.

"The Social Structure of Industry," address to Professor Cabot's Business Executives' Group, 5 December 1936.

"Social Behavior in Industry," *Harvard Business Review*, 1937–8, 16: 424–35.

"Of Words and Men," address to Professor Cabot's Business Executives' Group, 10 March 1940.

"Concerning the Nature and Usefulness of the Scientific Method," in AT&T, Personnel Relations Department, *Possibilities of Applying Scientific Method to Personnel Relations in a Business Organization*, New York, July 1940.

"Concerning the Interviewing Method and Methods of Diagnosing Problems of Individual Adjustment in a Business Organization," AT&T, Personnel Relations Department, *Possibilities of Applying Scientific Method to Personnel Relations in a Business Organization*, New York, July 1940.

"Analysis and Appraisal of Morale in a Business Organization," *Bell System Personnel Conference, Oct. 29 – Nov. 2 1940*, AT&T, 1940.

Management and Morale, Cambridge, Mass.: Harvard University Press, 1941.

"Group or 'Socialized' Behavior in Business Organization," in AT&T, Personnel Relations Department, *Personnel Counseling*, October 1941.

Man-in-Organization, Cambridge, Mass.: Harvard University Press, 1968.

The Elusive Phenomena: An Autobiographical Account of My Work in the Field of Organizational Behavior at the Harvard Business School, Boston: Harvard University, Graduate School of Business Administration, 1977.

Roethlisberger, F. J., and W. J. Dickson, *Management and the Worker: Technical vs. Social Organization in an Industrial Plant* (Harvard Business School, Division of Research, Business Research Studies, no. 9), October 1934.

Management and the Worker: An Account of a Research Program Conducted by the Western Electric Company, Hawthorne Works, Chicago, Cambridge, Mass.: Harvard University Press, 1939.

Slocombe, C. S., T. E. Torrance, T. N. Whitehead, and H. A. Wright, "Reactions of Employees," *Personnel Journal*, 1936–7, 15: 235–40.

Snow, C. E., "Research on Industrial Illumination," *Tech Engineering News*, November 1927, 257, 272, 274, 282.

Turner, Clair Elsmere, "Test Room Studies in Employee Effectiveness," *American Journal of Public Health*, 1933, 23: 577–84.

I Remember, New York: Vantage Press, 1974.

Western Electric Co., *Research Studies in Employee Effectiveness and Industrial Relations*, 1929.

Whitehead, T. N., "Psychology and Techniques of Discovery," *Journal of General Psychology*, 1934, 10: 364–75.

"The Scientific Study of the Industrial Worker," *Harvard Business Review*, 1934, 12: 458–71.

"Human Relations within Industrial Groups," *Harvard Business Review*, 1935, 14: 1–13.

"Social Relationships in the Factory: A Study of an Industrial Group," *Human Factor*, 1935, 9: 381–94.

"Leadership within Industrial Organizations," *Harvard Business Review*, 1936, 14: 161–71.

Leadership in a Free Society: A Study in Human Relations Based on an Analysis of Present-Day Industrial Civilization, Cambridge, Mass.: Harvard University Press, 1936.

The Industrial Worker: A Statistical Study of Human Relations in a Group of Manual Workers, 2 vols., Cambridge, Mass.: Harvard University Press, 1938.

Wright, Harold A., "Personal Adjustment in Industry," *Occupations*, 1940, 18: 500–5.

Index

Printed in the United Kingdom
by Lightning Source UK Ltd.
107475UKS00001B/114